D0910021

The Drama Is Coming Now

The Drama Is Coming Now

The Theater Criticism of

Richard Gilman,

1961–1991

Foreword by Gordon Rogoff

Yale University Press

New Haven and London

Copyright © 2005 by Yale University. All rights reserved. This book may not be reproduced, in whole or in part, including illustrations, in any form (beyond that copying permitted by Sections 107 and 108 of the U.S. Copyright Law and except by reviewers for the public press), without written permission from the publishers.

Set in Garamond and Stone Sans types by The Composing Room of Michigan, Inc. Printed in the United States of America.

Library of Congress Cataloging-in-Publication Data

Gilman, Richard, 1925–
    The drama is coming now : the theater criticism of Richard Gilman, 1961–1991.
        p. cm.
    Includes index.
    ISBN 0-300-10046-9
        1. Theater—United States—Reviews.   I. Title.
PN2266.5.G55 2004
792.9′5′0973—dc22
                                                                                    2003057638

A catalogue record for this book is available from the British Library.

The paper in this book meets the guidelines for permanence and durability of the Committee on Production Guidelines for Book Longevity of the Council on Library Resources.

10 9 8 7 6 5 4 3 2 1

No less than other men, the drama critic lives on hope. From week to week and season to season he feeds off the possibilities of things not yet seen and makes whatever peace he can with actuality. In September the promises are in the air, and the critic, for whom this time of year is the period of his most solid connection with the rest of humanity, follows the seductive balloons and the sky-writing over Broadway with senses nearly as agitated and heart nearly as open as the matron from Scarsdale or the buyer from Baltimore.

The sense of community will of course fade quickly. While waiting for seasons or curtains to go up the audience is fraternal, united, its common nature most pronounced and its pool of shared expectations most serene. But when that phase of primitive response to the pure, undifferentiated lure of theater is completed, then taste, sensibility, and intelligence take over and bring division and the end of democracy. Then the matron and the buyer live more or less comfortably in the present; the critic and the lover of dramatic art for whom "hits" and "smashes" appease nothing are reduced to naked hope.

Commonweal, Sept. 28, 1962

Contents

Foreword

Gordon Rogoff

At last, here is the Richard Gilman collection for which we've been waiting too long. Perhaps these essays and reviews, for all their intensity, wit, and fierce integrity, had to take second place in Gilman's mind to his lifelong passion for the plays and stories of Anton Chekhov. All who have known him have had to accept with resigned affection that we might never be so vividly alive, so sentient for Gilman as the great dramatist and storyteller who held sway over his imagination for so much of his working life. Who were we against the gentle, yet looming, vision of his truest teacher? Similarly, perhaps, even his own best work in journalism couldn't compete, couldn't be valued or live in the same world as Chekhov's.

Yet here it is, almost by default, a late-life rescue for some of the most trenchant criticism American theater has ever been lucky enough to receive. When he wrote about *The Seagull* as "a meshing of revelations, withholdings, recognition, everything serving as clues to the whole," he could have been offering a clear description of his own procedures. His thought, always driven by a weaving energy that has breadth, completeness, and a liberated attention to minute detail, never gives up just because the object of his disaffection might finally seem to be beneath his standards. As a character in his own Chekhov narrative he is found in these assorted pieces in the condition of "living within time"—

to use his phrase again—which is to say within the time he knows he must take to exercise the microscopic expansiveness of his critical attention.

What emerges invariably is a sense of balance and sheer common decency in all that he says, even when he simply won't book a seat on the great American hype-machine that insists on seeing good in everything. Not that he sees bad in everything. Far from it, he's a model of exquisite discriminations: Eugene O'Neill, for one, in *Desire Under the Elms* might suffer "failures of rhetoric at all the crucial points . . . its ponderous hefting of chunks of raw feeling and simultaneous hunger for an integument of significance . . . moving inexorably away from credibility or interest." That said, "he isn't false, though." Gilman finds "urgency and pressure and an artist's task, half-fulfilled." Generous, yes, but more than that, he's demonstrating the first line of critical responsibility: behind his mixed judgment is sensitivity for the dramatist without surrendering to the vacuous refusal of so many to notice the elephant in O'Neill's spacious room. Throughout these pages are many similar oppositions within the same critic. Even an early theatrical hero such as Tennessee Williams can't escape when his plays lose sharpness of outline, memory plays in futile search for what has long been half-forgotten.

Like all serious critics, and contrary to the popular myth, Gilman is at his best when responding to profound enthusiasms. His reach extends beyond Broadway's self-important and parochial concerns. Collected here are samples of a range comparable to Eric Bentley's: Brecht, Beckett (a natural quarry for Gilman's inquiries), Ibsen, and British playwrights, particularly Harold Pinter, who consistently engage him as he explores tensions between the old and the new. Again, he's a friend—even a disciple—of Joseph Chaikin, but that scarcely means that he falls into lock-step of any kind with Chaikin's early mentors from The Living Theatre.

And behind that particular antipathy is the genuine, complicated Gilman who delights in what might be called the agitation of the new while keeping a tight grip on all that he adores from the agitated, classical past. In his early days at Yale, he gave lectures on what he called *The Making of Modern Drama* (eventually published under that title), offering analysis of writers from Buchner to Pirandello as if they were newly minted from the page. In his hands, the modernists were born with Buchner in the early nineteenth century, the academic categories swept out of sight where they belong. Gilman's daring is always to disclose what goes against the prevailing image of writers at that time—Ibsen and Strindberg, for example—caught in the stifling confinements of photographic realism. He loves them for their successful encounters with an idea of theater formal enough to turn formulas upside-down almost without getting found out by the scholars. They might be "individuals caught in the fact" (Gilman borrowing from Henry James's views of Ibsen's characters) and the "fact" might be the inevitable limits to their experience, but as with Gilman's critical persuasions themselves, the limits are not allowed to interfere with the play of imagination.

These perceptions—and more—are caught in the wondrous fact of this page-turning collection. Gilman is that rare dramatic critic who respects the art so much that he won't let his intellect condescend to it. The result is that, despite his hesitancy over the years to see these essays once more in print, they stand up there with Chekhov and the others as more than just fleeting, journalistic occasions. Partly they do so through the continuing magic of his phrasing: the plays of Christopher Fry as "artsy-versy and mythy-mothy," the "urgent, intense, hard-breathing" of Arthur Miller's *A View from the Bridge,* Elizabeth Taylor in *The Little Foxes* coming on stage "heavy, panoplied, like a clipper ship under full sail, except that this is dry land." But apart from what might appear to be some easy targets, there is his greater mission to expose the pervasive cultural disaster that would even allow Taylor to make that entrance: a few lines later, he extends the charge to include Helen Hayes and Katharine Cornell as examples of "the nearly absolute inability of American audiences and most reviewers to tell good acting from bad." And since even generous collections can't include everything, I ought to recall one of my favorite Gilman lines about still another sacrosanct Broadway icon: about Jason Robards in Herb Gardner's *A Thousand Clowns,* he said that "directing Jason Robards must be like pushing heavy furniture around the stage." As Gilman writes in this collection (p. 207), "To be any sort of useful critic means one has to resist bullying from whatever direction it comes."

Beyond his gift for words that keep moving into complicated constructions while untangling their knots, and the straightforward statements, such as Strindberg embarking on "an adventure of sensibility," there is the startling reminder throughout that drama, likewise, is at its best when viewed by an adventurer of intellect. We cannot claim to be accustomed to this, though Gilman is plainly writing within an honored tradition that includes William Hazlitt, Edgar Allan Poe, Bernard Shaw, and so many of his contemporaries form Kenneth Tynan to Stanley Kauffmann. So, unaccustomed as we are, we can now give space in our minds to still another theater critic informed by all the arts and the wounded world surrounding our brief existence, taking from them a sense of renewal and possibility otherwise displaced by the rush of events.

Gilman is a major essayist, here showing his mastery of the short form while casting playful wisdom and serious humor over an everlastingly recalcitrant art. Reading even his lamentations is like reading the best dramatists at the height of their passions. Yet seen dispassionately, these pages are surely a part of Gilman's biography in action. Here are threads within threads, his prose commanding the full tapestry, a shock of color here, a delicate blending of textures there, all part of a meditative process that is at once lucid and muted, as befits not only Chekhov (by the way) but also the deeper regions of the art—and its performances—that keep telling him what he needs to know. Chekhov, Beckett, and the others may be his guiding emblems, but these pieces reveal him as their serene, if embattled, brother: even within the tradition of the unashamed intellectual as drama critic, Gilman can be seen here as an original, lavishing us with cascading images from a truly examined life.

About Richard Gilman

Richard Gilman was born April 30, 1925, in New York City to Jacob Gilman and Marion Wolinsky Gilman. He married Yasuko Shiojiri in 1992. He has three children (Nicholas, Priscilla, and Claire) from two previous marriages, in 1949 and 1966.

Educated in New York City public schools, Gilman attended the University of Wisconsin in 1941–43 and 1946–47, receiving a B.A. From 1943 to 1946 he was in the U.S. Marine Corps, Pacific Theater, honorably discharged at the rank of staff sergeant. He attended the New School for Social Research in 1947.

He was a freelance writer in 1948–54 and 1958–61; associate editor, *Jubilee,* 1954–57; literary editor and drama critic, *Commonweal,* 1961–64; drama critic, Channel 13 (PBS), 1963–64; associate editor and drama critic, *Newsweek,* 1964–67; literary editor, *New Republic,* 1968–70; associate editor, *Performance,* 1971–73; contributing editor, *Partisan Review,* 1972–80; drama critic, *Nation,* 1981–83.

Gilman was professor of dramatic literature and criticism at Yale University, 1967–99 (emeritus). He was also visiting lecturer in English, Columbia University, 1964–65; faculty of the Salzburg (Austria) Seminar, 1965; visiting professor of drama, Stanford University, summer 1967; visiting professor of theater arts, City College of New York, 1978–79; visiting professor, Columbia University, 1980, 1984, Boston University, 1984–85, Barnard College, 1987, Kyoto University (Japan), 1987; and McGraw Distinguished Lecturer, Princeton University, 1990.

Gilman is the author of *The Confusion of Realms* (Random House, 1969); *Common and Uncommon Masks: Writings on Theatre, 1961–1970* (Random House, 1971); *The Making of Modern Drama* (Farrar, Straus & Giroux, 1974, and nominated for the National Book Award; reprint, Yale University Press, 1999); *Decadence: The Strange Life of an Epithet* (Farrar, Straus & Giroux, 1979, and nominated for the National Book Critics' Circle Award); *Faith, Sex, Mystery: A Memoir* (Simon & Schuster, 1986); and *Chekhov's Plays: An Opening into Eternity* (Yale University Press, 1995).

He has written hundreds of reviews and essays in many magazines, including the *New York Times, Partisan Review, New York Review of Books, Atlantic, Dissent, Harper's Bazaar, New Republic, Nation, Village Voice, Performing Arts Journal, Commonweal, Commentary, American Film, Esquire, New American Review, Horizon, American Theatre, Tulane Drama Review, Newsweek, Saturday Review, Theatre Quarterly, Theater,* and *American Scholar.*

Gilman has received the following honors and awards and held the following titles: Rockefeller Grant, 1963–64; Guggenheim Fellowship, 1966; NEH adviser, 1970s; George Jean Nathan Award for Dramatic Criticism, 1971; Ford Foundation Grant, 1974; adviser, New York State Council on the Arts, 1974–75; NEH Summer Grant, 1977; fellow, New York Institute for the Humanities, 1977–80; Morton Dauwen Zabel Award from the American Academy and Institute of Arts and Letters for progressive criticism, 1979; President, PEN American Center, 1981–83—Vice President, 1983–86—Executive Board, 1985–88.

The Drama Is Coming Now

The Theater Criticism of

Richard Gilman,

1961–1991

Part One Essays and Articles

The Drama Is Coming Now

The spirit of an age is known to reveal itself in everything that the age conspires to say about its engagements with itself. We have spoken about ourselves, which really means that we have spoken *to* ourselves, more characteristically, more obliquely, more problematically, in painting and sculpture than in the other arts. Here our dialogue has been driven by a greater underground fury, frustration in apparent freedom; here we find the aggressive jest and the sense of exhausted yet tenacious conventions still to be overcome. The novel and the film are only occasionally used for their proper purposes, and when they are they approach the graphic arts and become our autobiography. The rest is noise. It used to be that the other arts aspired toward the condition of music, but it is more nearly true to say that they now wish to reach the condition of painting and sculpture. Picasso, Jackson Pollock, and Brancusi—with their solid, unhistorical, and nonexplanatory objects, their breaking of the mirror—are the sovereign examples.

And what about the theater? Even more heavily bound as it is to the social, to "communication," than the forms it resembles most, fiction and the cinema, it has fallen steadily behind an age in which the social is undecipherable and communication, like sleep, is impossible if you set out to achieve it. Where once the stage was the unparalleled means of a society's gaining a sense of itself and of all destiny, of life's winning through to formal and self-replenishing vision, it has become in all but a handful of its manifestations a wearisome repetition of what so many of its remaining devotees, like lovers blind to the withdrawal of love, continue to insist it is supposed to be. If it were not for the handful of plays (and they are the best plays of our time) that declare themselves to be other than what drama has always been taken for, we would be too bored and dispirited even to go on thinking about it. Yet there is something to think about, indeed by now something to overtake.

What we have to catch up with, we who are concerned with the theater and particularly with the theater in the United States where it has perennially suffered from the conviction that beauty originates in the pocketbook of the beholder and is a matter of seduction, is, at the very least, a consciousness of what has been happening to the bases of drama. We need an articulated consciousness, one that spreads among the practitioners and invades the theaters or, at any rate, one that cannot help being heard no matter what its efficacy will be allowed to be.

No one thinks we can create a new drama by fiat or speculation or through aesthetic manifestos or manuals of more promising techniques. But it remains true that we may impede the arrival or growth of any possible theater of truth and substance simply by failing to rid ourselves of the accumulated and inherited notions, which come more and more to resemble prejudices, which we have relied on up to now to carry us past the difficulties in the way of understanding the nature of dramatic art. In *Six Characters in Search of an Author* there is this admonition: "The drama is coming now, sir, something new, complex, most interesting." As spectators, participants, and evaluators we have not even begun to deal with the changes that have already taken place, much less prepare ourselves for what is newer still.

In America, of course, apart from the hermetic activity of the professionally enslaved, we almost never deal with new aesthetic phenomena until they have overwhelmed us with their multiplied presence, until, that is to say, they have become aesthetic norms. We continued to talk about Hemingway (and still do) chiefly in terms of his preoccupations, his values, obsessions, and possible neuroses until long after it was evident that his importance lay in his having changed the face of prose. *Axel's Castle* was a revelation to most of us, but the miracle was that nobody before Edmund Wilson had appropriated the material that had been lying so long at hand. Today we steadfastly ignore the new

French novelists, who are doing the most interesting work of the moment, and make a mountain out of an artistic molehill of a novel like *Ship of Fools.*

We write about the movies as sociologists or technicians or chroniclers of nostalgia, and mourn or praise like warring philosophers the disappearance of the human image from modern painting. Except in regard to poetry, where we have been blessed (or cursed) with the New Criticism's unflagging attentiveness, we have never had anything like that close, public, reciprocal relationship between aesthetic theory and practice such as the French, to take the supreme example, have never failed to keep up. There are those of us who are embarrassed or dismayed by such a liaison, but are we better off for having adhered instead to the two-fisted, red-blooded proposition that those who can, do and those who can't, teach?

The drama has suffered more than the other arts from the disjuncture between thought and activity that is so characteristic of our cultural life. The American drama is itself almost mindless; we weep for the intellectual deficiencies of Miller and Williams and for the existence of O'Neill as our monument to the hairbreadth victory of naked will and raw energy over language and idea, a victory that nevertheless leaves the major laurels on other brows. But our theater also suffers from a great reluctance to being *thought about,* except in the most sanctified and unoriginal ways. If the stage in America has produced so little that is permanent, revelatory, and beautiful, one reason for that is surely its aversion, which resembles that of "masculine" Americans to poetry or practical businessmen to Harvard theoreticians, to being discussed as an art, or at least as an art whose lineaments cannot be traced in all the standard, echobequeathing textbooks. If we set out to discover the art of drama on the theater shelves we are led to taking seriously Robert E. Sherwood and Sidney Kingsley, Lillian Hellman, William Inge, and Paddy Chayefsky.

It is doubtless also true that the notorious fate on American stages of the most important and life-giving European drama—our mangling, perverting, or simply letting go down the drain every valuable accession from abroad, from Ibsen and Chekhov to Brecht, Lorca, Beckett, Ghelderode, and Genet (we all have our memories of anguish in this regard)—stems far more radically from a failure of intellect, from a refusal to believe that intellect has anything to do with theater, than from a deficiency of mechanical skills or technique (which is in the end, however, almost nothing but a question of a certain kind of intelligence).

Intelligence is the last virtue we seek in our directors of "significant" foreign plays, for example. "Theatrical sense," éclat, professional briskness, inventiveness of the order of those star salesmen who "put over" a new product—these come first by a wide margin, on Broadway and, with its atrocious timidity and pretentiousness, Off-Broadway as well; and it is a measure of our hopelessness in the matter that when we do decide to make a gesture in the direction of mind we apotheosize a director like Tyrone Guthrie or José Quintero or Elia Kazan, bowing to them as if they were the Platos of the theater, when the truth is that they have become, if they were ever not, its Walt Disneys and Cecil B. De-Milles.

We have absorbed the European novel into our own, we have taken over and now outdistanced European painting, but a chasm remains between our theater, our conception of drama and theirs. We still do not understand what they are about; and we go on believing that we can effect our regeneration without such understanding. We wish to come to life again, or for the first time, without recognizing what the theater's true life is in our time. The point is that if the plays of Ibsen, Strindberg, Shaw, Chekhov, Pirandello, Brecht, Beckett, Ionesco, and Genet are permanent and inexhaustible, in themselves and especially in comparison with anything we have offered the world's stages, it is not simply because this European drama exhibits a greater complexity or a more direct involvement with crucial existence than our own, but because these plays in their various modes approach the theater as a means of *knowing* and not merely as a means of expression.

(But of course we may continue to comfort ourselves with the knowledge that the world makes a bigger thing of our accomplishments than some of us do. The world is wrong. If it pays extravagant homage to O'Neill, Williams, Miller, and now Albee, it is partly because an illusion is at work, the illusion of refreshment or inspiration from primitive sources common to minds tired of thought and subtlety, and also to minds that have never known them; the illusion that led Gide to call Dashiell Hammett our greatest novelist and other Frenchmen to adulate Horace McCoy; the illusion that leads a culture like Israel's, from the other extreme, to specialize in O'Neill in the belief that he is the shortest way back to the ancient Greeks and so to high "seriousness" on the stage.)

In Pirandello's *Six Characters* there is another moment of warning and illumination. At one point the stepdaughter protests against the attempt of the father, and by implication of the dramatist who has placed all six "characters" in existence, to make their story theatrically viable. "He wants to get at his 'cerebral drama,'" she cries out, "to have his famous remorses and torments acted;

but I want to act my part, *my part!*" The speech functions as one of the elements building the play to the realization of its theme, which may be described as the suffering produced by the conflict between levels of reality. But in its ironic suggestion that it is just the exigencies of the theatrical impulse that endanger the possibility of arriving at truth, the speech has a wider reference: it is expressive of the situation of modern drama, caught in a self-consciousness which it must draw upon to give itself strength, no longer straightforwardly celebrating the mysteries or dilemmas of existence but having moved to a position among them.

The speech also throws light on some of the problems of drama criticism in an age when the textbooks are exceptionally useless. We are still heavily involved, despite all the evidence to the contrary which continually arranges itself under our noses, in the fixed notion of drama as the enactment of passions, "cerebral" or otherwise, "famous" or, as is increasingly the case, quite the opposite. We go on thinking of a play as a structure in which to trap, shape, control, exemplify, and give significance to the major passions or to their perversions, which we further expect to embody themselves in the form of characters who will then work out their destinies along the unreeling line of a plot.

Yet if anything is true about drama as an art it is that it has passed through a transformation—has pressed its way through one—which has brought it to the condition of denying the usefulness of the passions as material, or at least their usefulness as long as they remain mummified within the inherited rigidities and spent predictabilities of traditional characterization and plotting. And this is one of the results of a more profound process. The drama, like the other arts, was alienated from itself and its immediate ancestry and then, subsequently, it recovered its own being through self-mockery, wit, fantasy, aggression, and ironic handling of its materials.

It should be a commonplace by now that all the representative art of our time is marked by a questioning—implicit or otherwise, comic mostly, extravagant, remorseless—of the very nature, purpose, and validity of art itself. We see this in the whole of twentieth-century art, from Picasso, Stravinsky, and Joyce to Kafka, Pirandello, Brecht, Mann, the surrealists, Jackson Pollock, the pop painters and sculptors (who are representative of the latest twist of the knife upon which art is impaled when it repeats itself too long), the a-novelists, Beckett, Antonioni, Ionesco, Nabokov, and Genet. This questioning is what fixes "modern art" and most radically separates it from what came before. From Ibsen's *When We Dead Awaken* to the poems of Wallace Stevens to Mann's *Doctor Faustus* the testing and interrogation of art can be observed in many concrete instances. But even when it is not the direct subject of the work it informs the creative action throughout the modern period. And that this examination stemming from doubt and despair should have led to a revivification of the imagination and its forms is surely one of the paradoxical glories of our notably inglorious age.

Pirandello was one of the most conscious of the artists who have made the imagination do new duty, struggling at each moment with its treacherous inclinations and forcing it back to the business of truth. To act out a cerebral drama or to present us with remorses and torments, *passions* which are arbitrary and selective and therefore certain to do violence to the wholeness of truth, the stepdaughter in his play is saying, is to make it impossible for me to act *my part*, my truth, which I only wish to offer as the direct revelation of myself, the unmediated history of what has happened, and not the dramatization, reductive and distorting, of someone's idea of the way things happen.

The tension is between art and life, between knowledge and actuality, and the spiral of irony and paradox rises to an extreme height because of the fact that the girl is of course a dramatic creation to begin with. As such, she is fighting for her life within a play which is in turn fighting for its life within a larger play—the play *itself*—which is struggling for its own existence . . . that is to say, struggling toward a dramatic mode which will enable it to overcome the obstacles blocking the way to truth.

The stepdaughter wishes, in other words, not to be a character, an arbitrary creation, but an identity, a reality, in the same way that drama, in Pirandello's practice, as in that of every other serious playwright of our time, wishes not to be the reflection of life, its staged version, but a reality, a counterpart or analogue. To act out known passions is to persist—as the most vigorous and original recent drama has told us by negation and new steps—in being the reflection of a life that in its loss of self-knowledge and confidence desires only to be handed back mirror images. These passions are useless because they are encrusted with a type of language that no longer describes the feelings themselves; beyond this they are fixed in those various flows of actions that have been repeated again and again because it is thought that there is no other way to present them. And it is these conventions, operating in the name of emotions, that serve to prevent any renewal or resummoning of passion from showing itself to us.

The analogy is, of course, with abstract painting's movement of repudiation and changed aims, its creation of a universe in which shapes, colors, and lines exist in their own right and not as the attributes or properties of objects that have their definition in the world of fact outside art. Such an analogy should not be carried too far; the best contemporary plays are not to be distinguished by their abstractness (the attempt at creating a theater of pure abstraction, in the manner of the experiments at the Bauhaus, the work of a playwright like Jean Tardieu, the Dadaists, or even Ionesco's slim, half-hearted, and mostly theoretical efforts in that direction, have resulted in not much more than some specimens of curiosa). Drama is nothing if not concrete. But there clearly are affinities between the relinquishment of subject in most recent painting and sculpture and the abandonment of character and the accompanying revolution in the concept of plot, character's milieu, that have come to be the characteristic features of certain dramas in our time. In both cases it is a matter of coming back to the truth, which lay disguised and impotent under the automatic functioning of convention. It is necessary to sketch the course of drama's entire revolution before returning to this rediscovery.

The theater is a way of knowing, a playwright is a mind. It has been more than fifteen years since Eric Bentley published *The Playwright as Thinker,* still one of the two or three most valuable works of American dramatic criticism, yet the only thing that seems to have happened is that we know the names now and have made uncertain visits to some of the places his pioneering on other shores opened up. The premise was so firm and lucid, the demonstrations for the most part so irrefutable. "The playwright must be a thinker not only if he wishes to be a propagandist. He must be a thinker if he wishes to be a great playwright." And once again, "every great writer is a thinker—not necessarily a great metaphysician but necessarily a great mind. Among the recognized great playwrights of the past there are no exceptions to this rule."

And yet we go our mindless way, chattering about "commitment" and "responsibility" as if they were not the most intellectually arduous endeavors, screeching about "robustness" and "passion," praising the most intellectually shoddy plays for their "power" or "vitality" or "sense of life," praising worse ones for their "thoughtfulness," unable to distinguish between thought and thoughts-in-drama, unable to take the yoke of "playwright of social ideas" from Ibsen, continuing to write such nonsense as Walter Kerr's dictum that the drama of ideas is one "in which people are digits, adding up to the correct ideological sum," and never seeing more than piecemeal and spasmodically that the drama in our time rides a revolution in ways of knowing and that its procedures follow stringently from that.

The Playwright as Thinker rose out of the observation that modern drama (1880 was Bentley's starting point, although he took the necessary look back to

Kleist's and Büchner's practice and Hebbel's and Schiller's theory) has been much more concerned with ideas than the drama of any previous age. If in fact ideas are the essence of modern drama, this did not mean, Bentley was at pains to point out—"pains" is devastatingly mild; "torments" would be more accurate—that these plays have been aridly intellectual or that they are lacking in emotions or sensuousness. What it did mean was that at a certain point in the nineteenth century, with Wagner and especially Ibsen, drama identified itself with the rising critical spirit: that attitude of analysis and questioning the pursuit of which meant a reconstitution of forms. From then on ideas, or more broadly, thought, became increasingly important as the substance of the revived theater. This was dangerous thought which attacked and threw up alternatives to the settled habits of mind and sight of both the audience and the theater which had for so long served it as a rite of confirmation and solace.

In Robert Brustein's splendid chapters on Ibsen and Strindberg from his forthcoming book, *The Theatre of Revolt* (a title that encompasses something even broader than Bentley undertook), we can see how this spirit of repudiation and urgent inquiry grew into the full-scale rebellion it has constituted ever since. The history of the theater over the last seventy-five or eighty years is in fact the history of that rebellion, but it is also the history of the refusal to recognize that the rebellion is all there is. For no art except the film possesses greater resources for the masochistic rejection of its own best possibilities than does the drama; that it is also theater makes it possible for us to resist revolution behind its physical arguments, its stages that must be enlivened and its rows of seats waiting to be filled, its economic exigencies and enforced obligation to what is immediately assimilable. The revolution remains outside, like the one in Genet's *The Balcony;* within, the life of illusion continues, the hall of mirrors goes on throwing back to its patrons the reflections they have always known.

Nevertheless, the revolution remains all there has been and all there is, even while the Pulitzer Prizes and Critics' Awards go on being punctually bestowed on what is mostly nonexistent. Being a rebellion of a double kind, throwing off desiccated theatrical practices in the wish to cast off the dead image of itself that life had been putting on stage, it necessarily changed the forms of drama at the same time as it changed its subject. This is of course what happens in every transformation in the arts, yet the drama seems to have difficulty in understanding that new forms and new subjects arise together and that the avant-garde, far from imposing itself like an invention, appears, as Ionesco has written, "of necessity. . . . It is self-generated when certain systems of expression are exhausted, corrupt, too remote from a forgotten model." No, it is not drama that fails to understand this but theater, that heavy institution to whom extreme conservatism is thought to be necessary for survival.

The well-made play depended for its acceptance on the belief that existence itself is well-made and that there is pleasure in witnessing clever demonstrations of the fact; the theater of intrigue, amorous confabulation, naked and solipsistic action, detection and denouement, and narrow psychological realism, depended on men's desires to see their lowly irrelevant dreams rehearsed or their physiognomies and psychic maps projected in a drama of repetition, reassurance, or that sort of titillating dangerousness that is also ultimately reassuring. When the drama of thought arose it was as a repudiation of such purposes and with the momentum of new ones. And just as it was the new purposes of Picasso and Stravinsky—their refutation of established belief and understanding, detectable behind the strange sounds and sights—that was so disturbing to their first audiences, so in drama it was the new intentions as much as the changed forms that "theater-lovers," professors, and reviewers found so objectionable, ostensibly on the ground that thought is nontheatrical but more profoundly from a distrust and hatred of ideas as the truly dangerous instruments of change and rehabilitation.

This is not the place for a rehearsal of the philosophic and aesthetic events that had preceded or were contemporaneous with those of the new drama— Marx's turning of bourgeois principles into the agents of their own destruction, Nietzsche's transvaluation of values, Dostoevsky's Underground Man, Rimbaud's *dérangement* in the interest of liberty, Zola's cruel realism Cézanne's overthrow of established appearance. But it is important to keep the drama, which has a way of remaining outside the intellectual histories, from escaping into an arbitrary fate. When the theater changed it did so in obedience to a spirit that was at work everywhere: what made the plays of Ibsen and Strindberg and Shaw so disturbing was that like occurrences elsewhere in art and thought they undermined a settled conception of moral and social existence, a complacency, a system for evading truth.

But the ideas of the new drama had, of course, to discover their proper mode of existence. The first observation we make about this is, naturally, that the new plays, the masterworks of the rebellion at least, were not "ideological," not forensic, did not constitute a theater of argument. Brustein has remarked, by way of delivering a final blow to the tiresome central canon of Ibsen criticism, that he was "much less interested in specific ideas than in a generalized insight," and this was true, to one degree or another, of all the playwrights who transformed the stage. In the rehabilitation of the world and the self (the self is, ultimately, what is always dramatized, as Ibsen knew) through using thought, through that necessarily self-conscious working of a way out of illusion and sterile gestures by putting the imagination to new uses, which has been the effort of art continuously since the nineteenth century, the drama played its part according to its nature.

Bentley has demonstrated that in the plays of dramatists as diverse as Ibsen, Strindberg, Shaw, Chekhov, and Pirandello ideas—new or recovered concepts of man, of fate, experience, truth—functioned as aspects of the imagination. Ideas were incarnated in the drama, infused with feeling, made to comment upon action and indeed, the transcendently revolutionary step, made identical with action. In his discussion of how Pirandello's achievement lay not in putting forth the intellect or reason as the subject of the drama but in fusing the intellect with passion, with "action," Bentley wrote that "it is the peculiar associations of thought—with suffering and joy, with struggle and primitive fears—that is characteristic of the new drama." "Associations" is perhaps too weak a word; "impregnation" would be better.

Thought is impregnated with feeling, and feeling is in turn directed and shaped by thought. The process differs widely from playwright to playwright, but the point to be stressed here is that you cannot detach the "ideas" of Ibsen or Strindberg or even Shaw from their dramatic milieus, as academic criticism continues to do, whether it wishes to be honorific or the reverse. What distinguished these plays from those of the dead theatre of their time was precisely that they were works which sought to *reinterpret* and *relocate* man. This is a thing you naturally cannot do by simply parading the traditional passions, but you cannot do it by arguing the case either. It is in the union of dramatic imagination with philosophic intention that the triumph of the modern stage lies.

We are severely embarrassed by the word "philosophic" as applied to drama; for professional theatre people it is the most damnable word they can imagine. Yet it is time for us to take Bentley's phrase and strengthen it to read "The Playwright as Philosopher," or even "as Metaphysician," since nothing better describes what modern drama is so crucially about. Let us go to a few authorities. "True poetry," Artaud writes and means true drama, "is willy-nilly metaphysical, and it is just its metaphysical bearing, I should say the intensity of its metaphysical effort, that comprises its essential worth." And Ionesco: "since the artist apprehends reality directly, he is a true philosopher. And it is the broadness, the depth, the sharpness of his philosophical vision, his living philosophy, which determine his greatness."

Ionesco goes on to say that the theatre "should avoid psychology, or rather give it a metaphysical dimension," and it is this action that can be traced in revolutionary drama from Ibsen on (where it was conducted within a naturalistic structure that seemed to exclude it), along with the corollary action of giving a metaphysical dimension to social existence, to struggle, to dreams, fate, and identity. The crude idea of a philosophic drama, one that *expresses* a set of ideas, is not in question here. The drama exists as an incarnation of a philosophy, a metaphysics, one that wishes to rediscover or "reinvent" man, to bring him again, in Artaud's words, "to his place between dream and events," to test him and put him under new obligations, to provide him with truer gestures and a less cowardly speech.

There is no wish here to force everything into an unyielding container, such as has been done with "absurdity," to speak only of the most current simplifying effort. The theater which has called upon a metaphysical impulse in order to resurrect itself has taken as many forms as there are minds at work in it. The metaphysical dimension of Giraudoux is very different from that of Sartre; Pirandello's does not resemble Cocteau's or Beckett's or Genet's. And there are those playwrights, such as Brecht and Shaw, for whom we have to stretch the ordinary usage of the word metaphysical to make it cover, as indeed it is meant to, concern with the nature of truth and a probing beyond appearances, since in such writers what seems to be on display is hard-headed, antimystical, practical thought, and insight.

But if we wish to keep the revolutionary theatre from disintegrating in our minds into arbitrary fragments and accidental virtues, if we wish to escape from the eternal sterile debate between naturalism and symbolism, poetic theater and realist theater, the epic and the lyric—those alternatives which in our time have more to do with details than with spirit—we need a word which will tell us what the revolution is about. And we need it above all if we are to understand and be capable of addressing the tremendous technical and procedural changes that have come over drama since Ibsen first put the practices of the boulevard and the data of the drawing-room into the service of poetry, that poetry which Cocteau described as "of the theater" and not in it and which Artaud insisted was, whether it considered itself to be so or not, inescapably metaphysical.

The changes undergone by plot and character transcend all others, and unite the revolutionary plays despite their differences. It is in the altered nature of these hitherto twin pillars of the traditional idea of theatre that modern drama's own metaphysical intention and aspiration are most centrally displayed. For the very idea of character and plot rests on a concept of man and existence, a belief in psychological coherence, in the continuity of experience and in the permanence of what is considered to be "human nature." When character disintegrates and plot, as "story," is abandoned, we are witnessing the dissolution of the very concepts which underlay their previous use.

We might say, if such terms would help, that modern drama is existential rather than essential, that it repudiates the typologies and narratives that an essentialist philosophy or attitude produces from its profoundest nature. The point is that from Ibsen on drama began to present characters who grew less and less "identifiable," less psychologically unified and socially coherent, less verisimilitudinous. It became increasingly difficult to put oneself in the place of the persons on stage, the dramatic and psychic energies being so widely dispersed among the roles, the entire structure tending more and more to resemble the relationships characteristic of poetry. That Ibsen's last plays are usually derogated by being called loose and symbolic is due in great part to their characters having slipped out of their conventional moorings in psychology and personality, to their having broken the stereotypes of action to become elements in what, as Brustein has said, was moving toward a "drama of the soul."

With Strindberg the process is accelerated. In the preface to *Miss Julie* he writes, "because they are modern characters, living in a period of transition more feverishly hysterical than its predecessor at least, I have drawn my figures vacillating, disintegrated, a blend of old and new." Fourteen years later he prefaces *A Dream Play* with a much more extreme description: "The characters are split, double, and multiply; they evaporate, crystallize, scatter, and converge. But a single consciousness holds sway over them all—that of the dreamer." In drama a single consciousness may always have been said to have held sway over the characters—the consciousness of the playwright, who chooses, arranges, and moves things along. But what Strindberg introduced was a sovereign consciousness *within* the play itself, in which the characters participated and which might be said to have constituted the subject and action of the drama.

Participating in such a subject, the characters were no longer substitute persons, no longer identifiable by comparison or reference to figures in the world. In one way or another, with digression into various psychological or social milieus,[1] with one or another degree of emphasis on the established conflicts— the new theater has moved away from the placing on stage of surrogate figures

---

[1] Even when the modern writer does go into psychological or social milieus, he is not returning to what we understand by "naturalism." The revolutionary and metaphysical impetus which is at the heart of modern drama works against verisimilitude and imitation. Pirandello's urban jousters with appearance, Giraudoux's mythic debaters, Genet's Algerian rebels, and even Ionesco's bourgeois heroes will *not* be found in the house next door.

for the audience. The culmination is with us now, in the great postwar triad of dramatists—Beckett, Ionesco, and Genet—in whose plays, otherwise so different, characters function as figments of a dramatic imagination that has passed entirely beyond psychology, beyond explanation, detection, or celebration, so that they remain free of *traits,* stuck on like labels, of personality (except in relation to one another), and of anchors in the usual conventions of history, society, or the stage itself.

As with character, so with plot, which is, of course, character in motion. Hebbel wrote that "drama should not present new stories but new relationships," and this is another mark of the drama of our time: that it has repudiated anecdote and tale. In the absence of conventional narrative the tendency is to look instead for allegory, as has happened in so much of the criticism of plays like *Waiting for Godot* or *The Blacks.* But such dramas will not yield to an allegorical interpretation, which has the effect of attempting to refill the spaces that have appeared in them because of their refusal to tell a story, their refusal to *progress.* As Jacques Guicharnaud has written of *Godot,* "it is not an allegory, an incompleted *Pilgrim's Progress.* It is a concrete and synthetic equivalent of our existence in the world and our consciousness of it." It is independent, entire, needing nothing from our filing cabinet of possible situations and denouements to justify itself. It *has* no situation and reflects none; it *is* the situation itself.

For the most part drama criticism has lagged behind drama. For a description of what has led to the creation of these plays without heroes or histories we might more profitably turn to the writings of a novelist like Nathalie Sarraute, to her explanations of the changes in thought and sensibility that have resulted in the revocation of narrative and the liberation of character from the necessity of being our reflection. She speaks of the representative new observer for whom works of art may no longer be restatements, no matter how adroit or sincere, of the known passions and their coherent destinies. "He has seen time cease to be the swift stream that carried the plot forward, and become a stagnant pool at the bottom of which a slow, subtle decomposition is in progress; he has seen our actions lose their usual motives and accepted meanings, he has witnessed the appearance of hitherto unknown sentiments and seen those that were most familiar change both in aspect and name."

If the drama has changed in obedience to this altered condition of perception and knowledge, which we may consent to or resist but which is with us nevertheless, it has been by no means a consistent, orderly, exclusive process; forms of theater overlay and jostle one another, nothing is ever entirely replaced. The theater of character and plot continues, sometimes successfully but no longer at the center of the dramatic imagination as it functions most acutely today. If such theater returns as our truest drama it will in any case be unlike its framed portraits; it too will have a metaphysical thrust, a pressure toward escape from the airless rooms of the "lifelike" and the recapitulated. The theater of Beckett, Ionesco, and Genet may not extend more than a certain way into the future; but there is no other kind of drama that seems prepared to do for us what Artaud cried out for: a sense of life renewed, a "sense of life in which man fearlessly makes himself master of what does not yet exist and brings it into being."

The American theater, with its endless concentration on means instead of ends, its cult of the actor as "expressive personality" which so unfits him for plays in which there is no personality to express but a condition to be exemplified, its refusal to take thought, its clinging to passion when passion is mere noise and to story when story ends in empty arrival—this theater which is our concern, our heritage, vocation, and residence, will live when it discovers and has the will to animate the narrow, fragile, dissociated, and yet, therefore, all the more revelatory existence that is the only true one the theater can have in our time. It may not happen; it has been the only wish of this essay to sketch the reasons for its not happening and the outline of the way it might.

Tulane Drama Review, Summer 1963

British Theater: Kinky, Arrogant, and Frankly Magnificent

One day early last March a prospective theatergoer in London (a person, let us assume, of more than routine taste and expectations) could have chosen from among the following offerings, almost all of them well acted, a few of them brilliant examples of regenerated theatrical techniques and directorial imagination: Harold Pinter's much debated new play *The Homecoming;* three variously accomplished but honest, energetic, and tough-minded dramas by relative newcomers—Frank Marcus' *The Killing of Sister George,* Edward Bond's *Saved,* and David Halliwell's *Little Malcolm and His Struggle Against the Eunuchs;* two solidly original works from the recent repertoire—Ann Jellicoe's *The Knack* and John Arden's *Serjeant Musgrave's Dance;* and a spectrum of generally competent and in some cases splendid revivals—Shaw's *The Philanderer, Man and Superman,* and *You Never Can Tell,* Wilde's *An Ideal Husband,* Gogol's *The Government Inspector,* Turgenev's *A Month in the Country,* Middleton's seldom performed *A Chaste Maid in Cheapside,* and, slipping a notch or two but still within the purlieus of civilized entertainment, Noel Coward's *Present Laughter* (his new offering, *Suite in Three Keys*—in three parts and spread over two nights—came in a few days later).

Besides all this, and depending on what the National Theatre was presenting that evening, he could also see Laurence Olivier in *Othello,* Albert Finney in the Feydeau farce *A Flea In Her Ear* and in Arden's *Armstrong's Last Goodnight, The Crucible* by Arthur Miller, Congreve's *Love for Love,* or Peter Shaffer's *The Royal Hunt of the Sun.* And elsewhere in town were a new and arresting production of *Hamlet* in which a young actor, David Warner, plays the Prince with startlingly contemporary gestures, a newly translated version of Hauptmann's comedy *The Beaver Coat,* Spike Milligan in *Son of Oblomov,* an exercise in sustained and spontaneous absurdity, and *Beyond the Fringe,* in its third or fourth change of company and targets.

If the next day this theoretical theatergoer of advanced taste had found himself in New York and had asked a knowledgeable friend what our theater had going of interest and value, he would have been told that the best things on in the colonies at the moment were the Royal Shakespeare Company's *Marat/Sade,* John Osborne's *Inadmissible Evidence,* Shaffer's *Royal Hunt,* and Arden's *Serjeant Musgrave,* the last, unfortunately, in an inferior production. There was also of course a great range of indigenous work to which he naturally would not want to subject himself.

The truth is that if the theater is a perennial invalid, as one of its hardiest clichés would have it, then the British theater at the very least and in more than one sense, can be said to be ambulatory. It travels well these days and at home is capable of sudden and impressive sprints down the hospital corridors before slowing down for more treatment. The British theater, for all the complaints one hears about it from its more dedicated practitioners and observers, looks very much from this side of the Atlantic like paradise. An Eden of uncertain ecstasy and somewhat besieged innocence, perhaps, but nevertheless a green and fertile place.

The view from here being very much like that from Death Valley, this may not seem especially resonant praise. Still, of all the arts, theater is the most imperfect, relative and unstable, unlikely to flourish for long anywhere and constantly in desperate need of new blood and fresh ideas. And that is what, since a certain day in 1956, the British theater has been getting, and what we, except for a few hermetic infusions from our native donors or at secondhand from London, surely have not.

The matter is not so much one of great plays having been written as of a strong, diversified, and animate theater having been created within the past few years. England has only one or two playwrights—Arden and perhaps Pinter—who come anywhere near being the geniuses of original vision and statement that Beckett, Genet, and Ionesco are. What it does have, however, is a continually augmented corps of competent dramatists who, working largely within established forms, have produced a body of dramatic literature which substantially outstrips our own recent work in interest and vitality. Besides Arden and Pinter there are Osborne, Shaffer, Miss Jellicoe, and Arnold Wesker, with all of whom Americans are familiar; but they are probably not familiar with Alun Owen, Henry Livings, Clive Exton, David Campton, David Rudkin, N. F. Simpson, Frank Marcus, and Edward Bond, together with a dozen or so others, all of whom, however much they may differ in manner and capacity, are serious, talented, and in possession of a sense of the stage as something more than a place for Pavlovian experiments in audience response.

Much more significant, what England has now is three state-subsidized theatres and an audience that goes to see plays of varying merit—contemporary works or classics, solid texts or pretexts for improvisation. The atmosphere permits new and risk-taking styles of performing, directing, and design.

Another bracing element of the British theatrical weather is the fruitful relationship between the stage and television and films. The Royal Shakespeare Company is itself making several films—both Shakespeare and contemporary. And unlike the situation in America, where television is a laughing stock as a serious art form, the best British actors and playwrights move easily into its purlieus.

Perhaps nowhere in the world is there a body of actors to compare in skill, robustness, versatility, and intelligence with the British, and nowhere are there wider opportunities to work continuously yet in vastly different roles. From the older but still flourishing generation of Olivier, Ralph Richardson, Max

Adrian, Donald Wolfit, Michael Redgrave, and Peggy Ashcroft, to Paul Scofield, Colin Blakely, Robert Stephens, Dorothy Tutin, Maggie Smith, David
Warner, Nicol Williamson, Albert Finney, Ian Richardson, Vanessa Redgrave,
Joan Plowright, Alec McCowan, and Geraldine McEwan—the list appears
endless. Nor is it easy to find anywhere a group of directors to match in inventiveness, daring, and knowledge of the stage's possibilities such men as Peter
Brook, William Gaskill, Peter Hall, and John Dexter.

The newer generation came almost literally out of a void. We can seldom fix
with such accuracy the onset of a cultural revolution or, as seems more appropriate a description in this case, a continuing and embattled insurrection, as we
can the beginnings of the New Age of British theater. When John Osborne's
Look Back in Anger opened at London's small Royal Court Theatre on May 8,
1956, everything was ripe for upheaval. England did possess a tradition of
drama as an art, a confidence in the spoken word; there were dozens of repertory companies throughout the country and several first-rate acting schools.
But acting as well as drama had long been arrested in conventional postures;
nothing new had stirred, it seemed, since Shaw and Gordon Craig.

That year, Arthur Miller was in London to oversee the production of *A View
from the Bridge* and attended a conference entitled British Playwrighting:
Cause Without a Rebel. Casting a protective eye toward Marilyn Monroe in
the stalls, sandwiched between two private detectives, Miller called the British
theater "hermetically sealed" from life. Even *Look Back in Anger,* he said, was
the same kind of play that we in America had developed and exhausted in our
socially conscious thirties. The English participants at the conference had to
agree. There was little at the time they could take pride in. Terence Rattigan's
reign over the British stage had not yet spent itself, a reign of teacups and genteel problems, tears shed easily and imagination never challenged. N. C.
Hunter was still writing bittersweet neo-Chekhovian comedies, filled with aging knights and dames who gave the impression that geriatrics was England's
foremost social study. The plays of Christopher Fry, all artsy-versey and mythy-
mothy, still had a hold on the sensibilities of middlebrow pretenders.

Look Back in Anger may have seemed an obsolete form to some, but it pre-
saged the future nevertheless. What the "brave, young" play, as Kenneth Tynan
called it, did, with its plunge back into actual speech, its faculties attuned to
kitchens and bathrooms instead of tea shops and salons, its then startling
rhetoric of public issues and private crises, was quite simply to force the English
stage to become aware of a social revolution. (So unyieldingly provincial was
the recent *Armstrong's Last Goodnight,* Albert Finney said they had to "translate

it back into English" when they brought it up to London.) Ten years later Osborne's play rather glaringly shows its deficiencies. But Osborne made it seem possible for young writers to work for the stage, now that it appeared to have a place for seriousness and contemporarity; he cut through the stifling atmosphere of "classical" acting by the kind of parts he wrote. His ideology may have been similar to our earlier social drama, but his manner was definitely English and distinctly contemporary. There were no inarticulate gruntings and gropings, no Actors-Studio-like yearning for motivation. There was, instead, a profusion of talk, some of it glib but most of it impassioned, which rested on an assumption that language itself is enough to entertain and enlighten.

What turned out to be even more promising than this play itself was its sponsorship. Journalists may have seized upon the catchphrase "angry young men" and thought they had pinned down a movement, but the directors of the English Stage Company (headed then by George Devine and now by William Gaskill), which produced *Look Back in Anger* as one of its first ventures in a scheme to rejuvenate the British theater through *literary* energies, had no such ideological or temperamental bias. They simply lent their theater's resources after Osborne to the best playwrights they could find. They welcomed innovation and chance-taking and have been rewarded for their openness by the plays of Arden, Ann Jellicoe, Wesker, Owen, and Simpson, most of whom the Court has continued to produce at very little profit, if any.

The same month as the Osborne opening another event took place which was to have almost as profound an effect on the entrenched system of British theater, and a few weeks after that still another. The first was the opening on May 24 of a play called *The Quare Fellow* by a hitherto unknown Irish writer named Brendan Behan. Originally little more than a set of chaotic notes for a dramatic piece, it had been shaped and given life by Joan Littlewood, who for eleven peripatetic years had headed—half guru and half drill sergeant—a group called the Theatre Workshop. Its principles rested mainly on the notion of no preconceptions at all, on the joys and terrors of improvisatory theatrical acts and on the spirit of unselfish communal enterprise, which then as now in the commercial British theater, as in our own to this day, was the last thing anybody was capable of. From the Theatre Workshop were to come over the next few years another play of Behan's, *The Hostage,* a piece by Shelagh Delaney, and, most impressively home-built and unconventionally ebullient of all, the musical *Oh! What a Lovely War.*

If the Theatre Workshop had shown Londoners the possibilities of imagination being exercised outside formal structures and texts, the appearance that summer of Bertolt Brecht's Berliner Ensemble reminded them of the splendors of cohesive group performing, precise, mutually reinforcing, able to animate texts with unerring skill and absolute control. Beyond that it convinced some Englishmen of the necessity for a publicly endowed and public valued theatrical institution. These Englishmen determined to break forever what Shaw had called the "eternal cycle of boom or bust," the responsiveness of the theater to no insistences beyond commercial ones.

In addition to the Royal Court, two such institutions did come into being, subsidized by public funds, and took up positions at the center of Britain's theatrical life, as preservers and interpreters of the past and fecund sources of contemporary energy and idea. The first was the Royal Shakespeare Company, which in 1960, with the appointment of the then twenty-nine-year-old Peter Hall as director, evolved from the old, static Shakespeare Memorial Theatre at Stratford and became the chief promulgator of new styles of directing and performance. The techniques were themselves the products of radical thinking about the nature of theater itself. Hall's ideas, and those of his colleague Peter Brook, were strongly influenced by the theories of Antonin Artaud, a Frenchman who had demanded that theater be an unrelenting assault upon the senses of the spectators. The audience was to be subjected to shock as often as possible and to surprises the rest of the time. Peter Brook foreshadowed this style in England when he directed Laurence Olivier at Stratford in *Titus Andronicus.* The blood and gore flowed in good measure and the test of the success of any single performance, it might have seemed, was the number of fainting ladies. Along with their revaluations and transformations of Shakespeare at Stratford, Hall and Brook began to put on contemporary plays at the Company's new branch, the Aldwych Theatre in London. From their efforts rose the great centerpieces of the present-day British stage: Brook's lean, oblique, blackly "existential" *King Lear,* his astonishing tour de force, *Marat/Sade,* and Hall's reworking, with John Barton, of Shakespeare's Henry VI plays and his *Richard III* into *The Wars of the Roses,* a combination of spectacle, drama, and physical experience.

The second "great battleship" of the British stage, as George Devine once called it, the National Theatre, opened its doors in 1963 as the successor to the moribund London Old Vic. Under the direction of Laurence Olivier, whose influence as mentor, exemplar, welcomer of the new, and irreverent revivifier of the old goes beyond that of any other person in the British theater, and with Kenneth Tynan as literary director, the National Theatre has produced a remarkable range of drama, in varying styles, from all periods of Britain's own theatrical past, as well as European classics and contemporary works by Arden and Shaffer. A kind of performing museum, with none of the mustiness the word implies, detached from ideologies and easy, reductive political stances, enabled by its subsidy, which this year is $364,000, to function partly free of commercial considerations, the Theatre provides an anchor, a testing ground, a source of style, and a principle of continuity for the theory and practice of drama in England.

Yet that this theory and practice, as exemplified by the National Theatre, the Royal Shakespeare Company, the Royal Court, and everyone who has been inspired, influenced, or merely prodded by them, remain minority enterprises is a truth reestablished every day. The West End theater, counterpart of Broadway, continues to be mostly occupied by plays designed for "Aunt Edna," the British equivalent for our little old lady from Dubuque, by American musicals, and by seemingly ineradicable theatrical anachronisms like Agatha Christie's machine-tooled thriller *The Mousetrap* and Marc Camoletti's subadolescent comedy *Boring Boring.*

There are signs however that the commercial establishment is at least partly on the defensive. A year or so ago the great "Emile Littler Row" erupted. Littler, head of the Society of West End Managers, issued a public protest against what he called "dirty plays," especially those of the Royal Shakespeare Company, and most particularly *Marat/Sade,* about which he remarked, in one of the most flaccid *J'accuses* on record, that there "is talk of flagellation and singing with gestures." This year the puritan voices were heard again, shaken into action by Edward Bond's *Saved,* in which, as an integral part of its theme, a baby is smothered to death in its crib by young hoodlums. Laurence Olivier seems to have had the last word on that; in a letter to the *Observer* he wrote that "*Saved* is not for children, but it is for grown-ups, and the grown-ups of this country should have the courage to look at it."

Whatever the censors and bluenoses may do, the English theater will continue to offer fare for grown-ups in the months ahead. Peter Brook hopes to do a documentary play at the Aldwych with actors from the Royal Shakespeare Company, a drama invented from his impressions of New York, from Pop Art and Happenings. Peter Hall promises a "surprise" contemporary play at Stratford (the rumors are that it will be about Vietnam). The National Theatre will offer Ostrovsky's *The Storm,* directed by John Dexter, and Olivier and Geraldine McEwan in Strindberg's *The Dance of Death.*

Courage does not seem to be lacking in the people who care about drama as an art in England. It can take the form, as it so often needs to do, of holding the so-called avant-garde itself up to attack. Recently Charles Marowitz, an extremely intelligent and radically oriented critic and director (and an American), mourned the death of the little-theater magazine *Encore,* which had exhorted, pushed, and pulled the best new theater in England through the events of the past ten years. Marowitz had this to say: "If there ever was a need for a critical theatre-Eye, a cultural vigilante, it is now when the English theatre is patting itself on the back for having produced great writers, fine companies, and first-class actors . . . and writers like Osborne and Pinter have become part of a new establishment." More pressure like that and a few years from now we may well be talking of the "New New English Theater," the one that came into being because of the complacency and inertia of the present one, which at the moment, however, seems to be resilient and energetic enough to hold on for a good long while. Long enough, at any rate, for Americans to realize once again the possibilities of fresh and exciting theater.

Still, in America there would seem to be little hope of raising a counterpart to the British theater soon. For one thing, America has not yet made the separation between Broadway and a true "theater"—a place of consciousness, art, *and* fun. For another, it is at the bare outset of a system of training from which actors and not "personalities" may arise.

Yet there are signs that the United States contains the seeds for a first, tentative growth. Its greater social diversity and freedom from tradition mean that odd, rough, energetic little theatrical enterprises are forever springing up. A chaotic but dynamic Off-Off-Broadway, working out of lofts, coffeehouses, and churches, has largely replaced the dormant Off-Broadway movement of recent years—it is significant that Joseph Chaikin, director of New York's radical and lively Open Theater, is in London this summer helping Peter Brook with *U.S.* If the kind of naïve, tempestuous, insurrectionary impulses that keep rising from obscure corners of the American stage could ever be fused with British technical capacity and intelligence, the U.S. might some day come to have a real theater, instead of merely the lights and CPA charts of show biz.

Esquire, July 1966

Growing Out of the Sixties

When I first talked to Erika Munk about the inaugural issue of *Performance,* we spoke of its having some such theme as "getting rid of the sixties." It seemed a good idea: a new magazine, a point in time not too far past the beginning of a new decade, presumably a rare opportunity to clear the air and the decks. But the rallying cry soon struck us as more than a little bombastic. Can we ever really "get rid of" the past, especially when it's so recent that the calendar is the only means we have of making sure there's a separation? And do we really want to wipe it out? Was it so bad, so misguided, is it such a weight on our backs now? Finally, is there even such a thing as the "sixties," a substantive with a fixed shape and clear outlines?

To think in terms of decades is of course simply a convenience. But what we call the sixties, whether or not they actually began in 1958 or 1959 and whether they are or aren't over, seems to me to be especially clearly defined as a chronological unit of consciousness and activity, a segment of time quite different from the immediately preceding chunk. And after everything is put in that minimal perspective which may prevent us from shouting as arrogant promulgators and partisans, this stretch of time can be seen to have been the most fertile period in the theater—or at least in thinking about the theater—since that equally innovative and dissident era, the twenties. At the same time I think something peculiar to the period (something that is peculiar to any artistic period) has indeed to be gotten rid of, if in a far less apocalyptic sense than I'd originally conceived. "Growing out of the sixties" is a modest and reasonable proposal.

What's ready for jettisoning, for leaving behind, nostalgically if we have to, are some of the illusions of those years, illusions which, it ought to be said, were in some sense necessary and inevitable and which it was precisely one of the functions of some of the period's best energies and minds to pursue, in order to try to discover what might not be illusory. If it's to educate us at all, the past seems to me valuable in just this way: that it can instruct us in what has been seen or felt to be real, what unreal, what in an indeterminate, still to be explored condition.

Nineteen sixty was the year I began writing about theater and drama, after having been for a long time relatively uninterested in them, like nearly all my intellectual and artist friends. I started with the illusions and appetites of the day, and with its experiences. In the winter I first saw *The Connection,* which had of course opened some months earlier but which was only now beginning to attract wide and serious attention. Sometime that summer the *Tulane Drama Review,* a magazine I had just become aware of, published Martin Esslin's essay on the Theater of the Absurd, the nucleus of the book that shortly followed. In the fall or the early winter of 1961 I learned about certain theater-like activities (I don't remember if they were called "happenings" yet) taking place at the Reuben Gallery on East Third Street, and went to see a few of them.

These three experiences of mine were no doubt duplicated, with variations, for a great many other persons to whom the theater around this time first began to appear *plausible,* an art capable of as much consciousness and serious imagination as any other. It was true that I had seen *Waiting for Godot* at its New York première in 1954 and had admired it enormously, had seen *The Chairs* and *The Lesson* a few years later and admired them, too, and had read Genet's *Death-watch* and *The Maids,* as well as Adamov's *Pingpong* and some other works which we were all to follow Esslin, with however many caveats, in calling "absurd."

But these plays had had their effect on me essentially as literature; when I thought of *Godot,* for example, it was in much the same terms as I did *The Trial* and *Amerika, The Confessions of Zeno, The Four Quartets*—the monuments of fiction and poetry I had been passionately visiting for years. I don't know if very many others had the same literary response, but I suspect there were more than theater intellectuals would have cared to admit. One reason for it, I'm sure, was the pitifully bad productions that we saw; there are times, as we all know, when Shakespeare is a lot more satisfying in one's armchair than on the stage. But these productions weren't arbitrary or accidental; they issued from a theatrical apparatus and morale that seemed wholly incapable of doing justice to texts of such imagination or of bringing into existence anything startling and revelatory on their own.

Gelber's play, and even more the Living Theatre's production of it, showed me the possibility of an American theater of originality and true contemporaneity, "committed" (although that was a word and an idea that were to cause trouble later on), tough, informal in the best sense, a source of vigorous consciousness. Esslin's essay, for all its Procrustean methods and the misleading implications of its title, was valuable above all for its investigation, the first full-scale one I'd come upon, of the theatrical background of the change in drama.

Happenings, although I was never to overcome an initial and instinctive antipathy for the atmosphere in which most of them were created and was to develop fairly solid theoretical objections later on, seemed to me when they began a really important new step toward breaking up the stage as an artificial place, the scene of aloof, static, self-contained works set there for contemplation. For I, like so many others, was moved at this time by the vision of a theater of activity, effectiveness, and a power of truly changing consciousness.

In that regard there was one other significant element of the atmosphere in which the decade began, and this was the presence of Artaud. *The Theater and Its Double* had been translated and published here in 1957, I think it was, but Artaud's influence was just really beginning to make itself widely felt around 1960 and 1961, and would of course reach a peak a few years later. I remember participating in a panel discussion of Artaud in 1962 and being greatly impressed if not surprised by the fervor his ideas aroused. I was fervent myself; Artaud, the hanging judge of the theater that oppressed us and the prophet of its resurrection after sentence had been carried out, inspired a kind of blind violent faith, was a cicerone to heroic positions, a mapmaker of the brutally "honest" future. But I also remember Mary Caroline Richards, the book's translator and one of the panelists, warning the audience that Artaud wasn't to be swallowed whole, that there were things wrong, holes in his thought, impossible prescriptions.

In one way or another nearly all the ensuing phenomena of the sixties rose out of the atmosphere and activity I've just briefly described. Another brief summary of what became the materials for a history of the sixties: the growth of an American drama of "absurdity" and, later, the ridiculous; the proliferation of happenings into many species of events, environments, mixed media enterprises, and the like, and their subsequent loss of éclat; the coming into being of more "committed" theaters like the Becks', and their own group's transformation into a peripatetic, fully missionary theatrical community; the arrival of a work—Peter Brook's production of *Marat/Sade*—in which Artaud's ideas at last seemed to be incarnated; toward the end of the period Grotowski's appearance in America and his wide impact, something that was in certain crucial ways a counterpressure to much of what had gone before.

Running through nearly everything was the desire, in no sense unprecedented in the theater but seldom before so passionate and millenary, to *reach* the audience, to shock, change, and convert the spectator and through him the world. During these years I was never free of a sense of one irony that lay in such an impulse and ambition. The serious theater in America had struggled for so long to get itself accepted as an art, to be thought of as being on the same level as poetry, say, or music. Now the action of some of its most gifted and dedicated people (and of the painters, sculptors, and musicians who had elbowed their way in with happenings) was to try to throw off the very notion of the aesthetic as a category and mode of experience and of the artist as the maker of impressive, fully autonomous and closed works, would-be "masterpieces," as Artaud had derisively called them.

That this deaestheticizing of the theater could be carried out to the point where the line between art and life would be obliterated was, I think, one of the governing illusions of the sixties. Around it other illusions clustered: the notion that political radicalism could be directly converted into theatrical élan and effectiveness; that theater could be a singular and powerful agency of therapy both for its practitioners and its audiences; that performance could base itself on a more or less unmediated exhibition of personal being—the actor as self-demonstrator.

Darko Suvin has pointed out how happenings, for all their antiaesthetic aggressiveness, possessed an aesthetics of their own, and how their eventual retirement to an existence as little more than an interesting footnote to dramatic history resulted from their lack of recognition of certain basic polarities—"emotion and reason, facts and values, objects and persons, estrangement and cognition, wit and language"—dichotomies which all the ardent wishing of our new *simplistes* hasn't begun to overcome and which remain as the source of all theatrical energy and indeed of all forms of imagination. I think that what was true of happenings was also true of performance theater, theater as community, theater as radical action.

Happenings were performed by "amateurs," as an element of the new hope for innocence. Elsewhere, among people of the theater, the new cult of the amateur spread for somewhat different reasons. It was an attitude conditioned, if not wholly brought into being, by nearly everybody's idea of what professionalism now meant: slickness, falsity, the artificial, the corrupt. I remember once engaging in a rather heated discussion with members of the Open Theatre, which I served for a time as a director and an "adviser," which meant someone sufficiently detached from the group's day-to-day training and sufficiently conversant with history to have a bit of perspective. Professionalism, I told the group, no doubt rather stiffly and not at all sure that I wasn't trying to convince myself, originally meant the quality or action of "standing up for" something; to profess a faith was to identify yourself as a believer, with all its consequences, to be a professor was to stand up for and with the particular knowledge you had. And in the vernacular a "real pro" still meant a person without any nonsense in his chosen field, someone capable, serious, and dependable.

My argument was that the group had to become more professional in these senses, that it ought to be more *skillful* than it had been, wholly competent to do what it proposed, and that its radical ideology and passion for social and psychic truth couldn't be replacements for technique and might in fact be standing in the way of its acquisition. Not that anybody was arguing for the absence of technique; but it was evident that for many of the members the word had become tainted, like "professionalism," with unsavory connotations. Never clearly defined, unconsciously held in some cases, the belief was present that technique ought really to be a function of ardor, of earnestness and political will, and that to pursue it for its own sake led to an emptying out of the soul, to a creative death.

I knew then, and was to be strengthened in the knowledge, that there is never any question of pursuing technique for its own sake, except, that is, where soul, art, creative intention are missing to begin with. It was to be Grotowski, more than any other force in the sixties, who would indicate what the problem actually is, how technique is related to spirit and how in the theater (in all the arts for that matter) spirit has no existence without process. "Sincerity and precision" was Grotowski's formula: honesty of feeling *and* the means for its exemplification; passion *and* the clear signs of its formal existence. The result of Grotowski's incredibly rigorous explorations was the appearance for the first time of what Artaud had called for—a theatrical language halfway between dream and reality.

As the decade went on one saw everywhere the growing primacy of the political impulse, or the theatrical impulse politicized and placed in the service of a radicalism that sought to affiliate itself with the broader radicalism outside. And one saw the emergence of a corollary impulse of communality; egalitarian, group-therapeutic, it pitted itself against the traditional aristocratic and hierarchic qualities of drama-as-art and above all against what was felt to be, because of the essentially contemplative nature of the consciousness and experience offered and enacted, a principle of merely personal and private salvation.

The theater as redemption. This heavy weight had more than enough people eager to impose it. Beyond any doubt the destiny and vicissitudes of the Living Theatre most centrally exhibit what the sixties were about in regard to the redemptive uses of the stage. In an interview in *The Drama Review* a couple of years ago Julian Beck described the group's transformation, which really began with its self-exile from America in the fall of 1967:

> We have been, since the late 1940s—what is the right word?—confirmed theoretical anarchists and activists but we were very much under the influence—after the war

and in the early fifties—of that critical attitude towards art which said: you cannot mix art and politics . . . they don't go together; they degrade each other. . . . I don't think we came to a breakthrough in the theater until we became frankly political. And when we insisted on saying politically what we wanted to say politically, we felt free enough to discover breakthrough ways of doing it.

Whatever the influence on them of the taboo against mixing art and politics, they had been at it before, having culminated with their production of *The Brig*, implicitly a thoroughly political work. But, as Julian said, they wanted to be *frankly* political, openly, messianically so. What's more, they intended their company to be in itself a sort of microcosm of the new society they wished to help bring into being through their work. The performances they gave in Europe and when they returned here, those revelations of their own creativity, morale, and values, were the putative instruments of the transformation of their audiences. By contagion, imitation, the chance to participate in theatrical occasions that were somehow "real," the audiences would be brought through the sea-change into what these prophet-demonstrators had already attained or were in process of reaching: new moral and social being. The world would change its face and its tune.

The illusion that this transformation could actually take place—that there was some true transfigured condition on the other side of the rhetoric and the rituals—was patently shared by a great many participants in and avid observers of the events at the Brooklyn Academy and elsewhere that fall of 1967. (Although it was to be true that at certain radical campuses the Theatre would appear backward, naïve, offering histrionics instead of actions.) "Freedom," "spontaneity," "love," "innocence," "breakthrough," "paradise"—the vocabulary was evangelical and apocalyptic, and political in the sense of having vague connections with the "revolution" going on outside. Yet it was also, with great irony, *personal*, a seduction toward an orgasmic release of the self, toward the validation of a new rhetoric of egoism and toward the end of *noncreativity*. "You are all artists," the antiaesthetic Becks proclaimed, borrowing the prestige, still powerful among the young, of the artist-idea, the old romantic vision of splendid, originating, untrammeled, world-defying selfhood.

In the atmosphere of the Living Theatre released, the orgy of breast-beating by certain critics and of moralistic denunciation by others, the nearly hysterical self-examination by many kinds of theater people, the placing of everything on a basis of either/or, responsible criticism seemed more than superfluous; it had the feel of heresy or, worse, blasphemy. In this air to make aesthetic judgments or even—being hip enough to shelve the word—judgments of a technical or procedural nature, was to be made to feel (if you were honest with yourself and if you had been, as I had, a supporter) churlish, misanthropic, a counterrevolutionary. Still, I made these judgments: on the positive side certain beautiful physical accomplishments, an ensemble cohesiveness; on the negative, verbal ineptitude and even degradation, hopelessly bad "acting" or such movements as were intended to replace acting, extremely naïve social and political attitudes. More important, there was another kind of criticism to make, and this was a judgment from a simple human standpoint, a perspective of ordinary honesty.

From this angle of vision the Living Theatre seemed to some of us to lie. To lie for the most part unconsciously, to lie perhaps in the name of some waiting truth, but to *not be truthful.* One evening as I sat listening to Julian Beck pleading for love in the world and with the audience "to help us love you" and then screaming "We're trying to love you!" with an unspoken "Goddamn you!" at the end of it, I was reminded of Danton saying to Robespierre in Büchner's play, "Isn't there something in you that whispers sometimes, 'You lie, Robespierre, you lie?'" For the terrifying righteousness of the Becks surely covered a radical hatred, as it does in all such prophets and rhetoricians of values. And this righteousness, the extreme absence of love in the very act of its being proclaimed, the aggression and contempt that hung in the air as its true composition, all seemed to be to bring down nearly every claim and aspiration of this theater whose central principle and justification was that of being "real."

It was never real, except in that sense in which things actually happened there; the group had landed in another kind of artificiality after its flight from the artifices of theater. Its vision, everything testified to it, was a construction of the will, not the sight of true, revivified existence. This was the revolution: to proclaim with absolute insincerity—"bad faith" in several senses—that the group and the audience were going to march on the Atlantic Avenue jail after the performance "to set free the prisoners"; to *speak of* doing away with money while charging high admission prices; to *assert* innocence while practicing deception and calculated exploitation of the audience's emotions; to offer as bodily and sensuous liberation a sad, dispirited milling about onstage, an underwear show, as Eric Bentley described it.

I don't wish to sound too hard or righteous myself. The Becks were no doubt more naïve than coldly mendacious, more self-deceived than vicious. But *there* were the illusions: on the Becks' part that they had indeed attained a new innocence and purity and that their rituals were more than contrivances, on the audience's that they had been truly changed. I remember sitting there, nostalgic, wanting *something* to be true, as the crowd shuffled around on the stage and went through the motions of fellowship and community, along with the motions of freedom—disrobings and posturings that to anyone not caught up in the group suggestibility were forms of painfully appropriated "spontaneous" behavior.

Later Grotowski would say in reply to a question about audience participation that his theater had tried it once, thinking it the au courant, democratic thing to do, but had discovered, a confirmation of what he had secretly suspected, that people invited up to a stage (or to a *playing-area*) to "do what they feel like doing" invariably act in imitative ways, in simulacra of gestures and movements picked up from others and especially from the examples provided by bad actors in the bad theater. It was something I was to be aware of later in the work of the Performance Group: their audiences filled the performance spaces with clichés; they had been released only into derivative, inauthentic acts.

But, then, their models had been the performers themselves. With all the good will in the world (and that of course can be challenged; I expect mine to be; I anticipate some responses to this essay: Menshevik, bourgeois pig, *Walter Kerr!*), it was impossible to watch and above all to listen to *Commune*—opened in winter, 1971; the sixties are still with us—without a heavy sense of the indestructible naïveté and sad playing at being original of those performers.

They gave us, as I said in a review, "their dumb biographies." Not dumb like Woyzeck, stricken by the conditions of existence, not like mute inglorious Miltons; they were stupid because they were trying so hard to be bright and original, to "feel," to "expose" themselves, to be "vulnerable," as Schechner has said. All values that you can't chase after, all abstractions that lead to fashionable inauthenticity. Their lives placed onstage and the staged flight from their lives that the performance also represented were full of received ideas, gleanings from the ethos, from psychoanalysis and encounter therapy, from the counterculture's arid political scatology, from Zen and the will-toward-ritual and the will-toward-myth, from Hesse and Tolkien and Norman O. Brown. From the headlines. When they were original, therefore truthful, it was almost always in a comic or parodic vein, which is to say when they had something formal to work with and against and therefore some tension was present.

Theirs was one of the radical illusions our theater has been gripped by and no doubt had to be. Under the intolerable pressure of a seemingly deracinated society and a politics of death, they wished to create new life of their own—mythic, an immediate psychic liberation, above all public, exemplary, to be shared—instead of reproducing, as in traditional formal theater, a life created elsewhere and therefore presumably unrelated to our own, to the *real* questions. ("I sometimes think I have failed my readers by not having answered the important questions," Chekhov once wrote, in error.) But they wished to produce this life in a theater while pretending it wasn't a theater, to perform while pretending not to be performers, to have audiences who were not to be spectators but cohorts; they wanted to exhibit themselves without having known or understood themselves. The other illusions followed: that statements are facts, that rhetoric is truth, that rituals can be devised like board games, that all selves are equally interesting, that freedom is equivalent to the gestures of freedom, that innocence can be willed, that love is easy and art—or imagination—or theater—or performance—is a matter simply of being yourself.

The audiences weren't changed, either, as they weren't by the Living Theatre or any other missionary group (I except the Bread and Puppet Theater, whose modesty, sacrificial qualities, and capacity to witness instead of exhort have given it real exemplary power). The believers were confirmed, the disconsolate briefly consoled, the radically naïve given a transient sense of sophistication, those in search of *frissons* a momentary exhilaration. That the audiences for this kind of theater have been so young and inexperienced isn't due to there having been uncovered a new, innocent, and uncorrupted public for the stage, as the entrepreneurs have so fiercely wished, but to the fact that such spectators have mostly come seeking *life,* or rather the appearance of involvement, the gestures of concern, the *acting-out,* on their behalf, and occasionally with their participation, of resentment, scorn, or suppressed passion—the acting-out, finally, of the love that is missing from everything else and of the fate that a repressive politics seems to have made it impossible for them to assume.

When the Performance Group was at its best it was occasionally antic, unexpected, moved by an energy that derived not from the members' "private lives," as Schechner wished and asserted that it did, but from their having thrown themselves into a wrestling match with the kind of intractable material represented by their *Dionysus.* The subject and myth stood outside, debilitated by time, no longer believed in; the Group threw itself against that and was able to create, along with the usual quota of unoriginal and hyperbolic acts of self-expression, moments of true theatricality, images of despair, hunger, erotic quest, thwarted violence, and, maybe best of all, comic exuberance. These moments took skill, consciousness; the rest issued from self-indulgence.

And also, it seemed to me, from fear. The fear of being left out, of not being with it, of not having an immediate effect: such a condition is characteristic of false or pseudo avant-gardes in every period and may temporarily corrupt the genuine. I remember sitting disconsolately in a London theater watching the Royal Shakespeare's *U.S.* A false event, a fake spasm, a politically induced tic. The powerful Company, famous and accomplished, its great *Lear* behind it, was now doing its American thing, being *au courant,* wanting to assume a responsibility and passion you could only sorrowfully conclude they didn't feel. They gestured in the direction of Vietnam, they labored at correcting our presumed lack of feeling and only succeeded in revealing their own. They ought to have made that absence their subject, to have been ironic or rueful. They ought to have been honest.

The story was going around of how on opening night, as the performers stared at the audience after some final skit or turn, Kenneth Tynan (propagator of another sixties illusion: eroticism as public birthright) had broken the miserable tension by getting up and asking: "Are you waiting for us or are we waiting for you?" After which, the spell in pieces, the spectators were able to shake themselves free of the wretched, meaningless burden of guilt and complicity which the performers, without having earned the right to insist on anything, had tried to impose on them. It may be that we ought to have felt guilt about Vietnam, but the final effect of the evening, on me at any rate, was to have my vision of Vietnam or any political reality blocked off by the sight of all those egos making capital of it.

If I say that the theater cannot and ought not be asked to make good the deficiencies of life, I mean that the experience of drama or of any art is not directly convertible into usable emotions, that the consciousness we gain, for all that we would wish it utilitarian, is ideal, a matter of paradigms, structures of perception, patterns of possibility. There is a central misunderstanding of Artaud, one to which he contributed by his frequently ill-considered rhetoric, that will throw light on what I mean. At his most precise, Artaud spoke of the rebellion of the senses and consciousness which the theater can bring about as "virtual." By this he meant what the dictionary does: "being in essence or effect but not in fact."

The point is that the theater cannot create a real rebellion, that nobody is inspired to rush from his seat to implement what he has witnessed or heard, that such changes as take place in consciousness are incipient, questions of essences, models for the change of consciousness in general. To believe that anything else is possible or desirable, that, for example, a theatrical work can inspire its audiences to a direct and efficacious action outside the theater or can succeed in instigating a permanent alteration in the real arrangements of the world, is to reduce theater to mere agitation—which is what there are enough people still happy to do—or to participate in the kind of radical illusion I've been talking about.

In a related area, to think that myths and rituals and the like can spring into being by fiat is to profoundly misunderstand their nature. The most "ritualistic"-looking theater of recent years, Grotowski's, is one in which the contemporary impossibility of myth and ritual is precisely what is recognized and made the source for productions based on a tension between the past—where myth and ritual are alive—and the present, where consciousness searches for connections, for roots. Our audiences haven't been participating in myths or rituals, but in games, and in self-deluding games at that.

Finally, to mix or not to mix art and politics is scarcely the issue. There is no proper subject for drama and no experience alien to its operations. But to wish to make theater do the work of politics (or the reverse: the notion of politics as "style," a heritage of the Kennedy years, seems to me another dangerous illusion) is to become susceptible to the very degradations that politics itself is marked by: the reductive, the simplistic, the received; and lying, inauthenticity, manipulation, egoism, cant. More than that, it is to subscribe to the illusion that Nietzsche pointed out when he wrote that "in the long run utility . . . is simply a figment of our imagination, and may well be the fatal stupidity by which we shall one day perish."

In the sixties, the troubled imagination, wanting to abandon its traditional function as creator of alternatives to what the world had decided was useful, wanting to be responsible and efficacious and immediately felt, wanting not to be imagination at all but presence, turned in many ways toward "reality." The irony is that reality isn't so easily appropriated. The point about art, the theater's or any other, is that it comes into being just because, as Camus said, "the world is unclear." The reality the theatrical messiahs of these last years have wished to conquer and exhibit, the reality they were so sure of, has turned out to be in their hands someone else's, something unreal, rhetorical, a figment. To grow out of the sixties may mean to begin working again toward the reality of the theater, which cannot save us but which may provide us with the images we need in order to know that we aren't saved.

Performance, Dec. 1971

Broadway Critics Meet
Uncle Vanya

It is often said of New York theater that the review of one critic (Clive Barnes in the New York Times*) can make or break a play. While there is some truth in this there are, in fact, a dozen critics writing for a wide variety of newspapers and magazines likely to review each new production. But how high are the critical standards? Martin Esslin has established a precedent in* Theatre Quarterly *of keeping London critics on their toes in his reviews of the reviews (of* The Lower Depths *and* Savages*). Here Richard Gilman extends the practice to New York by looking very critically at the critics of the star-studded Mike Nichols production of* Uncle Vanya, *which opened at the Circle in the Square—Joseph E. Levine Theatre, in June 1973.*

When it was first announced early last winter, there was already a smell of success about the all-star production of *Uncle Vanya* Mike Nichols was planning to direct. There's always the smell of success about all-star productions, whatever the record shows; after all, the word "star" is the very proclamation of triumph and *éclat.* And Mike Nichols is a star too—the very embodiment of the golden-handed director whose work in the theater and films can occasionally go a little wrong, but only in the sense that it's then seen as "not being up to his usual standard," which is considered to be the model of what taste and wit and ingenuity ought to look like on the stage or screen.

As I write this (in London, as a matter of fact) the production was indeed a spectacular success, the hottest ticket in town except naturally for a few of the bigger musicals. It had been announced for a limited engagement, but before I left New York I heard that the run might be extended—if, that is, the stars could find their way free of their commitments. The success, to come now to the purpose of this essay, is only partly the product of the reviews, which were extremely favorable on the whole. One had the feeling that those glittering names—George C. Scott, Julie Christie, Nicol Williamson, Cathleen Nesbit, Lillian Gish—would have carried the day against a chorus of execrations, had they been forthcoming. But the reviews *were* favorable, in most cases ecstatically so, and this made for the chief interest of the entire event, since the production, in my opinion and that of a solid minority of other observers, was nothing less than an artistic disgrace.

CRITICAL POWER STRUCTURE

Before I go into the details I ought, for the benefit of British readers, to present a brief sketch of the nature and power structure of reviewing in New York. For some years now there have been only three daily newspapers in the city, and of these only the *Times* matters in the commercial aspects of culture. In fact, the *Times* matters so much that a rave review of a play there can mean instant success, whatever the rest of the critics say, while a knock can close a production in two days. The power of the *Times,* scarcely credible to Londoners I imagine, even extends past New York and the United States. A few years ago the press director of the Stratford, Canada, Shakespeare Festival told me that the degree of success or failure of their seasons depended not on the reviews in the Toronto or Montreal papers but on those in the *New York Times,* and that the latter's notices had influence not just with prospective American visitors but with Canadian theatergoers as well.

The other two papers, the *Post* and the *News,* have respectively perhaps 10 and 2 percent of the *Times'* power. The *Post's* readers are (in rough sociological terms) middle-class, liberal, and Jewish, a theater-attending population to be sure, but almost all the *Post's* readers are known also to read the *Times* in the morning and to take their cultural clues from it. The *News* is the proletarian paper; its enormous circulation of over 2,000,000 daily would number, I venture to guess, not more than 1 percent who have ever attended a professional production in their lives, and this fact is acknowledged by the paper's traditionally running the shortest, most perfunctory reviews of Broadway productions and almost never noticing anything taking place anywhere else.

Besides the three "real" newspapers, there is something called *Women's Wear Daily,* a publication put out for the ladies' apparel industry, and its reviews do seem to have some sort of minor persuasiveness with the thousands of out-of-town buyers who can be found in the city on any particular evening and who need to find entertainment or have it provided for them by their manufacturer-hosts. Then there are the national weeklies, *Time, Newsweek,* and the *New Yorker,* only the latter, however, because of its compact affluent readership, having any measurable effect on the box-office. There are also two mostly local weeklies, *New York* magazine, a brash, pseudo-chic guide to the intricacies of urban living edited mainly for the upwardly mobile (who also read the *Times*), and the *Village Voice*, which offers by far the most extensive theatrical coverage of any publication in town, but is heavily oriented toward Off- and Off-Off-Broadway and has a young readership much more interested, theoretically at least, in art and experiment than in polished entertainment.

Finally there are the national political weeklies or bi-weeklies, the *Nation, Commonweal,* and the *New Leader,* all with tiny circulations and no influence on anybody, and the *New Republic,* with no influence either but with a tradition of having had for fifty years the best drama criticism in America—Stark Young, Eric Bentley, Robert Brustein, and, at present, Stanley Kauffmann. And apart from the medium of print, there are the television and radio reviewers, whose thirty-second to two-minute notices are almost never anything but intellectually nonexistent but whose power, particularly those on television, has grown to where collectively they constitute the only serious rival to the hegemony of the *Times.*

I can't tell you what the media reviewers specifically said, since I was out of town the night *Uncle Vanya* opened, but I gather that their reaction was universally positive and even glowing. Of the printed notices I've confined myself to, or been confined to (some of the weekly and bi-weekly reviews hadn't yet appeared when I left the States), ten from most of the journals I've mentioned, plus an additional piece by the Sunday, and former daily, critic of the *Times,* Walter Kerr, who has, as most of you know, the biggest reputation of any American journalistic reviewer, but whose situation as a kind of dispenser of afterthoughts to what Clive Barnes, the daily man, has already said leaves him with little real force now.

With certain exceptions (to which I'll come later) everything these reviewers saw was something I didn't see, and the other way round. I wasn't at all surprised by this, it having been my constant experience, both as an ordinary theatergoer and a practicing critic to find myself—in respect to the reviews—in the position of the character in a Chas Addams cartoon who is looking with a wide grin at an unseen stage (or screen) while everyone else in the theater is in tears. Or the other way round: as Brecht had his ideal epic-theater spectator say, I weep when they laugh.

If this sounds snobbish, I'm afraid my only defense is to quote Max Beerbohm's remark to the effect that popular journals generally hire for their drama critics men whose taste is as close as possible to that of the public, and to add that (as H. L. Mencken said in another connection) the bad taste of the American public in matters of theater can never be underestimated. The truth is that there has never been an intelligent body of theatrical opinion in America; no one seriously interested in the stage pays any attention to the reviews, or rather such people look to the one or at most two capable critics who happen to be practicing at any one time, invariably in the smaller journals of opinion.

THE CHEKHOVIAN CLICHÉS

In any case, what I saw that night (the production had been running for about ten days—an important point to which I'll return) was, to put it as flatly and simply as I can, a travesty of Chekhov's great play. To begin with the text: that it *is* a great play none of the reviewers cared to deny, although in some especially illiterate quarters the acknowledgment seemed to come with that air of received information that surrounds such words as "classic" and "masterpiece." Moreover, almost none of the reviewers failed to offer us the clichés of Chekhov criticism; they spoke of his "lovely" qualities, his "humanity," the way he moves between "tears and laughter," the way his plays deal with "defeated" lives, with "boredom" and the destruction of hopes. None of them, not even Stanley Kauffmann, whose review in the *New Republic* was along with Walter Kerr's piece far and away the most intelligent and perceptive, said the important non-clichéd thing about *Uncle Vanya:* that like the other three last great plays of Chekhov it is not about failure but about *stamina.*

Kauffmann can be excused because he pretty much assumed a knowledge and opinion of the play on the part of his readers and so spent most of his space on the production (although he was the only critic to mention the very useful fact that *Vanya* is a rewriting of *The Wood Demon;* one had to assume that most of the critics had never hear of the earlier play). For different reasons from Kauffmann's, the other critics also spent most of their space on the production, their motives being, it seems clear, to get as quickly as possible to an area where their lack of knowledge and original thought wouldn't matter nearly so much: the acting and directing, subjects about which it's generally held in America that every man is his own expert and that no special training is required in order to be one.

Nichols' direction—to take up that first—lacked any sense of coherence, any integrating principle; his performers were allowed to occupy their little fiefs on the stage and do their things there, which is to say play *their* roles as they conceived them, with no evident awareness of a dramatic scheme embracing all, or of a texture of which they were together to contribute the palpable design. Scenes succeeded one another like automobile crates being loaded onto a ship; large blocks of action (or, at least as often, inaction; one of the worst aspects of the production, in the classic tradition of Chekhov misperformance, was that it made the self-declared boredom of the characters boring, something which only Kauffmann and Kerr seemed to feel) followed in no line of consciousness, with no sense of composing a whole.

CONTRADICTIONS OF AN ALL-STAR ENSEMBLE

Besides Kauffmann, only one other reviewer seems to have seen this lack of a through-line. That was Martin Gottfried, the *Women's Wear Daily* critic, whose aspirations to intellectual seriousness are well-known but whose equipment, and perhaps situation, have seldom supported them. Gottfried wrote that "Mr. Nichols has directed the play one scene at a time, one actor at a time. Of all playwrights, Chekhov needs such staging the least. His plays cry out for ensemble performance by the actors and of the material." Apart from the fact that I don't have an idea what that last phrase might mean and that I can't imagine any playwright needing "such staging" at all, the observation was accurate and useful to have. Gottfried, however, spoiled the effect of this and several other strictures he made by going on to be carried away by the glamour of the whole thing; he thought the stars contributed the "show business glitter and personal charisma that is as important to dramatic theatre as it is to a musical," and that "their presence (they aren't stars for nothing) . . . is what our theatre needs more of."

Well, that's straightforward enough: Gottfried wants the coruscating presence of stars in our otherwise unglamorous theater, and if he doesn't see the contradiction between wanting that and ensemble playing too, neither did most of the other reviewers. In their case, however, they thought they had both, and made a point of how wonderfully well this production escaped the pitfalls of egoistic playing. Brendan Gill's review in the *New Yorker* spoke for the great majority: "a cast so eminent it might have been assembled in a daydream (but) the performers . . . are by no means celebrated names stalking a stage in order to be gawked at and applauded. Under the direction of Mike Nichols, they make up a company that invests a great play with more than its usual power to move an audience."

I'd like to know how Gill has determined *Uncle Vanya*'s "usual" power of affecting its audiences, but then I'd also like to know how one might gawk at and applaud a stalking name. Gill's style is generally one of the better instruments to be found among the corps of reviewers, but *Uncle Vanya* seems to have had the effect of driving everybody's style into new and strange corners, even those which one would have thought hadn't an inch to move around in. My favorite examples are Jack Kroll (the *Newsweek* reviewer): "Chekhov's characters are like neurons in a giant brain whose prolonged, self-generated thinking has resulted in a stupor of subtlety"; the *Times'* Clive Barnes' description of Vanya and Astrov as representing "the folly of indecision on the one hand and of circumstances on the other"; and the *Post'*s Richard Watts' remark that Chekhov "couldn't help bringing in his basic fondness for the Russian people."

SENSATION VERSUS SINCERITY

Apart from the general acclamation for the ensemble work—which in America, I might say, is usually seen whenever a company of actors arrives at the theater at approximately the same time and does not refuse to take cues from one another—there was the question of the individual performances. Here the pull of the stars was most patently in evidence, and here could be seen a wonderful instance of what Henry James once called the American theater-going public's inability to distinguish consciousness in acting from "sensation." I don't know if the British public is any better at this, but I imagine that a good number of your critics are better at it than most of ours.

The most sensational of the performers was of course Nicol Williamson, who appropriately received the lion's share of the plaudits. Williamson, as British readers of this article know better than I, is an extraordinarily uneven performer who badly needs a firm directorial hand, but here was given a pat on the rump and told to take off. Brendan Gill amusingly, if with a central failure of aesthetic understanding, said of him that "nothing could prevent his purchase of a bus ticket from Perth Amboy from becoming a melodrama of almost unbearable intensity." The failure of understanding lies in the fact that the intensity of melodrama is always bearable, it being the nature of the genre to be so; dramatic art at its truest is what is unbearable, in the sense that we don't know how to bear it with our ordinary emotional equipment and so have to expand our awareness to encompass it—we have to change.

Williamson's performance—energetic (frenetic is really the word), funny at moments, entirely self-indulgent—was precisely the chief element turning the play toward melodrama. Sprawled on the floor in one scene (he was forever draping himself over furniture or trying to climb nonexistent walls) he reached out to clutch the ankle of the aloofly passing Julie Christie, the Yelena of the production—a gesture that struck me as more suitable for an attempt to dissuade the villainous landlord who has just ordered everybody out into the snowy night than as an indication of hopeless infatuation. But this excessively broad performance delighted everybody, even Kauffmann (who was the only one, however, to point out that Williamson looked much too young for Vanya's forty-seven). The adjectives were "virtuosic," "magnificent," "marvellous," "inspired," and so on. And one reviewer, Jack Kroll, basing his opinion on a recording of the famous British production of the early 1960s, declared that Williamson's "surpassed Michael Redgrave's fine performance."

ACCOLADES FOR THE ACTORS

The other male lead, George C. Scott as Astrov, came in for more restrained praise, although John Simon in *New York* magazine thought him Williamson's superior and the equal of Olivier in the production referred to above. Comparisons between Scott and Williamson ran through many of the reviews, a peculiar circumstance which struck me as an indication of the effects of the star system at its most pernicious. Clive Barnes spoke of Williamson as an "internal" actor and of Scott as an "external" one, a mild enough if not especially useful distinction. But Brendan Gill called Scott a "match" for Williamson, Martin Gottfried said that Williamson "simply acts circles around Scott" and "blows him right off the stage," and Ted Kalem in *Time* spoke of their scenes as having "the charged intensity of *mano a mano* contests between bullfighters." Only Walter Kerr, who thought Scott a bit too detached from the proceedings, and Kauffmann, who thought (as I did) that he had "no *idea* of the part, no intent or subscription; he just scans the surfaces for chances to score," escaped both the tow of Scott's reputation and the temptation to see acting as a kind of sporting event, with winners and losers.

When it came to the rest of the company, opinions were a bit more divided. Three or four of the reviewers engaged in that wonderfully inane practice of covering four or five performances with a single adjective: "Barnard Hughes as the professor, Cathleen Nesbitt as a widow, Conrad Bain as an impecunious landowner and Lillian Gish as an old nurse are fine"—Watts in the *Post;* "Barnard Hughes is fine . . . and there are excellent contributions by . . . Bain . . . Gish . . . and . . . Nesbitt"—Douglas Watt in the *News;* "Hughes, Bain, Gish and Nesbitt play to perfection their roles as respectively"—Gill; "The smaller parts are all nicely filled"—Julius Novick in the *Village Voice.*

Actually, these smaller parts were all badly, or rather blindly filled. Kauffmann pointed out that Barnard Hughes as Serebryakov "is merely a fussy old crank, devoid of (the requisite) benevolent pomp and unctuous oppression."

And John Simon, in perhaps the most devastatingly negative remark any reviewer made about any performer (Simon is notorious for his conservative tastes and acid tongue), said that "Lillian Gish seems to me an actress whose usefulness ceased with the passing of D. W. Griffith."

The only real disputes, though, were over Julie Christie and Elizabeth Wilson, who played the extremely important part of Sonia. In regard to Christie, where she wasn't thought to have been "fine" and to have made an outstanding "contribution," her admirers succumbed entirely to her looks. "Lovely indeed," said Watts; "exquisitely beautiful," said Novick; "phantasmally beautiful," said Kroll. John Simon, in league with the truth, called her "almost amateurish"; Walter Kerr thought her "bland," as did Clive Barnes, and Kauffmann, once again the most perceptive of all, described her as having "all the impact of a faded fashion model."

The case of Elizabeth Wilson is central to the whole disaster. She is an actress with a reputation for comedic flair, which is scarcely what she is called upon for here. As if trying to keep her natural bent in severe check, she plays Sonia with a fiercely "spinsterish primness," as Julius Novick said, which has the effect of entirely perverting the role, destroying the qualities of innocence, slowly being instructed in the realities of the world and of durability under siege which distinguish her from the "bored" or hapless others and make her the play's true centre. A number of reviewers (Novick, Kauffmann, Barnes, Kalem, and Simon) pointed out that she was much too old for the part—she is supposed to be in her early twenties and looked forty-five—but only Novick and Kauffmann were illuminating on how fatally wrong she was in realms beyond the physical.

THWARTED THEME

I spoke before of *Uncle Vanya* being "about" stamina and not failure. In this connection the proof, if any were needed, of Nichols' complete failure to understand the play is given in a very minor incident concerning Sonia which nobody else seems to have noticed. During the scene of violent recriminations between Vanya and Serebryakov, the one that culminates in Vanya's failed attempt to shoot the professor, the nurse, a representative like all of Chekhov's aged servants of time endured, soothes the horrified girl with the wonderful lines: "Don't be upset, my dear. The geese will cackle for a while and then they'll stop. They'll cackle and then they'll stop cackling." In other words, you do not oppose the voices of the exacerbated and the frantic; you outlast them.

I quote these lines from Ronald Hingley's translation from memory, but I believe they're reasonably accurate. In the Nichols production, whose translation is by one Albert Todd, described as an expert in Slavic languages, and Nichols himself, and is racy, colloquial ("let's face it," someone says) but generally not too disturbing, the incident is left out almost entirely, the nurse simply shouting at the disputants at one point, "you're all a lot of geese." A small point, perhaps, but it seems to me a crucial one. Together with many of the other failures of understanding I've mentioned it indicates how this *Uncle Vanya* has been approached blindly, its subtleties erased and depths papered over.

One more note: I mentioned that I saw the production at its ninth or tenth performance. A friend whose mind I respect saw it on the second night, admired it, heard my anathemas, went back, and agreed that it was pretty awful. He accounted for this by saying that since Nichols had left after the second or third performance to attend a film festival somewhere in Italy or Eastern Europe, the actors, particularly Williamson, had gone haywire. I don't believe it, though I respect the irony of the reversal of the usual claim that productions ought to be seen after they've "settled down." I think my friend, who is a brilliant novelist but a very amateur theatergoer, was impressed, as many of the spectators seem to have been, simply by hearing the words of Chekhov, that vague figure of our artistic education, spoken aloud and clearly. And I also think it a splendid illustration of our theater's practice of irresponsibility that, even if it were true, Nichols should have jetted off to his festival after two days. I remember Jerzy Grotowski sitting night after night at the performances of his Laboratory Theatre, taking notes, being in charge. A high standard to set for the theater, of course, but unless we have one like it we're fated to the unrelieved disgracefulness of this all-star production. Still, as I said, I'm sure Nichols' early escape was only the finishing touch to his artistically criminal work.

Theatre Quarterly, Feb.–April 1974

The New German Playwrights:
Franz Xaver Kroetz

"I am a theater person who mistrusts nothing as much as the theater," Franz Xaver Kroetz told an interviewer a few years ago. The assertion brought the young German playwright into some very good company. At one time or another during their lives as dramatists, Büchner, Strindberg, Chekhov, Pirandello, and Brecht expressed sentiments of the same order; Ionesco has revealed his abiding disappointment in the life he witnessed on the stage; and Kroetz's own brilliant contemporary, Peter Handke, has made disbelief in the ordinary practices of the theater a ruling element of his dramaturgy. It would seem as though the drama, to a much greater degree than the other arts, requires of its geniuses an at least preliminary attitude of skepticism, contempt, and even revulsion.

The reason for this isn't hard to find. Along with opera, its related form, drama is the bourgeois art par excellence, the one most tempted toward the reinforcement of existing cultural values and so, by extension, of social and moral values, too. The matter is more subtle than ideology or any form of direct persuasion; what theater does, when it is operating to deaden consciousness, to act as a consoling and confirming ritual, is to reproduce an *expected* life, to present models of experience (or wishes, dreams) which the audience has already had and about which it has already come to conclusions. Again, it isn't a question of obvious comfort or palliation; "painful" plays, dramas about suffering of one kind or another, may also be bourgeois—in the sense of being complacent, essentially optimistic, unable to imagine life otherwise than as it has been known—as long as the depicted suffering fits easily into preexisting molds. There is a place for suffering in any well-rounded bourgeois education.

In a prefatory note to his short play *Heimarbeit* (*Homeworker*) Kroetz has composed a terse manifesto for all his work, a statement that reveals the particular basis of his mistrust of the conventional theater at the same time as it sets out the ground on which his distinctive imaginative sympathies rest and from which they seek their objectifications. "I wanted to break through an unrealistic theatrical convention: garrulity. The most important 'action' of my characters is their silence; and this is because their speech doesn't function properly. They have no good will. Their problems lie so far back and are so advanced that they are no longer able to express them in words."

A drama built on silences. A theater of the inarticulate. Such is the ironic achievement of this playwright who is scarcely thirty and has already established himself as a wholly unexpected and astonishing force in his native theater and is likely to do so soon in theatrical consciousness everywhere.

Set until very recently (the change is greatly significant and I shall take it up later) in the urban lower-class and poor farming milieus of his Bavarian childhood and youth, Kroetz's plays offer what would seem to be a chamber of horrors of violence and scatology. A spinster returns from her factory job one evening, goes through her precise rituals of lonely domesticity, and then calmly, gravely, kills herself. A script calls for a man to masturbate and defecate on stage (in production of course the actions are simulated or shown indirectly) and for a girl to foul her pants from fear. There are abortions or attempted ones in several plays. A dog is shot in another; a man and a woman use each other as targets in a deadly game with a rifle; an infant is murdered; illegitimacy, adultery, perverse sexual acts run through all the texts. Everything is dumb, animal-like, without any dimension of "mind."

Knowing only this much, one might properly conclude that Kroetz represents a retrogression, a movement back to a grim and fatally circumscribed realistic mode. Or, on a coarser level of response, such as that which greeted the opening of *Homeworker* in Munich in 1971, when Catholic organizations among others picketed the theater and rotten eggs were thrown at its façade, one might see no overriding artistic purpose in the display of such "tasteless" and malodorous material. Yet there seems to me no question that Kroetz is among the most remarkable new writers for the stage of the last fifteen or twenty years, and by new I mean in sensibility, vision, and technical procedure. To begin to know how this may be so, despite the appearance of datedness or crude sensationalism which any summary of his plots and dramatic incidents would present, we have to return to the note to *Homeworker* I quoted before.

Kroetz's great quiet originality lies in the fact of his having broken through, as the note tells us he wished to, a theatrical convention—an iron principle would not be too strong a term for it—that has held dominion over the stage throughout almost all of its history and in nearly every one of its sectors, transcending questions of style and theme and coming almost to represent dramatic reality itself. "Garrulity," he calls it, affixing a pejorative connotation to what we have always thought of simply as speech, dramatic utterance, oral expression on the stage. So unquestioned has been the existence of speech, dialogue, as the central agency of dramatic values, the chief means by which consciousness is shaped in the theater, that to accuse it of being "unrealistic," misleading, a convention and not the precise heart of the matter, is to seem to be quarreling with the very nature of the theater and of drama as a form. Yet we ought to know from our own lives, even if we lacked a theater to bring it formally to our attention, that garrulity—the overabundance of speech, its runaway mode—is designed to hide truth even more than to reveal it, and to mask the hiding: "methinks he doth protest too much" is a response to garrulity having been found out. To speak too much serves to cover up with words the holes in our existence, the spaces of unmeaning or of meaning too painful or dangerous to be permitted lineaments.

It is these spaces, these holes, that Kroetz's plays can be said to offer as their dramatic vision or actuality. A paradox? A contradiction in terms? How does vision arise from emptiness or substance from absence? Well, so nurtured are we on a belief in language as the most direct instrument of meaning in any literary work (and drama, while a peculiar form of literature, an enacted one, we might say, is nevertheless literary) that we find it dizzying to try to imagine how its absence or, more accurately in regard to Kroetz's plays, its maimed presence might be more significant and evocative than its fullness. The richer the language, the greater the work, we think; Shakespeare is the criterion and the apex. And this is all very well and true, except for the moment, the repeated moments in the history of the theater, when garrulity takes over, when there is too much being said.

A starting point for an understanding of what this "too much," this excess of utterance might be, as Kroetz conceives it, lies in another remark to an interviewer that "my figures are incapable of seeing through their situation because they have been robbed of their capacity to articulate." The word "robbed" alerts us to the political dimension of Kroetz's theater, but for the moment the thing to see is that the statement could function by inversion as the most concise possible history of traditional "high" drama, for that might be defined precisely as the *seeing through* of situations, replicas or analogues of those experienced in life, on the stage.

To do this one needs speech, which is to say the power of naming the condition one is in (if not directly then by verbal structures that create it metaphorically; the most "eloquent" plays do it just that way), of making distinctions both within it and between it and other states, and therefore of making it, in theory at least, useful: instructive, purgative in Aristotle's sense, eye-opening in Brecht's, in every case part of the formal stock of human awareness. And, Kroetz is saying, until now, throughout the long reign of the theater as a cultured activity, such a power has been the possession only of the privileged, in an economic sense, surely, but in a wider one as well. It has belonged to the more or less articulate, by definition. Drama in this view has consequently offered us, in a way that transcends subject or idea, a world in which characters, deputies for the rest of us, own from the start the means of making their situations known, of expressing them, so that whatever else a play may be it is essentially a process of bringing this knowledge into the light.

What is more, the knowledge is itself privileged, the self-awareness of those human beings in the guise of stage characters whose social existence, and so whose existential space, is wide enough to permit thinking about, giving names to, and so truly experiencing—although not of course necessarily "solving"— their predicaments: Lear's knowledge that he has lived not wisely but too well; Norah's that she must leave her husband in order to find out what she is. If such knowledge is continually being corrupted and turned into bravado by garrulity (in the commercial theater garrulity is all there is) which papers over the chasms and so hides reality at the same time as it seems to proclaim it, the principle re- mains undisturbed that it is only through language that the attempt to know can be made, and the belief is firm that drama is one of our chief means of or- ganizing this expressive intent.

Now this doesn't in any way mean that there have been no poor or stultified inarticulate characters is drama. The point is that where they exist they have not been at the center of the work and have been surrounded by characters who can speak and so carry the burden of verbal meaning, or else, as in Tolstoy's *Power of Darkness,* O'Neill's *Hairy Ape,* or Gorky's *The Lower Depths,* they have been given a passionate "popular" utterance of their own and so made articulate after all. The one great exception might seem to be Büchner's Woyzeck, yet even this unprecedented figure of the oppressed and victimized possesses speech, bro- ken, tormented, mad if you will, but greatly evocative speech nevertheless. On a more debased aesthetic plane the poor and outcast have usually been given an articulateness that is the product of romantic invention, the fake urban lyricism of Odets or the cracker-barrel loquacity of plays like *Tobacco Road.* In any case, the condition of being truly unable to utter one's reality has never been a cen- tral element of any play, has never, one can almost say, been a subject.

In place, then, of characters whose command of language is their precondi- tion for being characters and who talk so that we may "appreciate" them (ap- preciate: to judge with heightened perception and understanding) and so pre- sumably be made more conscious, Kroetz has created figures whose speech does nothing either to bring forward ideas or perspectives on their condition or to cover it up, and in fact only "expresses" it negatively by its injured or inadequate quality. They seem to speak only because people do speak, struggling to find some connection between words and the internal conditions or facts of the world which make up their situations; they speak, one feels, because not to speak at all would be the conclusive evidence of their despair.

In the opening scene of *Michi's Blood*, a scene which with characteristically quiet irony Kroetz calls *Table Conversation*, a man and a woman, lovers or at least sexual intimates, exchange these words:

MARY. Once we've got a room you can go to the john.

KARL. 'Cause it's cold there.

M. A person just can't take everything lying down.

K. Right.

M. 'Cause you're a filthy pig.

K. That's what you are, what's that make me?

M. You're off your rocker.

K. That's what you are, what's that make me?

M. You're horny, but you can't get it together.

K. That's what you are, what's that make me? I don't give a shit.

M. Don't eat if it don't taste. Think I'd stop you?

K. Not you, cause I wouldn't ask.

M. Don't bother eating if it don't taste.

K. Tastes O.K.

M. You don't love me no more. That's it.

K. If you're so smart.

Later, after the woman has revealed her pregnancy, the man gives her a crude abortion. A scene called *Finding the Truth* goes as follows, in its entirety:

M. Can I tell you something?

K. Why not.

M. I've got a pain.

K. Then pull yourself together, you'll manage, just don't think about it.

M. Right. One should never lose hope.

K. So what do you want?

M. I just don't know anymore.

K. Probably something stupid anyhow.

M. Right. 'Cause I forgot.

K. Always gotta add your two bits.

M. Why?

K. There!

M. 'Cause I'm human too.

K. That's something.

Now the painfulness of these exchanges arises from their substance, naturally, but even more from their relation to the play's events or, more accurately, the expected significance of those events and their "values." In the first scene the quarreling lovers (if we can call them that—their relationships mocks all the classic, lyrical attributes of the word) stumble verbally round one another, exchanging blows of sad, depleted forcefulness, blows without point, delivered in the dark. The clichés, the repetitions of banalities, the bromides all testify to the stricken nature of their speech, not so much its lack of expressiveness— that is obvious—as the entire absence of originality, the queer and terrifying sense it gives of not having been created by them but of having instead passed through them, as it were. It is as though their language has been come upon, *picked up,* scavenged from the gray mindless stretches of a mechanical culture.

In the second scene the pathos of this derivative, radically inappropriate speech is still deeper. We know from what has gone before that the woman is anguished over the abortion, or rather we have to intuit it since she is wholly unable to express it in terms we would think appropriate. The man, for his part, is embarrassed, frightened, bellicose; but once again these emotions and attitudes have no appropriate style, no diction we can accept as directly constituting the experience, the way traditional drama has always organized its effects. The clichés and fragmented responses, the sad aphoristic wisdom ("One should never lose hope!" Kroetz's plays are full of such sayings in the mouths of victims) move to fill the space between feeling and event, but the gap remains intact. And it is from this abyss that there rises the extraordinary sense in the spectator of being present at a sort of fatal accident, a crack-up at the edge of truth. "'Cause I'm human too," the woman says. We know she is, but the sorrowfulness of the remark is that she has been injured past the capacity to demonstrate it.

If the damaged speech of Kroetz's characters is their most striking departure from conventional stage figures, it doesn't mean that the physical in his work is any less original. If anything, the physical action in these plays is more mysterious and disturbing than the verbal, not so much in its substance as in the ways it is disposed. Where the connection between speech and physical action in traditional drama might be said to be that of comment and reciprocity—an "acting" out of the verbal, a "speaking-out" of the material, in Kroetz's plays this relationship is ruptured; the two orders of expressiveness never fuse, never offer direct perspectives on one another. Nothing is done as a *consequence* of something having been said, or the other way round.

The clue to this strange new relationship of speech and act lies in Kroetz's remark about the most important "action" of his characters being their silence. For these silences, the gaps within or the truncations of their speech, make for an almost unbearable tension on the stage, a pressure of the unsaid—of the unable to be said—that weighs upon every movement or gesture, and all potential ones, and infuses them with a quality of extreme nakedness, radical isolation. Bereft of the "cultural" covering in which dramatic actions are ordinarily sheathed, the matrix of articulated ideas, attitudes, perceptions, comment, and so on, these physical events take place, so to speak, inexplicably, like eruptions from the darkness, pure, horrifying acts of discrete and seemingly motiveless violence.

The most extreme of them, the murders, rapes, assaults that fill his plays, come at a point when the felt inadequacy of the characters' language, the frustration they cannot name (and still worse, cannot even imagine with a name, since that would be to possess some part of the language whose lack is their very condition) bring his characters to pass over the boundaries of the "civilized." It is as though the tension created by their inarticulateness, the profound occlusion of consciousness in them, can only give way to the "reliefs" of brutal motions, to a catharsis in which nothing is purged but something infinitely painful is, at least, attested to.

This deeply subtle relationship of speech and gesture in Kroetz's plays, this atmosphere made up so largely of the implicit and unannounced, make their strange power and effectiveness unusually difficult to convey through brief quotation or the description of single actions. Still, a scene such as the following one from *Farmyard* offers us a narrow way into the depleted, stricken world his imagination has come upon. A middle-aged farmhand has taken the young, retarded daughter of his employer to a country fair. They take a ride on the "ghost-train" and when they emerge from the tunnel the girl is evidently in distress:

SEPP. What's the matter?

BEPPI. (Walks stiffly.)

S. Something's hurting you?

B. (Denies it.)

S. You dirtied your pants. You did. Come on now. Were you scared?

B. (Completely confused.)

S. Come on now we'll clean you up. (They go behind a tent or away from the crowd.) Here now let's clean you up. Here, wipe yourself with these leaves. (She cleans herself, diarrhea runs down her legs.)

S. You shit your pants. Here let me. (He cleans her up.) Take off your pants, you can't do it that way. (Beppi cleans herself with his help.) Wipe yourself with this. Here let me. (He takes his handkerchief and wipes her with it.) It's all right again. Come here. (He takes her and deflowers her.)

The scene is of course harsh, unsettling, "embarrassing" to witness. But what strikes one throughout is the entire inability of the girl to speak about or to the situation (although she is slightly retarded, she is in no sense a mute) and the man's extreme matter-of-factness in his speech to her, a matter-of-factness that is greatly at odds with what the theatrical spectator is conditioned to expect and that prepares the way for the brutal abruptness with which he takes the girl's virginity. The cold terse stage direction in which this is indicated is an exemplary instance of Kroetz's methods (if that is the right word; I would prefer to say his angle of vision): the absence of either preparation or aftermath, the refusal of comment, the sudden, isolated, terrifying act of violence. An actor or director might wish, out of obedience to notions of proper "theatricality," to insert some stage business between the last line of the dialogue and the rape, but it is precisely Kroetz's genius to cut through such dramatic integument in order to present the most naked, unmediated, and, to the degree that this is possible, *unaestheticized* gesture and image.

This cold, grave quality of Kroetz's plays, their eschewal of judgment, argument, and authorial bias, the absence in them of any trace of tendentiousness, of "color" and emotional solicitation of a traditional kind, and, finally, their extreme simplicity of incident and iconography, are what so sharply distinguish them from the species of drama we have historically called "naturalistic." Apart from a mutual repudiation of fantasy and the elevation to the status of characters of previously excluded beings—the poor, the outcast—his plays have almost nothing in common with the dramas of classic naturalism, Zola's, say, or Hauptmann's. Above all, they do not share traditional naturalism's dream of a quasi-scientific imperium, its enslavement by what Delacroix called "the fetish for accuracy that most people mistake for truth."

By the same token, Kroetz's work protects itself through its internal dispositions, its sense of mysterious fatality and inassuageable pain, from the charge of sensationalism, of an intention simply to shock, although the accusation continues to be made. His plays are as far from *Tobacco Road* or any newer mode of sexual "frankness" on the stage as it is possible to be; they may seem to be dealing with some of the same materials and ambiances, but the difference is of the order of that between C. S. Forester's and Joseph Conrad's treatment of the sea, an absolute difference of size, mind, and moral imagination.

In fact, the disturbance Kroetz has caused, as well as the welcome given to him by more discerning minds, goes far beyond the immediate physical data of his plays to the broader implications of his style and the aesthetic and cultural significance they radiate. The truth is that his breaking of moral and social taboos, his unhygienic displays and feral anecdotes, are in the service of a far more subversive vision than they mount up to in themselves; his presence speaks of a wider imaginative change in German theater—so often a force for change in the universal stage—than one could discover by a recounting of his "stories."

Homeworker was one among a number of unsettling new plays that appeared in Germany at the end of the sixties and the beginning of the seventies and were the work of a wholly new generation of German-speaking dramatists of whom Kroetz is likely the most gifted and surely the most original. Men born during or just after the war, the group includes Martin Sperr, Wolfgang Bauer, and Rainer Werner Fassbinder (who is better known in the United Sates for his films), and while they differ widely among themselves in matters of style and sensibility they also share certain deep affinities. They are all to one degree or another left-oriented in politics; they employ vernacular speech in preference to any sort of literary language; they have set themselves against the use of the stage as a source of what they consider debilitating illusion; and, most significant for their creative morale and imaginative independence, they have been freed—by acts of will as well as by chronology—from the previous era of devastated German consciousness.

This group of writers, to whom only for the sake of a convenient identity we might give the collective name of "new realists," constitutes I think the most vigorous and in some ways innovative movement in the theater since the renaissance of the British stage which was carried out fifteen or twenty years ago in the early plays of Osborne, Pinter, and Arden. The more pertinent comparison, though, is to the appearance in Paris in the early fifties of what we have come to call—at the cost of as much confusion as the term new realists is likely to cause—"absurd" drama, the revelatory, unexampled plays of Beckett, Ionesco, and others. For what these young German playwrights have been doing, Kroetz most forcefully among them, is the same kind of life-giving work as that of their antipodal predecessors in France: the extrication of the theater from its own assumptions, from received wisdom and settled notions of what drama is and may do.

These writers make up, that is to say, an avant-garde, but one which neither proclaims itself as one nor bears the obvious distinguishing marks of such an enterprise. There ought to be nothing surprising in this; it is outsiders who usually give avant-gardes their name. And in regard to the signs by which they will be known, it is one of the grand subtleties of culture that the truly newest forms generally owe their animating principles to achievements reached in the past and often appear to us as old, although with a strange, unaccountable light flickering over their surfaces, the light of something newly seen.

In the case of these new German playwrights the debt is to the old and for the most part underground tradition of the *Volkstück,* or "folk play," which was not, as its name suggests, a work of naïve authorship, rising from some memorializing or celebratory impulse among simple people, but the highly conscious creation of sophisticated writers for the theater. Its chief characteristics are that it concerns itself with the lives of common people and that it is written either in dialect or in one or another kind of colloquial language, in opposition to the *Hochdeutsch* or high German in which the overwhelming majority of German plays have always been composed.

The form was introduced in Vienna in the early eighteenth century by a writer named Josef Anton Stranitzky, and carried to a full development by the nineteenth-century Austrians Johann Nestroy and Ferdinand Raimund. Then after a long period of neglect it was revived in the twenties and thirties of this century, chiefly by the gifted German writer Egon von Horvath (whose neglect here—he has scarcely been translated—is a minor cultural mystery). Von Horvath, who died young in 1939, wrote plays whose characters were mainly petty clerks, small shopkeepers, housemaids, hustlers, grifters, and the like, the marginal, tamped-down people of modern urban life, and which were free of the didactic moralizing that had marred the work of Nestroy and Raimund.

Von Horvath's influence on Kroetz and his fellow neo-realists is clear and acknowledged by them, but their most direct and powerful predecessor, as they unreservedly avow, is a writer with a strange, painful history who figures in only the most marginal accounts of twentieth-century German literature and is entirely unknown here. Marieluise Fleisser, who died in 1973 at seventy-one,

wrote plays, as well as novels and stories, about the most oppressed of characters, the socially insulted and injured, employing a coarse, ragged vernacular for
their speech and exhibiting them in an atmosphere of spiritual desolation. The
victim of psychic disorders and domestic turbulence, at various times of censorship, and almost throughout her career, of public indifference, she was "re-
discovered" in the late sixties by Kroetz, Fassbinder, and others and has since
enjoyed a certain vogue. Before her death she met Kroetz, who has carried her
vision and techniques to a much more extreme point. She called him "the dear-
est of her sons" and went on to say, with an understatement characteristic of
both him and herself, that "he cares about the others."

This caring, which is clearly so much more than abstract concern for the victims of social and economic injustice, has, as I have tried to point out, entered
Kroetz's work without fanfare or any kind of declaratory impulse whatsoever.
And it is just this quality of austere detachment, the placing before us, without
comment or the least grain of theatrical seductiveness, of imaginative evidence
which makes up a stringent, self-validating dramatic whole, that helps lift these
plays out of what we might call their "local" status, their possible existence as
case histories.

For however specific the milieus of his characters may be, however identifiable they are according to our typologies of social organization, dramatically
they exist as deputies (Kroetz's own word for them) for all of us. They have particularly grave afflictions and employ their own blind means of combatting
them, but they stand the way we do—the articulate, readers, writers, audiences—in the face of the chasm between language and truth, self-awareness
and fate, closer to the extreme edge of course but not constituting a different
species. They speak, or struggle to speak, for us all.

Still the judgment I have just offered is essentially an aesthetic one, and the
theater is notoriously a place where aesthetic reality has a hard time making itself known. Our compulsion to construct moral hierarchies among human beings has been given particular encouragement in the theater—heroes and villains, the absolved and the condemned; it is one of the subtle bourgeois
conventions of the stage at which Chekhov, as he tells us, used to "swear
fiercely." And though the phenomenon is scarcely confined to the theater, the
medium is especially disposed toward the corruption of a "virtue" such as pity
into a sense of superiority or, at best, into a mode of proper, civilized, ineffectual response; you pity the sufferer, who remains in place for your pity to exercise itself upon.

In the light of these things the crisis of conscience that overtook Kroetz several years ago is far from surprising. A mistruster of the theater, a man of strong leftward leanings, he had seen behind the suffering of his characters an expropriation, a "stealing" of their language, as he called it. He had seen politically, in other words, and because, as he thought, "my pieces keep producing primarily apolitical pity," he took certain steps to try to correct that. In 1973 he joined the West German Communist Party, and though he has claimed that he has experienced no pressure, that he has been encouraged to write in the "same way as before," the fact is that his writing has changed drastically.

The first indication of this was his having written (a few months before his formal entrance into the Party, but when he was well along toward the decision) an unabashedly "agitprop" work called *Münchner Kindl*, a play about the housing situation in Munich and the growing concentration of land and capital in the hands of a few oligarchic families, which contains a direct call to tenants and the exploited generally to join the Communist Party. His most recent play *Das Nest* carries him further along the retreat from his earlier stance of pure untendentious vision as well as, thematically, from his icy tales of the dispossessed. A drama about ecology and the conflict between values and power, its characters are of the middle class and have no difficulty at all in "expressing" themselves.

But perhaps the most disturbing evidence of Kroetz's change is in his having rewritten an earlier work in order to make it conform more closely to his present belief and attitude. This play, originally called *Men's Business* (an ironic title conveying Kroetz's erstwhile deep sense of women as even greater victims than men), ended with a shocking, unbearably painful yet superbly revelatory scene in which a couple play a "game" with a rifle and so allow their mute antagonisms and unfulfillment to find their fatal expression. Kroetz has retitled the work *A Man, A Dictionary*, which comes from a nearly untranslatable folk saying, and much more radically, has eliminated the culminating scene and given the play a more or less "happy" ending.

Kroetz is young, and he cares. We have to sympathize with him in his dilemma and refrain from condemning in the name of "art" what seems to be a movement toward an obvious and unresonant facticity. Some time ago he spoke poignantly of what lay behind his changed position: "My pieces are oriented on very Christian conceptions: they appeal primarily to empathy, to love among people, to insight, to understanding, to giving something up of one's free will, to improving something of one's free will; they are touching, they do not agitate, offer no solutions, and therefore lend themselves particularly well to being absorbed as a kind of warm breath."

If he fails to see the truly remarkable dimensions of his earlier accomplishment, its revolutionary shift in consciousness and powerful, exemplary beauty, he is surely justified in his suspicions of the fate of any kind of imagination in the world of institutionalized culture. Like other writers before him (Tolstoy comes immediately to mind), he is caught between his social awareness and concern and his *prédilection d'artiste.* Whether or not his new mode of didactic dramatic invention will be permanent is beyond even our speculation. Meanwhile the earlier plays remain, testing us, challenging our habits, harsh, unaccomodating, and heartbreaking.

Partisan Review, Autumn 1976

How the New Theatrical Directors
Are Upstaging the Playwright

Shortly before his recent resignation, Joseph Papp announced plans for a thoroughgoing renovation of the Vivian Beaumont Theater at Lincoln Center. The Beaumont would be remodeled, Papp said, with a view to making it a directors' showcase, while the Public Theater, Papp's other fief, would remain primarily a place for writers. This is a curious separation, but behind it is a large cultural idea—Papp's wish "to create a bridge between the avant-garde theater and the conventional" one. At the center of this ambition, not unknown in modern theatrical history, was his intention of presenting perennial works in ways that would "shatter convention—classics treated by modern minds."

Such shattering and treating would be at the hands of directors, of course, and Papp has already done a great deal to strengthen those. Directors are enjoying a new and perhaps unprecedented eminence in the American theater these days, to the point, some say, of threatening to "take it over." One has an image of the Mafia moving into the Bronx or Scarsdale, and so an impulse to call Papp the godfather of the development. The past season's productions at Lincoln Center by Andrei Serban of *The Cherry Orchard* and *Agamemnon* and by Richard Foreman of *The Threepenny Opera* are centerpieces of this movement toward directorial hegemony over a large sector of our theater. And Papp reported that both Serban and Foreman figured prominently among a group he was considering for work at the altered Beaumont.

Others were Joseph Chaikin of the erstwhile Open Theatre, Richard Schechner of the Performance Group, Peter Schumann of the Bread and Puppet Theater, and Lee Breuer and JoAnne Akalaitis of Mabou Mines, together with more traditional workmen like Michael Bennett, deviser of *A Chorus Line,* and Mike Nichols. One wouldn't have been surprised to have seen Tom O'Horgan sneak in somewhere, or assignments given to English directors like Frank Dunlop, whose *Scapino,* an innovative rendering of Molière's *Les Fourberies de Scapin,* was such a hit in New York a couple of years ago.

Whomever Papp might have chosen, it's abundantly clear as this season ends that not since the 1950s, when a corps of professionals like Elia Kazan, José Quintero, and Alan Schneider were working at full steam, have directors had so much power and prominence. So-and-so's production of this or that, so-and-so's vision, so-and-so's concept: the cachet is all with the director now, it appears, to the detriment, many would argue, of the playwright. In that regard a significant difference shows itself between the earlier echelon of star American directors and the one now gaining or consolidating power. (I include Serban because nearly all this young Rumanian's major work has been done here.)

I spoke of Kazan and the others as "professionals" and did not mean by this a contrast with any sort of amateur. The point is that those directors were theatrical freelancers, established (and more or less establishment) talents who lacked any far-reaching aesthetic of theater, or at any rate never enunciated one, and who were willing and able to take on whatever of interest and/or profitability came their way. In contrast, almost all the directors Papp names and others whom he might have, such as Robert Wilson (who is, of course, also a writer) and André Gregory, have been or are still connected with theatrical groups at one distance or another from the commercial center; gurus or at least intellectual forces, they have worked with people who share their approach to theatrical art, their theories of staging, and to one degree or another their distance from what they would all doubtless agree in thinking of as the "bourgeois" stage.

The earlier directors worked mainly with new plays by living playwrights or, as in the case of Quintero's efforts on behalf of O'Neill, with late and theatrically not-yet-realized plays by recently dead writers. For this reason the conventions Papp quite rightly inveighs against—the pieties encasing the production of almost all classics from the Greeks to Pirandello and Brecht—were not a problem for them; what they had to assault or outflank were the habitual deficiencies of American stage imagination, in particular our tradition of the director as most usefully a traffic cop. This meant that for all their distinctive styles and notable energy and for all their occasional forays into the playwright's province (the most flagrant example being Kazan's jostling of Tennessee Williams's texts toward greater commercial éclat), they were measurably subordinate to the writers they were hired to serve.

In contrast, for the type of director who is making himself felt these days, the play, especially the accepted classic, is less in need of being faithfully served, that is to say respectfully and straightforwardly transmitted, than of being given life, in the problematic pursuit of which liberties are often taken of a kind that can outrage purists but also dismay the thoughtful. Without making judgments yet of specific productions, I want to emphasize at this point the "avant-garde" nature of these directors' background and angle of approach. Behind the new impulse toward vividness, originality, and emotional "relevance" in staging, particularly the staging of classics, is a sense of theater as having been feeding on its own exhausted values. Dissimilar as their own work may be, these directors share in regard to classics a notion of texts buried under successive layers of presentational cliché for the overthrow of which a certain degree of daring and even at times recklessness is thought to be essential. Director's theater in its most specific meaning refers to a body of stage work created by directors who owe at least as much to the visual arts, dance, and music as to traditional drama. More broadly, the phrase refers to a tendency, increasingly evident lately, for directors who stage other people's plays to take liberties with texts, especially of classics, to place their own contribution on a par with the dramatist's and sometimes beyond. What its defenders say is that director's theater has heightened the theatrical values of contemporary plays and, most important, given new life to classics, by refusing to be bound by tradition, which, in such a view, is really frozen convention.

Director's theater has also rejected certain rights—of texts, of authors—one would have thought inviolable. Peter Brook, some of whose own Shakespearean productions have been superb, has said, "I do not for one moment question the rewriting of Shakespeare," and Jonathan Miller, the madcap physician turned director, has flatly stated, "I don't believe one has any duty or obligation to an author, once he's dead. The play becomes a public object. One should be able to do to it exactly what one wants."

Though this isn't quite as appalling and indefensible a statement as it might seem, it does represent a directorial arrogance that makes itself felt at the leading edge of the theater everywhere these days. Louis Jouvet, a fine director as well as actor, once wrote: "Almost all directors after a few years of modest service dream of showing their nature and the scale of their imagination. . . . They are seized with a violent desire to make over masterpieces and to express at last their own personal perceptions. . . . The profession of the director suffers from the disease of immodesty."

Such a cast of mind is understandable. They have all worked at the implementation of more or less pure and immediate theatrical or histrionic vaules, for which texts are often simply pretexts, occasions for little revolutions in staging and performing. They have been used to being "creators," not simply intermediaries or the equivalent of orchestral conductors. And they have all in one way or another been affected by, and in some cases contributed to, the age's periodic waves of radical thinking about the theater, thinking that for several generations has so largely been a product of the directorial mind itself.

It would doubtless surprise the ordinary theatergoer to learn that the very notion of a director as a distinct figure is scarcely a century old. Until well past Shakespeare's time, as far as we know, performances were organized and shaped, in so far as they were shaped at all, from within, by one or another member of the acting company, whose task seems to have been simply to see that what needed to be done was done, at the right time and with as little confusion as possible.

Later there appeared in England and elsewhere the "actor-manager," a star performer who ran a company and dictated the nature of productions, usually disposing their elements so as to set off his or her own talents and charms. It wasn't until the mid-nineteenth century, when Samuel Phelps did some pioneeringly careful productions of Shakespeare in London, that directors in anything like the modern sense came into being, and it wasn't until the 1870s that the Duke of Saxe-Meiningen would startle the theater world with his well-drilled troupe, whose work aimed at creating for every production a unitary, coherent effect.

At the end of the century, with groups like André Antoine's Théâtre Libre and the Moscow Art Theater of Stanislavsky and Nemirovich-Danchenko, directing became a primary component of all theatrical work, including the most narrowly commercial. More than that, the director began to be a chief source of theatrical ideas, so that the history of twentieth-century theater is at least as much one of directorial theory and practice as of dramatic innovation.

Stanislavsky, Meyerhold, Gordon Craig, Artaud (who didn't direct much but became the master of others who did), Brecht (in his directorial role), Grotowski, Brook: Whether or not they called themselves or were called directors, they make up the great line of modern directorial thinking, whose chief tenet is that every production has to have an "idea" behind it, that texts have to be interpreted, or *reinterpreted,* and not simply placed literally, faithfully on stage. Meyerhold, Stanislavsky's brilliant, wayward disciple, and the man from whom true directorial megalomania might be said to have sprung, even had himself listed in the programs of plays he directed at his theater as "author of the spectacle."

Since then the practice has spread of billing the director above the playwright or, as with Shakespeare and others, attaching the director's name to a particular production. We speak of Brook's *King Lear,* Franco Zeffirelli's *Romeo and Juliet,* Andrei Serban's *Cherry Orchard.* This has connections with the older practice of affixing a star performer's name to a role he or she has become famous for: Kean's Hamlet, Olivier's Richard or Henry, Duse's Mrs. Alving. But it has even stronger affinities with the way film directors take or are given credit (or blame) for their works. A major element in the rise of director's theater has been the craving of theater directors for the kind of independence, the creative leeway, that some of their film counterparts have always been given.

The obstacle in the way of this is simply the enormous difference between the functions of the screenwriter and the dramatist. Films aren't primarily made up of literary materials, but of visual components and the relations between them, and it's the film director who largely selects and orders them. On the stage, where the play, the text, *is* (or was) the thing, the director hasn't originated the work but is there, theoretically at least, to serve it.

The traditional obligation of the director, once he emerged, was to take charge of a body of actors while subordinating himself to a text, in somewhat the same way a conductor does to an orchestra and a score. His task, as the stage designer Lee Simonson said about Saxe-Meiningen, was to "visualize an entire performance and give it unity as an interpretation by complete control of every moment of it." Even more fundamentally his job was to move a text from, so to speak, paper to boards, to give it palpable existence.

It's just this question of how texts can and ought to be brought to physical life that's been at the center of theatrical theory and experiment since the time ended when all the animation that was wanted was the presence and mystique of star performers. There are still stars in the theater, of course, but for any intelligent or not wholly commercial director, stars can as easily injure a production—by overriding the text, tipping everything their way—as give it truth and force. Indeed, the rise of the director stemmed in part from a revolt against the star system in favor of ensemble playing. The irony is that the director has become the new star; *his* presence; *his* interpretation, and often *his* mystique are what rule.

All right. He has a case. Nothing is drearier than the sort of traditional, literal-minded production of Shakespeare or Chekhov, say, that bases itself on detailed research into Elizabethan England or turn-of-the-century Russia and presents the play as though it were a museum piece. And nothing is more limiting than the "accepted" way to stage anything. Times and perceptions change and the way we do plays ought to change with them. For new plays there's no history of production, so we should be free to risk whatever might "work."

So then, armed with the justification that audiences are irritated or bored by conventional renderings of the classics or straightforward mountings of any play, the auteur-director (to borrow a term from films) feels free to devise or invent what will wake them up. A crucial fact about plays as scripts lends itself to his ambition: Between any written text and its physical realization on stage is a zone of uncertainty, incompleteness, an area where interpretation is precisely what's necessary. To take some examples from stage directions: Shakespeare's *Henry V* says merely "a field in France"; Chekhov's *Cherry Orchard* says "in the distance the outlines of a large town." The director has the obligation to "create" or suggest France or the town, and the opportunity to do it in whatever way he wants.

Going deeper, we find ever more subtle and ambiguous areas between written texts and plays on stage. In recent years we've come to use the term "subtext" to indicate the life implied beneath or behind the dialogue and the indicated physical actions; this existence, so the notion goes, is in rather the same proportion to the total life of a play as the visible part of an iceberg is to its total bulk. It has been precisely in the region of subtext that the auteur-director has been able to exercise his wildest inventiveness and so to commit his greatest crimes.

From the beginning of this development it was inevitable that there would be conflict between the director and the playwright or, in the case of the classic repertoire, the defenders of a "proper," sanctified style and approach. Between any playscript and the physical stage is a zone of ambiguity and doubtfulness, an area where language doesn't always suggest its own unmistakable incarnation, and where the director is therefore on his own. Yet there are indications he has to follow. Chekhov's quarrels with Stanislavsky over the latter's readings of his plays as "heavy dramas," the Russian expression for tragedy, are familiar history, and there is further evidence that Stanislavsky, along with his heroic capacity to fill the stage with life, had a dangerous tendency to dictate the idiosyncratic life he wanted to find. "A stage direction or a single phrase in a play called forth all sorts of images in his mind," an assistant of his once said, "and these very often played havoc with the author's text."

The more fecund the directorial imagination, then, the more likely is the text to suggest subterranean and decisive truths about itself, something we have learned to call the subtext, but also to suggest what the author may not have at all intended and may bitterly oppose when it reaches the stage. I don't know if Fernando Arrabal saw O'Horgan's recent production of *The Architect and the Emperor of Assyria,* but if he did he would have witnessed half a dozen plays, only one of which he wrote. Overdirection, O'Horgan's besetting vice, is also to one extent or another that of many of the most prominent new directors (especially when they are let loose on a classic), as underdirection, or complete infertility, is the malady of most conventional ones.

For these new directors doing too much to a text, above all familiar ones, is the vice of their previous virtue. In their work with their own companies or associates, often on texts of their own or the group's creation, or in relaxed situations with a text as the ground of an experiment, such as Serban's work at La MaMa, it was scarcely possible to do too much, since what was wanted was the bringing to theatrical life of something that had either not yet existed or did so in a rudimentary, "open" form. But classic texts exist and have their rights.

There are limits to what may be done to a text and these are set within the text itself. They have to do with coherence, aesthetic appropriateness, plausibility; and with the imaginative and intellectual vision of a work, its tone, weight, and individuality. These make up the "life" that has to be respected. There isn't any single *right* way to do Shakespeare, for instance, but there are wrong ways, and updating is almost always one of them. When, in a production of *Hamlet,* Laertes appears in white flannels and carries a tennis racquet, and Fortinbras is accompanied by British tommies with a walkie-talkie; or when, in a far-out *Macbeth,* the witches are seen on two television screens, anachronism, discordance, idiosyncrasy reign, and a new vision, inferior in its very *au courantism,* is substituted for the old.

Peter Hall, a great Shakespearean director, has said, "I think that doing Shakespeare in modern dress is on the whole crazy. . . . Though it illuminates

. . . it always cuts off much. It is a direct and crude way of making *some* signals work." The signals Hall means are those that have to do with "relevance." The hope is that substituting contemporary dress, speech inflections, physical objects, current references, and so on, for those of the original text will allow greater access to the play's life; it will overcome the archaisms. But where is that life to be found except in an intricate embodiment of its own contemporaneity? What's cut off is the mesh of relations among speech, gesture, and action, the very sense of life, the great paradigmatic visions that are, beyond the lines themselves, Shakespeare's poetry. What's removed, in the interest of timeliness, is the timeless.

"It is a strange role, that of the director," Peter Brook has said. "He does not ask to be God and yet his role implies it." However the position is attained, if you find yourself God, the temptation is either to abdicate or to roll up your sleeves. In regard to new plays the temptation is to try to make them appealing by strategies of seductive and often excessive staging which may do violence to subtle or quiet values in the text while eliciting the raves of shallow critics. For classics the temptation, wholly legitimate to begin with, is to move against traditions of staging and performing which have hardened into dogmas.

The benefits of this refusal to do things as they have always been done are clear enough; Peter Brook's radically austere *Lear* and his radically flamboyant *A Midsummer Night's Dream* are examples. But the risk is that in trying to revivify—as though they were dead—plays by Aeschylus or Shakespeare or Chekhov the director ends by replacing the writer's imagination with his own. Max Reinhardts all, directors are encouraged today in this species of arrogance by many complex factors, of which the most obvious are the star syndrome affecting all who work publicly and the prevailing mood of audiences, for whom classics are more than ever synonymous with boredom and cultural duty. The wish to be entertained in the theater isn't to be questioned, but problems begin, as Brecht pointed out, with notions of what is entertaining. It's here that Papp's bridge-building ambitions run into difficulty. On one bank of the broad river is his audience for "conventional" theater, an audience for whom entertainment is essentially spectacle or vicarious, predictable sentiment, and who want their classics shaped toward these ends; on the other is that much smaller "avant-garde" audience for whom the entertaining must also be the imaginatively true, the dramatically unexpected.

The irony is the reception of Serban's and Foreman's productions at Lincoln Center this season, of Schechner's *Mother Courage* at the Performing Garage, and of O'Horgan's everywhere is that for the most part they were popular with conventional audiences and critics and vigorously disliked by the theatrical avant-garde. The latter, an ill-defined group to be sure, can be minimally described as those who welcome change in the theater and value risk-taking in its practices. Artaud and Brecht are still its gods, along with Jerzy Grotowski and to a lesser extent Brook; Robert Wilson and Foreman in his Ontological-Hysterical Theater work are among its new enthusiasms.

The point is that it hasn't been fossils or zealots of the status quo who have objected most strongly to these recent displays of directorial egoism. The issue isn't originality versus archaism but originality that remains in coherence with a text against that which distorts it and may evey destroy its true life. It goes without saying that there's no fixed "meaning" to a classic play or a good new one for that matter; the argument isn't over that. But there surely is a sense which a play asserts an atmosphere, a tone, a specific weight, an angle of vision. These are the things a director has to discover and find the means to express; the process oughtn't to be one of superimposing life but of revealing the life that is there.

Serban's *Cherry Orchard* is a notable instance of a directorial mind substituting itself for the playwright's, of a concept trampling over a dramatic fact. From the set design, spectacular in its own right, brilliantly calculated to draw oohs and ahs but drastically out of keeping with Chekhov's complex, subtle realism, to the dominant farcical tone which is a perversion of Chekhov's description of the play as a "comedy" (which he undoubtedly meant in the Dantean sense, not that of Feydeau), the intrusion of characters—the boy, the toiling peasants, the White Rock girl who kneels beside Firs at the end—unknown in the text until now, and the factory in the background to add a note of menacing industrialism where Chekhov implies no such thing, the production systematically subverts the play we have known. It was this sort of thing that Chekhov tried to guard against by calling the play a "comedy" so as to prevent Stanislavsky from directing it as a heavy, somber sociological drama.

To superficial minds this subversion is all to the good; we are tired of conventional Chekhov, the argument goes, weary of the lugubrious solemnity with which he is always played; we want to see him come alive. Well, the alternative to lugubriousness isn't this sort of dragooned animation, these arty capers with their lightness in every detail, the delicate tensions between past and future, gain and loss, appetite and necessity that aren't Chekhov's meaning but the constituents of his vision and what he fought for against Stanislavsky's urge to turn the play into something singleminded and bulky. Following on Stanislavsky's heels, Serban has turned it into something diffuse and antic, which is new all right but not better.

Such free readings of texts as I've described may not seem to suggest havoc, but they're almost always part of a larger action, in which the highest crimes of director's theater take place. This is the matter of shifting plays from their original settings or, most radically, their original times. The justification is always "relevance." Behind the transposition, say, of Chekhov to the antebellum South, or Shakespeare to the 1890s, is the idea that the plays can't live without such modernization or relocation, can't "speak to us" in their original lineaments and settings. And this in turn implies that the classics are in need of rehabilitation, as though they were wounded, decrepit, abject victims of time.

What are we to say of this? Does time cripple novels or poems, so that we can no longer read them? Does it injure music so that at some point it can't be listened to? Are old movies unviewable? The auteur-director of a modernizing bent would argue that these analogies are false, since literary texts, musical scores, and films are finished objects, fixed and impossible to alter (except by a bowdlerizer's scissors), while written plays are sets of suggestions for their own enactment. When Jonathan Miller asserts that plays on stage can be anything one wants, he's speaking from a common belief that plays are only alive on the stage and that it's the director who's the chief conferrer of that life.

This argument contains some truth but it's also full of half-truth and false premises. To begin with, there's the question of what we mean by "life." Of course the stage contains physical life while texts do not. But does this mean that written plays have no life at all? The fact that we read many plays with great pleasure (often more than we get from bad productions) establishes that there is a life on the page, an *artistic* life. And the relation between this type of existence and the physical one that unfolds on stage—also artistic but in a different manner—is what ought to determine the extent of directorial freedom.

With *Agamemnon* Serban extends his abuse of the classics. In this case he and his coworker Elizabeth Swados don't so much violate the text as smother it under the weight of a theatrical apparatus that contains every cliché of "advanced" directing one can think of. For such clichés do exist and Serban ought to know about them, since his erstwhile mentor, Peter Brook, once issued a terse warning against them. "As long as we retain any sneaking belief," Brook wrote, "that grotesque masks, heightened makeups, hieratic costumes, declamation, balletic movement are somehow 'ritualistic' in their own right and consequently lyrical and profound—we will never get out of a traditional art-theater rut." An exact description of *Agamemnon*. Artiness, not art: this is the culmination of directing which doesn't listen to a text but dictates to it. And it is directorial artiness that, if anything, is taking over the theater.

When Serban was at La MaMa he did better, more restrained and cohesive work. The same is true of Foreman on his own grounds. The deadly combination, it would seem, is that of the almost unlimited resources of a theater like the Beaumont together with the always smoldering ambitiousness of directors. In such surroundings, or in the atmosphere of boom or bust that continues to pervade the theater on Broadway and off, directors, their gaze split between the work and its potential reception, will go on thrusting themselves forward as the saviors of playwrights who are presumed unable to make it on their own. The director as creator of his own text may add to the life of the stage, but as usurper of another's he diminishes it.

Years ago Jean Vilar, one of the best and most modest directors of the century, wrote in regard to producing Shakespeare that "the text is there, rich in stage directions embodied in the lines themselves . . . one need only have the sense to follow them. Whatever is created, beyond these directions, is 'direction,' and should be despised and rejected." What we are seeing these days is direction in that invidious sense. Vilar went on to call for a "theater of simple effects, without pretensions, accessible to all." For us to have such a theater directors will have to regain a modesty they show every sign now of regarding as an archaic and wholly irrelevant virtue.

But directors aren't the only culprits. What feeds director's theater in one of its forms is a widespread present dislike for or boredom with history. History doesn't speak to us, people say, meaning the past in all its forms and therefore classics as well. Why do Shakespeare at all then? Ah, but Shakespeare's wonderful, a genius—except that he's outdated, arthritic with old age. So he's given contemporary attire and accents, made to look and sound like the life we know. (Except for some of the language, but a little editing can help.) He's rendered *unhistorical,* another victim of the erosion of our sense of time.

Is the alternative to this the type of museum production of Shakespeare—or any playwright—that was described before? A model exists to prove it isn't: Peter Brook's aforementioned *King Lear* of the middle 1960s. It was an immensely original production, but its originality didn't consist in modernizing Shakespeare or making him relevant. Brook's daring move was to strip the play of all the conventional theatrical baggage, the panoply and excessive detail—of costumes, props, etc.—that so often make seeing Shakespeare far more tedious than reading him. The acting, too, was subdued, lean; there was nothing conventionally "Shakespearean" about it, no grandiloquence or underscoring of emotion. The result of all this was to allow the language to shine through as it rarely does on stage, to give us the play in its true life.

One can't be optimistic that directors will curb their itch to express themselves in the guise of revealing the play. One force behind the growth of director's theater is the present cult of personality, together with the belief in a right to do "one's own thing" in every area high or low. At the turn of the century, Jacques Copeau, a director and leader of the new theater in France, saw the first signs of what would develop into phenomena like director's theater. "Let us hope," he wrote in warning, "for a dramatist who replaces or eliminates the director, and personally takes over the directing; rather than for professional directors who pretend to be dramatists." After all this time, it isn't going to be easy to dislodge the pretender.

Editor's note: This article was drastically cut down in the *Times.* Reprinted here is the full text, approved by Gilman with some minor deletions.

New York Times, July 31, 1977

Out Goes Absurdism—In Comes
the New Naturalism

There are never any clean, decisive endings to eras in the arts, but it seems evident that the age of the "absurd" in drama is rapidly drawing to a close. Little spasmodic instances of theatrical absurdity will no doubt continue to show themselves here and there for a time, but the vigor and fertility of this movement, or genre, or, perhaps most accurately, enterprise of the great imagination are surely at a point of exhaustion.

The great figures whose names were associated with it from the beginning, Samuel Beckett and Eugène Ionesco, continue to write but are no longer sources of bafflement or revelation to audiences nor startling, brilliant mentors, mines of possibility for young dramatists. Their influence, particularly that of Beckett, by far the greater artist, has long since been assimilated into the general aesthetic of theater. *Waiting for Godot* and *Endgame* have reached a classic status, while the early plays of Ionesco, like *The Bald Soprano* or *Victims of Duty*, are still effective but are beginning to feel more like historical documents than the astonishing, subversive works they were once rightly taken to be.

More generally, there is visible now a shift away from what we have thought of as the mood of absurdity, that oblique or inverted way of regarding experience and shaping dramatic artifacts which, when it announced itself a generation ago, seemed to many of us to constitute nothing less than the resurrection of the stage. Theatrical excitement, or at any rate interest, has shifted toward other modes, to the point where to be "absurd" these days is to risk being considered old hat. Such are the rhythms of fashion, as well as the deeper ones of artistic change.

The most extreme avant-garde movement in drama these days lies of course in the so-called Theater of Images, the work of playwright-directors such as Robert Wilson, Richard Foreman, and Lee Breuer, whose emphasis is on a painterlike disposition of theatrical elements into nonnarrative, heavily visual constructions, with a corresponding subordination of plot, plot-related language, and "action" in the traditional sense. This kind of work owes a good deal to absurdity obviously, but at least as much to developments in the other arts, especially dance and painting.

In another, opposed direction, the theater has moved into what can be called a "new naturalism," something marked by the return of dramaturgical intentions and procedures that were thought to have been superseded. Plays like Ronald Ribman's *Cold Storage,* Albert Innaurato's *Gemini* and *The Transfiguration of Benno Blimpie,* even such a slight play as D. L. Coburn's *The Gin Game,* the works of David Mamet and of the British writers Simon Gray and David Rudkin, dissimilar in many respects and of varying merit as they are, are all more or less well-made, all to one degree or another sequential, logical, immediately apprehensible, "straight."

On what, I think, is a level of greater originality but still within this ambience of the straightforward and the rejection of fantasy or pure invention are the plays of David Storey and, even more impressive, those of the group of young, socially committed German playwrights of whom Wolfgang Bauer and Franz Xaver Kroetz are perhaps the most gifted.

As absurdity has worn down, to be replaced as the dominant mode of dramatic expression by the types of theater I have cited, certain ironies have exhibited themselves. Most flagrantly, both the average theatergoer and that species of critic or reviewer whose job, as Max Beerbohm once said, is to serve and preserve average taste, have come to honor or at least accept the "absurd" only after its energies were clearly flagging, and they have always had difficulty in distinguishing its real achievements from imitation or outright fraud. The success, either critical or commercial and in some cases both, of plays like Edward Albee's *Seascape* or Tom Stoppard's *Travesties* represents, I think, the triumph of imitative or spurious absurdity. Reviewers for whom *Waiting for Godot* was "not a play" (in the way that for most of Picasso's early critics his work was "not painting") and who thought *The Chairs* or *The Lesson* was mere nonsense found these later works impressive examples of absurdity. In reality, Albee's play was pretentious, pseudo-metaphysical, and artificially mysterious, and Stoppard's was witless, juvenile, designed to flatter and cajole the vulgar and half-educated.

To be sure, high praise for such works is common enough in artistic history. A revolution is finally perceived, the apparatus of prize-giving and official commendation moves into operation—when the revolution is in a decaying state or is factually over.

But what in fact was that revolution like? What was it like to have been present at its beginnings and through what we can think of now as its "heroic" days? And what has been its legacy? To begin with, it was—like all such moments of cultural change—confused, full of bewilderment for many, rage for others, and passionate excitement for a minority. When *Waiting for Godot* opened in New York in 1955 (it had had its American premiere a few months earlier, in Florida strangely enough) some of those in the first audiences knew they had come into the presence of a great work, although it was not so easy at first to know why it was one. For some students of the drama, the event was comparable to that April day in 1923 when Pirandello's *Six Characters* opened in Paris and, as a French critic declared at the time, "the modern theater was born."

Yet, if the term "absurd" was not yet in use, most theatergoers and reviewers responded to the new plays as though they indeed made up a theater that satisfied the dictionary definition of the word: "contrary to reason, obviously false and foolish." Audiences during the brief run of *Godot*, which had opened on Broadway when it might have been better served in more modest surroundings, muttered, coughed, nudged one another, and drifted out in large numbers long before the curtain. (A few years later, I sat by as a huge theater party of clubwomen marched out in near-military formation after ten or fifteen minutes of a production of *Endgame* at The Theater of the Living Arts in Philadelphia.)

The confusion and dislike extended to critics and performers. Marya Mannes wrote in her review of *Godot* in the *Reporter* magazine that she doubted whether she had ever seen "a worse play." Norman Mailer allowed that there might be something to the play but wrote that he considered its enthusiastic admirers to be "snobs, intellectual snobs of undue ambition and impotent imagination." There is a credible story that Bert Lahr, who played Gogo in the Broadway production (and played well), said afterward, "I didn't understand a goddamned thing." About the same time, Ionesco's first plays were being greeted by general incomprehension and hostility, one noted reviewer going so far as to publish swatches of dialogue from one play in an effort to establish that they weren't funny; they were extremely funny.

Still, as Beckett and Ionesco, along with some lesser but still innovative new French writers like Arthur Adamov, Robert Pinget, and Jean Tardieu, came to be treated with increasing respect and admiration in some scholarly and intellectual circles, the winds of fashion veered. The descriptive phrase "Theater of the Absurd" immediately fixed itself in the consciousness of the educated public upon the appearance in 1961 of Martin Esslin's book with that title. Esslin had borrowed the word "absurd" from Albert Camus, who had in turn taken it from Kierkegaard. Stripped of its religious and metaphysical implications, the word functioned in Esslin's hands as a means of identifying a new kind of dramaturgy. Too many new kinds, it turned out; as one critic remarked at the time, Esslin made all interesting avant-garde plays of the past thirty or forty years sound as if they had been written by the same person.

In any case, "Theater of the Absurd" entered the language, to be employed, in much the same way as the adjective "kafkaesque," to denote segments of "real" life, disjointed or impenetrable experiences. And the misunderstandings multiplied. In 1962, the Cherry Lane Theater in Greenwich Village hung a banner over its marquee with the message and rubric "Theater of the Absurd" and put on a series of eight or nine new plays so diverse as to make it possible for only the widest net to cover them.

But "absurdity" has always been a wide label, the loosest of terms. That this was so helps account for the proliferation of imitations, a whole genre of the pseudo-absurd taking shape once the atmosphere was open to it. Ionesco had said that for his part he was not colonizing a realm of chaos or arbitrary actions nor excluding the psychological from his work, but offering "a *different* logic and a *different* psychology" (italics mine.) But an innovator can scarcely expect to control what he has released. For many playwrights of differing talents, the absurd meant absolute freedom. One had only to be illogical, nonconsecutive, "zany"; since there seemed to be no more rules, an anarchic spirit held sway.

Most of the counterfeits were swiftly forgotten, but some, like Arthur Kopit's *Oh Dad, Poor Dad, Mamma's Hung You in the Closet and I'm Feelin' So Sad* (Kopit was later to move into imaginative veins closer to his real talents and capacities), Murray Schisgal's *Luv* or Bruce J. Friedman's *Scuba Duba,* managed to seduce some critics and audiences into thinking them "absurd," when the truth was that they were foolish.

So powerful was the pull toward the absurd at one time in the 1960s that even resolutely conventional playwrights were caught by it. Both William Inge and Lillian Hellman had their fling at the new genre, Inge with a play called *Where's Daddy?* and Hellman with one called *My Mother, My Father and Me* (the domestic or parental motif in pseudo-absurdity was strong at the time; Kopit's *Oh Dad* and Charles DiSenzo's *Big Mama* are other examples). The Inge and Hellman plays were severe embarrassments, the only discernible value in their having been produced being the grant of new evidence, if any were needed, that to be truly absurd was a question of vision and not of coy or antic dramaturgy.

Now, I don't wish to seem to be defending some notion of "pure" absurdity, to retroactively be guarding the gates against theatrical barbarians. The point is that whatever absurdity was, there was never a *theater* of it, but simply a diverse, unprogrammatic, and quite spontaneous movement—in the sense of a step or stride, not a cultural crusade—away from traditional forms on the part of a small number of original minds, and a consequent burgeoning of works in the new vein by lesser minds and in some cases by outright mimics.

Writers like Beckett and Ionesco, as different as they are from one another, had come to feel the historic procedures of the stage as restrictions: its need to be immediately "lifelike," its reliance on narrative, its unfolding through sequential cause and effect, its principles of necessary "conflict," "denouement" and the like, and its penchant for moral, psychological, or social explanations or solutions. What the early absurdists, as well as the younger writers who were influenced by them, shared in varying degrees was, essentially, an absence; unlike each other, their works were also unlike traditional plays, and so seemed to many people to be unlike drama at all.

Their revolution was by no means unprecedented. A half-century earlier, Strindberg's preface to his *Dream Play* contained passages that read now like a prediction of the future dramaturgy: "Time and space do not exist . . . imagination spins and weaves new patterns of memories, experiences, unfettered fancies, absurdities and improvisations." And Pirandello, Brecht, Ghelderode, and the Surrealists had offered their own alternatives to dramatic conventions, while a prophetic figure like Artaud proposed their even more radical overthrow.

What was different in the plays of Beckett and Ionesco from those of their avant-garde predecessors was, most obviously, that they were structurally more extreme, they dispensed more completely with considerations of orderly plot, character development, progress toward a dramatic climax, and so on. Beyond that, they seemed to lack even minimal points of reference to the world outside the theater; Ionesco's *Jacques* or Beckett's *Happy Days* unfolded not as a dramatic tale that we could enter vicariously and with whose characters we could identify—who could identify in the familiar sense with the fire chief in *The Bald Soprano* or the roomer in *The New Tenant,* with Nag and Nell in *Endgame* or Didi and Gogo?—but in a metaphorical universe alongside our own.

This was in fact the key to understanding these plays: they were self-contained; they didn't *comment* on our experience or seek to heighten or rearrange it, but created rich new patterns of experience itself. As Beckett said about Joyce, they were not writing "about" something, they were writing something. At a period when writing *about* things on the stage took the form usually of domestic melodrama, a time when the British theater was ruled by what someone has called the Pax Ratiganus, the French by the mildly witty, mildly adventurous but thoroughly traditional plays of Jean Anouilh, and the American by the limited perspectives of Arthur Miller and Tennessee Williams (which is not to deny the latter's force), absurdity came like the discovery of a new continent.

The region has been thoroughly explored and now, as the name and the actuality fade from celebrity, what has been left to us? The handful of great plays is there, and there is seldom more than a handful of great plays in any era. What is perhaps more important is the way in which absurdity has influenced many writers who have remained closer to earlier epochs. Harold Pinter is a case in point. It serves no purpose to call him an "absurdist," but he is not likely to have written as he has, or as well as he has, without the example set him by those who were.

Landscape and *Silence,* and *Old Times,* the most recent works of his we have seen, may derive in their silences, their disjunctions, and lack of a prominent "plot" as much from Chekhov as from Beckett, but it is hard to imagine their movement beyond a detailed, identifiable social setting into a world of fable and elegiac rumination without Beckett's having been there before him.

There are a number of younger playwrights here and elsewhere who have profited by that example, too. The imagination has been stretched, made more supple, and drama itself potentially made more spacious and intrepid. American playwrights like Sam Shepard, Maria Irene Fornes, Rochelle Owens, Jean-Claude van Itallie, and Ronald Tavel come out of a line of absurdity, whatever their particular visions and however much they may have modified their earlier, more extreme experiments. And at least one impulse of absurdity, its rejection of obvious plot and storytelling, has, as I said before, been passed on to the theater of Wilson and Foreman.

But the direct mode of absurdity seems to have run its course. There is no simple answer to why this should be so, but certain observations might be made. To begin with, revolutions or even major changes in the arts have generally followed a rhythmic, some would say cyclical, destiny. Art is never "progressive"; as Ionesco once remarked, artistic innovation is always in some manner a return to forgotten truths. Once that return has been accomplished, once, to take the case of dramatic art, its brittle artifices and congealed practices, its psychologizing and philosophizing (rather different things from psychology and philosophy) have been exposed and cleared away so that the stage's imaginative actions can again be felt as revelation, there is no need to keep attacking a defeated enemy.

More than that, the movements of artistic experience and desire are such that when something has been out of favor, it tends to come back precisely because in the interval it has taken on a new strangeness. Art, after all, is a way of looking (the theater, Ibsen said, is a place for seeing, the Greek root of the word) and what has not been looked at for a time becomes oddly new.

This is what has happened in some areas of painting, where the body and objects appear to us now, after their long exile, in new, almost visionary light. And it is happening in fiction, too. A book like Joseph Heller's *Something Happened* is not a regression to a dated naturalism, as so many disappointed readers thought, but a work of new realism, one distinguished by its immensely sober acceptance of some painful, obvious, yet suppressed human truths and an almost incantatory invocation to their reality.

In the same way, the "new naturalism" in the theater is not retrograde; only an inflexible and programmatically avant-garde critic or spectator would think it was. This new desire for the actual world in dramatic art is in a much more supple sense of the term avant-garde, since, stripped of its aggressive, military connotations, all the term ultimately means is a refusal to repeat what has already been done. The new naturalism is new in that it has shed its predecessor's infatuation with pseudo-scientific explorations and its ideological ambitions; it refuses, the best of it at least, to comment or judge, a repudiation it has almost certainly learned from absurdity, and so presents to us an unbiased universe of dramatic events in which we may see ourselves once more without distortion.

The kind of "distortion" that absurdity brought into being was necessary, healing in a profound way; it was an indirection seeking direction out. The world had been obscured by conventional ways of looking at it. But the world turns, responding to our attention. Hegel once wrote that "the known, just because it is the known, is the unknown." For those who may rejoice in the end of absurdity as a return to the norms of drama, the implications of that remark ought to give pause; the norms, in theater, as in life, are what are forever in question. At the heart of the best absurd drama was a recognition of this. Whatever comes next will surely be saved from ignorance by absurdity's having shaken the known, unexamined world.

New York Times, March 19, 1978

The New American Playwrights: Sam Shepard

Not many critics would dispute the proposition that Sam Shepard is our most interesting and exciting American playwright.

Fewer, however, can articulate just where the interest and excitement lie. There is an extraordinarily limited and homogeneous vocabulary of critical writing about Shepard, a thin lexicon of both praise and detraction. Over and over one sees his work described as "powerful"—"brutally" or "grimly" or "oddly" powerful, but muscular beyond question. Again and again one hears him called "surrealist" or "gothic" or, a bit more infrequently, a "mythic realist" (the most colorful appellation I've seen, affixed to Shepard by our most rococo reviewer, is the "bucking bronco" of American theater). To his detractors he is always "obscure," usually "willfully" so, and always "undisciplined." But even some of his enemies acknowledge his "theatrical magic," always with that phrase, and admirers and some enemies alike point to his plays' "richness of texture," always in those words.

The same sort of ready-made language can be found in discussions of Shepard's themes or motifs. Nearly everyone is agreed that the great majority of his plays deal with one or more of these matters: the death (or betrayal) of the American dream; the decay of our national myths; the growing mechanization of our lives; the search for roots; the travail of the family. (The trouble is, this cluster of related notions would apply to a good many other American writers as well.)

Most critics find it hard clearly to extract even these ideas from Shepard's plays, many of which are in fact extraordinarily resistant to thematic exegesis. Shepard's most ardent enthusiasts have got round the problem by arguing that he isn't (or wasn't; there's been a significant change in his latest plays, which I'll take up later) talking *about* anything but rather *making* something, a familiar notion in avant-garde circles and, as far as it goes, a correct one. They point out that his genius lies not in ideas or thought but in the making of images; he speaks more to the eye, or to the ear (in terms of expressive sound, though not necessarily in terms of immediate sense), than to the mind.

I don't fully accept this argument, though I see its virtues, and I do share in some of the prevailing uncertainties. I don't mean that I'm uncertain about the value of Shepard's work, but I find the question of "themes" troubling, primarily because I detect a confusion in *him* about them. But the real difficulty I share with many critics isn't so much deciding what the work is as knowing how to write about what it is. How to wield a critical vocabulary that won't be composed of clichés and stock phrases, how to devise a strategy of discourse to deal usefully with this dramatist who slips out of all the categories?

I hold Shepard before me as the subject of this essay. There he is, changing his skin as though by an annual molting; seeming, and often being, disorderly, sometimes to the point of chaos; obeying—until recently at any rate—no fixed or familiar principles of dramatic construction; borrowing, like an exultant magpie, from every source in or out of the theater; being frequently obscure, though never, I think, "willfully" so.

If there's a more nearly perfect exemplar of a cultural education gained ("absorbed" is a better word) in the fifties than Sam Shepard, I can't imagine who it might be. I first saw him at the Open Theatre in 1965, a James Dean-like youth with an un-Dean-like intellectual glint in his eyes. Even after I'd overcome my initial dismay at such easy and untutored confidence, it took me a while to see that there wasn't any reason he couldn't be a playwright or anything else. For the fifties, out of which he came, or sidled, was the era in which two things started to happen of great importance to our subsequent culture. One was that the distance between "high" and "low" in art began to be obliterated, and the other was that the itch for "expression," for hurling the self's words against anonymity and silence, began to beat down the belief in the necessity for formal training, apprenticeship, and growth, that had always been held in regard to drama or any art.

Shepard is much more than the product of these developments, but they do infect or, from another judgment, animate him in profound ways. He was born in Illinois but grew up in Southern California, and that vivid, disastrous milieu has been the psychic and imaginative ground of all his plays, whatever their literal geography might be. He has said that he lived in a "car culture for the young" and that the Southern California towns held a "kind of junk magic." In a few autobiographical fragments and elliptical interviews he tells of a life resembling that in the movie *American Graffiti*, only tougher, shrewder, more seeded with intimations of catastrophe in the midst of swagger.

Shepard seems to have come out of no literary or theatrical tradition at all but precisely from the breakdown or absence—on the level of art if not of commerce—of all such traditions in America. Such a thing is never a clean, absolute stride away from the ruins; fragments of tradition, bits of history, cling to every razed site and to one's shoes. But in his case one does see a movement with very little cultural time at its back, or only the thinnest slice of the immediate past, a *willed* movement, it might be said, for one sometimes suspects Shepard of wanting to be thought sui generis, a self-creation. That he must, for example, have been influenced by Jack Gelber's 1959 play *The Connection,* by some of Ronald Tavel's work, by certain aspects of Pinter, and, more recently, by Edward Bond, as well as by elements of what we call theatrical "absurdity," are things he has never mentioned.

What we do know is that in a sense he's a writer in spite of himself. In 1971 he said that "I don't want to be a playwright, I want to be a rock and roll star. . . . I got into writing plays because I had nothing else to do. So I started writing to keep from going off the deep end." Naturally, there's much disingenuousness in this, something tactical, but it oughtn't to be disbelieved entirely. Shepard's plays sometimes do give off a whiff of reluctance to being plays, a hint of dissatisfaction with the form. And his recent incarnation as a film actor increases our sense that he's had something else, or something additional, in mind all along.

For what was true for him when he started (as it was true for the general culture in its youthful sectors), was that a mode of expression existed more compelling, more seductive, and more in affinity with the outburst of the personal than writing in the old high formal sense. In light of Shepard's rock ambitions, listen to him on the genre. It made, he said (without punctuation) "movie theater books painting and art go out the window none of it stands a chance against the Who the Stones and Old Yardbirds Credence Traffic the Velvet Underground Janis and Jimi . . ."

Nevertheless Shepard did pluck drama from outside the window and become a writer. But the influence of rock is major and pervasive, if most direct in his early plays. It can be seen in the plays' songs, of course, but also, more subtly, in a new kind of stage language, contemporary in a harsh, jumpy way, edging, as both rock lyrics and rock talk do, between pseudo-professional argot and a personal tone of cocksure assertion. It is almost hermetic at times, but one can always detect a type of savage complaint and a belligerent longing. Thematically, rock, or rather the legendary status of its star performers, provided the direct subject of *Suicide in bFlat* and *The Tooth of Crime.*

But rock isn't the only musical style Shepard employs. A whole range of other genres can be found: modern jazz, blues, country and western, and folk music of several kinds. Shepard has always claimed, or others have on his behalf, that these musical elements are as important to many of his plays as their speech, and that the same thing is true for his decors. Indeed it's difficult to imagine much of his work without its music, by which I mean that it's not an embellishment or a strategic device, in the manner of Brecht, to interrupt the flow of a sequential narrative, but an integral part of the plays' devising of new consciousness.

Shepard's physical materials and perspectives come largely from developments in the graphic arts and dance during his adolescence and early career. He has said that Jackson Pollock was important to him, but what seems more active in his sensibility are emanations from the "happenings" phase of painting and sculpture, collage in the manner of Johns and Rauschenberg, and the mixed-media experiments of the latter artist with John Cage and others. His sets reveal all these influences at two extremes: their occasional starkness, a bare space in which lighting is the chief or only emotive or "placing" factor, and their frequent stress on dirt, *dreck*—the kitchen of *4-H Club*, "littered with paper, cans, and various trash," or the set for *The Unseen Hand*, composed of an "old

'51 Chevrolet convertible, bashed and dented, no tires . . . garbage, tin cans, cardboard boxes, Coca-Cola bottles and other junk."

More generally, in regard to subject and reference, to iconography, we can observe a far-flung network of influences, interests, and obsessions that have gone into the making of Shepard's work. The most substantial of these are the car or "road" culture of his youth, science fiction, Hollywood Westerns and the myth of the West in general, and television in its pop or junk aspects. Besides these Shepard himself has mentioned "vaudeville, circuses . . . trance dances, faith healing ceremonials . . . medicine shows," to which we might add telepathic states, hallucinatory experiences (drug-induced or not), magic, and witchcraft.

Eclectic as all this seems, something binds it together, and this is that nearly everything I've mentioned is to one degree or another an interest or engagement of the pop and countercultures that had their beginnings in the fifties. When we reflect on what these movements or climates have left us—their presence is still felt in the form of a corpse not quite grown cold—a set of major impulses immediately emerges: a stance against authority and tradition, anti-elitism, the assertion of the untaught self in impatience and sometimes mockery.

But one sees in it all too—something most pertinent to a rumination on Shepard's plays—another and more subtle configuration: a world of discards and throwaways, of a *nostalgie de la boue* appeased by landscapes filled with detritus and interiors strewn with debris, of floating images, unfinished acts, discontinuity and dissonance, abruptnesses and illogicalities; an impatience with time for proceeding instead of existing all at once, like space; and with space for having limits, fixed contours, and finality.

This in large part is Shepard's theatrical world. I said that his plays emerged far more from new movements outside the theater than from within it, but what really happened can't be that clear. If he's never acknowledged any debt to the so-called absurdists, or to any other playwrights for that matter, whether or not he learned directly from them scarcely matters. He learned alongside them, so to speak, or in their wake, in the same atmosphere of rejection of linear construction, cause-and-effect sequences, logical procedures, coherent or consistent characters, and the tying of language to explicit meanings that distinguished the new drama from its predecessors.

Except for its final phrases, a note to the actors preceding the text of *Angel City* might have been written by almost any avant-garde playwright of recent years, and in fact goes back in its central notion to Strindberg's revolutionary preface to *Miss Julie*. "The term 'character,'" Shepard wrote, "could be thought of in a different way when working on this play. Instead of the idea of a 'whole character' with logical motives behind his behavior which the actor submerges himself into, he should consider instead a fractured whole with bits and pieces of character flying off the central theme. Collage construction, jazz improvisation. Music or painting in space."

What distinguished Shepard's plays from most others in the new American repertoire was their greater vivacity and elasticity, even more their far greater impurity, the presence in them of so many energies and actions not previously thought properly dramatic. More than any other American playwright of the sixties, he broke down the fixed definitions of the dramatic. But doing this brought risks. He has said he wants to create "total" theater, and this ambition is both the spur to his triumphs and the clue to his delinquencies. For total theater, where everything is present at once, can result in a canceling-out, a murk and confusion.

If the American theater was ready for Shepard's wayward gifts, it was because it was ready for anything in the emptiness in which it then existed. In the late fifties and early sixties our theater was just beginning to catch up with developments in arts like painting and dance, and with the revolutionary changes in drama that had taken place in France with Beckett and Ionesco and, more modestly, in England with the early Pinter. Albee's first plays, Gelber's *Connection,* and the work of the Living Theatre were all signs and artifacts of a stirring here that was to result a couple of years later in the burgeoning of Off and Off-Off-Broadway. A major aspect of this was the creation of experimental, insurrectionary groups like the Open Theatre, the Performance Group, and others.

Shepard's first plays to be staged were done in New York in late 1964, and it's no accident that a few months later he appeared at the door of the Open Theatre, for that body of actors, directors, and writers was one of the centers of the upheaval.

This isn't the place for an extended discussion of Shepard's debt to the Open Theatre, nor are the intellectual transactions between them entirely clear. What can be said is that Shepard learned something important about "transformations," one of the group's main lines of exploration into both the psychology of the actor and the relationship between acting and formal texts. Briefly, a transformation exercise was an improvised scene—a birthday party, survivors in a lifeboat, and so on—in which after a while, and suddenly, the actors were asked to switch immediately to a new scene and therefore to wholly new characters. Among the aims (which were never wholly clear) were increased flexibility, insight into theatrical or acting clichés, and more unified ensemble playing.

Shepard carried the idea of transformations much farther than the group had by actually writing them into his texts, in plays like *Angel City, Back Bog Beast Bait,* and *The Tooth of Crime,* where characters become wholly different in abrupt movements within the course of the work, or speak suddenly as someone else, while the scene may remain the same. Besides this, Shepard has maintained a connection to the Open Theatre's Joseph Chaikin, collaborating with him on two theater pieces (*Tongues* and *Savage/Love*).

More than that of any important playwright I know, Shepard's work resists division into periods, stages of growth or development. The only exceptions to this, once more, are the latest plays, which do seem to constitute a rough phase. Unlike the serial way in which we arrange most writers' work in our minds, the body of Shepard's writing seems present itself to us all at once, lying rudely sprawled across our consciousness, connected in all its parts less by organic adhesion than by a distinctive ebb and flow of obsession. Shepard doesn't move from theme to theme or image to image in the separate plays; he doesn't conquer a dramatic territory and move on, doesn't extend his grasp or refine it. What he does from play to play is lunge forward, move sideways, double back, circle round, throw in this or that, adopt a voice then drop it, pick it up again.

Most of his plays seem like fragments, chunks of various sizes thrown out from some mother lode of urgent and heterogeneous imagination in which he has scrabbled with pick, shovel, gunbutt, and hands. The reason so many of them seem incomplete is that they lack the clear boundaries as artifact, the internal order, the progress toward a denouement (of some kind: a crystallization, a summarizing image, a poise in the mind), and the consistency of tone and procedure that ordinarily characterize good drama, even most avant-garde drama of the postwar time.

Many of his plays seem partial, capricious, arbitrarily brought to an end, and highly unstable. They spill over, they leak. They change, chameleon-like, in self-protection as we look at them. This is a source of the difficulty one has in writing about them, as it's also a source of their originality. Another difficulty is that we tend to look at all plays for their single "meanings" or ruling ideas but find this elusive in Shepard and find, moreover, his plays coalescing, merging into one another in our minds. Rather than always trying to keep them separate, trying by direct plunges into their respective depths to find clear meanings tucked away like kernels within gorgeous ragged husks, I think we ought to accept, at least provisionally, their volatility and interdependence; they constitute a series of facets of a single continuing act of imagination.

Beyond this, and as an aspect of it, we have to see Shepard's work as existing in an especially intricate and disorderly relationship with life outside the theater. Such a relationship obviously is true of any drama, but in Shepard's case it shows itself as a rambunctious reciprocity in which the theatrical, as a mode of behavior, takes a special wayward urgency from life, while the living—spontaneous, unorganized, and unpredictable—keeps breaking into the artificial, composed world of the stage.

There is a remark of John Cage's that's especially pertinent here: "Theater exists all around us and it is the purpose of formal theater to remind us that this is so." Much of Shepard's energy and inventiveness are given (undeliberately, of course: as part of the action of being an artist) to this kind of reminder; his theater is as much about theater as about the "real" world. Above all, it's about performing, and here the relations between art and life become particularly close.

There are indeed themes in his work—sociological, political, and the like—but the plays aren't demonstrations or enactments of them; they exist as dispositions, pressures, points of inquiry. And if there's any overriding vision it's this: our lives are theatrical, but it's a besieged, partly deracinated theater we act in. We want, as though in a theater, to be *seen* (the Greek root of "theater": a place for *seeing*), but there are great obstacles to this desire.

If it's not useful to search for the specific meanings of all Shepard's plays, then their general meaning or significance (or perhaps simply what these plays cause in our minds, what Henry James called the "thinkable" actions of drama) is something else. I want to start on the way toward that by contemplating the surfaces of this ungainly body of drama, and what more immediate data are there than Shepard's titles?

Most of his titles float, bob up and down from the plays on shorter or longer strings. They appear as aggressions, put-ons, or parodies, but almost never as traditional titles in some direct or logical connection to the works. They seem crazily theatrical in themselves; they scare you or break you up before the curtain has even risen: *Dog; Killer's Head; 4-H Club; The Holy Ghostly; Cowboy Mouth; Shaved Splits; Fourteen Hundred Thousand; Back Bog Beast Bait; The Tooth of Crime; Blue Bitch; Action; The Mad Dog Blues; Angel City; Geography of a Horse Dreamer; Operation Sidewinder; Curse of the Starving Class; Forensic and the Navigators; Icarus's Mother.*

I don't know if it has pointed out how these titles resemble the names of rock groups, or pieces of graffiti, or certain writings on tee-shirts. They don't denote finished, discrete dramas as much as a continuing action, a calling of attention; they're less identifications than announcements.

This is also true of his characters' names, which are like knives, road signs, or trademarks. There are some prosaic ones—Ed, Frank, Jill, Becky, Stu—but with these we think Shepard is playing a joke. The real names are and ought to be: Cherry and Geez and Wong; Shooter and Jeep; Shadow; Beaujo and Santee; Forensic; Galactic Jack; Dr. Vector; Tympani; Hoss and Crow; Salem and Kent; Kosmo and Yahoodi; Miss Scoons; Sloe Gin Martin and Booger Montgomery; Gris Gris; Ice; Blood; Blade; Dukie; Dude. There are very few last names, for like the titles they're less identifiers than assertions.

It's as if these characters had named themselves or gone behind the playwright's back to get named by some master of hype, some poet of the jukebox. They're like movie starlets and a type of star—Rock, Tab, Tuesday; they're like rock personalities, even bands. Their names seek to confer one or another quality on their persons, soliciting us to read them as dangerous or alluring or zany—in any case as original. This is a function of nicknames or pseudonyms at any time, but in Shepard they're the names first given; his characters start with a flight from anonymity.

Some of them smack of science fiction, others of pop sensibility. They're partly japes, sly mockeries of staid naming in theater and life. Yet most of them aren't just tactical but move in our minds like signals from a particular human and geographical environment, one that vibrates simultaneously with sadness and violence, eccentricity, loneliness, and self-assertion, bravado and the pathos of rootless existence. The "real" place is California and the Southwest; the site in our minds is American toughness and despair, danger and isolation. I think of rodeo riders, poker dealers, motorcycle gangs, bar hostesses, gangsters' sidekicks, hotrodders and drifters, killers on the plains, electric guitarists in roadhouses. And I think of the stars who would wear such epithet-like names if they didn't have to use reasonable ones.

In laying such emphasis on these names I naturally don't mean to suggest they can bear a weight of interpretation of the plays, only that they can help us toward the dramatic center. For if something like a "quest for identity" is central to Shepard's vision, as I think it is, then names, first clues to identity or its lack, are greatly instructive.

Now "quest for identity" is a flaccid term in popular psychology and perfunctory cultural criticism, and it has of course to do with the question of "who am I?" But is this a useful or even a true question, especially in the theater? Can we ever, in life, know who we are except in a formal, abstract way, as the result, say, of a Cartesian inquiry, a religious definition, or membership in a human category? Might not the true questions in putting forth the self, certainly in the theater but also in life with its theatrical hunger, be "who do I seem to be?" and "what am I taken for?" And might not the quest for identity really be the quest for a *role*?

I intend nothing pejorative by this, nothing having to do with "role-playing" as a neurotic maneuver; but rather that we either take our places in a drama and discover ourselves as we act, or we remain unknown (as some indeed choose to do). In the reciprocal glances of the actors we all are, in our cues to dialogue, the perpetual agons and denouements that we participate in with others; identities are found, discarded, altered, but above all *seen*. Not to be able to act, to be turned away from the audition, is the true painful condition of anonymity. But to try to act too much, to wish to star, the culmination and hypertrophy of the common desire, is a ripeness for disaster.

I think Shepard's shamanistic or totemistic names are the initial signs of his art's fundamental impulse. The selves behind the names, the characters, are avid to be but above all to be *seen* to be. I know this can be said in one way or another of the substance of all formal theater. Jarry once said that a playwright wants to "unleash" his characters on a stage, and Robbe-Grillet said of Beckett's Didi and Gogo that they have to "ad lib for their very lives." To write plays is to invent characters to live more visibly and perilously than oneself.

But what is remarkable about Shepard's plays is the way they display the new raw unstable anguish and wit that marks the self seeking itself now, and that they display with such half-demented, half-lyrical force the things that oppose this quest, its exacerbated American circumstances, which Shepard's own new raw questing sensibility has made its scene, obsession, and poetry.

I believe that all Shepard's themes or motifs can be subsumed, even if loosely and with jagged projections everywhere, by this perspective. Consider the question of "roots," so stark or shadowy in his plays. To have roots is to have continuity and so a basis on which to act (a step to a step), to act in both senses of the word. Not to have roots is to risk acting on air. This is why I think the facts of Shepard's literal and cultural background are important. He couldn't have come from the East or North or at another time. In the West rootlessness is far more widespread and for many almost the condition of life. But at the same time the West, particularly California, is the place where, most acutely, visible success, gestures of self, personality, fame are means, conscious or not, of making up for or disguising the lack of roots.

Isn't it also the place—as a metaphor beyond its klieg lights and therapies and bronzed bodies—where energy and anguish, talent and emptiness, the hope of a name and the corruption of a self are the matings from which come a special piercing sense of dismay, which may be one thing we mean by the destruction of the "American Dream"?

"Identity" and "roots" merge as themes in Shepard. For if the American Dream means anything more than its purely physical and economic implications, it means the hope and promise of identity, of a "role" in the sense I indicated before. Inseparable from this is the hope of flexibility, of suppleness in the distribution of roles—the opportunities of being seen—such as was largely absent from the more fixed and closed European world. In turn this promise, sometimes fulfilled, is met with the ironic condition of rootlessness, lack of continuity and ground. The effect of this in Shepard's theater is either to crush or literally deracinate—tear the mind from *its* roots—the seeking self or to hyperbolize it into flamboyance, violence, or the ultimate madness, the fever for what we call "stardom."

The very "rootlessness" of Shepard's theater, its springing so largely from a condition outside the continuity of the stage, is a source of the difficulty we have with it, as it is also a source of its dazzling disturbances. But inside his theater, within its own continuousness, a tragicomic drama of names and selves unfolds. I think of the frantic efforts of so many of his characters to make themselves felt, often by violence (or cartoon violence—blows without injuries, bullets without deaths: dream or make-believe, something filmed), of the great strand in his work of the ego run wild, of the craving for altered states of being and the power to transcend physical or moral or psychic limitations—and the very alterations and transcendences of this kind carried out in the plays: the transformations, the splitting of characters, the masks, the roles within roles, the mingling of legendary figures with invented ones. And I think of the "turns," the numbers, the oratorios and arias, and especially the monologues or soliloquies that aren't simply contributions to the plot but outcries of characters craving to be known.

The monologues take many forms. One is a kind of technical disquisition, such as Jeez's on deer-skinning in *Shaved Splits* or Howard's on flying in *Icarus's Mother.* They may be prosaic or bizarre but they have the effect of claiming for the speaker an individuality based on some sort of detailed knowledge. More often the monologue is simply a "story," matter-of-face or exotic, which may or may not contribute to the plot, but which always serves to distinguish the speaker as a voice, as someone with *something* to tell.

Occasionally such a monologue will contain within itself a crystallization or recapitulation of the play itself and of Shepard's angle of vision. A speech of this kind is Shooter's in *Action* about the risks and necessities of acting:

> You go outside. The world's quiet. White. Everything resounding. Not a sound of a motor. Not a light. You see into the house. You see the candles. You watch the people. You can see what it's like inside. The candles draw you. You get a cold feeling being outside. Separated. You have an idea that being inside it's cosier. Friendlier. Warmth. People. Conversation. Everyone using a language. Then you go inside. It's a shock. It's not like how you expected. You lose what you had outside. You forget that there even is an outside. The inside is all you know. You hunt for a way of being with everyone. A way of finding how to behave. You find out what's expected of you. You act yourself out.

Another is Miss Scoons on the dream of stardom, in *Angel City:*

> I look at the screen and I am the screen. . . . I look at the movie and I am the movie. I am the star. . . . For days I am the star and I'm not me. I'm me being the star. I look at my life when I come down . . . and I hate my life when I come down. I hate my life for not being a movie. I hate my life not being a star. I hate being myself in my life which isn't a movie and never will be. I hate having to eat. Having to work. Having to sleep. Having to go to the bathroom. Having to get from one place to another with no potential. Having to live in this body which isn't a star's body and all the time knowing that stars exist.

The monologues are most often tight, staccato, gathering a strange cumulative eloquence. In their varied voices they reveal as nothing else does Shepard's marvelous ear, not for actual speech but for the imagined possibilities of utterance as invention, as victory over silence.

Everything I've been discussing converges in *The Tooth of Crime,* which I think is Shepard's greatest achievement, the one play which is most nearly invulnerable to charges of occlusion or arbitrary procedures, the one that rests most self-containedly, that seems whole, inevitable, *ended.* It contains his chief imaginative ideas and obsessions at their highest point of eloquence and most sinewy connection to one another. It exhibits his theatrical inventiveness at its most brilliant yet most uncapricious and coherent, and it reveals most powerfully his sense of the reciprocities of art and life. A splendid violent artifact, it broods on and wrestles with the quest not simply to be known but to be known inexhaustibly, magically, cosmically: the exaltation and tragedy of fame.

For this drama of confrontation between a rock "king" and his challenger, Shepard calls on an astonishing range of sources. The chief plot action, the eventual "shoot-out," is borrowed of course from Western movies and legends. But the play is more than its narrative; or rather, the true narrative, the tale of consciousness, is of the vivacity and anguish of the swollen name, the self propelled into a beleaguered exemplary condition in which the general need is fulfilled for some selves and names to be transfigured so that others may at least elbow into their light. The mobile levels of discourse, the amazing variety of textures serve to proffer and sustain a painful, refulgent myth, itself drawn from a public mythology, that greed for and apotheosis of *status* that began to gather intensity some years ago and rages without let-up now, so that we meet its vocabulary everywhere: "We," "Us," "Superstar," "King of the Hill," "Number One."

On a bare stage with its only prop an "evil-looking black chair," or throne, Shepard composes a drama whose main impulsions are the rage for competing, the savage jostling for the top that strangely implies there isn't enough fame to go round; and the dehumanizaton induced by celebrity, which converts true actions into poses, frozen stances. Hoss, the menaced king, says at one point that he'd be "O.K." if he "had a self. Something to fall back on in a moment of doubt or terror or even surprise." And when Crow, his rival, who has been talking in a murderous insider's jargon, speaks normally once, Hoss says: "Why'd you slip just then? Why'd you suddenly talk like a person?"

The contest employs various "languages," some actual, others invented or mythical, to display the half-real, half-imagined ways we define ourselves by vying. The gunfighter metaphor is central, but there's also car talk, where you rap through rare makes and horsepower, and a range of images from sports. Shepard brilliantly places the event in a deadly sci-fi world where computers determine rankings and an interplanetary commission guards the rules or "codes." Against this Hoss, who retains something of the older humanness, speaks of a time when "we were warriors" not incarnate appetites, and when there was a correlation between style and being. In a greatly revealing speech he indicates the new distance between authenticity and appearance: "Just help me into the style. I'll develop my own image. I'm an original man, a one and only. I just need some help."

In the play's climactic moments Hoss makes a last effort to reestablish his rule over the new soulless domain where nothing is valued except the deified name. He describes himself as a "true killer" who "can't do anything false," who's "true to his heart . . . his voice . . . pitiless, indifferent and riding a state of grace." Upon which he breaks down and cries over and over, "It ain't me!" The last word is Crow's, the victor: "Didn't answer to no name but loser. All that power goin' backwards. . . . Now the power shifts and sits until a bigger wind blows." The power, the force of ego turned ruthless and mechanical, will reign in a world without grace or true light; only the blinding sterile "stars" remain in their pitiless hierarchy.

In his last three plays Shepard has withdrawn noticeably from the extravagant situations, the complex wild voices and general unruliness of the earlier work. His themes, so elusive before, seem clearer now, if not pellucidly so; his vision dwells more on actual society. Physical or economic circumstances play more of a part than before.

I said before that one has to go beyond the economic implications of the "American Dream," but you do start there. Having money is both a form of and a means to identity; it lets you act. More than that, money makes itself felt in America as a chief agency of the distortion of the human theater; it forces people into roles and out of them, and by its presence or absence it dictates the chief values of our dramas. The very pursuit of it, beyond sustenance, flattens out selves, converts them into instances of success or failure, makes the play we're in single-minded and soulless. Still, as Freud once said, money isn't a primal need of the psyche, and it isn't one for Shepard's characters.

In *Curse of the Starving Class* the family is poor but not hopelessly so; their material need isn't so much the question as the instigation to enact a deeper need. They're starving but not really physically. The set is a kitchen, images of food and eating abound, but the weight isn't on physical hunger as a motif and nothing indicates this better than the incident when to a depleted larder Weston brings an enormous number of artichokes. The absurdity of this is evident, but what it reveals is the way food operates as a metaphor for a quest and not its aim.

What they're really starved for is selfhood, distinctiveness, satisfying roles. On any level they refuse to be of the starving *class*. As Emma insists, they're different from those who are starving as a function of their *status,* their definition, which is obscurity. They struggle to emerge, be seen by others, escape from being members of a class, a category.

The "curse" is the dark side of the American Dream and is manifested in its victims partly through standardization, and the quantification of values imposed by lawyers, developers, admen, and the like (the "zombies . . . they've moved in on us like a creeping disease," Wesley says), and partly by the very distortions of the craving for selfhood that results in ill-fated measures to achieve it. Apart from Wesley the members of the family come to disastrous ends or these impend; only he, the quiet, somewhat deadened, unambitious one, has the right, if uncolorful, idea. He wants to remain on the seedy place, to extend such roots as there are. He will settle for that role, that tiniest of bit parts.

In *Buried Child* the family to which the son, Vincent, returns is also poor, or marginal, but this isn't their *dramatic* condition. Vincent discovers that they don't know him, that in fact they're locked together in unknowingness, in a fixity of objectless rage and spiritual lameness. A struggle ensues between what we might call principles of movement and arrest. After fleeing the maimed scene, Vincent comes back to take over: "I've got to carry on the line. I've got to see to it that things keep rolling." The father, the incarnation of discontinuity, shouts that there's no past to propel a future. In the face of a photo from his youth, he insists: "That isn't me! That never was me! This is me. This is it. The whole shootin' match."

The mysterious field behind the house that everyone knows to be arid nevertheless produces vegetables in abundance. The fantastic field is a metaphor for fecundity, of course, and at the same time works as a hope of future life against the bitter, hidden truth which emerges at the end in the form of the murdered, "buried" child. The childhood buried in the adult who has refused the connection and so the continuity? An image of the secret life of families, burying the issue of their lovelessness? I don't think the symbol or metaphor is susceptible of neat interpretation. But it remains, as does the play with all its loose ends and occasionally unconvincing events—Vincent's violent change near the end, for example—strong and echoing in the mind.

In its straightforwardness and sparseness of action *True West*, Shepard's newest play, is surely the least typical of all his works. Its protagonists, two brothers who somewhat resemble Lenny and Teddy in Pinter's *Homecoming* (as the play itself also resembles Pinter in its portentous pauses and mysterious references), clash over their respective roles. Lee, the drifter and man of the desert, envies Austin, the successful screenwriter, and takes over his position by selling a producer on an "authentic" Western, one, that's to say, drawn entirely from his own matter-of-fact and therefore nonartistic, uninvented experience.

Austin, not an artist but a contriver of entertainment, nevertheless represents the imagination against Lee's literalness. Their battle shifts its ground until Austin, in the face of Lee's claim that his story reveals the "true" West, retorts that "there's no such thing as the West anymore. It's a dead issue!" The myths are used up. Still, his own identity has been found within his work of manipulating popular myths and he finds himself draining away under the pressure of Lee's ruthless "realism." The play ends with Austin's murderous attack on his brother, a last desperate attempt to preserve a self.

A last word on *Tongues* and *Savage/Love*. Both are more theater pieces than plays. They're the outcome of Shepard's and Chaikin's experiments with a dramatic form stripped of accessories, of plot elements and physical action, reduced to essentials of sound and utterance. When they rise, as they sometimes do, to a point of mysterious and resilient lyricism, they reach us as reminders at least of Shepard's wide and far from exhausted gifts.

I suspect he'll astonish us again.

Sam Shepard: Seven Plays, 1981

Part Two **Production Criticism:**

American Drama

Wilder's *Plays for Bleecker Street*

Thornton Wilder is probably our culture's finest living example of *faute de mieux*. He is our stage philosopher, in the absence of any other, our house allegorist, the man we turn to for civilizing counterinfluences to the practices of the new barbarians. He is much loved by the reflective, the humanistic, the homespun, the quietly patriotic, the slightly disenchanted, the moderately iconoclastic, and all who crave "satisfying evenings in the theater." All of which is not to say that he lacks real virtues; there is no denying that he is one of our most accomplished stylists, whose easy art is hard to dislike and harder to dislodge.

At least it is hard to dislike *Our Town* and *The Skin of Our Teeth,* and they continue to hold tenaciously to their places in the American repertoire. But *Plays for Bleecker Street,* Wilder's first appearance in some years, is another matter. These three one-acters, for all that they exhibit some of their author's ingratiating qualities and possess a good deal of the virtuosity of their predecessors, recommend themselves in the end rather strongly to our distaste, since—all the hullaballoo to the contrary—they are thin, strained, ultimately vacuous, and without power to obtain the least grasp on our imaginations.

They are the first plays of a cycle, or rather several related cycles, which

Wilder has been working on for a long time and which he clearly intends to be his *summa*. Their titles ought to have forewarned us. For in composing a series called "The Seven Ages of Man" and another called "The Seven Deadly Sins," Wilder betrays his obsession with numbers, which is an aspect of his strong Platonic bent. He once wrote that the key words in *Our Town* were hundred, thousand, and million, by which he meant that the play was concerned with quantities, generalities, and universals, the specific data—Grover's Corners and its inhabitants—serving as instances and objectifications of the broadest kinds of truth and laws.

Wilder, it seems clear, is forever seeking such instances, or exemplifications, for the illustration of large, preexisting ideas, or categories of ideas (the process is evident in *The Bridge of San Luis Rey* as well as in the plays). Together with his allegorizing, which springs from it, and his use of a vocabulary of truisms and clichés inserted into contexts of incongruity and mellow irony, which fleshes it out, this Platonic habit of thought constitutes his stock-in-trade as a dramatist.

It has had its successes, carrying *Our Town* along the broad, gently flowing quasi-philosophical stream that made its specific banalities endurable, and lending to *The Skin of Our Teeth* its partially redeeming quality of epic speculative nonsense combined with humanistic affirmation. But in the new works, perhaps because of their brevity, the weaknesses of this kind of imagination—its tendency to drown the particular in the general and its attenuated sense of conflict—are much more sharply revealed.

The first playlet, *Someone from Assisi,* which is listed as Number Four, or "Lust," from "The Seven Deadly Sins," suffers from more radical deficiencies than even those, and actually seems beyond critical analysis. In it Wilder has attempted to illustrate the sin by dramatizing its effects, having St. Francis, in the plenitude of his revolutionary asceticism, encounter a woman he had seduced during that rake's life before his conversion and who is now mad as a consequence.

What results, after some extraordinarily banal and flaccid dialogue, during which nothing is either tested, explored, or given point, is a heavy-handed coming down on the idea that the saint, in his shame, now possesses the fullness of poverty—nothingness. The impression one carries away, however, is of nothingness in the dramatic not the theological sense, and the sin the play seems to have grown out of is, sad to say, not lust but sloth.

"Childhood," Number Two from "The Seven Ages of Man," is considerably better. Here Wilder is back in his element—that sea of fantasy in which only objects with portentous exteriors but hollow centers can safely float—and his wit and learning, which are those of a combination cracker-barrel philosopher and psychiatrist, or alienist, from about 1913, have a chance to flower. His children act out their perverse games ("Hospital," "Orphans") under the eyes of their uncomprehending split-level parents, and the whole thing has a degree of humor and wispy charm. But the informing idea—that parents are "just people in our game, you're not alive"—is neither original nor profound, so that one feels at the end like crying out, with that wiser, legendary child, "But he's naked, can't you see?"

Finally, "Infancy," Number One from "The Seven Ages." It is quite funny, in a broad farcical style—that is the first thing to say for it. The second is that it is surely a piece of ingenuity to have grown men, in bonnets and baby carriages, playing infants. But though the situation permits Wilder his broadest effects and we do laugh, it comes with embarrassment, as though some rather inferior response had been set off. Beyond that, the play's governing notions, in this case that infants know and want more than we think they do and that they and we would exchange roles of it were possible, aren't very satisfying.

Perhaps they would be if something had been found to make them more dramatically viable, to give them more presence. But they, and the men in the carriages, and the mother and nurse and policeman, and all the characters from the other plays, finally exist as schemes in a mind, as conceits, as Platonic essences. And of course nobody has ever seen one of those.

Commonweal, Feb. 9, 1962

Kingsley's *Night Life*

Scanning Broadway, the eye of the ironist is immediately rewarded, filled, satiated in quick time: there is so much generosity. So far this season we have had plays of ideas in which no one thinks, comedies from which humor has meticulously been excluded, stars who are five-pointed disks of blackness, other-directed directors, sex without love, love without sex, and sex without sex. We have also had hit flops, like *Mr. President,* which nearly everybody hates but which is sold out for all eternity, and flop hits, such as *Who's Afraid of Virginia Woolf?* which almost everybody admires but which is too "disturbing" and "negative" for the tastes of demos. And we have also had plays like *Night Life,* around which the mists of irony swirl like complex and deadly gases.

During the intermission at *Night Life* a woman was heard to remark that Sidney Kingsley's drama was "simply too avant-garde" for her. A female Rip Van Winkle, she must have awakened, at the sound of the curtain going up, from a sleep that began in 1925, or at the latest 1936, since *Night Life* is a stage work of such outdated sensibility, exhausted rhetoric, and antediluvian technique that to consider it advanced can have no other rational explanation. And Kingsley has surely shared the lady's sleep, his dreams filled with the early O'Neill, with Edna St. Vincent Millay and Maxwell Anderson, with the Group Theater at its ideological worst, with his own paleolithic *Men in White* and *Dead End* and with John Dos Passos' *U.S.A.*

Kingsley's self-styled "new kind of drama" takes place in a microcosmic U.S.A., the "key club" in New York City. Now I have never been inside a key club, but I do not believe that Kingsley has been inside one either, unless he spent part of his long sleep there. For one thing, I happen to know that such establishments have girls in bunny or other costumes, and there just aren't any tomatoes, except customers, to be seen in this one. And for another, it doesn't seem likely to me, no siree it doesn't, that a key club should be the arena where the most pressing personal, national, and universal problems are thrashed out, made to yield up immense rhetorical and dramatic consequences, and ultimately resolved.

Even so, how ineptly is the implausibility put forth, how primitively does Kingsley's sad, arrested sensibility and gelid craftsmanship, which have been superseded by a dozen more pertinent kinds, arrange the evening's procedures. The single two-leveled set is filled with Representative People—a ferociously ambitious labor leader modeled on Jimmy Hoffa, a lawyer whose idealism has been shattered by the world's corruption and the H-bomb, a lesbian movie queen, a middle-aged couple who are discovering terrible things about one another, various personages identified in the programs as "Frenchie" and "gigolo" and "Harry's girl," who pullulate and mill around and interrelate and have empathy and rapport, or show us that they lack them.

The dramatic focus—and this is one of the purportedly new dramaturgical elements—continually shifts, in Kingsley's hunger for "totality," from one character or characterological nexus to another, the utterances move from un-felt dialogue to equally unfelt and pretentious asides and spoken thoughts, the tone from bawdy to bloodthirsty to earnest to mystical to melodramatic. Throughout, a pianist knocks off pop or blues melodies, joined occasionally by a girl singer and once by the entire clientele, which does a very energetic twist—all this constitutes the other piece of theatrical trailblazing. In the end everything is set right: the labor leader is revealed in his True Colors, the lesbian gets her Comeuppance, the lawyer has his Faith restored, the couple is reunited in Death, and Kingsley has conquered darkest, most complicated, and multi-farious America.

Most of the reviewers who had qualms had them about Kingsley's structure, that is, his admittedly brilliant inventiveness was thought to result in some-thing not quite coherent. But it was generally agreed that he has a fine ear for speech (examples: "You battled your way to the top"; "You're a worthy antago-nist"; "Deep down inside, as a human being, you're . . ."), a profound aware-ness of psychological truth (viz.: the movie star is asked about her suicide at-tempt: "Why did you do it? You have everything"), and the keenest sense of contemporary anguish coupled with the wit to express it (*ecce:* "We can't get through—words don't mean anything any more" and "I don't want kids be-cause I have a vision of a man with a pointed head pressing a button and my children frying").

I am not ordinarily for the young on principle, but a play like *Night Life* next to, say, *Virginia Woolf,* cries out for a generation to get the hell out of the way. Kingsley has every right in the world except one to feel the way Ibsen did when he wrote *The Master Builder.* What disqualifies him, of course, and leaves him wholly naked to the onrushing juveniles, is the fact that he was never Ibsen. He was only Elmer Rice.

Commonweal, Nov. 23, 1962

O'Neill's *Desire Under the Elms*
and Sherwood's *Abe Lincoln*
in Illinois

I would not wish to discourage the average theatergoer from seeing José Quintero's open-stage rendering of *Desire Under the Elms.* If you are an average theatergoer, you are probably rather in awe of O'Neill and consider this play a modern classic, so that attending it is in the nature of an act of piety. Well, if you perform it, you will be rewarded by a production mounted with force and quite vivid detail and by some extremely interesting and energetic characterizations by George C. Scott in the role of Ephraim and, on a much smaller scale, Clifford A. Pellow and Lou Frizzell as the sons Simeon and Peter.

There are some soft spots, however. Rip Torn is an actor of special intelligence, but as Eben he is too introspective and directs too much of his utterance into his beard to hold his end up well, while Colleen Dewhurst, ordinarily a performer of immense talent and vitality, is curiously muted and monolithic as Abbie. More disturbing is the open stage itself; it keeps trying to turn this heavy, coarse, brutally elegiac play into something more like an allegory of early America by Martha Graham. Her presence would not be altogether out of place, though. There are so many things to remember—where to stand, when to move so that every section of the audience gets its share of you, how and where to make your exits—that a choreographer is required to keep the cast from slithering, hopping, and dancing out of control.

But what is most difficult for me—a nonenthusiast of O'Neill—to overcome, is a feeling that this tragedy *manqué,* with its failures of rhetoric at all the crucial points, its vastly irksome "be ye's" and "hisn's" and "allus's," its ponderous hefting of chunks of raw feeling and simultaneous hunger for an integument of significance, is moving inexorably away from credibility or interest. A noted critic-director recently described it in my presence as a "beautiful" play; I wanted to say to him, but held myself back, that he has a beautiful fidelity to relics. At least it isn't false, though; it represents urgency and pressure and an artist's task, half-fulfilled—as was almost always the case with O'Neill—but attempted and full of achievements along the way.

It is harder to arrange devotional exercises for Robert E. Sherwood than it is for O'Neill, who for all his faults was a genuine playwright and wrote some plays that unlike *Desire Under the Elms* can still engage us. What Sherwood wrote I find it difficult to say, but he apparently retains his hold on *someone's* imagination, his having won the Pulitzer Prize some twenty years ago serving to keep the legend bright in certain quarters. He won it for *Abe Lincoln in Illinois,* and that play may now be seen again as the first offering of the Phoenix Theatre's re-descent upon the Lower East Side. It is hard to say whether the play or the production is more preposterous, but the competition does have the effect of spreading our pity evenly between our fathers, who apotheosized Sherwood, and some of our contemporaries, who have wished to resurrect him.

The banality, the folksiness, the tedium, the reliance on our good will and investment in Lincoln rather than on one's own imagination! The cutting down of Lincoln to the level of Broadway theatrics, his personality a compound Daniel Boone and Edgar Guest and his destiny a matter of getting shoved along by his ambitious wife! *Alors,* the performances, the staging win after all: they make an unpleasant play detestable. Stuart Vaughn has directed and set the work in epic style, which is the equivalent of playing *Uncle Tom's Cabin* as though it were *Mother Courage.* And Hal Holbrook, that master of the arts of make-up, has contrived to look like Lincoln, move like Andy Griffith, and speak like Tennessee Ernie—in Illinois.

What a race of children we must be to have once admired and to tolerate now this thoroughgoing insult to intelligence and taste. But perhaps we value freedom of speech and expression more than anything.

Commonweal, Feb. 15, 1963

Inge's *Natural Affection*

Toward the end of *Waiting for Godot* Estragon remarks to his companion, "We always find something, eh Didi, to give us the impression we exist?" To which Vladimir replies (impatiently, Beckett indicates) "Yes, yes, we're magicians." In the face of Arthur Miller's long silence and Tennessee Williams's disappearance into the mists of Nirvana, it is William Inge to whom the American theatergoer must increasingly look for the impression that he or she exists. Inge is a good man for the job, a real professional who always manages to find something or other in his bag, some emotion or other, some domestic or country passion or other—the point about giving an impression of existence is that the elements that go into it are interchangeable.

The impression of existence afforded by Inge's latest play is built around the conflict between maternal feeling and responsibility, the "natural affection" of the title, and sexual feeling, which as we all know is not to be thought of as natural in present-day America. That conflict is the center of the play, the thing that satisfies the textbooks, but of course Inge knows how to give an impression of complexity, too, the thing that satisfies the newer textbooks. So he has spliced in a number of subsidiary thematic strands, including such sure-fire impression-givers as "human loneliness," the failure of communication, and the jockeying for dominance that goes on between men and women who earn unequal amounts of money.

The play is rich in the impression of a robust, flavorsome, accurate speech, such as is ordinarily to be overheard between the head lingerie buyer for a Chicago department store, a woman in her late thirties with a long since vanished husband and a son away at reform school, and the slightly younger foreign-car salesman who is living with her. There is a wonderfully convincing impression of life swirling between these two, gay, hard-nosed, sentimental by turns, and only after this has been brilliantly established is the deeper impression—that of life's unfathomably sorrowful dilemmas—allowed to supervene.

The one selected by Inge this time, the aforesaid conflict between a mother's heart and a mistress's, leads straight to disaster, than which there is nothing better calculated to give a jim-dandy impression of existing with all stops out. The boy comes home, and since there is only one bathroom and one crisp end to the roast beef—incontrovertibly hard facts we all face at one time or another—presents his mother with a choice. If she keeps the boy she will lose her lover (he is waiting for the chance to open his own Cadillac agency before proposing marriage, since the fact that he is from an inferior ethnic group—the name is Slovenk, as in Kowalski—naturally has to be obliterated through chromium and much horsepower before wedding bells can be allowed to sound); if she opts for the latter, the boy will have to go back to the reform school, which, we have been made to know, is no Summerhill. Why the trio couldn't have simply moved to a larger apartment, since space seems to be at the heart of the tragedy, is never satisfactorily answered.

At any rate, the tragedy is there and will be heard. After much backing and filling, the woman finally chooses the boyfriend, announcing her decision in a speech which for its impression of a tragic dimension to existence has seldom been surpassed, even by this magician: "I'm not going to throw away the rest of my life on a smelly, rotten, dirty kid I never wanted in the first place." From then on fate works itself out in a majestic simulation of fate working itself out. The rejected boy descends to the level whereon all men who do not have the impression of being loved are to be found; he commits a senseless murder, shocking the audience and, presumably, his mother when she finds out, into an awareness of how necessary it is to keep up impressions.

The cast of this entertaining movie is remarkably good. Kim Stanley, who used to be an actress before she became an Actress, handles the woman's part with Pavlovian ease and security: tears, blowsiness, camaraderie, maternal concern, the torments of being the head buyer when your inamorata is only a Volkswagen salesman, all exhibit themselves on schedule and with precision. Harry Guardino is properly Ingean as the dumb but sharp, tough but good-hearted boyfriend. Gregory Rozakis plays the son with commendable belief in his reality. And Tom Bosley, as an aging neighbor who is representative of another sort of failure in love and to whom are entrusted certain central profundities of Inge's dramatic vision, best expressed in the lines "Life is miserable . . . everything is crazy and mixed up," appeals strongly to our sense of the roundedness of the occasion.

Natural Affection will make you know you are alive and that life is a damned serious matter. That is to say it will do these things if, like the majority of the theatergoers of America, you have no other way of finding out.

Commonweal, March 1, 1963

Baldwin's *Blues for Mr. Charlie*

James Baldwin is a hero, a prophet, an enormously effective essayist, a routine novelist and, it turns out, an inept playwright. But in the impure world of the theater a deficient play can be a sufficient sociological event, a public ritual which reduces the purposes of drama to those of a political rally or a show of arms. Such is the life of *Blues for Mr. Charlie;* crude, belligerent, naïve, constructed out of unassimilated grievances and untransformed pain, it may have seemed a liberating act for its creator but it is an imprisoning one for us. The audience on opening night, one observer remarked, appeared to be composed mostly of Black Muslims or white masochists, the former being steadily confirmed in their narrow anger and the latter in their enervating guilt.

Baldwin has loosely based his play on the case of Emmett Till, the young Negro whose murder in Mississippi in 1955 resulted in the swift acquittal of his accused slayer and the man's subsequent avowal of the crime. The central events are the same: the return to his Southern hometown of a Negro youth who has been North; his refusal to behave with traditional deference; his shooting by a white supremacist; the trial and acquittal; the final unrepentant admission of the murder. Within this narrative framework Baldwin has composed a rough, coerced ballet of interracial relationships, a *danse macabre* between partners, one of whom is suffused with rage, frustration, and grief and the other with arrogance, indifference, or guilt. At one point the stage is literally divided between "Blacktown" and "Whitetown" with the groups rhythmically changing sides.

This cleavage and rigid opposition are at the heart of the play. It is astonishing that a sensibility of Baldwin's alertness should fill the stage with stereotypes, moving like animated biases or figments from a dream of self-congratulation. They are crude lay figures: the Southerner who lusts after Negresses; the Uncle Tom; the alcoholic, genially philosophical Southern white liberal; the wise old mammy. And there are clichés within clichés: the Uncle Tom who comes through in the crisis, the liberal who finks out at the end. For them Baldwin has provided a rhetoric which is occasionally and only for the Negroes pointed and uncontrived, but which much more often is inherited banality. A girl remembers the dead boy: "One day, I'll recover. I'm sure that I'll recover. And I'll see the world again—the marvelous world. And I'll have learned from Richard— how to love. I must. I can't let him die for nothing."

To stage this ideological scenario, director Burgess Meredith has reverted to a production style that had its heyday in the 1930s, that of the old, exhorting Federal Theater, with elements of German expressionism and of the Marxist "agitprop" play. Characters move forward to deliver soliloquies; groups wait at the back while a scene unfolds in the foreground; music breaks in and dies. Derivative as this is, however, its effect gives the work what physical vivacity it has—a straightforward naturalism would have been disastrous. And Meredith has elicited some superior performances from his Actors Studio company, chief among them Al Freeman Jr.'s energetic portrayal of the victim and Diana Sands's superlatively lyrical and passionate rendering of his girl.

Yet everything alive and spontaneous in *Blues for Mr. Charlie* is intermittent and accidental. What is steady and basic is Baldwin's perpetuation of the deadliest abstractions of the interracial situation. Over its fateful dilemmas and agonized impasses he has thrown a net of quarter-truths and outright myths. His Negroes, so unmistakably mouthpieces, are forever indicting the white man—Mr. Charlie—for his effeteness, sexual incapacity, and ghostly life, and insisting that he is singlemindedly intent on their oppression. And his white men are engaged either in mechanical demonstrations of barbarism or degrading exhibitions of a futile sense of shame. It is easy to say that Baldwin has become a Negro chauvinist, but something more is at stake. In *The Fire Next Time* he wrote that "whatever white people do not know about Negroes reveals . . . what they do not know about themselves." To turn the dictum around and apply it to him is to come upon the crucial failure of his play. It is just the responsibility of the artist to *know*, to transcend the limitations of his physical condition in order to reach truth. Everything else is sentimentality, the outcome of what W. B. Yeats called the will's doing the work of the imagination.

Newsweek, May 4, 1964

Hansberry's *The Sign in Sidney Brustein's Window*

To write, to be an artist, is to sit in judgment on oneself, Ibsen once remarked, and as a supreme artist he knew how agonizing, but liberating, the process was. There was surely a dry agony in Lorraine Hansberry's writing of *The Sign in Sidney Brustein's Window,* but because the play is a vicious sitting in judgment on others, personal liberation was impossible from the start. As for the spectator, embarrassment, pity, sorrow, and anger are the emotions proper to the occasion.

There is a sort of inverted miracle in the way Hansberry manages to distort so many things—taste, intelligence, craft—and be simultaneously perverse as dramatist, social commentator, political oracle, and moral visionary. A further miracle is her union of bitchiness with sentimentality. But it is borrowed bitchery, for in her incredibly awkward drama, in which scene stolidly follows scene like a row of packing cases and character talks to character like droning telephone poles, Hansberry plunders from every playwright around, most thoroughly, Edward Albee.

The play can be said to be about the editor of a weekly New York newspaper who joins a local political crusade, is disillusioned, then revived by the knowledge that "love is sweet, flowers smell good, and people want to be better." But Hansberry is a master at changing the subject, so that there is a plethora of entirely separate plots: a domestic drama; an interracial one; the tragedies, respectively, of a goodhearted whore, a fainthearted queer, and a lily-livered liberal; the melodrama of a blackhearted dope pusher, and the tragicomedy of a cheated-on wife.

Yet none of this suggests the uses to which Hansberry puts her dragooned themes. They serve exclusively as containers for her venomous anger: she hates homosexuals, liberals, abstract artists, nonrealistic playwrights, white people unwilling to commit suicide, Albert Camus, Jean-Paul Sartre, Samuel Beckett, William Golding, and, especially, poor, plundered Edward Albee. Hansberry ostensibly wants to attack sham and hypocrisy, but her lack of charity chokes the play and becomes itself an intellectual vice which, ironically, stings her with its backlash. Her attack on "success" name-drops furiously, and her savage assault on intellectuality brandishes every intellectual catchword that can be snatched from the Zeitgeist.

Hansberry once wrote a play, *A Raisin in the Sun,* which in its small domestic compass was something of a judgment on the self. In turning into a cocktail-party shrew, in shifting her suffering to the backs of others, in using every easy trick to destroy what threatens her, she has betrayed not only the function of art, but social responsibility, political possibility, her own cause, and, most radically, herself.

Newsweek, Oct. 26, 1964

Lowell's *The Old Glory*

Last week in an Episcopal church near Broadway the American theater was given an improbable impetus toward maturity. The occasion was the first full-scale production by a nonprofit, partly church-sponsored group called the American Place Theater. The play was poet Robert Lowell's first, *The Old Glory.* But the light that rose from both occasion and drama spread far beyond the modest auditorium.

The Old Glory is in two subtly related parts, the smaller, *My Kinsman, Major Molineux,* being based on a Hawthorne story, and the larger, *Benito Cereno,* on the short novel by Melville. Yet they are no mere adaptations, since Lowell has in transmuting fiction into drama infused the works with a new and singular life. Together they compose a dark, menacing, yet also greatly luminous image of the American experience, its origins in violence and naïveté and its quest for a reconciliation between power and the troubled, unready American soul.

A "political cartoon" is how Lowell modestly described "Major Molineux," with its outsized gestures and rough typology of America on the eve of rebellion. Robin, a boy of eighteen, comes with his younger brother from the country to Boston to seek their relative, an agent of the king. The atmosphere is one of eerie myth and turbulent caricature, with pre-Revolutionary Boston symbolizing the City of Man. A ferryman resembling the legendary Charon warns the brothers of obscure perils, and they are plunged into the complex, tormented life of the City, as commedia dell'arte figures—a parson, a prostitute, a rich man—swirl around them with enigmatic speech and hostile faces.

"Everyone answers me in riddles," Robin says, but later adds that "we're learning how to live." What they are learning is the impossibility of innocence. When they come upon their kinsman, he is the victim of a lynch mob; tortured, bleeding, yet still swearing allegiance to the king (and by extension to civilized values and continuity), he is mocked by the citizens who knew him as a good man but now demand his death as a tyrant. "Whatever we do is our own affair, the breath of freedom's in the air," someone sings. As the boys stand gazing at the dying man, the truth takes shape that nothing is one's own affair, that the attainment of freedom is always haunted by the death it imposes on others.

In *Benito Cereno* innocence again confronts the true conditions of existence, this time in the person of an American captain whose ship has met a Spanish slave trader off Trinidad. On boarding her he finds a scene of desolation: her captain, Benito Cereno, seems to be dying, her crew has been decimated by scurvy and storms, her cargo of slaves reduced by half. Yet Captain Delano, outwardly a figure from a boys' book about the Marines storming Tripoli, is troubled by a sense of hidden corruption and threat. "God help me, nothing's solid," he exclaims.

He is right: the ship has actually been taken over by its Negro slaves, who have tortured and killed their Spanish masters. In a sequence of astonishing power the revelation is made, and Delano stands facing his enemy with an anguished question. "Who would want to murder Amasa Delano?" he murmurs, echoing pristine American innocence. There is hatred in the world, and subterranean gatherings of violence; the loving and the violent stand locked in an eternal embrace whose acceptance is the mark of maturity. In the last scene of this amazing play, as Delano gives the only answer of which he is capable—reluctant but emphatically efficient violence—we are shaken to the depths by what we have seen of ourselves.

The triumph of *The Old Glory* is total, flowing centrally from Lowell's magnificently literate text, but incorporating all the arts of the theater, from staging to costuming and lighting. Jonathan Miller, British writer- and wit-turned-

director, has staged both plays in an exactly appropriate style, the first with a wild, hallucinatory energy and the second in a slow, brooding tempo that springs free its final terrors with overwhelming force. And the acting is impeccable throughout; to cite Lester Rawlins for his superb performance as Delano and Roscoe Lee Browne for his brilliant work as the leader of the slave rebellion is only to recognize the greater richness of their roles.
Newsweek, Nov. 16, 1964

Miller's *Incident at Vichy*

The best thing that can be said of Arthur Miller's new play is that it marks a slight step up from the depths of *After the Fall,* just as its production by the Repertory Theater of Lincoln Center marks a mild recovery from the company's recent disastrous rendering of *The Changeling.* The next best thing one can say for *Incident at Vichy* is that watching it is like seeing a second-rate but superficially engrossing movie about the Nazis, such as Hollywood used to make in 1942 and 1943. Melodramatic, tendentious, dated, it holds our attention not by what happens inside the drama but by something outside from which it draws its effects—our knowledge of the enormity of what happened, our instant response to the sight of a Nazi uniform. In such peripheral and borrowed ways Miller's new play manages to stave off full calamity, but it is nothing like a satisfactory achievement.

The scene is a "detention room" in Vichy, France; the time is September 1942. A group of men has been rounded up by the Germans, with the cooperation of the French police. It soon becomes clear that the hunt is for Jews; word comes to the waiting men that the rumors they have heard about extermination camps are well founded, and the play now turns to a series of portrayals of their varying attitudes toward the "incomprehensible" fact. For with one exception the men are indeed Jewish, hence, presumably, at the center of the historic agony and, as characters, at the promising service of a playwright's passion and imagination.

Yet almost nothing is dramatized. Miller does bring in a figure from those 1942 movies—the troubled, non-Nazi German officer—and constructs a scene in which the man's self-hatred and thwarted decency generate a fair amount of power. But almost everything else is posture—the men taking stances of victimization, evasion, cowardice, defiance, and so on. And after that Miller turns to a debate—which once or twice approached trenchancy but which far more often is windy and self-righteous—about the nature of Nazism and the proposition that we are all responsible for having allowed it to happen.

There are two chief participants in these forensics: an Austrian prince, the only non-Jew among the prisoners, who is the incarnation of refined, fastidious, liberal opposition to Nazism, and hence for Miller is a deplorable ally, just as the refined white liberal is for James Baldwin. Speaking for Miller himself is a psychoanalyst, that old literary standby—the tormented, questing intellectual who seeks to push issues to their limits. But as the evening moves on (the play is only an hour and a half long) it quickly becomes evident that those issues have been pushed by other hands: echoes of the controversy over the Eichmann trial and of Rolf Hochhuth's *The Deputy* reverberate through the theater like reproachful voices whispering, "Zeitgeist-robber!"

"They do these things not because they are Germans but because they are nothing," the psychoanalyst says, and the thesis of Hannah Arendt's book on Eichmann rises ghostlike to the mind. "Nothing is forbidden any longer," the prince complains, and Dostoevsky's *The Possessed* receives its latest rifling. "There are no persons anymore," the German officer laments, and everybody's secondhand philosophy of modern man's predicament comes packaged to the stage. And finally, in the play's climactic scene, Miller's poverty of ideas is naked: the prince sacrifices himself so the Jewish doctor can live, a duplicate of the last piece of action in *The Deputy.*

Now, nobody would wish to find fault with Miller's subject or quarrel with his right, and even duty, to grapple with issues so fundamental as the ones he raises, even though their contours have changed over the last twenty years. The theater desperately needs to become again the forum for the boldest confrontation with the truths of history and the moral life of man in society.

But the point is that Miller doesn't grapple with his issues, he scarcely even raises them; above all, he doesn't give them dramatic life, so that his words hang in the air like hoarsely delivered sermons, and his ideas emerge without outline or weight, like a rhetoric of private neurosis and anguish struggling to become an important public statement. And the fact that the theater is the most public art leads Miller to try to implicate us unfairly in his personal problem of inarticulateness and philosophical confusion; we are never drawn into a drama, but only prodded, cajoled, accused into an artificial and temporary remorse. "We are all scum," someone says, speaking for the author. But in this play he has not earned the right to say it.

A word about the acting and direction, which represent a considerable improvement over anything the Repertory Theater has thus far done. Harold Clurman has staged *Incident at Vichy* with an eye to keeping its rhetorical gassiness from carrying it right out the exits, and with a minimum of stagy effects. And the company is at full strength, still a low standard by anyone's ideal of repertory acting, but unembarrassing and adequate for the job. David Wayne and Joseph Wiseman are especially competent, and there are decent performances in lesser roles by David Mann, Hal Holbrook, and David J. Stewart. One wonders, however, how long the best people at Lincoln Center can continue to persevere among the worst.

Newsweek, Dec. 14, 1964

O'Neill's *Hughie*

During the last five or six years of Eugene O'Neill's creative life, from the late 1930s to 1942, he wrote his most durable plays—*The Iceman Cometh, Long Day's Journey into Night, A Touch of the Poet.* He had come finally into his true art, shedding the grandiosity and pompous rhetoric of plays like *Marco Millions* or *Strange Interlude,* taking up subjects about which he felt deeply, instead of merely yearning toward. *Hughie* comes from this period, but, unfortunately, scarcely shares in O'Neill's late-won power and assurance. Barely an hour long, it was written in 1942, the only completed work of a projected, experimental eight-play series. Having never been performed here (it was done in Sweden in 1958), it is worth seeing, but only as a fragment from a troubled and uneven life-work.

Into a seedy New York hotel comes Erie Smith, a small-time Broadway gambler. The year is 1928 but the man exudes the aura of flashy bravado and pinched hopes that surrounds the grifter in any era. He addresses a long monologue to the night clerk, a defeated, apathetic man, on the subject of the former clerk, a man named Hughie who has recently died. Hughie was naïve, mediocre, impressionable, a perfect "sucker," but for that very reason a perfect foil for Smith's need to dazzle someone, to feed another's fantasies and thereby strengthen his own precarious hold on life. After the monologue, in the play's only real action, he shoots craps with the clerk, having awakened him to the shabby, hopeless, yet somehow sustaining myth of gambling, the—excitement of the Big Time, vicariously lived.

It is pretty thin stuff, made thinner by our knowledge that O'Neill was to treat the same theme far more substantially in *Iceman.* The one thing that carries the evening through is the performance of Jason Robards as the gambler. Not that it is an exciting performance, but rather a fascinating exercise in "correct" playing. That is to say, Robards does the role to perfection—since he offers an enormously competent reading of a set part. When he slaps his thigh it is with Falstaffian authority; when he describes some girls he has known as "raw babies," he keeps the "raaawwww" going until it sounds like red meat. What is remarkable in acting of this kind is that since it is never less than rich, broad, and absolutely safe, it never manages to offer a single surprise or moment of discovery.

Newsweek, Jan. 4, 1965

Miller's *A View from the Bridge*

Ulu Grosbard, in his revival of Arthur Miller's *A View from the Bridge,* gives an exemplary demonstration of the way a director can function as life-giver. To consider the revival of *A View from the Bridge* is to gain an insight into the art of direction. Miller's play is anything but a masterpiece. Urgent, intense, hard-breathing, it aspires to tragedy without the equipment to achieve it, since it suffers from a basic failure of vision, a muddled grasp of how psychic action relates to existential truth, and an insufficiency of language rich enough to support its theme. Yet the tragic story of Eddie Carbone, the Brooklyn longshoreman who cannot allow himself to become conscious of his incestuous love for his niece and thereby brings about his own destruction, does have a certain potential physical life, a sensual reality which makes it viable for the stage.

What Grosbard has done is to make the play work at the top of its capacity, converting it into an almost wholly satisfying theatrical experience, if not a revelatory one. And he has done it by freeing the plays' physicality and giving it shape, at the same time as he ushers into visibility such strands of meaning and thought as Miller was able to weave into the drama. His greatest feat is resisting the temptations to indulge in stage business, to make the action even harder-breathing than the text asks for, to have his actors express themselves like people from "real life" instead of as instruments of a dramatic vision. Continually reining in, cutting off scenes before they can overflow into bathos, and imposing a deft, quick movement on the action, Grosbard, aided by an extremely good cast headed by Robert Duvall and Jon Voight, has brought off a minor miracle.

Newsweek, Mar. 15, 1965

Baldwin's *The Amen Corner*

Under the pressure of his own myth and status as Negro spokesman and prophet, James Baldwin has allowed his powers of self-criticism to atrophy. A writer more severe with himself, less concerned with role-playing, would not have wanted a work like *The Amen Corner* to represent him—except as a private exercise in becoming a playwright. And the drama is, in fact, an early work, written in 1953, just after Baldwin's first novel, *Go Tell It on the Mountain,* which it strongly resembles thematically. It is not false or hysterical like his second play, *Blues for Mr. Charlie.* It is merely inept and tedious, making earnestness do the work of imagination.

The setting is the same as that of the novel and, in large part, of Baldwin's own early life: a storefront church in Harlem. Its minister is a woman, intense, determined, seemingly on fire with the Lord. She has brought up her son, a talented pianist, to walk the strictest path, holding out to him the negative example of his father, a jazz trombonist who left the family years before and is now dying somewhere, from "sinfulness," as she says. Early in the play, the man puts in an appearance and is indeed seen to be dying, although not, we are quickly assured, from sinfulness.

In the drama's main action—the subsidiary one is the effort of a claque of small-minded parishioners to oust the minister from her post—the father accomplishes a double revolution. He springs the boy free to lead his own life in the world and converts his wife from a loveless spirituality to an acceptance of the joy and pain of being human.

Such are the play's themes, unexceptionable if hardly original. Its dramatic life is another matter. For Baldwin, playwriting seems to be a matter of finding opportunities for speeches, set-pieces in which a particular attitude or emotion is proclaimed, as though from a pulpit. The mechanism sometimes works; there are several affecting moments in *The Amen Corner.* But it works without relation to any context, so that the high moments are buried in long stretches of clumsy, groping exposition, of irrelevant detail and lifeless movement.

And Baldwin, serving himself badly enough, is further ill-used by the direction of Frank Silvera, who plays the father with some vigor but has staged the play stiffly and uninventively. As for the rest of the cast, it is no more than adequate. Bea Richards in the crucial role of the minister is physically arresting—

taut, sculpted, primitive—but her high-pitched, incantatory, uninflected speech soon grows monotonous and predictable, exactly as the play does. *Newsweek,* Apr. 26, 1965

Inge's *Where's Daddy?*

William Inge's forte has always been the conjuring up and apparent exorcism of childhood fears and adult anxieties. His plays slide past the pain of existence while ostensibly confronting it and arrive safely at reassurance, leaving the impression that some arduous process of maturation has been gone through. Confined to this small domestic realm, Inge has at least been master of his intentions. But when he steps outside into the world of ideas, social movements, and intellectual currents, he is lost. His new play *Where's Daddy?* attempts to be terribly modern, au courant, and complex, and succeeds only in being preposterous.

The comedy-drama centers on a battle of the generations. Youth is represented by a post-teen couple who are having a baby but have decided, in accordance with the "new morality," that love is out and personal fulfillment in. Maturity is impersonated by the girl's mother, a matronly square, and the boy's former guardian, a fiftyish homosexual, literate and civilized. The latter two are horrified, from their different vantage points, by the couple's decision to separate—the boy, a budding star of television commercials, to seek his fortune unencumbered, the girl to hand the baby over for adoption and go it alone.

Obviously, this being an Inge play, none of these horrible things is going to happen, but along the way he manages to throw in comments and tableaus having to do with every aspect of modern social life imaginable. It is difficult to know, so inept are the play's mechanisms, when Inge is being mocking or straightforward, but it seems clear that among the things he abhors are young people's "selfishness" and "immorality," psychoanalysis, the plays of Samuel Beckett, television commercials, and contemporary "crisis theology." "It's no good these days to be shocked at anything," the matron remarks, but Inge is clearly shocked by a world rapidly invalidating the homespun pieties of his own psyche and grasp of reality.

For Inge, all in favor of "responsibility" and "love" and "joy" and "generosity," turns everything finally toward these abstractions. In the end, his young people turn out to be "nice" and "responsible," so that the older members of the cast can sigh in relief and go back to their knitting and pre-Freudian cosmology.

The one saving grace in a notably graceless evening is Hiram Sherman as the wise old homosexual. A real pro, he fashions a completely convincing portrait—delicate and sharp, witty and baffled—of the outsider who maintains connection with some central human values. For the rest, there is Betty Field in a strained, monotonous performance as the mother; Robert Hooks and Barbara Ann Teer as a pair of neighbors who are Negro so Inge can show he is aware of the racial crisis; and as untalented a tandem as Broadway has recently seen, Barbara Dana and one Beau Bridges, as the incarnation of Inge's saccharine theory of what the young are really like.

Newsweek, Mar. 14, 1966

Albee's *A Delicate Balance*

Alienation, terror, the hunger for roots, sexual warfare, self-deception—these have been Edward Albee's themes ever since his auspicious debut with *The Zoo Story* seven years ago. They are the themes, in one form or another, of most serious drama and literature in this century—and of a great deal of pseudoserious, imitative work. Albee's imitations may frequently be skillful and entertaining but they are imitations nevertheless—of Strindberg, O'Neill, Genet, Ionesco, and now of Harold Pinter and, most heavily, of himself. His latest play, *A Delicate Balance,* is effective and interesting up to a point; but the point is precisely the line which separates the appropriated, the derivative and general, from the new, the independent, the specific and self-propelling.

In the kind of urbane living room which has become Albee's unmistakable scenery, six characters enact a parable of human responsibility and estrangement. The atmosphere at first is that of Noel Coward laced with a bit of the domestic savagery of Albee's own *Virginia Woolf.* A wealthy middle-aged couple go through a long and boring recapitulation of their circumstances, which include their mutual tolerance, if not love, their well-rutted habits, the disturbing presence of the wife's alcoholic sister and the equally disturbing existence of their thirty-six-year-old, much-married daughter. But then, in the kind of movement which in all of Albee's plays marks an uneasy transition from realism to fantasy, the couple's best friends burst in, having been frightened by some mysterious power. They bring with them a whiff of Pinter and their quasi-metaphysical presence provides the generator for the subsequent events.

They have come because they are afraid to be alone and have decided to live with their best friends, since what is friendship for if not to provide what is needed? Taken aback, the couple find themselves assailed from another quarter when their daughter, having left her fourth husband, arrives home and demands her room—her haven from the "dark"—which the friends have moved into. The wife, hardheaded, practical, the fulcrum of the "delicate balance" between the family and the outside world, wants the friends to leave; her husband, tortured by his realization that he doesn't love them, insists that they stay in order to oppose by will the constriction of his feelings. In the end they go, for everyone has come to realize that they are all incapable of love, that their friendship has been a matter of habit and convenience and contains no principle of sacrifice, and that, in the end, "the only skin you've ever known is your own."

It is this latter kind of cliché that is all too prominent in Albee's rhetoric—whenever, that is to say, he aspires beyond the hard-bitten repartee with which he alone feels comfortable. "When all the defects are admitted, memory takes over and corrects facts and makes them tolerable," someone says. This inflated dialogue attempts to fill in for true action, both physical and verbal—to state the case which Albee has not otherwise succeeded in making. For a "case" in drama is something realized, incarnated, made palpable, so that there is no division between theme and procedure. In *A Delicate Balance* the division is extreme.

And yet there are several moments in which something direct and authentic breaks through. One is a scene in which the husband, solidly and adroitly

played by Hume Cronyn, recounts an anecdote, reminiscent of the long central one in *The Zoo Story,* about a cat which unaccountably stopped liking him; another is his passionate, broken plea to the friends to stay. Rosemary Murphy, playing the conventional role of a wise drunkard with unconventional wit and force, provides a few more, as do Henderson Forsythe and Carmen Mathews as the friends. As the wife and daughter, however, Jessica Tandy, with her narrow range of movement and voice, and Marian Seldes, with her forced hysterics, seem to epitomize the forced and narrow side of Albee.
Newsweek, Oct. 3, 1966

Terry's *Viet Rock* and van Itallie's *America Hurrah*

When the Yale School of Drama invited the Open Theatre to stage Megan Terry's *Viet Rock,* it gave recognition to one of New York's most original and vigorous new theater groups. A loose aggregation of actors, directors, and playwrights, the group has worked mostly in a downtown loft and in coffeehouses since its founding in 1963. Last week two plays opened Off-Broadway which were almost entirely the work of Open Theatre people and principles: *Viet Rock* and Jean-Claude van Itallie's *America Hurrah.*

One of these principles, operating in both plays, is that of "transformations," a shifting, fluid movement within a play by which actors change from role to role without transition, scenes merge, and physical actions often run counter to speech. The intention is to break up the conventions of ordinary narrative drama, in which one character equals one imaginary person and scene follows scene like steps in a logical demonstration.

Van Itallie's three short plays, whose dominant intention is to satirize aspects of American life, make up one of the most impressive debuts in a long while.

Two of the playlets are flawed, but forgivably so: van Itallie's craftsmanship is still searching for control and his satiric sense is far from free of cliché. *Interview* is a highly stylized, intricately choreographed exercise in urban loneliness and depersonalization. *TV* is an essay on the chasm between our daily lives and the debased dreams of popular culture.

What is arresting in them is not so much the points they score—off employment agencies, television, the Johnson family—as the effects they reach through their experiments with the nature of the stage. "Characters" in drama, they keep saying, need no longer be finished replicas of people from "real" life but rather fragments, archetypes, monsters, masks. The third playlet, *Motel,* realizes this superbly. A huge papier-mâché "doll" covering a live actor represents a motel manager who drones on about her place's elegance, its home-away-from-hominess, while two more dolls, a man and a woman, enter silently, strip to their underclothes, and slowly, terrifyingly, with unreal movements, wreck furniture and scrawl obscene messages on the wall as the sales monologue goes on. This is a compelling image of American violence all right, but on a much deeper level—it is an extension of our powers of envisaging ourselves.

Megan Terry's *Viet Rock* is far more ambitious than *America Hurrah,* but though its strengths are often similar it gives off a pervasive aura of amateurishness such as van Itallie's work seldom does. Its nearest counterpart is *Oh What a Lovely War,* which was created improvisationally in Joan Littlewood's workshop just as Terry fashioned her play in the Open Theatre's. In it a young, earnest company enacts a fable or dream with music about the Vietnam war, tracing a handful of American soldiers from induction to the fighting and interspersing a good many topical skits—a Congressional hearing, an antiwar demonstration—along the way.

At moments the play captures the harsh, jangly beat of this strangest of wartimes. At other times the sheer energy and conviction of the cast carry the audiences upon a real tide of theatrical pleasure. But it doesn't carry them for long or to any memorable destination. Terry, who has written better plays, is frequently sentimental and obvious, but what is worse, she seems to be writing about the war from the headlines, from what others have felt and said about it. *Oh! What a Lovely War* was about World War I and conveyed the specific terrors, idiocies, and pain of that specific war. *Viet Rock,* for all its topical references, is at bottom merely an antiwar play, falling back on all too easy statements and gestures.

Newsweek, Nov. 21, 1966

Lowell's *Prometheus Bound*

Robert Lowell's "imitations" are actually new works which take the structures and themes of classic poems and convert them to Lowell's own, contemporary uses. The same is true of his "adaptations" of plays, his *Phaedra* and his newest work, *Prometheus Bound*. In its world première last week at the Yale School of Drama, the play revealed itself to be not much more than the skeleton of the Greek original, filled out with Lowell's own imagination, which sometimes adheres closely to Aeschylus but more often veers sharply in very un-Greek-like directions.

The evening was puzzling, difficult, full of superb moments but also of stretches of barren event, enormously interesting in its ambitions and its central enterprise but not quite managing to bring it off. With its pure lyricism and nearly complete lack of physical action, *Prometheus Bound* is one of the hardest of all Greek tragedies to stage for modern audiences, and Lowell's free, colloquial, "existential" version doesn't make the problem much easier. It does, however, suggest a line of approach, which director Jonathan Miller has energetically followed.

To get past the sterile faithfulness of most productions of Greek tragedy, he has replaced the original's windswept mountaintop and gloomy rock with a seventeenth-century castle keep—a brilliant, towering set by Michael Annals, with flaking dusty gray brick walls, enigmatic statuary in niches, and two huge chains running from floor to flies like a cold symbolic armature of fate—and dressed his actors in dusty unkempt gray costumes of the period.

Lowell's construction follows the bare Greek outlines: as punishment for bringing fire (intelligence) to men, Prometheus is chained to a rock by Zeus, where he is visited by "seabirds" who function as a chorus; Ocean, the god who urges him to submit; Io, Zeus's former earthly lover; and Hermes, Zeus's messenger who brings a last appeal for submission. Lowell follows the structure of some of the original speeches, and there is a scattering of Aeschylus's lines, but everything else is almost pure Lowell.

Where Aeschylus shaped an elemental conflict—intelligence versus might, man's finiteness versus God's omnipresence—and looked forward to an eventual reconciliation, Lowell's *Prometheus* is a mostly dark, anguished poem (the writing is actually in a kind of loose, imagistic prose) about suffering, death, and tyranny. Far more than in Aeschylus, Lowell's Zeus is a political tyrant, "blind with power," and at the same time he is a deity resembling the "helpless" God of certain contemporary theologies. And Prometheus is not so much Zeus's fierce adversary as he is a witty, mordant rebel, like a hero in Dostoevsky or Camus.

As Miller steers the play through its long arcs of lyricism and elegy and smaller ones of acrid commentary—"Cruelty is [Zeus's] form of courage"—and relaxed banter—"Why should I go on talking about monsters? When you have seen one, you have seen them all"—the work seems more and more to fall into a succession of shapely, intense but isolated dreams. This conception yields some splendors. In a beautiful long speech, Irene Worth as Io contrives to fashion a complete, miraculous little drama from what is essentially a narrative. And Kenneth Haigh as Prometheus also does some memorable work, including a soliloquy on death in which he tells Io how her own body, "that hound-pack of affliction," will close in "to kill you."

It is difficult to see how or why Miller might have "jazzed up" the play. Quietness, immobility, inwardness, make their own appeal to the mind. But perhaps the trouble is just there: *Prometheus Bound* in its ancient mythic incarnation remains available almost wholly to the mind—not the senses, except that of hearing. Whatever Lowell's poetry, distinguished as it is for the most part, has added or changed, his *Prometheus* remains uncomfortable on the stage, and at home in some much more private realm. Unlike his masterly adaptations of stories by Hawthorne and Melville, which were the basis of his brilliant trilogy, *The Old Glory,* the new work does not quite break out into its own hard, inescapable dramatic action.

Newsweek, May 22, 1967

The Living Theatre on Tour

When the Living Theatre left America for Europe four years ago I was among those who wished them well in their self-exile and, as it seemed to me, their opportunity to find out what they were really about. I'd always been troubled by them, having admired them more, I suspect, in theory than as an actuality. I defended them as often because of their detractors—most of whom represented everything sterile and commonplace in the theater—as because of their own occasionally memorable productions— *The Connection, The Brig.*

Their regular (and belligerent) lapses of taste, intelligence, even simple skill never convinced me of some splendid amateurism full of redeeming spontaneity and unacademic prowess, nor were those lapses ever entirely offset by the group's energy, daring, and originality, whenever the latter quality sporadically showed itself. And the way they mixed theater and politics, or rather the way, in that earlier incarnation, they *didn't* fuse them but seemed torn between opposing claims so that they would drop their stage activities, no matter who suffered—actors, audiences with tickets in hand, playwrights—to go off on a march, or would break an aesthetic unity to register a protest, seemed to me irresponsible, adolescent, and, most crucially, ineffective.

Now they are back, Judith Malina and her husband Julian Beck and about thirty members of a company that is at least as much a community, a practicing, striving peripatetic utopia. From the reports one heard of their European progress they had changed drastically. They had become wholly, furiously political, for the first time a true collectivity that presented its own visions and imaginative enterprises instead of doing other people's plays, however radical those works and their staging might be. It's true: they have changed, the four years of wandering, full of triumphs and outrages, during which they shaped their new nature before European audiences whose own theaters apparently possessed nothing so far out or so *self-willed,* have brought the Living Theatre back to us as something giving off a hard, continuous pressure to take sides.

"Reality" is what the Living Theatre is all about now; apocalyptic, tendentious to the point of violence, a self-generated and self-validated juggernaut of revised sensibility and renewed humanism, the company comes at its audiences charged with mission. This is what it hopes you will undergo: not performance, presentation—an active shaping for passive onlookers—but action itself, in which all participate, boundaries break down, and company and audience enter into a new and mystical collectivity, germ center of a coming better world.

The audiences so far, at Yale and the Brooklyn Academy of Music, have been almost entirely young, open (to something if not necessarily to the Becks), irreverent and aggressive, politically worked up and intellectually skeptical, audiences of potential dadaists, komsomols, and insurrectionaries. To be something new, or to think you are, to get out of the rut, to change the rules and therefore the experiences are the principles and impulses at work everywhere—with the theater, that place of egos in propinquity and of immediate statement, being one of the chief arenas.

I saw three of the four productions in the Theatre's current repertoire, missing only *Frankenstein* (which some persons I respect tell me is the best; but then, others I respect think it the least). *Antigone,* which is Judith Malina's translation (and rewriting) of Brecht's adaptation of Hölderlin's German version of Sophocles, and which is directed by her and her husband, is the only "play" of the three, and it does its best to keep from being any kind of straightforward one. The Becks are involved here with that animus against the classics that is only partly a matter of anti-intellectualism or of an extreme bias toward the contemporary, its other being justified boredom with the way plays like this are perpetually presented: according to someone's idea of how Greek "dignity" and "majesty" must have exhibited themselves theatrically in their actual time.

Thus there is nothing artificially dignified and certainly nothing majestic about this production; a great many risks are taken, there's no hesitation in skewing the plot around to point up the most contemporary (and obvious) issues and fiddling with the texture to release an up-to-the-minute aroma, and the very pace and movement—jagged, febrile, insouciant—reveal a wish to interrupt and sabotage the stately, solemn, boring measures of Greek tragedy as a *cultural inheritance.* To this ambition I was sympathetic, as I was to the occasional purely physical éclat that the Becks have always proposed as their chief theatrical virtue and which takes the form of inventive groupings, movements off the stage and into the theater-building-as-the-world, communal sounds and postures, of despair, anguish, frenzy, and so on, in which the chorus becomes the body of the feeling rather than its commentator.

But the play is nearly intolerable whenever it has to be *acted,* whenever lines have to be uttered and consciousness invoked. It was evident to me from the beginning that whatever else it is the Living Theatre is unbelievably untalented in the rudimentary processes of acting—speech, characterization, the assumption of new, invented being. Malina and Beck are the worst offenders: as Antigone she is alternately coy, neurotic, wild-eyed, and impish, a happy heroine, while he plays a preposterously monstrous Creon, modeled largely on Lyndon Johnson as MacBird. Heavy-handed, amateurish in the full pejorative sense, making its political points (and I don't imagine I have to report what *they* are) with the utmost sneering self-righteousness, this *Antigone* reveals, wherever it "speaks," that the group's strength must surely lie somewhere else.

It lies theoretically in its rituals, its raids on the expectations of some audiences and on the preparations other audiences make for being changed, or for being made to feel *alive,* in its proposition that reality is in need of new morale and that society, sick and loathsome, needs regeneration through "honesty," "openness," and "sincerity." Thus to place itself before audiences as colleagues and fellow-sufferers, to gather the spectators in or, alternatively, to battle with them, to provoke, needle, exhort, preach, cajole, shame, and caress, to lay itself bare, to be sacrificial and incorruptible and redemptive *in the middle of society,* is what the Theatre organizes itself so strenuously to do. A serious undertaking, an ambition having nothing to do with entertainment or feats of skill or coldly formal art served up from a distance . . . and it is all brought down by a näiveté of monumental proportions and a self-love that wholly undermines any pretense of love for us.

In *Paradise Now,* the group's latest and most ambitious production, everything flaccid and indulgent and embarrassing about their work is on display. In the series of rituals, games, group embraces, "spontaneous" exercises, and colloquies with the audience, the possible virtues—the achieving of true, uncoerced, felt community, the reenergizing of political attitudes through accurate and hitherto unknown gestures and utterances of indictment, repudiation, alternative morales—are continually brought to ruin by that näiveté and that self-love. Every so often a truly affecting, even lovely image is shaped; the company, which does respond as a trained organism and is commendable in its submission of the parts to the whole, arranges itself silently as an anguished exemplary body of victims or moves about the theater with the simple gravity of a religious procession. And every so often, at a moment of silence in every case, I felt myself moving out in love toward the sheer, impracticable, beleaguered hope that some kind of community was really forming, and toward the group and the Becks themselves, remembering all the hard times, wanting the thing to be redemptive, purgative, and new.

But the talk, the pompous, self-righteous, clichéd talk! The talk that separates and kills as effectively among leftists and radicals as among the "enemy," the talk that reinforces complacency at the very moment it's trying to unsettle and prod, that brings the darkness closer through its utter blindness to the political and social realities, that says what we already know, what we've found useless *as talk.* "To reinvent love," they chant, "to do useful work," "to get rid of central control," "to spell out paradise." "The day we stop using money" is the day of paradise, we're told. "Be the black, be the poor," we're told, and someone unfriendly yells out, "why are you charging admission?"

"Fuck the Arabs . . . fuck the Jews" they bellow in a painful attempt to indicate their impartiality in the interests of human solidarity, an attempt made even more painful by their next piece of information: "Fuck means peace." "This theater is yours," we're told, "this theater is for creating a better world," and except when something unconscious takes over, when self is forgotten or overcome and the audience feels for a moment that the roots of its humanity, poor, starved roots, are mysteriously being watered, it may be that, in spite of the assault from the group, the better world is all easy rhetoric: easy statement, the easiest of statements. "Talk to your neighbor on the right, fascist!" one of the company tells somebody. "Stop thinking about yourself and think about the dying!" and someone unfriendly hollers, "what have you ever done for the dying?"

And then Julian Beck says that there are 20,000 policemen in this city, "who will form cells to change their consciences," and a printing press is brought on stage and the company shows some members of the audience how to use it for the rhetorical elaboration of the better world. And in an absolutely flawless cameo of irresponsibility, Beck, long lank hair falling back from his great bald crown, prophetic and furious, announces that there are "1,500 prisoners in the Atlantic Avenue jail a few blocks from the theater, who will free them?" "We're going to march on the jail and free them later tonight, who will march with us?" Of course no one marches, of course the prisoners remain. Easy, irresponsible, outrageous.

The next night I saw *Mysteries and Smaller Pieces,* which I liked more, or rather disliked less, because while the group still involved the audience in its fiercely adolescent declamations ("stop the war," "don't vote," "abolish the state," "abolish money"), it spoke less, turned more to what it does best—theatrical games and exercises, having fun with precisely the kinds of actions "serious" theater anathematizes: they blow their noses over and over, an action as important as any other; they marched around the stage in marvelous useless precision; they "passed" each other emotions and gestures as in a warm-up for an athletic event. The last piece of action, a long mimesis of our social despair and the horrors of our impersonality, in which members of the group "die" in agony at various points in the theater and are carried stiff and strangely remote by others in the company to be piled in a pyramid on stage, was solemn and affecting, and, what's more, a true theatrical action, a new one.

Yet it seemed to me as I walked out afterward that even here something centrally confused and contradictory about the Living Theatre showed itself. For if theater, as I think it must, has to renew itself by dealing with the problem of illusion, with, that is, the at least partly discredited tradition of impersonation, of pretending to be someone else (which film, for one thing, gets around through its very abstraction, its mythic reality), then what is the point of miming dead men or any other kinds of actual beings? If you are to rouse and change audiences, for political purposes or more generally humanistic ones, by putting yourselves in front of them as your own selves, exemplary but also familiar, doing the things the spectator would presumably do if he weren't a spectator and soliciting him to do them, to come up on stage, to sing along, to take off his clothes (*Paradise Now* contained, as Eric Bentley's pointed out, not a show of nudity but one of underwear), then why impersonate anything, why pretend? If the point is to break down the artificial distinctions, to make theater into actuality, to implement John Cage's observation that life is everywhere dramatic and the function of art is to indicate that this is so, then why "act" at all? I think this confusion stems from the Becks' fundamental ignorance of what is happening both in their theatre and in the world, and even more from the group's fantastic self-love and self-pity. For if the Living Theatre were truly interested in others or even in peace and human love, they would *see what they are doing* instead of plunging forth unappeasably in their fixed conviction of their own righteousness and of the wrongness or inadequacy of everyone they appear before (one gets the feeling that they're uncomfortable in the face of the many members of the audience who are clearly in sympathy, as though something precious in their self-consideration as noble outcasts, unique critics, were being threatened). Having made certain moves in the direction of a theater freer of artificiality and closer to the realities, they continually move off into their own amazing artifices and unrealities. Their arrogation to themselves of peace, love, freedom, unsupported by anything earned, anything achieved, or anything newly discovered about those conditions of humanity ("What have you done for the dying?"—a nurse does more), their wanting it both ways—to be a theater of public and political use and at the same time to be a community in search of its own salvation, the two things not being necessarily consonant and in this case being flagrantly at odds, all this is painful to see and experience. We're all waiting for the future to take hold in the theater, for politics to be cleansed and revivified by art or any other means; nothing like that is going to come from people who cannot see beyond the mirror.

"It's not a show, it's the real thing," a member of the group shrieked during *Paradise Now.* No, it's not the real thing, it's a show.
New Republic, Nov. 9, 1968

The Performance Group's
Commune

In the commentary which accompanies the recently published book of photographs of *Dionysus in 69* Richard Schechner writes: "Most important by far is our struggle to expose our feelings, to reveal ourselves, to be open, receptive, vulnerable; to use impulse and feeling in our work. And to believe that excellence in art is, ultimately, a function of wholeness as a human being." Although the members of the company have mostly changed from those of the earlier production, there isn't any reason to suppose that the Performance Group doesn't want its new work, *Commune,* to exemplify the same qualities and live in the same spirit.

For the most part it does live this way, or at least tries to mount such an existence. And so it directly raises all the questions which would only be present in a negative form if the work were cold, inhibited, aloof, and protected—the qualities, presumably, of the kind of formal, institutionalized theater the Performance Group has set itself to oppose. How does being "open" and "exposed" really function in dramatic or aesthetic actuality? What is "vulnerability" if it's to be anything more than a bit of adolescent morale? Are impulse and feeling only available in the theater through a programmatic decision? Is excellence in art to be so easily identified with wholeness as a human being, or might it not be the outcome precisely of a lack of wholeness, the compensation for an otherwise intractable deficiency? In the *Dionysus* book Schechner goes on to tell us that for all its partial successes the work foundered because it needed "an innocence that a long-run play cannot have," as well as "a willingness to participate within the terms of the production that audiences do not have." Now Schechner is notable for the extent and general accuracy of his self-criticism, but I can't help feeling that he is being disingenuous here. I thought *Dionysus* failed—if we can still use a word like that—for the same reasons that *Commune* fails even more completely, because of inherent difficulties, something infertile and self-defeating operating at the center, and not because of having run up against any stony methodological or societal resistance.

To begin with, the innocence—freshness? spontaneity? freedom from commercial calculation or the cupidity of professionalism?—which Schechner sees as being possible only in a random or discontinuous theatrical operation is, as far as I've been able to see, a myth and not a demonstrated truth. Happenings were never innocent, nor are the species of single-shot or short-run stage enterprises we can see all over lower New York. A long run may deaden or corrupt, but a short run is no guarantee of anything pristine. In our theater the ravages of ego and the delusions of "self-expression" are at work independently of time or occasion, and the commercial structure is at least as much a result as a cause.

The myth is much larger than a question of physical procedure. Like so many of the yearnings that provide our new theatrical activities with both their energy and their frequent principle of disaster, the quest for innocence has much more to do with life than with art, especially in the case of works which, like the Performance Group's, wish so strenuously to annihilate the distance between themselves and ordinary experience. Stanislavsky once wrote that "people are always attracted by what they have not, and actors often use the stage to receive there what they cannot get in real life." From almost all our recent stage phenomena of performance-theater, audience participation, games, and rituals there rises, along with undeniable daring and vigorous search, an atmosphere of surrogate behavior, a sullen or hyperthyroid but always *willed* esprit, narcissism masquerading as "openness" and exhibitionism as honesty.

Different as they are, *Dionysus* and *Commune* share a common and continuous aspiration: to exist as an event ranging itself alongside those of life, to involve the spectator in new or revived myths, to employ the stage as an arena instead of as a place at which to stare. And both works try to cut through the distinction between performer and self, between the presentational and the phenomenological, that has kept the theater "irrelevant." The notion of amateurism enters here, as a mode designed to combat the fractionalization of the self and the inauthenticity of action that the professionalism of the formal theater is supposed to have engendered.

The night I attended *Commune* was as far as I know an entirely typical one. From the moment I walked in and was *ordered* to take my shoes off and leave them with a heap of others by the door (a snowfall lingered on the streets and I had a moment of panic), the atmosphere struck me as composed of one part hushed reverence, one part authoritarianism, and one part titillating adventure. An image that came to mind late was of having been put in the hands of people who were operating a combination Buddhist temple and house of orgies; I suspected I wasn't going to get away without undergoing something of the cross-cultural disturbance this implied.

Sit anywhere, you're told, and you find a place somewhere in the environment of platforms, ladders, catwalks, and wooden constructions—a large rolling affair that suggests the sea is the central object—which I found the most satisfying element of the evening, as Grotowski found the environment for *Dionysus* the only thing about the work that pleased him. And then you wait, looking around, taking stock of your fellow spectators or acolytes, who are mostly very young, inexperienced, radically uncertain of what is expected of them, nervous or full of adolescent bravado, above all touchingly (to you, the jaded critic) innocent of all ordinary theatergoing habits. Well, this isn't a theater but a place of real if exotic life. Or so the attenuated premise maintains.

The event begins slowly and pleasantly with the members of the company strolling about and softly singing "The Big Rock Candy Mountain." I have sat down on a platform at floor level, a bad choice as it turns out. But for the first few minutes, while the audience finishes drifting in and the pile of shoes grows toward the ceiling, my vantage point has its uses. I study intently a heavyset teenaged girl in tight black slacks as she clambers up a ladder a few feet away and gets good looks at the company members, who sometimes have to step over my feet on their rounds. Across the room I notice a man I decide to keep my eye on, an elderly fellow with an obviously youthful heart, who is later to join in everything, the young audience's unlikely chief representative.

Now the singing ends and the members of the group begin to chant or deliver in singsong a series of monologues. "I came and decided to be an actress, I was really sick of the commercial theater," one girl tells us, and others lay bare their recent pasts, making references to the group, to Schechner, and to productions like *Makbeth* and *Dionysus.* They are offering us their autobiographies and it is supposed to accomplish a number of things: to present the company as nonprofessionals, evangelical dropouts; to frame the work as an endeavor to overthrow performing, to establish relevance and immediacy and, it must also be, vulnerability. As they go on I glance at a wall where *Commune*'s company is listed, a roster of real and invented names: David Angel, Mischa, Jayson, Susan Belinda Moonshine, Bruce, Fearless Jim. And I read that the "text [has been] compiled from various sources and group improvisations."

We are getting acquainted with these performers-who-aren't-performers, and it seems to me that we already know too much. I'm caught, sitting here in this big room which makes me think of an Indian cliff-city, between feelings of sympathy and abstract goodwill (I want this kind of theater to work, I'm against a lot of what it's against) and a real dislike for these dumb, predictable biographies full of the Zeitgeist, of *notions* of freedom and itches for self-expression. If only the members of the group were more interesting, I think, if their lives were more original, their personalities subtler or more powerful.

Then I see myself for a moment as stuck in an outmoded expectation. They're not supposed to be original or subtle or powerful, that's the old theater of striking personalities, and so on. These people are representatives, delegates from our own lives and communal experience. But then I remember Grotowski's observation about how our lives are full of clichés and imitations, so that the actor's task is a kind of unlearning, and I reflect on the idea that originality needn't be undemocratic or aloof or cultish. And that it's something hard-won.

The company members now begin putting on shoes from the pile and passing out others to the audience. The idea is to break down more barriers, and also to strike a temporary blow at private property; "everything belongs to everybody," an actor intones. I feel another, clearly retrograde, twinge of anxiety; my shoes are new and expensive, and besides I have unusually wide feet. But since I came in early my shoes are at the bottom of the heap, and before they get that far the actors move on to new things, into the invented portions of the production, with the audience continuing to exhibit an awkward, half-embarrassed good nature.

The sources of the test that is now enacted include the Bible, *Moby Dick,* and the Manson murder case. From the ensuing mélange of transformations of the company into historical and mythical personages and into animals, of mimings of birth and sexual acts, mock religious ceremonies, and political parodies, I'm able to determine a number of themes and impulses. The central thrusts are toward the breaking of taboos and the release of inhibitions, along with the making of a "statement" about the horrors of our public times. Some of it is inventive and occasionally successful as sheer minor spectacle. I like a moment when an actress, Joan MacIntosh (immeasurably the most talented member of the group and the only one whose name I remember), recites in thickest Brooklynese, "Gimme ya tired, ya poor, ya huddled masses . . ." and a crazy snaking procession to the accompaniment of "Columbia the Gem of the Ocean." I find a sort of gentle wit at other times.

But not once do I have the feeling that the audience is being ushered into the mythic dimension that is so ardently being sought or that the rituals have any reality beyond that of a longing to have rituals. Someone strays from the seats and joins a group of the performers. They sit with their arms round one another, and the experience is that of witnessing not communion but a sad, willed simulacrum of it.

Beyond this, what undermines the physical vivacity (when it *is* vivacity; at times it seems to me a headlong, indiscriminate, strangely mournful attempt to establish high spirits by force) is the production's verbal poverty and derivativeness. There is nothing mocking or parodic about lines like these: "The point of death is rebirth"; "Marlboro country is everywhere"; "Jayson knows the truth because he knows nothing"; "Everything in life is in and out"; "Total paranoia equals total awareness"; and "If man would strike let him strike through the mask." These expressions, and dozens like them, constitute the production's conscious wisdom, offered with that air of portentous discovery that character-izes so many naïve theatrical activities which refuse the job of self-examination in the very name of self-revelation and aren't able to see that theater, like any art, is a means of changing the self and not merely exposing it.

In general the production works best when it isn't trying to be profound and apocalyptic, a not very demanding observation to make. More interesting than that, it works best whenever it has something entirely independent of the per-formers' egos or life histories to play with and against. In this way, the musical elements of the evening seem to me most satisfying of all; these folk songs and spirituals, inserted into a context that releases them from sentimentality and overfamiliarity, provide a tension between the artlessness of most of the pro-ceedings and a formal, inherited, impersonal dimension of expression. This tension, the taut ground on which discovery can take place, is what *Commune* otherwise badly lacks, as all those works lack it which want so desperately to be direct and spontaneous and testamentary without honoring the artifices that alone make those things possible.

The difference between *Commune* and Grotowski's work (I think the com-parison justified because Schechner is at least nominally the closest thing to a Grotowskite we have here) is that the Laboratory Theatre is instigated by the dual and inseparable principles of *sincerity* and *precision,* which might be trans-lated as honesty and technique, while the Performance Group, in lacking tech-nique—formalization of impulses, clear signs for feelings—lacks, finally, hon-esty as well. It comes back to what I said earlier about the necessity of extricating the self from clichés and imitations, from any "ruling spirit" of the age. It isn't enough to be open and vulnerable and all the rest of it; what you have to have is the daring and canniness and painfully won skill by which the personal is rescued from acquired notions of what is personal and the merely idiosyncratic is transformed into the exemplary.

At one point in the evening a young man sitting next to me, who had been observing with increasing dislike my unobtrusive note-taking, leaned over and fiercely whispered, "How can you enjoy the show when you're so busy writing everything down?" to which I shot back, "How can *you* enjoy it when you're so busy being aware of me?"

In fact, he hadn't been enjoying it, at any rate not in a way the Performance Group theoretically would admire. He had been reacting the way a Broadway spectator responds to *his* kind of consolations and exotic presences. He had yakked at dirty words, yelled "Wow!" at a nude scene, twitched with self-satisfaction on hearing Anti-Establishment views expressed, and done all this with a beady-eyed attention to what others in the audience were doing, including me, and with that violent determination to have a good time, to belong and be with it, that reveals no sort of open spirit or impulse toward the communal but their terrifying absence. He wasn't refusing to participate within the terms of the production; he was, unfortunately, all too much a part of them.
The Drama Review, Spring 1971

Chaikin's *Tourists and Refugees No. 2* and Hellman's *The Little Foxes*

Since 1977, Joseph Chaikin has led a collaborative theater effort at La MaMa called the Winter Project. Actors, directors, designers, and musicians work for about three months a year on materials of their own devising, occasionally incorporating lines contributed by well-known writers. *Tourists and Refugees No. 2* is the third offering of the enterprise. I missed its predecessor, *Tourists and Refugees,* but saw *Re-Arrangements* in 1979, and *No. 2* seems a big advance over that. Some of Chaikin's weaknesses, or those of the people he attracts, are to be found in the new piece, but these are easily outweighed by its strengths. I doubt whether we'll see any more original and satisfying theater for a good while.

As the title suggests, the piece is divided into two parts, though these aren't clearly separated. To the accompaniment of jagged, inventive music by a small ensemble, six actors, most of them veterans of Chaikin's Open Theatre, slip in and out of a variety of roles, none of them named (the program lists them as "the woman with gray hair," "the man with black hair," and so on), and none of them constituting "characters" in a conventional narrative. What they offer are skitlike episodes, turns, epiphanies, self-contained soliloquies or fragments of speech. All of this is designed to exhibit certain fundamental or noncontingent realities in opposition to the way social or political forces have organized reality.

In its sounds and images the work deals with the *nature* of being a tourist or a refugee, two polar categories of being away from one's home. Without at all doing it neatly, the two actions or conditions fall into a tragicomic relationship, and it was the comic, or tourist, aspect I found most impressive. This is in line with my sense of Chaikin's previous work, including *Re-Arrangements;* to be serious for him is often to be political, which means to be grim and at the same time sentimental—a not uncommon conjunction. In the present piece the refugees are too often, and too easily, seen as victims of "fruit companies" and "multinationals," as well as of that action of capitalism that "creates needs, tastes, longings." Visually there are too many heads shrouded with cloths—for an image of facelessness, I suppose.

But even in these segments there are some affecting things, including one scene in which people driven from their homelands are "interviewed" for radio or television. They speak no words, making only strange, agonized sounds, while the interviewer "translates" as though they are offering real sentences: "live another day . . . to spite the enemy . . . to tell a story."

In the "tourist" sections, the wit and invention flower. Among many things I could mention is a running number in which a group of tourists (visually the most touristy travelers imaginable) are led by a tour guide in slow motion across the stage, the world's stage, as it comes to seem. The guide intones a litany of questions—"Have you seen any natives since you arrived?" "Are there any natives where you come from?"—and later, on seeing a figure dancing or writhing on a platform, the tourists call out: "Are you a waterfall? A native? An angel? What's the life like?"

Another splendid bit is a long, lunatic monologue by Ray Barry (it's unfair, I know, to single him out by name; the other five actors are every bit as good), who—in drag and with a wig falling over his face—extols the virtues of "getting away," "getting some sun," seeing the world, visiting the graves of the famous—"Stalin, Mao, Hegel . . . walk right on the bones." Still another triumph is a scene in which a tourist is asked about his sexual fantasies by a native and launches into a horrendous nonstop account that would put de Sade to shame. All of which makes me want to give the group some unsolicited advice:

go with the humor, which is really much more destructive in breaking up the logjam of perception afflicting us all.

A few weeks ago I promised to report on Elizabeth Taylor's stage debut; I hereby make good my vow.

Edmund Wilson once remarked that after flipping through an issue of *Life* magazine, any issue, he felt as though the culture depicted in its pages was entirely unreal, as though he were being shown a civilization he simply couldn't recognize. After seeing Taylor in *The Little Foxes,* after reading the reviews, almost all of them laudatory and some of them ecstatic, and after learning that she was nominated for a Tony award as Best Actress, I feel the same as Wilson; the culture out of which this incredible event could arise is as alien to me as that of Zimbabwe; more alien, for I imagine I share some general values with the people there.

Having once described the acclaim for Lauren Bacall as a case of the empress's new clothes, what am I to say about Taylor, in whom the discrepancy is greater still between what she is and what she is taken to be? One suspects she is a bad actress from the moment she comes on stage, heavy, panoplied, like a clipper ship under full sail, except that this is dry land. But only when she begins to speak, in the role of the avaricious matron in Lillian Hellman's exhausted melodrama, can you determine just how bad she is.

Not even competence, not even bare adequacy. Her voice is gratingly high-pitched and her utterance is on one monotonous note, except for an interrogatory swoop at the end of nearly every line. She screeches or shrieks at moments when the script lets her know that "emotion" is required; she has the uncanny knack of emphasizing the wrong word or phrase in almost every bit of dialogue; each time she turns to a fellow actor, prepared to emote, the operation seems to take fifteen minutes. She has no sense of timing, no sense of verbal rhythm. When she says, "I wish you were dead," the resonances are those of the 1890s, and the snarl on her face is from the same period. The only thespian virtue I could detect in her is that she doesn't forget her lines.

How, then, account for the huzzahs? Either I'm wrong, along with the handful of friends and acquaintances with whom I gathered in traumatized silence during the intermissions, or all the others are: the flatterers, the blind people, the corrupted, the venal. At my most charitable I put down at least part of the éclat as being due to the nearly absolute inability of American audiences and most reviewers to tell good acting from bad. This is what gave Helen Hayes and Katharine Cornell their eminence, and this, compounded by the florid circumstances of Taylor's debut and the charisma manufactured elsewhere, is what makes for her standing ovations.

But there's also a conspiracy, conscious or not, to turn everything to account. I think of "Engine Charlie" Wilson's notorious remark about what's good for General Motors being good for America; substitute "Elizabeth Taylor" and "Broadway" in that sentence and you have what's happened. That and syco-phancy too. When Taylor came on stage, the audience rose in an ovation, a thing that sometimes happens when "stars" make their appearance. But then, from somewhere behind me I heard someone shouting "Bravo!" Before she'd said a word, done a thing! An *a priori* bravo! Nothing could better have exhib-ited the demented, noxious quality of the event or testified more truly to the collapse of all our theatrical standards.

Nation, June 20, 1981

Hwang's *The Dance and the Railroad* and *Family Devotions*

David Henry Hwang is a twenty-four-year-old native of Los Angeles and the son of immigrant Chinese-American parents; his plays, all of which deal with the experiences of the Chinese in America, have been receiving considerable at-tention and praise. One of them, FOB (which stands for "Fresh Off the Boat"), won an Obie last season, and two others. *The Dance and the Railroad* and *Fam-ily Devotions,* are presently on display at the Public Theater.

The Dance and the Railroad, which has been running for some time, is a short play whose two characters, named John Lone and Tzi Ma (which "hap-pen" to be the names of the actors performing the roles), enact through dance, mime, acrobatics, and speech a tale of political versus spiritual values—a muddy tale, I must say. Lone and Ma are workers on the transcontinental railroad (the time is 1867), and the action takes place on a mountain overlooking the work site. A strike has been called, and the two men are divided over its usefulness and especially over the eventual compromised settlement.

They are connected by the admiration of Ma, the younger man, for Lone, who had been a leading opera performer in China and who, disdaining his fellow workers as "dead" men, spends his time on the mountain practicing dances and other routines. The men's deadness results, he says, from the fact that they work only because "the white men force them to," whereas he lives because he "can still force my muscles to work for me." Ma objects to this, but he is powerfully attracted to Lone's physical prowess and begs to be taken on as an apprentice, his goal being stardom and pots of money when he goes back to China. Lone does take on Ma, a clumsy fellow, and much of what interest the piece has rests on the discrepancy between Lone's "purity" and dedication and Ma's worldly ambitions.

There are some rather impressive acrobatic turns by Lone and some mildly amusing physical byplay between him and Ma, but the work is painfully deficient from a verbal standpoint, when it isn't pretentious. "The mountain is millions of years old," one of the men says. "Its wisdom is immense." As I said, the narrative is murky, having something to do in the end with Ma's denunciation of Lone for his political and economic naïveté and the latter's returning, whether chastened or not I couldn't tell, to his lonely exercises. Lone—the actor, that is—also directed the play and wrote the music; he won an Obie last season for this performance, but from what I saw it must have been for his gymnastic feats.

Family Devotions, which has recently opened, is also short but has much more going on in it, though to no greater point, as far as I could see. Set in southern California at the present time, it concerns a Chinese-American family (there's also a Japanese fellow, a relative by marriage) who seem to be living well in their ranch house—they talk about tax shelters and the like, dress in crisp tennis clothes, and have elaborate barbecues on their patio—but turn out to be bitterly divided in their values. The younger people are the most Americanized and materialistic, while the older generation, in the persons of a mother and a grandmother, represent a spiritual dimension.

The spirituality isn't Chinese, however, but some form of Protestant evangelism—in other words, something borrowed, Western, and "inauthentic." At least this is the argument advanced by a new arrival, a relative visiting from China. This uncle, who seems to accept Communism primarily because he accepts China, confronts the family with their "betrayal": "If you deny those who share your blood," he says, "what do you have in this country?" This is the playwright's point of view, too, and he works hard at an intricate plot which culminates in a melodramatic revelation of an even deeper kind of inauthenticity: the women's religiosity has been based on a lie. It would be unfair of me to reveal its nature, but I will say that the whole episode struck me as arbitrary and unconvincing.

Even so, inferior plots don't always result in inferior dramas; there are possibilities of rich textures, resonances, and acuity of performance, all of which can rescue delinquent stories. But *Family Devotions* has none of these virtues; the dialogue strains alternatively after wit and profundity, the physical actions long to be farcical or grave but are merely foolish or lugubrious. And the production itself is so inept, from the graceless movements of the performers to the Charlie Chan or Fu Manchu accents some of them employ, that one might suspect director Robert Allan Ackerman of a parodic notion, were not the whole enterprise so patently in earnest.

It's this earnestness, this "good intention," that I think is a major reason for the critical and popular enthusiasm for Hwang's work. The response is chiefly to the *fact* that, for the first time, a Chinese-American playwright is speaking his mind about his own people and America; another minority is being heard from. We've seen this happen in recent years with black, Chicano, feminist, and gay writers, and no doubt it happened years ago with Jewish ones. In almost every case there's been a lowering of standards, not surprising to be sure, yet dispiriting nevertheless. A bad playwright or, in the case of Hwang, a crude and thus far unskillful one, can only be encouraged in his or her inadequacies by this triumph of politics over dramatic art. Or have we reached a point where to say this is to risk appearing both elitist and naïve?

Nation, Nov. 21, 1981

Fuller's *A Soldier's Play*

After fourteen seasons, the Negro Ensemble Company can no longer be regarded as an exotic enterprise on the fringe. The NEC came into being because the established American theater didn't seem to have any place for the black experience. So the group proceeded to carve such a place for itself, with determination if not always a clear notion of what it was doing. Its stance was either aggressive, that of an adversary, or defensive, which meant insular and self-validating; it stumbled, fell, rose, and kept going.

Never quite a true ensemble, in that it frequently brings in performers for particular productions, the company has had difficulty creating an identifiable style, a way of doing things unmistakably its own. If it still has that difficulty, at least its repertory has become much more flexible, so that its socially oriented realism has lost some of the pugnacious, parochial quality that once marred it.

Charles Fuller's *A Soldier's Play,* the opening production of the NEC's fifteenth season, is exemplary of this change and, as I see it, this growth. A flawed but estimable play, it's about the black experience but is supple enough in its thematic range and social perspectives to treat that experience as part of a complex whole, as part of American reality in its widest sense. To be released from an adversary position may mean a loss of fierceness—it certainly means a reduction in ideological thunder—but it can make for an increase in subtle wisdom and intellectual rigor.

Not that *A Soldier's Play* is a triumph of the dramatic imagination. But it is intelligent and morally various enough to overcome some basic uncertainties and remnants of the NEC's older confrontational manner, and so commend itself to our attention. Set in a Louisiana army camp in 1944, the play deals with the fatal shooting of a black sergeant (reflecting the times, blacks are called "negroes" or "coloreds"), a martinet who, out of shame at his people's seeming acceptance of their inferior status, is tougher on his own men than are their white officers.

He's far from likable, but when he's killed and the culprits aren't found, the mood turns ugly among the black soldiers. At first, the Klan is suspected, then some white officers, but the brass wants no trouble and the incident is shunted aside. Finally, an investigator is sent from Washington, a black lieutenant with a law degree from Howard University. His relationship with the white captain previously in charge of the case makes up the moral and psychological center of the drama, which on one level proceeds as a moderately absorbing detective story.

The captain, an earnest liberal, is convinced he knows who the killers are but feels his hands are tied, and he grows impatient with the black officer's slow, careful inquiry. The real problem, however, is the dislocation the captain experiences in his abstract good will. "I can't get used to it," he tells the black man, "your uniform, your bars." Still, he comes to accept the investigator, whose mind is much more in tune with reality than his own and who eventually brings the case to a surprising conclusion. Along the way there are some deft perceptions about both political and psychological matters, and a jaunty historical sense: "Look out, Hitler," a soldier says, "the niggers is comin' to get your ass."

The biggest burden the play carries is the direction of Douglas Turner Ward, the NEC's artistic director, who is also a well-known playwright. Ward manages the many flashbacks, through which the action is propelled, with a heavy hand: lights go up or down with painful slowness, figures from the past *take their places* obediently in the present. There are also some soft spots among the performances and an unpleasant ending, or coda, in which the black officer gratuitously reminds his white colleague of the lessons taught and learned. Yet in its calm concern for prickly truths and its intellectual sobriety, *A Soldier's Play* elicits the audience's approval, if not its boisterous enthusiasm.
Nation, Jan. 23, 1982

Guare's *Lydie Breeze* and Shepard's
The Unseen Hand

In comparison with most European cultures, America has a thin tradition of playwriting; a native drama did not come into its own here until nearly the end of the last century. One result of this is that we tend to overvalue the work of those American playwrights who do have talent: we create instant masters. O'Neill's inflated reputation is the chief example. More recently, Arthur Miller and Edward Albee have suffered from the same early critical overestimation; the harm in Miller's case showed itself in his paralysis in the face of what was expected of him, and in Albee's, in his repeated and doomed attempts to live up to his reputation as an innovator.

Drama critics, detesting a vacuum, find writers to praise and elevate into mastery (literary critics are somewhat more restrained). I was put in mind of this situation when I saw John Guare's new play and read the notices of my fellow reviewers. Nobody is quite saying that Guare is the new Strindberg or Beckett or even O'Neill (although Jack Kroll, *Newsweek*'s indefatigable rave-bestower, comes close), but with a few honorable exceptions the play has been applauded astoundingly beyond its merits. As far as I could see, *Lydie Breeze* has no merits. What it does have is an elaborate fraudulence: false lyricism, false philosophy, borrowed plot elements and characters, an impression of depth with no substance at all. In short, the play is just the sort of thing that perpetually takes in critics avid for eulogizing.

Guare's play is set in a decaying house on the beach at Nantucket in 1895. The title character has been dead for some years, a suicide following her husband's murder of her lover, but her presence is felt—or is supposed to be felt—everywhere. The husband now lives in this house under a curse (the first of many literary scavengings, this one from O'Neill, if not from the Greeks or from the Greeks via O'Neill) with his teenaged daughter, who is or isn't half-blind, and a maid-tutor, who is or isn't Irish. They are visited by an older daughter who works in Washington for a senator, and by several young and older men who have various functions in the creation of plot and atmosphere.

The atmosphere is New England Gothic, for the most part, although it spills over into Norwegian Gothic, which brings us to the question of plot. Apart from O'Neill, the writer whom Guare has rummaged in most busily is Ibsen, plucking themes, incidents, and even phrases of dialogue from *Ghosts* and *The Lady from the Sea,* although *Rosmersholm, Little Eyolf,* and *John Gabriel Borkman* make substantial contributions too. I won't attempt to summarize the narrative use Guare has made of these appropriations and of his own singularly flaccid inventions, except to say simply that *Lydie Breeze* is a lurid tale—something having to do with revenge, fatal love, hauntings, a case of syphilis, and political matters concerning William Randolph Hearst.

Ludicrous plots are likely to result in ludicrous dialogue, and that's certainly the case here. A small anthology of lines delivered with orotund solemnity:

"The only power is the power that comes from being around power"; "We are what we are for only a few moments in our lives"; "Ghosts will follow you anywhere"; and, my favorite, "America could have been great but we never trusted our dream." While I'm on the subject of language, I might mention the bemusement with which I heard these 1895 characters saying "frig off," "sucker" and "wise up," among other anachronisms.

Louis Malle, the filmmaker, has directed the play in a frenetic fashion, perhaps thinking he was doing another *motion* picture. I admired only the shrewd, supple performance of Josef Sommer as the widower-father-murderer, and was especially disappointed by Ben Cross, who did such lovely work in the movie *Chariots of Fire;* here, in the role of the murdered man's son come back for vengeance, Cross only strikes poses with his etched profile. Malle was the director of *Atlantic City,* for which Guare won an award for best screenplay. I didn't think much of that film: spurious originality, borrowings, a thin air of being "with it." Upon rereading most of Guare's plays after seeing this one, I think that description holds up for his entire oeuvre.

There's a nice revival going on of a play by a writer who does deserve our esteem and plaudits—or did, since his recent work has shown a loss of imaginative vigor. Sam Shepard's *The Unseen Hand* isn't one of his richest or most accomplished pieces, but it's wholly characteristic of his late-early or early-middle period, and it offers a good deal of high-spiritedness and verbal fun. Shepard's dominant themes and iconography are on display: uprootedness, science fiction as contemporary mythology, our culture of cars and violence. A cast of five does well by the deliciously named characters—Sycamore, Blue, Willy the Space Freak, and so on—and the set and direction, by Dorian Vernacchio and Tony Barsha, respectively, have the proper qualities of raunchiness, camp, and mad excess.

Nation, Apr. 3, 1982

Miller's *A View from the Bridge*

A magazine editor once suggested I write an essay called "The Indestructibility of Reputation in the Theater or, Once Famous, Always Famous." We'd been talking about Tennessee Williams and Arthur Miller, neither of whom had, at the time, written even a passable play in years, while their reputations, in the public mind at least, remained constant. In the decade or so since that conversation, Miller and Williams have continued to turn out sorry plays, as has Edward Albee, the three of them forming a triumvirate of world-renowned inept American dramatists.

They weren't always inept, of course. In the first half of his career, Williams produced plays rivaled in our theater only by O'Neill's late work; Albee's first plays were fresh and important. I'm less sure of Miller. *Death of a Salesman* survives as a reasonably effective domestic drama, but *The Crucible* has always struck me as strained and false, as have *After the Fall* and *A View from the Bridge*—which drama of illicit passion in Brooklyn is once more on Broadway in a production that originated at the Long Wharf Theater.

I once had a certain affection for *A View.* The first time I saw it was in 1962 at the Sheridan Square Playhouse, where, after much rewriting, it was being given its first American production since its failure on Broadway some years earlier. In retrospect, though, I wonder if my opinion was unduly influenced by the fact that this production introduced two splendid actors who went on to better, or at least bigger, things: Robert Duvall as Eddie Carbone and Jon Voight as Rodolpho. Even in that less sophisticated theatrical age, the play's shortcomings were evident—its suspect lyricism and equally suspect anthropology, its confused aspirations toward tragedy—but there was something about it that I and others thought rugged and "sincere," qualities which have always been associated with Miller, the Honest Abe of our theater.

Twenty years later I find it hard to understand my earlier esteem. The ruggedness strikes me now as clumsy and simplistic, the sincerity as bathetic. The lyricism, whose chief articulator is the lawyer, Alfieri, seems false and more sophomoric than ever: "This is the gullet of New York, swallowing the tonnage of the world"; and "I confess that something perversely pure calls to me from his memory—not purely good, but himself purely, for he allowed himself to be purely known." The anthropology, the whole business about tribal memories and mores, is arbitrary and unconvincing.

Miller's introduction to the 1961 paperback edition hints at what's wrong with the play and, indeed, with nearly all his work. He speaks of the "larger-than-life attitude which the play demand[s]," of the "myth-like feeling of the story" and of his hope that through his play we will become able "to understand ourselves a little better not only as isolated psychological entities, but as we connect to our fellows and our long past together."

Miller has always aspired to push his basic naturalism into poetry and philosophy, to make his quite conventional grasp of existence yield up wisdom. A far from mean desire—but he just doesn't have the talent. *A View,* a muddled and textbookish tale of sexual desire, is in no way "larger-than-life," and the effort to make it so is precisely what makes it so melodramatic.

This effort toward grandeur is what makes almost everybody in the cast act so ponderously, as though they've been entrusted with the myth Miller speaks of—or perhaps it's the myth that the play is a great American classic that has them all emoting with such elocutionary zeal. Saundra Santiago as Catherine, Eddie's niece and object of desire; Alan Feinstein and James Hayden as the illegal immigrants; Rose Gregorio as Eddie's oppressed wife; Robert Prosky as Alfieri—they try so hard and so ineffectually to make poetry out of banality.

And then there's Tony Lo Bianco as Eddie. Ordinarily a competent actor, Lo Bianco is astonishingly hamhanded here. The most charitable explanation for the exceedingly odd busyness with which he invests the role—he's forever twitching, hunching his shoulders, swiveling his head, gesturing, hopping—is that he suspects its thinness and is trying to compensate with frenetic physical activity. At points the performance struck me as modeled (unconsciously, no doubt) on Henry Winkler as the Fonz: The "Hey*uh*" with cupped hand outthrust, the lifting of the chin in interrogation or defiance. The evening's most embarrassing moment is the phone call Eddie makes to the immigration authorities to betray the illegal immigrants: in the hoarsest of anguished whispers Lo Bianco breathes, "I wanna report something," speaks his piece and then backs away from the phone booth, hands outstretched in horror at what he's done.

Why is the production such a hit? I don't think there's any mystery. Miller's reputation is fixed—once famous, always famous—and *A View from the Bridge* is one of the plays it was based on. Beyond that, a hunger exists among reviewers as well as the Broadway establishment for "hits," especially in a season as empty as this one. "Broadway has found a much needed evening of electric American drama," Frank Rich wrote in the *New York Times.* "Broadway isn't dead," said Pia Lindstrom on NBC-TV; "Hurrah, excellent theater has returned to Broadway," said another television reviewer; "I was so happy to see this kind of drama coming back to Broadway," said still another. Poor Broadway! Artistically, at least, it's more often injured by its friends than by its detractors.

Nation, Mar. 5, 1983

Norman's *'night, Mother*

The hyperbole machine is operating on Broadway again. Upon a modest two-character play with nothing flagrantly wrong with it—but not much to get excited about, either—the reviewers have lavished nearly their whole stock of ecstatic adjectives, to which encomiums a Pulitzer Prize has just been added. Even before Marsha Norman's *'night, Mother* reached New York City, Robert Brustein likened it to *Long Day's Journey into Night.* (That Brustein's American Repertory Theater had given the play its premiere, in Boston, might have had something to do with that wild comparison.) Well, O'Neill's best play and Norman's do have something in common: they both bring us unpleasant news about the family.

The play takes place one evening in a house "way out on a country road" in the South. A middle-aged woman and her thirtyish daughter live here. The mother is silly, self-indulgent, and totally reliant on her daughter in practical matters; the daughter is heavyset, slow-moving, and morose. Early in the evening she informs her mother that she is going to kill herself that night. "I'm tired," she says. "I'm hurt. I'm sad. I feel used." From then on the play details the mother's frantic efforts to dissuade her daughter and the young woman's stolid insistence on carrying our her plan.

The mother makes absurd suggestions: the daughter could take up crocheting; they could get a dog, rearrange the furniture. The younger woman grimly makes her preparations, showing her mother where things are in the kitchen, telling her how to pay the bills, and so on. As the mother begins to grasp her daughter's seriousness, her arguments become the "reasonable" ones any civilized person would make, but the daughter beats them back, saying she wants to turn life off "like the radio when there's nothing on I want to listen to."

Up to this point the play is moderately interesting as a moral inquiry (do we have the right to kill ourselves?) and moderately effective as a tale of suspense. But then the women begin to talk about the past, the daughter's childhood in particular, and what emerges is commonplace and predictable. I don't mean their lives are commonplace and predictable—that's a given—but dramatically the play falls into domestic cliché. The mother confesses that she and her husband, the girl's father, had no love for each other and, in response to the daughter's lament, says, "How could I know you were so alone?"

Next we learn that the daughter suffers from epilepsy. She says it's in remission and isn't the reason she is killing herself, but the fact of the illness, and especially the fact that the mother for a long time hid the truth about it from her, enters our consciousness as a diminution of mystery. So too does the daughter's admission that her own husband left her partly because she refused to stop smoking.

The effect of these revelations is that the suicide becomes explicable on the one hand—epileptics, neglected children, and abandoned wives have a hard time "coping"—and ludicrous on the other—if nicotine is more important than marriage, what can you expect? The play might have had a richness, a fertile strangeness of moral and philosophical substance, had the suicide been undertaken as a more or less free act; had Norman not offered as the executor of this fascinating, dreadful decision a character with so many troubles. When the shot sounded (from behind a bedroom door) I wasn't startled, dismayed, or much moved; it was all *sort of* sad, *sort of* lugubrious.

Norman writes cleanly, with wry humor and no bathos. Kathy Bates as the daughter and Anne Pitoniak as the mother give finely shaded performances. But the only way I can account for the acclaim *'night, Mother* has been getting, besides the hunger for "important," "affecting" dramas that gnaws at our educated theatergoers, is that this domestic tragedy doesn't succumb to the occupational disease of its genre: an "uplifting" or at least a consoling denouement. But what a negative virtue that is, and what a comment on our impoverished theater! Yes, the play's *honest,* yes it's sincere; but have we reached the point where we find such minimal virtues something to rave about?

Nation, May 7, 1983

Foreman's *Egyptology*

Richard Foreman's special kind of avant-gardism is more than fifteen years old. By now, it has made whatever mark it's going to—and that's considerable. I used to think his Ontological-Hysteric Theater was merely an eye-catching appelation, but it turns out to be shrewdly descriptive of his work and ideas. The ontological element lies in his forcing audiences to respond only to what they see and hear—what exists on stage—instead of experiencing theater through a screen of preconceptions and expectations. The hysteric element is his pushing things to extremes: dissonant sounds; violent, unsequential movements; a jangle of words, gestures, and emotions.

Foreman's latest work, *Egyptology*, poses the same problems as all his creations, which means the one thing a spectator ought not do is try to make rational, narrative sense of what goes on. I don't mean you should accept the piece as a purely visual and aural phenomenon, bizarre but "important," the way people do who think they ought to like Foreman but don't; the point is that whatever intellectual sense you make of it is at best arbitrary.

Across a gloomy, grimy, blackish set with a small bar and piano to one side and a hospital room to the other, an Egyptian sarcophagus in a corner and the walls festooned with skulls, skeletons, black feathers, and a picture of Mickey Mouse, strolls a portly man in a smoking jacket and a red fez. A diplomat? An Egyptian diplomat? Jungle sounds are heard: bird calls, barks, growls, the shrieking of . . . what? The company assembles, the women in tacky twenties' dresses at first, the men in this and that (one's costumed as a weightlifter or strongman); at various times the cast wears Egyptian headdresses or false faces, and carries toy dogs, ice-cream cones, or razors.

A woman (Kate Manheim) dressed as an aviator and a man (Seth Allen) dressed rather like an SS officer are the only two "characters" who keep a single, if uncertain identity. Much frenetic activity ensues, the group being moved around or stopped in their tracks by whistles, bells, and gongs—a familiar Foreman device. Violence is a central theme of the little playlets or sequences they enact; the piece ends with the company squared off in boxing stances.

"Egypt!" someone cries out at one point. Egypt is indeed a motif, if only as a madly imagined place. The aviator says, "I'm too involved in flying over Egypt to pay attention to the pyramids," and I interpret that as a clue to the work: we're all too involved in what we're doing to *see* anything. But I won't press it.

As the piece goes on (it's only a little over an hour), fragments of meaning swirl around, statements or rather verbal scraps are offered: "It was important to me to be a traitor to my own people"; "There is a turbulence in me that I don't think is controllable." Perhaps the most revealing lines, or at least the ones that struck me as central to this occasionally exciting, occasionally arch, and mechanically avant-garde work about dread, lust, and despair are these near the end: "Will the world continue forever?" "I don't care." "A proper response."

Nation, July 9–16, 1983

Part Two **Production Criticism:**
Brecht and German

Dürrenmatt's *The Physicists*

In *The Physicists,* the Swiss playwright-novelist Friedrich Dürrenmatt has added a political dimension to the traditions of the intellectual thriller. The truest criminality and madness, he suggests, lie in the modern superstate whose god is efficiency and whose rationale is the maintenance of systems for atomic annihilation. But the play is a flawed, unstable amalgam of expert stagecraft and ultimately hollow thought.

The scene is an insane asylum where three eminent nuclear physicists are confined. One, Beutler, thinks he is Isaac Newton; another, Ernesti, believes himself to be Albert Einstein; and the third, Mobius, claims that King Solomon appears to him in visions. Much of the early action is taken up with an investigation of the murders of three nurses, one by each of the physicists. But halfway through, the detective-story atmosphere changes to that of a moral and philosophical drama, yet one without the intellectual power to sustain it.

The physicists are revealed as impostors, playing at madness. Mobius is the greatest genius alive and he wishes to deny the world the increased potential for destruction which his radical discoveries have created. Beutler and Ernesti are scientist-spies assigned by an Eastern and a Western power to try to win Mobius for their country's cause. But it is Mobius who wins, persuading them to stay with him in the asylum behind their masks of lunacy, so as not to add to the world's store of suicidal knowledge. Having built to this climax, Dürrenmatt ingeniously erects another: the asylum's chief doctor, a hunchbacked spinster, is exposed as *really* mad; she has stolen Mobius's formulas and plans now to use them to gain absolute control of the world.

What Dürrenmatt is saying, in the first place, is that knowledge cannot be suppressed, and, beyond this, that the contemporary world is so organized that no individual's moral decision has any effect—madmen are waiting to step in when reason has made its gesture. The first point is valid, if obvious. But the second begs the central question of responsibility and choice, turning over the issue of human survival to an area of insanity and irrationality which cannot be affected by thought—or by plays. Furthermore, as an image of despair, it lacks even the originality that might have given it a cautionary value.

Yet if the play has no intellectual weight it might have had a theatrical existence as a fairly taut and disturbing thriller. Dürrenmatt is adept at structuring tension, and Peter Brook, who directed, is a master of stage vividness. But he has worked with a cast which—with one exception—doesn't have the range and subtlety to make Dürrenmatt's black humor come alive. Jessica Tandy and Hume Cronyn play the mad doctor and Beutler with the monotony and obviousness of stock-company stalwarts, and George Voskovec as Ernesti offers merely a handsome imitation of Einstein. Robert Shaw, as Mobius, is left to carry the load. A finely honed actor with strength and subtlety to spare, he is up against the inexorable fact that he has only a quarter of the play's lines.

Newsweek, Oct. 26, 1964

Brecht's *Baal* and *The Exception and the Rule*

Bertolt Brecht was one of the handful of great playwrights who gave size and sinew to the contemporary theater, but Americans are never going to know about it if the newspaper reviewers have their way. After years of mocking (and misunderstanding) his theories of drama and resenting his Marxist leanings, they now find him "interesting" and "provocative," by no means a giant such as Neil Simon, but not to be despised either. Two current Off-Broadway productions of Brecht plays aren't likely to take business away from *The Odd Couple,* but for anyone who cares about drama as something more than diversion, they are noteworthy events.

Baal, Brecht's first play, written in 1918 when he was twenty, is an astonishingly complete, sophisticated, and self-assured achievement. Brecht had served as a medical orderly in World War I, and his experiences, while never directly exploited, suffuse the play with an awareness of how inadequate were both traditional realism and conventional romanticism to express the war's epic nihilism and deracination.

Baal is a hugely enigmatic figure, gross but magnetic, who incarnates the spontaneous life of the senses but also the anguish of human finiteness and mortality. Like an elemental, amoral force, he snaps up bodies and souls, a mighty seducer who nevertheless keeps jogging "toward the cure of the disease," the cure being death. After episodes which involve him in lust, perversion, betrayal, and finally murder—yet which are modulated by his radical innocence into a strange beauty—he dies in lonely squalor. Upon his end, the sky, "young and naked and immensely marvelous," looks down in serene indifference.

The Exception and the Rule is from Brecht's middle period of the late 1920s and early 1930s, when he was writing "didactic" plays, inspired by Marxist principles but transcending ideology. Set in a fantasy Asia, it concerns the trip across a desert in search of oil by an avaricious Western trader and his gentle coolie porter. With water running out, the coolie offers his employer the last of his own, but the latter mistakes the gesture for a threat and kills him.

At a subsequent trial the merchant is acquitted, on the ground that as the world is organized, along class lines and with unbridgeable gaps resulting from man's self-interest, he "had to feel himself threatened" and thus had to protect himself. That is to say, where violence is the rule, it is logical to expect violence, kindness being the "exception" which one cannot rely on. But far beyond this cynical "social" lesson, the play echoes with disturbing implications about the relationship of morality to logic and of abstract humane values to the concrete pressures of materialism.

Neither production is fully expert, but both plays receive better treatment than Brecht ordinarily gets in America. *The Exception and the Rule* is closer to the proper balance of elements—grotesque humor and accurate sociology, incantation and tough vernacular. Director Isaiah Sheffer has found an appropriate desert-like décor and the right sort of choreography—a slog-slog-slogging take-off on Kipling's *Boots*—and his production, though somewhat slow, boasts a superb performance, stylized, delicate and immensely original, by Joseph Chaikin as the coolie.

Gladys Vaughan's *Baal* suffers from a jumble of styles and a misguided attempt to find American equivalents for Brechtian qualities—lumberjacks talk like hillbillies, a German girl sounds like a Bronx teenager. Yet the company is high-spirited and dedicated, so that a good deal of *Baal*'s excitement, the excitement of a revolutionary act of dramatic art, gets through.

Newsweek, June 7, 1965

Grass's *The Plebians Rehearse the Uprising* and Docudrama

The setting of the play is a theater in East Berlin, the time 1953. Bertolt Brecht, greatest of modern German playwrights, is rehearsing his Berliner Ensemble in his own version of *Coriolanus*. They are working on a scene about a plebeians' revolt in ancient Rome. Outside, a real rebellion is going on—the workers' uprising against the Russians and the East German government. The two realms, art and history, are brought suddenly into conflict: rebels burst into the theater with a demand that Brecht use his influence on behalf of the revolt. From then on a drama unfolds which examines and harshly judges Brecht's historical actions, his canny, ambiguous attitude toward the uprising and refusal to fully support it.

Entitled *The Plebeians Rehearse the Uprising*, the play, which opened to considerable excitement in West Berlin last week, is by Günter Grass, Germany's leading postwar writer. At the curtain a youth stood up in the balcony and shouted, "My God, that was bad," and part of the audience booed Grass when he appeared. But at least as many cheered, and the critical response, while negative on the production, was on the whole favorable to the play and in some cases glowing.

The *Frankfurter Allgemeine Zeitung*'s Dieter Hildebrandt wrote that "the stage was dominated by a dramatic structure and . . . sense of reality which makes Peter Weiss's *Marat/Sade* seem like a flop." *Die Welt*'s Friedrich Luft, dean of German critics, called Grass's work "by far the best, most intelligent of the new collection of German documentary plays."

The German theater, in the doldrums aesthetically and intellectually since the war, has come to be dominated by dramas that employ the facts and documents of recent history. Seldom transformed by the artistic imagination, these plays depend on raw, brute actuality for their effect.

The movement began in 1963 with Rolf Hochhuth's *The Deputy*, a dramatized indictment of Pope Pius XII's alleged failure to speak out against Hitler's destruction of Europe's Jews. Since then Hochhuth has been joined by Weiss, whose *Marat/Sade* is not strictly of the genre but whose *The Investigation*, a play based on the Auschwitz atrocity trials, most certainly is; Heinar Kipphardt, author of *In the Case of J. Robert Oppenheimer*, a "scenic report" on the scientist's 1954 security hearing, and *Joel Brand—The Story of a Deal*, a play about Adolf Eichmann's attempt to trade the lives of a million Jews for 10,000 army trucks; Felix Lützkendorf, whose *Dallas, November 22nd*, a melodramatization of Lee Harvey Oswald's life, received the worst reviews in recent German stage annals; Hans Hellmut Kirst, a popular novelist who turned to the stage with *The Revolt*, a drama about the abortive July 20, 1944, plot against Hitler; and Günther Weisenborn, author of another documentary about that plot called *Valkyrie*.

The torrent shows no signs of slackening. Weiss is hard at work on his most ambitious project, a "musical" reworking of the *Divine Comedy*, in which Dante will "react to what is hell and what is paradise today." Hochhuth is writing a play that will examine the morality of bombing civilians in wartime. And a good many other writers are speeding up similar "documentary" labors. As Joachim Kaiser, critic of Munich's influential *Süddeutsche Zeitung*, told me, "I'm afraid we're going to be burdened with many more such plays in months to come."

Kaiser, a thirty-seven-year-old cultural dynamo who heads the opposition to documentaries, insists that the plays "don't do justice to the horrendous reality of the facts they relate," and adds: "What we need is more thought, not more SS men running from left to right stage." Munich director Fritz Kortner argues that "no compilation of facts and documents can replace a writer's own power of conviction . . . a direct presentation of evidence that the Nazis were bad is neither literature nor art." And Harry Buckwitz, director of Frankfurt's Municipal Theater, sums up the antidocumentary position: "The documentarists make it easy for themselves. Instead of distilling their material into a viewpoint, they put raw facts onstage and expect to convince. It won't work."

But for a great many theatergoers it *has* worked. While some audiences appear to have been bored or baffled by the documentaries (which have been by far the most frequently performed plays in Germany the past few seasons), others have left the theater tight-lipped, drawn, obviously shaken. And a recent public debate on *The Investigation* drew more than eight thousand young Berliners. Hans Werner Richter, ex-officio "father" of postwar German literature, explains the phenomenon as "a natural outgrowth of the effort to comprehend what happened in Germany, an artistic and political need."

Erwin Piscator, the aging director who was a leading experimentalist in the 1920s and who returned to Germany in 1962 after a long exile in the United States and Western Europe, is the genre's most ardent champion. Piscator, who gave their first productions to *The Deputy* and *The Investigation* at his Freie Volksbühne Theater in Berlin (his enemies call it the Piscatoire), asserts that "this form was adopted because the facts of our great catastrophe overwhelmed the writers. They had to start with careful documentation. . . . I never thought people would come to see *The Investigation,* because the material was so horrible. It means the public wants to be informed, to become acquainted with the truth about the Nazi period."

Yet the roots of the German documentary movement go deeper than the immediate past, with its guilts that have to be faced and exorcised. History itself has always been one of the German deities. "World history is the world's last judgment," said the poet-playwright Schiller. And in 1835 Georg Büchner, the short-lived genius whose play *Danton's Death* placed the French Revolution under deep moral scrutiny, wrote that the playwright "is nothing but a writer of history, except that he stands above the latter in that he creates history for the second time . . . instead of characteristics, he gives us characters; instead of descriptions, he gives us living figures."

For writers like Weiss and Hochhuth, the intention seems to be to create history as though for the first time, that is to say, reproduce it. What matters is the sheer unopposable weight of the facts, their "higher reality." And this higher reality is usually in the service of a hoped-for political reformation; it is no accident that nearly all the documentary plays are by writers with one degree or another of socialist orientation.

In this respect, the new German drama resembles the left-wing "agitprop" theater of the 1930s, a theater aimed at immediate effects which could be translated into action. But the new documentary plays, less arty and more impersonal than the 1930s works, may represent an impulse as much of despair as of hope and commitment. The despair is about art, about the imagination's role in the consummately difficult task of changing the world. Art seems helpless, so perhaps facts will prevail. "It is a typical German attribute," a Munich critic said recently, "to try to solve on stage those problems . . . for which no adequate solution can be reached in life."

The documentarists are aware of their vulnerability to the charge of masking their lack of talent through recourse to history. Hochhuth has stated his hope that there will be fewer plays by authors who lack the ability to translate documents into real theater. But this is what he himself lacks: *The Deputy,* for all the political furor it caused, is a bad play. And Peter Weiss's close friend and fellow writer Peter Härtling put the case against Weiss's Auschwitz play and, by implication, the whole documentary movement, most kindly but also most effectively: "Auschwitz was indeed an Inferno, but Peter Weiss is no Dante."
Newsweek, Jan. 31, 1966

Brecht's *The Caucasian Chalk Circle*

Despite his narrow devotees and narrower detractors, Bertolt Brecht's plays live on their own rich merits. That Brecht was one of the masters of modern theater no serious student of the drama would dispute; what is arguable is the nature of his achievement, especially the relationship of his theories to his practice. Nearly all the bugaboos about Brecht concern these theories—"epic theater," "alienation principle," and so on—and all too frequently Brecht is praised or damned not for what he did but for what he is supposed to have done or what he wished to do.

Brecht's plays give pleasure, both intellectual and sensual—this is the first thing a playgoer should know if he is to make his way past the cultists and the carpers and go straight to the experience. And none of Brecht's works gives more pleasure than *The Caucasian Chalk Circle*. Written in 1944–45, it has been performed many times by American colleges and repertory companies, but never until last week in New York, where it was presented by the Repertory Theater of Lincoln Center.

Brecht called *Chalk Circle* a parable, and in one sense it is. Spiritually though not programmatically Marxist, the play's central theme is that of ownership and possession. Based on an anonymous fourteenth-century Chinese play, which in turn resembles a legendary judgment of King Solomon, the drama concerns a peasant girl who, fleeing a revolution in thirteenth-century Asia Minor, takes with her and nurtures the abandoned infant son of the deposed governor. Some years later, the wheel of power having reversed itself, the child's actual mother sues for its return, but loses when it becomes clear that Grusha, the peasant girl, loves the child far more. "What there is," the play concludes, "shall go to those who are good for it, children to the motherly . . . carts to good drivers . . . the valley to the waterers."

There is nothing sentimental in all this. Early in the play, as Grusha is debating whether she should risk herself for the child, a "storyteller" who functions as both narrator and author's voice sings about "the seductive power of goodness," and the play exhibits throughout a high ironic sense of what it costs to be good in a world of power and avarice. This theme merges with that of the nature of justice—one of the great scenes of the play has to do with the installation as a judge of a drunken rascal named Azdak. A combination of Groucho Marx and Robin Hood, he proceeds hilariously to rock the ship of state, dispensing justice with a fine eye for the fact that justice is one thing for the rich and powerful and quite another thing for the poor and unarmed.

Chalk Circle is an amazingly balanced dramatic feast, blending lightness of spirit with a rigorous sense of actuality, a fusion of techniques from melodrama, farce, spectacle, and folk-play, strict modernity together with a firm hold on perennial truths, gaiety and sadness, lyricism and sobriety. All this makes it an unrivaled contemporary play, closer perhaps to the dream of Shakespearean fullness than anything written in this century.

Unfortunately, the Lincoln Center production does only the barest justice to Brecht. A fine adaptation by Eric Bentley, handsome costumes and masks for certain of the players, one or two decent performances, and no egregious lapses of taste—such are its limited assets. But Jules Irving's direction displays little sense of Brecht's qualities: for a chorus he uses something resembling a night-club combine, for a storyteller, a portentous intoner instead of a dry observer. The great scenes are swallowed up in a general imprecision of movement and relationship, the sets are either too literal or too artily suggestive, and Brecht's irony and pathos are both lost in the absense of any controlling style. And the performances, except for Robert Symonds' shrewd if not especially robust Azdak, Elizabeth Huddle's earnest though uncompelling Grusha, and minor portrayals by Ray Fry and Michael Granger, reveal once more how far the Repertory Theater is from the level of acting its superb choice of plays demands.
Newsweek, Apr. 4, 1966

Brecht's *Galileo*

Though it of course draws on history, Bertolt Brecht's *Galileo* isn't a "historical drama." In writing a play about the struggle of the great seventeenth-century mathematician and astronomer with the Roman Catholic Church and his subsequent public recantation of his radical theories, Brecht dealt with complex issues of conscience and social policy. The most multileveled of his major works, *Galileo* is also a self-portrait: of a canny man, a sensualist, thinker, activist, egoist, who is perpetually divided among these various selves.

The play rests on a knife-edge of possible misinterpretation. Without Brecht's irony and antiromantic stance, it can become historical pageant or, more damagingly, a polemic that beats the deadest of horses—the church's onetime repression of science. Cunningly enough, the Repertory Theater of Lincoln Center has managed to perpetrate both these maimings in its current production.

On the surface everything seems to go along unalarmingly. John Hirsch's direction is careful, measured, almost stately, and the acting is a good deal more competent than usual at Lincoln Center. The visual panoply is rich and authentic: sumptuous Venetian, Florentine, and papal costumes, a multitude of impressive heraldic objects, a veritable museum of astronomical instruments. As pageantry, this *Galileo* certainly works.

The trouble is that it also works as a certain kind of 1930s humanist movie— say, Paul Muni in *The Story of Galileo*. Such is the portrait shaped by Anthony Quayle. A solid actor in the tradition of basso-profundo eloquence, Quayle gives an earnest, straightforward performance that misses all the role's nuances and, above all, obscures the deep central division in Brecht's protagonist.

"In spite of all, he is a hero," Brecht told his Berliner Ensemble when they were rehearsing the play before his death, "and in spite of all, he becomes a criminal." In Quayle's performance there are no "in spite ofs"; as a hero he is all open, uncomplicated energy and command; as a criminal he is utter abjection and defeat. Nothing in this conception prepares the audience for Galileo's recantation, which comes as an arbitrary, external event, just as the production itself is entirely external, a pep talk, a history lesson, a costume ball.

Newsweek, Apr. 26, 1967

Büchner's *Woyzeck* and *Leonce and Lena*

German drama has for a long time been among the most fecund in the world and at the moment is perhaps the richest, most innovative of all. At the back of this is Georg Büchner, that remarkable, unaccountable genius who died at twenty-three in 1837, leaving only three plays. Büchner was wholly unknown for almost fifty years until he was discovered by Hauptmann and other naturalists in the 1870s, but since then he has been a boundless source of inspiration and ideas for German-speaking playwrights from Wedekind to Brecht and down to Peter Handke, Thomas Bernhard, and Franz Xaver Kroetz.

Before the middle 1960s, when Jules Irving and Herbert Blau began their ill-fated regime at Lincoln Center with an ambitious (and, sadly, inept) production of *Danton's Death,* Büchner was almost unknown here. Since then we have had several productions of *Danton,* even more of *Woyzeck,* and one or two of *Leonce and Lena,* Büchner's only "comedy" and least regarded work. Now, an enterprising group in New York City called the Classic Stage Company has given us a double bill of *Woyzeck* and *Leonce and Lena,* and for all the production's shortcomings I'm grateful for its presence.

The CSC's *Woyzeck* is the less effective of the two, particularly when compared with some recent productions, including one at the Public Theater a couple of years ago with Joseph Chaikin in the title role, and the movie by Werner Herzog, which was almost a filmed stage play. (The best production I've seen was by the Bavarian State Theater some years ago.) For one thing, the company's small stage and penchant for mostly black and white decor ought to serve for intimacy and a necessary degree of abstraction, but instead feel at variance with the play's gritty, claustrophobic texture and depths of social horror. It's all too cold here, too much on the surface, too spick-and-span.

Another problem is what the company does with the text. As is well known, the twenty-seven or twenty-eight short scenes were left at Büchner's death in no fixed sequence, and this has resulted in a certain liberty for interpreters. In this case, Christopher Martin, who directed and made a new English version, has chosen to end the play with a scene I think should logically and aesthetically have come earlier. What's more, he has the play's last words—a description of Woyzeck as "the dogmatic atheist, tall, haggard, timid, good-natured, scientific"—spoken by one of the other characters, whereas in all other versions it's a stage direction, a summing up on the part of the author.

As for the English itself, Martin's rendering is mostly satisfactory, although there are several places where his choices seemed to me wrong, or inadequate. One is in the scene where Woyzeck has been knocked down by the drum major, who has been cuckolding him, and utters the most astounding and hair-raising understatement: "one thing after another." Martin has him say "after *the* other," which misses the effect of the conventional phrase, which we use to describe the ordinary knocks of experience and which in this context of suffering and despair is therefore so shattering to hear. A small point, perhaps, as is Martin's "when we poor people get to heaven we'll have to work the thunder" for "*help with* the thunder," but such distinctions distinguish great translations from merely serviceable ones.

The acting is of the same serviceable order, except for Karen Sunde. She plays Marie, Woyzeck's common-law wife—whose infidelity brings about her death at his hands—without charm or passion. As Woyzeck, Robert Stattel is energetic and clear—too clear, as it happens. He lacks the grimy, afflicted, sad-sack, yet burning quality of this character of "double nature," this victim of the way things are. He doesn't seem to hear "a terrible voice." He isn't mysterious enough, the way, for example, Chaikin was in an otherwise nondescript production. Chaikin, puffy, sweating, stammering, was a splendid incarnation of this first antihero in drama, a painful, immensely disturbing presence, whereas Stattel, competent as he is, makes you have to go back to the text to complete his character.

For all my strictures, I admired the company's vigor and willingness to take chances. The risk is even greater with *Leonce and Lena* than with *Woyzeck,* since the former work is so infrequently done and seems so thematically and procedurally remote from Büchner's other works. Yet the play has been unjustly neglected (I undervalued it myself for years) and when done right reveals a wonderfully witty side of Büchner, what we might think of as his powerful sense of absurdity (a century before the theatrical genre was so named) in its lighter or less somber mode. The current production has flaws but I thought it lively and effective, very much in the right spirit.

Leonce and Lena is a play about an invented kingdom in which the vices of real kingdoms are exposed. Büchner's political sense, so highly developed and so unprogrammatically radical, here works mockingly with both the actualities of power and the theatrical tradition of plays about power. The cast mostly performs smoothly and well and is distinguished by the presence of a really fine comic actor named Eric Tavaris in the important role of Valerio. With skills ranging from those of a vaudeville hoofer to a medicine show hawker, with something of the Borscht Belt *tummler* thrown in, Tavaris is a distinct pleasure to watch.

Nation, May 30, 1981

Brecht's *The Threepenny Opera:* Preview

One day in the summer of 1973 I got out of the subway at Berlin's Friedrich-strasse station, turned over my passport to submachine-gun-wielding East German guards (I'd, gulp, get it back later), and walked out into Bertolt Brecht Platz. Then, in the ornate, surprisingly small Shiffbauerdamm theater, surrounded by a few dozen tourists and several hundred young soldiers bused there on a cultural "outing," I watched the Berliner Ensemble perform Brecht and Kurt Weill's *Threepenny Opera.* Brecht had been dead for seventeen years and the production had rather the feel of a museum piece, but it was the Ensemble, after all, doing the play as he'd wanted it done, abrasively and raunchily, and I was enthralled simply to be there.

I hadn't known what was playing when I rushed off to the theater—where for the last few years of his life Brecht worked, for the only time, with a company all his own. It was fitting that *The Threepenny Opera* should be on. Though it is far from his best or most important work, it is far and away his most popular, the one the average educated person will know if he or she knows nothing else about Brecht. (Louis Armstrong singing *Mack the Knife* was the rage a while ago.) Its spirit and intentions—at any rate the ones he began it with—are quintessentially Brechtian.

I was reminded of my visit to the Berliner Ensemble by two new incarnations of *The Threepenny Opera,* the stage production directed by John Dexter that opened here this week and a film version by the Israeli, Menahem Golan. From what I know or have heard about both, the ironic history of *Threepenny* since it opened in 1928—the almost complete reversal of Brecht's hope for a particular kind of success—should have some new and juicy episodes for us to contemplate.

This ironic fate is partly Brecht's own doing. When Elisabeth Hauptmann, his longtime collaborator, made a German translation of John Gay's *The Beggar's Opera,* Brecht saw it as an opportunity to test his slowly developing theories of epic theater—a mode opposed to the comfortably smooth-flowing dramatic—and to indulge his increasing, Marxist-oriented detestation of the German bourgeoisie. He would turn Gay's eighteenth-century satire on Italian opera and the morals of the aristocracy into an assault on modern upper-class hypocrisy and, by the way, on the flaccidity of musical theater, one of its chief divertissements. He wanted to show, he wrote later, "the close relationship between the emotional life of the bourgeoisie and that of the criminal classes."

But just as was to happen later with *Mother Courage*—which Brecht intended as a grim object lesson in the havoc caused by a business mentality but which audiences responded to as the portrait of a heroic woman— *Threepenny* immediately became a favorite of the very audiences it had been meant to discompose and shame. And just as Brecht unavailingly rewrote parts of *Mother Courage* in order to diminish empathy with its protagonist, he would change some lyrics in *Threepenny* to cut down on sympathy for its characters and even warn against going after the "little crooks like Mackie" while being indifferent to the big ones like the Nazis. That didn't work either.

A normally hidden aspect of toughminded, ascetic, revolutionary Brecht is his hankering for fame and riches (Weill was more open about his own). The secret emerged several times but never more unwittingly and with such embarrassing implications as when he proudly wrote in the same essay in which he spoke of his "stripping bare of the middle class corpus of ideas" and tastes, that *The Threepenny Opera's* songs "found a wide public—a lot of people sang them to piano accompaniment or from records, as they were used to doing with musical comedy hits." Just so, but it certainly wasn't what he'd originally set out to give them.

Edward Bond, a great admirer of Brecht and much influenced by him in his own plays, once wrote unhappily about the middle-class audiences "chewing their chocolates in time with Brecht's music." The music was Weill's of course, but the composer gave Brecht exactly what he wanted. The result was a triumph of entertainment, pleasure, over social revelation and ideology. In July 1945, in ruined Berlin, a makeshift production of *Threepenny* ran at the Hebbel theater. A witness wrote that "the people loved the show . . . the house was packed." At Mackie and Mrs. Peachum's song about eating first and morality afterward—a key Brechtian political notion—there was "mad applause." When Brecht, in America at the time, heard about it he tried to have the show closed, as did the Russians, but it kept going.

Yet despite the play's defiance of its author, the text still has a good deal of bite. The sad fact is that production after production has taken even this harshness away. A case in point is the renowned version that ran at the Theater de Lys from 1954 to 1961. Marc Blitzstein's score, *from* or *after* Weill, and somebody's direction, *in the manner of* Brecht, thoroughly denatured the work. In my Brecht seminar at Yale recently we played portions of the Blitzstein score and then Weill's music; the difference was that between Wonder bread and dense pumpernickel.

Another way in which so many productions have injured or perverted the original is the casting of a glamorous, "dynamic" performer as Mack. The Dexter production is best known at this point for having Sting in the lead; the new film has Raul Julia, but features Roger Daltrey, once of the Who, as the Street Singer with the role "beefed-up" from the original. In both Gay and Brecht, Mack the Knife is described as middle-aged, fat, balding—in short, a very proper businessman-thief. This is central to at least one of Brecht's intentions: that the audience not see Mack as a romantic figure but as a replica, outside the law, of the predatory barons of industry within it.

I don't know anything else yet about the stage *Threepenny*—my misgivings may indeed be unfounded—but the film would seem to be a compendium of ways to eviscerate and trivialize what is, after all, a still robust work. Its director boasts of having elaborate, meticulously realistic Victorian sets when Brecht called for near abstraction, bare sets, a few grungy props; it employs an orchestra of up to thirty-five musicians when Weill wrote for twelve or fifteen. And it gets in, for contemporary pertinence, the atomic mushroom cloud and has beggars wearing shirts proclaiming "make love, not war."

And so the depredations continue. A musical play that broke the formulas goes on being handed back to them; what was supposed to be, and partly was, disturbing and strange is tailored to meet our need for being stroked with the familiar. Still, as I've said, the blame is partly Brecht's and the trouble began early. In Paris in 1930 the twenty-five-year-old Jean-Paul Sartre was seen leaving *The Threepenny Opera* delightedly singing the songs, just another contented bourgeois theatergoer of the sort Brecht professed to despise.

Village Voice, Nov. 14, 1989

Part Two Production Criticism:
Russian and Scandinavian

Chekhov's *The Seagull* and
Ostrovsky's *The Storm*

Three swallows do not make a samovar, but the Off-Broadway scene has more of a Russian flavor than usual these days. It isn't news when someone takes another fling at *The Seagull,* nor does the simultaneous presence of a trio of dramatized short stories of the master quite constitute a trend. But Ostrovsky's *The Storm* at the same time? It's a good thing the DAR doesn't hold its spring get-togethers in New York.

Still, some sort of investigation seems in order. Let us begin with the fellow-travellers: Joseph Buloff is clearly a subversive type. Why otherwise, when a half-dozen of Chekhov's amiable one-actors are available in splendid translations (by Eric Bentley and Theodore Hoffman), did he think it desirable to go to the great man's short fiction for his scripts? It's true that Anton Pavlovich did that himself once or twice. But dear Mr. Buloff, there's a difference. He came back with plays, not dramatized anecdotes. And he and Stanislavsky and Nemirovich Danchenko would never have allowed even these ephemera to be played in so broad and schmaltzy a Yiddish Art Theater style as you affect.

I will say in your favor, though, that the third piece, the one about the henpecked husband in the music shop, does mount up to something: not of course to Chekhov the dramatist, but at least to a *divertissement* of a modest and non-traitorous kind.

The Seagull? Well, it is tedious to have to say once again that Americans, with all the good will in the free world, can't seem to get Chekhov right. Though I'm not unhappy on this occasion, I have what is undoubtedly a subversive attitude of my own, which is that I would rather see mediocre productions of Chekhov (and Ibsen, Shaw, Pirandello, and even Shakespeare, for that matter) than not to see them at all or than to see the glittering new dramas of our *kitsch*-bound popular theater. Which is not to say that actively bad or perverted versions of the masters do not make me miserable.

The difference is that at those times when a company is struggling honestly with the text and has brought to it a degree of skill, humility, and nonslavish respect, we are at least afforded an encounter with the mind of the creator, with his intention, and with fragments of his vision. And we can often fill in the rest. The point is that great plays are literature, or have become it (which is a proof of their greatness), although most theater professionals and some critics keep on insisting that a play has no life except a physical one: they would be on safer ground if they confined their argument to the question of degrees of life and understood that only inferior plays cannot exist at all between covers since, being nothing but notations for action, they have to get their life entirely from players and managers.

Unconscionably sketchy as this doubtless is, I offer it in explanation of my being able to sit through the Association of Producing Artists' production of *The Seagull* in a fair state of contentment. For there were enough deficiencies to satisfy the most relentless purist. The APA company is a better than average troupe, with some talented people who are learning to play together. But as so frequently happens with plays of this stature, their *Seagull* was a dissonant affair that rocked internally from the meeting of diverse dictions and acting styles and kept slipping from one atmosphere to another, from decadent Southern to decadent British to decadent St. Tropez.

Clayton Corzatte played Treplev with an interesting angularity, his clipped, measured-out speech maintaining a line of expression above the actual lines, but he grew monotonous and artificial. As Nina, Rosemary Harris was a bit too English, too much the sprite released in the drawing room, and as Arkadina Nancy Marchand was more Miami Beach modern than St. Petersburg imperial, although in her climactic scenes with her son she did manage to rise into true feeling and a coherence with the play. For the rest, Paul Sparer's Trigorin drew too heavily upon Barrymore-like leers and eyebrow-raisings, Jerry Jedd's Masha was hoarsely neurotic rather than dessicated and painful, David Hooks's Dorn introduced a Midwesterner-educated-at-Harvard note, and only Page

Johnson as Medvedenko and Earl Montgomery as Sorin struck me as fully up to their roles.

Nevertheless, despite this mélange and despite the updating which resulted in pedalpushers for Marchand and sneakers for Sparer, and a loss of the denseness of Chekhovian time and place, the evening, as I've said, was endurable. We were given an adequate rendering of those incredibly swift transitions by which Chekhov constructs his dialectic of human fate, and enough legibility of speech and gesture to see how the full vision was intended to take shape. Most of all, if we bent to it and had the score in memory, we could hear the music, the first movement of that great symphony, fashioned from silence and indirection as much as from straightforward sounds, in which Chekhov blocked out in advance almost everything we continue to want to listen to.

I did not have the same sympathy with the new Repertory Theater's production of *The Storm.* Let us congratulate the company for even thinking of putting it on. But they are not nearly as talented a group as the APA, and their director, John Hancock, had very much less understanding of what lay in his hands than the APA's Ellis Rabb had of what was in his. You may bill Ostrovsky's play as a "romantic drama of forbidden love" in order to pull in the peasants, but you had better not play it that way. For as D. S. Mirsky, that wobbly historian of Russian literature, half rightly said, *The Storm* is a "great poem of love and death, of freedom and slavery," and it has to be presented with both its poetry and its ideas uppermost.

Ostrovsky, the creator of a truly national Russian theater and the most performed playwright in the USSR today, wrote his masterpiece in 1859, so that it falls almost exactly between two other monuments of Russian drama, Gogol's *The Inspector General* and Tolstoy's *The Power of Darkness.* In its grotesque elements and savage fantasy it derives from the former, and in its realistic aspects, its particularized arraignment of greed and materiality, it anticipates the latter. What it doesn't do is rest upon its ostensible story, the ill-fated love affair to which Hancock has subordinated everything else.

He does this in the first place by cutting in the wrong spots, in the speeches of Kulygin, the voice of reason coming at the play's center from one side, and in those of Feklusha, the mad emanation from folk religion and superstition, coming at it from the other. Second, he has Kabanova and Dikoi, the twin embodiments of heavy, mindless avarice, the deadly anchors in material tyrannization and social changelessness, play their roles like querulous fussbudgets instead of Karamazov-like monsters, surrealistic and unappeasable nightmares.

And finally he doesn't allow the love affair itself to play its intended role as part of a revelation of fatality, the perennial tragedy of body versus spirit in which the spirit's efforts at transcendence or escape are hopeless as long as it does not recognize that it must somehow learn to inhabit the same house.

For Ostrovsky was really an antiromantic; his lovers are ineffectual and offer no antidote to their poisonous surroundings. In an Ibsen-like movement his play traces the disastrous consequences of our not facing the truth about ourselves. The "Storm" will break and destroy us not because we have dared to defy convention but because our romantic defiance is itself a convention. A magnificent idea, tremendously moving when well and faithfully executed. Perhaps we should ask the NKVD to investigate why it wasn't.

Commonweal, Apr. 20, 1962

Chekhov's *The Three Sisters*

Maxim Gorki remembered how his great contemporary Chekhov used to say sadly: "Ah, my friends, how badly you live." The theme is echoed by Masha in *The Three Sisters* when she cries out: "My life is all wrong!" Life is lived badly, wrongly, not so much through errors of judgment or a perverse will but because of a crack at the center of existence. And this schism between ideals and action is what Chekhov saw so clearly, beyond the social malaise he also saw, all of which he embodied with such quiet majesty in his art.

Nowhere is there greater majesty or fuller substance than in *The Three Sisters*. These qualities issue from Chekhov's incomparable ability to make physical data yield moral truth, domestic irritation dilate into the great cage of universal suffering and beleaguered hope, and a single moment beat with the immeasurability of time itself. Almost nothing "happens" in *The Three Sisters*, but there is a psychic and spiritual eventfulness so dense, yet so clear and delicately organized, as to make the play one of the miracles of drama.

Yet it is just this miracle which makes the play so hard to do. The Moscow Art Theater lived for Chekhov and created an acting style expressly for his work; the Actors' Studio, whose production opened last week on Broadway, lives for other things, and its style of acting, for all the talk about it, is little more than an eclectic, haphazard set of specialties. If creating an ensemble meant no more than assembling an all-star company, this production would be a glory.

But as in that other recent all-star production, John Gielgud's *Hamlet,* the effect of *The Three Sisters* is inorganic and jarring. Lee Strasberg has not so much directed the play as arranged it. Some of his individual scenes work beautifully—the image of the sisters clinging together and mingling their realities at the play's end is especially unforgettable. But too often they function in isolation, so that the single effect is never managed for long. Furthermore, Strasberg, at his best in handling groupings and visual arrangements, exhibits a failure of nerve at the play's moral core; one senses in the reliance on violent speech and gesture, and the abrupt introductions of bits of color—traveling musicians, carnival mummers—which break the prevailing mood, a fear of subtlety, an itch for guaranteed effects.

The company is quite as uneven as the direction. There is a disturbing mélange of accents, from Tamara Daykarhanova's authentic Russian tones to Kevin McCarthy's all-American twang. But the weaknesses go deeper. McCarthy's jovial, smoking-car manner is all wrong as Vershinin, the army officer who dreams of a future of rational dignity. Shirley Knight is a pallid, monotonous Irina, the youngest sister, who yearns for Moscow, illusory source of life and hope. Robert Loggia plays Solyony, the eccentric lieutenant, with far too broad a villainy. And Barbara Baxley is almost ruinously bad as Natalya, the bourgeois viper who fastens a deadly grip on the sisters' house.

As balances, there are Geraldine Page, adequate and occasionally fine as Olga, the sister who keeps things going through her attachment to "duty"; Gerald Hiken, who plays Andrei, the ineffectual brother, with the right edge of hysteria; Albert Paulsen, touching and inventive as Masha's cuckolded husband; and James Olson, quietly effective as Irina's doomed fiancé.

Then there is Kim Stanley. With her performance as Masha, the sister who is closest to the play's center, she confirms her position as our greatest actress. When he was working on the play, Chekhov wrote to his wife, the actress Olga Knipper: "Oh, what a role there is for you in *The Three Sisters!*" Stanley seizes this role and takes it to its limits. From the opening scene, where she lies on a couch without speaking, she dominates the stage in her silences as in her speeches. It is a performance of such intensity, depth, complexity, and imagination that it comes close to enkindling the production. At the very least, it touches it with splendor.

Newsweek, July 6, 1964

Chekhov's *Ivanov*

Sir John Gielgud has done the theater invaluable services, from setting a high standard of controlled and clear acting to paying intelligent homage to the classics throughout his career. At first glance it would seem that he has performed another welcome act of piety in reviving Chekhov's early and seldom-produced play, *Ivanov.* Yet pious acts can also be ritual acts, unconsidered, stiff, and perfunctory. To see *Ivanov* at all provides a certain pleasure, since even lesser Chekhov shines with wisdom and humanity. But to see it as Gielgud has staged it—heavily, literally, without style or zest—destroys nearly all the pleasure.

Ivanov concerns a Russian landowner in his late thirties who is suffering from a failure of will, energy, and love. Intelligent, physically healthy, at one time alive with plans, but now apathetic and demoralized, he is the prototype of the cultured Russian of the late nineteenth century, the man aware of the need for action but powerless to act. His estate is rundown, his Jewish wife, whom he had married in a moment of openness and social courage, is dying of TB; yet he avoids her and all his responsibilities, muttering, "I've no heart to believe in anything . . . I don't understand."

Other people think they do understand. To Lvov, a young, seemingly idealistic but actually poisonously self-righteous doctor, Ivanov is simply a wickedly selfish fellow; to Sasha, a neighbor's young and vital daughter, he is on the contrary a victim, a sensitive, misunderstood man whom she can save by her selfless love. In these varying conceptions of Ivanov, Chekhov exposed both the illusive nature of reality and the tendency to classify people as villains or heroes, which he detested in life as in art.

Ivanov has clumsy elements, and nothing clumsier than the pistol shot with which the hero melodramatically ends his tortured life and the play. Almost everything which was later to be subtly implicit in Chekhov, all the interrelationships and tenuous strands of perception out of which he built his masterpieces, is all too explicit here, and the structure, with its traffic of entrances and exits and its rhythmic climaxes, betrays Chekhov's apprentice status.

Yet Gielgud's production makes *Ivanov* seem clumsier than it is, less relevant and less poetic. In the acknowledgments to his published adaptation of the play he thanks the Moscow Art Theater for sending him photos of the original production. And that is what it resembles: with its cardboard-like "picturesque" sets, its rigid lines of movement, its flat, unmodulated rhythms and largely elocutionary performances, it smacks of a museum piece. Gielgud himself plays Ivanov with restraint but also with extreme monotony and lack of verve. Jennifer Hilary exhibits some vigor as Sasha and Roland Culver is effective as her father. But Vivien Leigh is embarrassingly weepy and stagy as the dying wife, and most of the cast seems to be merely going through the motions of fidelity to a neglected drama.
Newsweek, May 16, 1966

Strindberg's *The Father*

The Father isn't one of August Strindberg's most invulnerable pieces of theater, but its writing was a decisive act, marking as it did an acute turning point in his career and prefiguring almost all of what he would later realize more fully. Before it, his dramatic writing had been mostly romantic tragedies in a largely derivative vein. He had, in fact, written no plays at all during the previous three or four years, a period when he described the stage as "reprehensible" for its resistance to the kinds of new consciousness that fiction and poetry had long since begun to assimilate and express.

But something had been taking shape in Strindberg, an adventure of sensibility. In 1886 he had completed an autobiographical novel, *A Madman's Defense*, which he described as "an analysis of the soul, psychological anatomy." Then early the next year he wrote to a friend that he had invented a new dramatic genre, "the battle of the brains." *The Father*, he went on without the slightest slip into false modesty, "is the realization of modern drama and as such is something very curious. Very curious because the struggle takes place between souls. It is . . . not a dagger fight or poisoning with raspberry juice as in *The Robbers*. The French of today are still seeking the formula, but I have found it."

What he had found, of course, wasn't a formula but a new dramatic subject and procedure, which he was to take even further a few months later with *Miss Julie* and much further still in the dream and chamber plays of his richest periods. *The Father* is enshrined in the textbooks as Strindberg's first "naturalistic" play, but the term is one of those misleading appellations with which cultural history is filled. For no sooner had Strindberg been described as a naturalist than he repudiated the word, calling himself instead a nynaturalist, a "new" one—a writer with different aims, and consequently different methods, from those of the quasi-official movement.

The realm *The Father* enters isn't sociological but psychological and personal (a number of lines and speeches are taken directly from *A Madman's Defense*); yet the psychic materials, extreme and turbulent, are used for no sort of clinical investigation or portraiture, either of a doomed marriage or of the larger reality of conventional sexual warfare. For the captain's obsession with whether or not he is biologically his daughter's father and his battle with his wife over the girl's soul are the occasions for the play, not its subject; they're the thematic planks on which the deeper, more mysterious drama can be erected. And this drama goes past the questions of sexual legitimacy and marital strife to the question of existence itself, the ultimate unknowability of human motives and desires, the terrifying strangeness of the "other." That sexual differentiation is otherness in its most profound form was precisely to Strindberg's purpose; in the largest sense his "illness" was less his famous misogyny than a furious, exacerbated dream of exposing all the world's erotic secrets.

The Father is a difficult play to stage well, in part because of its unruly emotional substance and in part because Strindberg had not yet mastered his new methods, his "formula." To put it briefly, this consisted in an abandonment of progressive, linear plot; a perspective on human motivation that saw it as multiple instead of unitary; and—as he expressed it in his preface to *Miss Julie*, the play in which the new procedures would fully flower—the avoidance "of the symmetrical, mathematical constructions of French dialogue" in favor of allowing his characters' "minds [to] work irregularly, as they do in real life." In *The Father* these departures from conventional dramaturgy were incomplete and not fully integrated into the play's thematic structure.

For all that, this important work can be done a good deal better than the Circle in the Square is doing it. Blame for a production as lacking in heat and distinctiveness, as flat and unevocative as this one, is usually diffuse, spread among many elements of the enterprise. But that isn't the case here. There's nothing flagrantly wrong with the direction by Göran Graffman, a Swedish actor-director with wide experience in modern classics. He has no radical "concept" to impose on the text and his clean style lets the latter speak. The set is spare and works well. And the players, for the most part, are up to their tasks. Frances Sternhagen always troubles me a little with her Anglicized diction, pitched somewhere in mid-Atlantic, but she plays the wife with force and precision. And Pauline Flanagan, that good veteran, is really fine in the small but central part of the old nurse.

But for *The Father* to be staged without an actor in the title role makes for a rather large handicap. I don't know what Ralph Waite is thought by others to be (factually, of course, he has for years played the patriarch of the Walton family on television: play one father, play them all) but he isn't an actor in any way I recognize. He exhibits no understanding of the text. He enters into no transactions, emotional or otherwise, with the other members of the cast. He seems to obey wholly arbitrary principles of timing, gesture, and facial expression and, in short, offers a performance which instead of developing merely begins and then, an hour and a half and a great many characterless pieces of action later, ends.

Since the captain is on stage most of the time and during all the crucial scenes, and since he is the locus of all the play's significances and tonalities, Waite's presence is a continuous fatality. There ought to be a slowly accumulating sense of terror and despair, the weaving of a thick texture of spiritual entrapment, but there is only a thin skin of menace, a murky atmosphere of disaster for whose understanding one has perpetually to return to a memory of the text before this incarnation. It's difficult to imagine what those spectators who come without such knowledge but with good will can possibly make of it all.

Nation, Apr. 25, 1981

Ibsen's *Peer Gynt*

When in the winter of 1868 news reached Henrik Ibsen in Rome that *Peer Gynt,* published a few months earlier in Copenhagen, had been assailed by most Scandinavian critics as "unpoetic," by which was meant unartistic, he wrote to a friend: "If my play isn't poetry, then it will be; the definition of poetry will have to be changed to conform to my play." The imperial manner wasn't foreign to Ibsen, and in this case, as in most others, it turned out to be justified. *Peer Gynt:* the centerpiece of Ibsen's oeuvre; the amazing picaresque journey into the ego and the soul whose protagonist stands with Dostoyevsky's and with Baudelaire's poetic "I" among the first exemplars of the modern self in literature; the first movie script, as someone has said, written thirty years before the first movies.

The text of *Peer Gynt* is more than two hundred pages long; the settings shift from the fjords and mountains of Norway to the deserts of North Africa; scenes take place in underground kingdoms, on ice pinnacles, in trees, up in the air; there are explosions, a shipwreck, an episode in a madhouse, violent deaths. No wonder Ibsen himself once said, "I don't think the play's for acting." But it is, with all the immense strain it puts on the ingenuity of actors, directors, and designers, and Ibsen knew it could be done. But that it's done infrequently shouldn't surprise us, nor is it remarkable that it's almost never produced in its entirety.

What makes the production of *Peer Gynt* by the Classic Stage Company so noteworthy is precisely that it's the first uncut version ever put on in New York City (in the United States, so far as I know) and only the sixth or seventh of any length. The play is being done in two parts, which may be seen on consecutive evenings or at matinee and evening performances on weekends; the whole thing runs about four and a half hours. Like the famous 1971 Berlin production by Peter Stein—to whom Christopher Martin, who has directed this one, acknowledges a debt—the work has been divided into eight "scenic chapters," four to a segment, instead of the text's five acts. And like Stein, Martin uses a number of actors to play the title role, in this instance four, to Stein's six. The idea has a lot to recommend it.

The rationale is that since Peer is a character without a true self, to have him played by different actors is thematically coherent. But, as is true of many aspects of this production, a shadow falls between the idea and its implementation, between intentions and results. I'll return to the four Peers in a moment, but first I want to take up some other aspects of this puzzling production, which satisfies and disappoints by turns.

Consider the physical decisions that Martin and his designer, David J. Goldberg, have made. It's surely right that with their minimal resources and in the CSC's small space they should have gone mostly for austerity and abstraction—no real sets, almost everything functional, with props brought in by the actors for each scene. Rope structures serve as trees, a billowing cloth as the sea, canvas shapes as mountains. Fine. But then why do they use projections only in the first sections of Part II, projections—mainly of Egyptian vistas—which moreover are never integrated into the stage action and instead work as distracting illustrations? And why do they go for such hurly-burly realism in the shipwreck scene, where the thunder blots out more than half the speeches?

This inconsistency, or dissonance, mars the production throughout. Some scenes are done cleanly, with sureness of touch; others are either muddled or wholly lacking in vigor and shape. Among the latter are the scene in the troll kingdom, the madhouse episode, and the scene with Anitra in the desert. The last two occur in Act Four of the original text, admittedly the weakest part of the play (Ibsen, aware of this, once suggested that an operetta might be made of it), but there's no excuse for making things worse than they are. There's no excuse, really, for what lies behind the production's many inadequacies: the startlingly uneven quality of the acting. The CSC is supposed to have rehearsed *Peer Gynt* for some ten months, but the radical incapacity of so many members of the company is a handicap no amount of time can overcome.

To go back to the four Peers: One is shockingly inept, another totally nondescript, the third has some talent and a bit of stage presence, and only the fourth, Ray Dooley, who plays section four in Part I and section five, which opens Part II, does full justice to the wonderful role. Dooley is sharp, energetic, intelligent; he clearly understands Peer, whose definition of courage is "to move with uncommitted feet among the tricky snares of life" and whose final revelation is that he's like the onion he peels near the end, all layers and no core. Patrick Egan does better in the final section than in the first, offering something of Peer's edgy exhaustion as his odyssey winds down. Tom Spackman, who does sections three and six, is a mere reciter of lines, while David Aston-Reese (sections two and seven) tests your patience every moment he's on stage, so inexpressive is he, so thoroughly *wrong.*

Among the rest of the company, which doubles and triples up, there's mediocrity and in a few instances something worse. Tom Spiller plays the troll king like a sleepy Hell's Angels leader, and Brian Lawson, with his high, wispy voice, manages to detract from Father Moen, Master Cotton, and Dr. Begriffenfeldt. The women are especially weak: Karen Sunde's Mother Aase is all wide eyes, open mouth, and monotonous delivery; Ginger Grace's Anitra offers some strange, ostensibly erotic movements and an accent indeterminable even by Henry Higgins. Patricia O'Donnell as Solveig smiles radiantly much too often, although she does periodically work up a radiance from somewhere deeper. And only John Camera—as Solveig's father, Hussein the scribe and the pastor—joins Dooley and Egan in giving solid performances.

Having said all this, I can still argue that this *Peer Gynt* should be seen. There's something admirable about the CSC's earnestness and dogged fidelity to the text and about what I have to call, not sneeringly, their amateurism. There may be moments when you'd rather have the written text in front of you than be forced to watch the stage, but still, it's all there. And there are some fine sequences. The last section is particularly good, doubtless because Egan, Camera, and Dooley (who doubles up in the lovely role of the button-molder) are all prominently at work. Ibsen's sprawling, glorious dramatic poem finally comes through in these scenes, which almost wipe out the memory of the histrionic misdemeanors that have preceded them.

Nation, Dec. 19, 1981

Ibsen's *When We Dead Awaken*

For some reason, there have been an extraordinary number of Ibsen productions during the last year or so. We've had *A Doll House, The Lady from the Sea, John Gabriel Borkman,* several *Hedda Gablers,* the uncut *Peer Gynt,* and *Ghosts,* to which we can now add *When We Dead Awaken.* I don't know what caused this spate of interest—the seventy-fifth anniversary last year of Ibsen's death?—but whatever's behind it, the phenomenon is welcome. There was a time not so long ago when Ibsen was as scarce on our stages as the Wakefield mystery plays.

The Open Space Theatre Experiment's *When We Dead Awaken* is, despite one significant weak spot, among the best productions of an Ibsen play in this country. (The British and German renditions have always been better.) If *Ghosts* is among Ibsen's most popular plays, moreover, *When We Dead Awaken* (the twelfth and last in a cycle of prose dramas of which *Ghosts* is the third) is, along with *Little Eyolf*, his least appreciated drama. No matter that Joyce thought it a stupendous work and set out to learn Norwegian after reading it in translation, or that no other play of Ibsen's comes closer to revealing the springs of his art. It's a difficult play to do, a mysterious play, one often wrongly called "symbolic," by which is meant vague, cloudy; the truth is that it's poetic in the deepest sense. Like the three plays preceding it (which begin with *The Master Builder*), *When We Dead Awaken* is rooted in Ibsen's final struggle between what he perceived as the demands of life and of art; also like the previous three, this play serves as a kind of atonement and at the same time a supremely painful acceptance of loss.

Still, it *is* hard to do: all those mountain scenes, culminating in the fatal avalanche; a minimum of action, by conventional dramatic standards; a basic premise that the central characters are already "dead," having murdered love or been accomplices in the crime. But it can be done, and the director of this production, Stephen Zuckerman, has proved it beautifully. The spacious, open set has only a ramp to suggest the movements up and down the mountain that are both theme and action; there is no attempt to convey the avalanche (Zuckerman gives us that apocalyptic moment by projecting bursts of light upon a scrim); delicate, abstract movements within the long duologues release the high lyricism of the language and avoid the sort of oratory that results from a misguided attempt at naturalistic speech.

With one exception, Zuckerman's actors are more than equal to the task. As Arnold Rubek, the sculptor who is Ibsen's nearly exact surrogate—the artist who has sacrificed human love for his work—Tom Klunis deftly manages the passage from arrogance to remorse. Nicholas Wyman is a fine, strapping, totally unsentimental Ulfhejm, the bear hunter who's the incarnation of natural appetite. And Anne Twomey is magnificent as Maja, Rubek's young wife who thirsts for freedom (a direct dramatic descendant of *The Master Builder*'s Hilde Wangel). Lovely sharp features, a husky voice, a dancer's command of space: everything physical is right. And everything in her uninhibited but precisely bounded performance testifies to a firm sense of the character.

Alone among the cast, Kim Hunter falls short of what's required. This former screen actress has stage presence, but it seems codified: a star's regal walk, a great lady's deliberate speech. As Irene, a former model of Rubek's whom he used and then discarded, Hunter has little intensity and not much grasp of the role. By turns melodramatic and, strangely enough, campy, she stands out unpleasantly among her colleagues. Hers is a tough role, it's true, but one still wishes for something better, something that would have made this *When We Dead Awaken,* admirable as it is, wholly right.

Nation, Feb. 2, 1982

Ibsen's *Ghosts*

When I left the theater after seeing the current production of *Ghosts,* I felt an unhappiness that had two sources. The larger, more generalized one concerned the invariably shoddy way we do Ibsen (as we do Chekhov, Strindberg, Pirandello, and the like) and the implications this has for our sense of the cultural past. The more circumscribed feeling resulted from the casting of Liv Ullmann, a fine actress on the screen and probably in the theater too—that is, in her native language and milieu—but misplaced here, embarrassingly so.

But first a word about the play, which, along with *A Doll House* (not *A Doll's House*—a mistranslation), is undoubtedly the most frequently performed of Ibsen's works. At the time of its writing (1881), he was still struggling to get beyond the procedures of the French *pièce à bien faite,* whose very "well-madeness" resulted in mechanical unfoldings and melodramatic points of crisis. *Ghosts* is therefore somewhat retrograde in its dramaturgy, although not at all in its imaginative and intellectual substance, its central theme being possession by the dead past and the consequent need for radical honesty to get free of it.

Everything that can go wrong with a production of this rich, important play goes wrong here. To begin with, there is no direction—not inadequate or misguided direction but none at all. John Madden, the original director, quit or was fired only a few days before the opening and was replaced by John Neville, who plays Pastor Manders.

Whatever the cause, the result is disastrous. The production has no energy, no rhythm, not a shred of cohesiveness. There are egregious physical blunders: a character remarks on the "bright, beautiful day" while through the windows we see only blackness; Mrs. Alving asks for a lamp to be brought in although the stage is already flooded with glaring light. There seems to have been a breakdown of the most fundamental kind.

Then there's the translation or "adaptation" by Arthur Kopit, who seems to have a deadly hand in a great many theatrical enterprises these days. There have been at least five major translations into English of *Ghosts* (and all of Ibsen's prose plays), from William Archer's earnest, awkward version in the 1890s to Rolf Fjelde's crisp, accurate rendering of several years ago. Astonishingly enough, Kopit (whom one assumes doesn't read Norwegian) seems to have gone back to Archer or at least to a translation from his period. From "foundling-home" for "orphanage," to "cleave to" one's husband for "stand by" him, his version is absurdly archaic. More than that, it's often foolishly literal, as when Oswald says, "I thought it was the study you were in."

No direction, a stilted translation—even the most gifted performers couldn't be expected to overcome such handicaps. Nobody comes close in this *Ghosts*. Jane Murray's Regina is perfunctory and pallid, lacking all the flouncy petulance and canny vivacity of Ibsen's character. As Oswald, Kevin Spacey exhibits torment, but it seems to stem less from the role than from his discomfort in playing it. And Neville—a journeyman British actor with an Old Vic voice and a matinee idol's profile—does Manders in exactly the wrong way, making him alternately a fool or a monster and thus destroying the credibility of Mrs. Alving's regard for him.

Which brings me to Liv Ullmann. It is difficult to say if she has any understanding of her role—that partly heroic, partly terrified woman working through strata of lies toward a hold on truth. Ullmann's English is so heavily accented, so bound to a Scandinavian singsong rhythm, that her lines offer neither emotion nor thought but merely the process by which they've been learned. Beyond this problem with speech (or maybe because of it), she is physically stiff, graceless, demonstrating no command of the space she's in, appearing instead to take refuge in some of its corners. It made me unhappy to see her name being exploited this way, and I hope she'll forgive me if I say it ought to make her unhappy too.

Nation, Oct. 2, 1982

Part Two **Production Criticism:**
French Matters

Arrabal's *The Automobile Graveyard*

What a distance for better or worse there is between the average play in print and on the stage. And how much greater is the distance likely to be when the stage is an Off-Broadway one. Several years ago Eric Bentley wrote, concerning the languishing state of the theater, that if Broadway tended to do trivial things well, Off-Broadway did important things badly. If anything, the situation seems to have become worse; the acting, directing, and general professional quality of the commercial theater is of a robust, if hermetic, excellence this season, while Off-Broadway exhibits one embarrassment after another. And one of the chief ways in which we are embarrassed is by the spectacle of blatant infidelity to the nature and intentions of particular dramas. Infidelity, not merely ineptitude. The latter is forgivable, if painful to see; the former seals up the gates of mercy.

The Automobile Graveyard is an extreme case in point. This two-act drama by the young Spanish playwright Arrabal is not a masterpiece nor is it quite the "astonishing" work that the publishers of its printed version claim it to be. But it is certainly an impressive piece of theater, full of wild energy and black humor, bitterness, mockery, and terror, and an innocent despair of the kind felt by children, who cannot fathom either the suffering they undergo or which they themselves cause. In short, it is original and distinctive, with dimension and a multiple life, an infinitely worthier play than the gaseous or obese psychological or sociological dramas that abound in our theater of safety and repetition.

At least that is the opinion of one reader of the published play. But as staged at the 41st Street Theatre, as directed and performed there in the first New York presentation of any of Arrabal's work, *The Automobile Graveyard* became a travesty of itself, having been rendered almost unrecognizable, having been, deliberately and obscenely, murdered. Not since I saw Lorca's *Blood Wedding* mangled on the stage of some tiny theater in the Village a few years ago have I been present at so thorough and unrelieved, so perversely ritualistically thorough and unrelieved a misreading and misstaging of a play. And that includes David Ross's unhappy *Ghosts* of this season.

It is doubtful if the cast, with one or two exceptions, had enough basic professional competence to handle even a much less demanding task (the feminine lead, for example, lacked the very rudiments of the actor's craft). But what made it impossible for them to give us even a crude approximation of the play's life was a directorial intention that was opposed at almost every turn to that of the author.

The spirit of *The Automobile Graveyard* is one of dream, more nearly nightmare; but not loose or impressionistic, nothing Saroyanesque about it, rather something sharp and agitated though controlled, with the clean, fatal, adamant lines of an obsession and the intellectual innocence of a child's universe—a real child not a theatrical one—in which there are no such things as symbols, only images of greater or lesser splendor or frightfulness.

What director Herbert Machiz has done to Arrabal's fable of madness, terror, brutality, and beleaguered hope, a fable whose avowed or unacknowledged roots are in Beckett, the Marquis de Sade, Brecht, and Alfred Jarry, is dissipate its obsessive energy, convert its dark wit into slapstick, construct symbols out of its irreducibly unsymbolic texture, and in general deliver up a shapeless, self-contradictory, and self-defeating work. On a textual level, for instance, he has made a number of changes, all in the direction of his conception of the play as cocky, ultracontemporary, and beat—something by Gregory Corso—whereas it is actually agonized, unlocalized in time, and "absurd," that is to say, interested in creation by radical inversions and mockery and not in representations of attitudes.

To further his notion he has had the three musicians who constitute the drama's center play rock 'n roll where the text calls for a "Louis Armstrong blues"—surely a very different thing—and has, in his rapacious desire for the timeliest posturings, introduced a number called "Graveyard Twist." Again, because *The Automobile Graveyard* is on one of its levels a retelling of Christ's Passion, he has seen fit to add to the parallels, which Arrabal displays with the utmost naïveté and casualness (the effect being, incidentally, to relieve the play of its potentially blasphemous character), one egregious instance being an elaborate "last supper" where the text had merely indicated that the characters are to eat peanuts.

I have not space to list all the points at which director Machiz stuck his ragged-edged sword into the body of Arrabal's play. But there is still an opportunity, which I won't forego, to mention that in a few places something survived. One was due to Kim Swado's properly surrealist and strident, almost poster-colored, set. The other was to be found in two performances: those of Harry Basch as Milos, the valet and waiter who presides over the auto graveyard whose wrecks are inhabited by men and women who simply go on doing what humanity cannot refrain from doing while around them unfolds terror and the death of innocence; and of Estelle Parsons as Lasca.

Parsons especially struck me as understanding what the play was about. She tried to give to her role its intended quality of controlled and yet violent derangement, of Berlin-circa-1925 smokiness and neurotic mythology, of cruelty and erotic, actually sadomasochistic, fury, all of it of a direct, apparitional intensity, as of a child's unmeliorated vision. She tried to avoid naturalism so as to step out larger-than-life, like the sort of mask-at-the-window which is one aspect of what Arrabal sees. She tried, in short, to exist at a point halfway between the recognizable and the fabulous, the psychological and apocalyptic. That she succeeded as well as she did is a tribute to her insubordinate nature, considering the orders that must have been issued by her sergeant.

Commonweal, Dec. 8, 1961

Ghelderode's *Hop, Signor!*

This magazine recently carried a moving remembrance and appreciation by Samuel Draper of the late Belgian playwright Michel de Ghelderode. Draper is the president of a society devoted to Ghelderode's work and to spreading knowledge of it in America, which is a very laudable activity. But I'm afraid the organization is falling down on the job; a real live-wire, red-blooded outfit would surely have been out in force a few weeks ago, throwing a picket line around the Cricket Theatre, where *Hop, Signor!* was being given its first American presentation. For to call yourselves "Friends of Michel de Ghelderode" and not do your utmost to keep the innocent and trusting away from what was beyond doubt the worst production of any play by any important contemporary since Lorca's *Blood Wedding* suffered its martyrdom a few years ago, can't help but put your charter under a cloud.

Hop, Signor! is clearly not one of Ghelderode's best or biggest works, but it seems to me an entirely representative one which might have served as a good introduction to the playwright's strange and lavish world. For it is about death and the life of the senses that death negates, and also about the tension and necessary relationship between good and evil, appetite and renunciation, hope and despair—all the polarities between which Ghelderode's dialectical imagination erects bridges—and it partakes of that lurid, violent atmosphere composed of processions, carnivals, masks, death's-heads, gold and purple tapestries, dwarfs, crucifixes, swords, wine-flasks, beatings, outrages, brutal cries, tendernesses, and hieratic smiles, which one continually encounters in this theater of extremity and paroxysm, where anguish and hope are bound together by the most resilient dramatic means.

You could have gotten only the merest intimation of these things from the Cricket production, and not even that much if you came to it, as most of the audience necessarily did, without any knowledge of Ghelderode on which to base judgments about losses, misconceptions, betrayals, and the like. I was therefore not quite so befuddled nor eventually so comatose as my companion, to whom Ghelderode was completely new and who said to me afterward that although he had received a hint from time to time of something unusually rich in texture and dramatic vision, it hadn't been nearly sufficient to keep him awake.

I'm afraid that any further Ghelderode productions in this country are going to have to contend with the apathy and irritation induced by this one. It wasn't that we were asking for the moon; I at least had no real confidence that any Off-Broadway company could do full justice to the Belgian's intricately composed patterns of conflict, his oracular and pell-mell language, or his theology which, even more than Claudel's, dares to come to earth and grapple with matter, with the "magnetic power of sin" and the fact that in our lives Heaven and Hell are seldom separated by more than an inch. But such absolute cataclysms of speech, movement, pace, such inspired mis-direction, such a thorough-going rout of theatrical art?

I am unacquainted with Philip Meister's directorial background, but I can only assume it was gained in professional basketball or possibly the game-rooms of cruiseships, since his idea of dramatic movement is to have everybody race furiously up and down the stage or mightily in place, and his criterion for the effective delivery of lines and for ensemble playing is based on sheer velocity, each performer being under orders to pass the ball back as swiftly as it has come, until the audience finds itself wondering why the Boston Celtics should be wearing those funny medieval costumes. But those performers: Cousy and big Bill Russell would really have been preferable.

Jane White, whose role is central, is listed in the playbill as running an acting school, which presents us of course with an embarrassment of possible epigrammatic revenges, but I will content myself with saying that I have never seen an actress whose voice and body were in such disharmony or whose miscalculations about the best way to be tragic, or comic, or seductive, or reflective, or earthy were so gross. As for the rest of the cast, after a hot race I have decided to award my anti-Tony (a small dun-colored figure with its head in a sack and its five-thumbed hands spread out palms upward) to John Granger, whose Executioner resembled nothing so much as a spastic weightlifter who has taken elocution lessons from Lawrence Welk, although he was hard-pressed by Howland Chamberlain, who played Dom Pilar with some extraordinary movements of the scalp and certain voodoolike bodily convulsions that must have had every doctor in the audience on the edge of his seat.

If I sound bitter it's because I simply can't understand why with something like nine thousand actors struggling to find work in New York, Off-Broadway should exhibit the worst of them week after week. Or why plays like Ghelderode's, which need all the sympathy and understanding and talent we can bring to them, should invariably wind up in the hands of directors like Meister.

Perhaps Draper's society can be expanded, armed, and sent out to befriend not only Ghelderode but all those great contemporaries whom we are turning more and more into caricatures.

Commonweal, June 1, 1962

Anouilh's *Traveller Without Luggage*

Jean Anouilh has had more of his plays produced on Broadway than any other living dramatist, for several excellent reasons. To begin with, he is extremely prolific (some twenty-five plays since his debut in 1932), but more important he is an extraordinarily skillful craftsman who may be depended on to keep his conjuring acts going at the highest level of technical ingenuity and smoothness. Yet he is not a great playwright. The envy of more original but more disorderly minds, he is, in the best sense of the word, an inheritor, a refined product of the theater and of civilization in general, which means that he is never a true disturber of the peace or a charter of new dramatic territory. And he is afflicted from time to time, as all thoroughly civilized men are, with a relaxation of vision, a last-minute softening which tends to negate whatever stringency and acuteness he has attained along the way.

Traveller Without Luggage, which was written in 1936 and has now been translated and adapted by Lucienne Hill, reveals the exact contours of Anouilh's sturdy professionalism, as well as the imaginative limitations he has seldom been able to transcend. Expertly constructed along the lines of a mystery story, it concerns a French soldier who has lost his memory after being wounded in World War I. Eighteen years later, at the age of thirty-six, he has been taken from an asylum to meet an aristocratic family who believe he is their lost son and brother. For some time they, and the audience, are not sure he is the one, a vein of suspense Anouilh adroitly mines until, in a leap beyond that simple mechanism, he turns the doubt to more complex uses.

But they are not complex enough; they end by begging the question, which has now become whether or not the man will accept his past, as the family reveals it to him. It is an ugly one; he was a violent, willful youth who delighted in trapping small animals, was responsible for a crippling injury to his best friend, hated his mother, and, just before going to war, stole his brother's wife. But since he cannot remember it, he has a choice of living without such a past. "I am the only man with a chance to start anew," he says. And that is what he does, Anouilh arranging matters by means of a deft but shallow piece of dramaturgy which leaves behind it all sorts of unexplored psychic areas and unconfronted enigmas of the self.

For in the interests of a harmonious structure and a mellow, civilized play of mind, Anouilh has shirked the radical implications of his theme. The deep relationship of a man to his past, the possibilities of change and renewal, the nature of the truth once it has passed into history, the difficulty of accepting our actions as in some sense irrevocable—these things he shunts aside or glosses over. "That devouring thing you call a past," the amnesiac says; but in Anouilh's hands the past is little more than a graceful notion, the occasion for a display of mildly philosophic urbanity.

And yet within its restrictions *Traveller Without Luggage* could be far more effective than this production allows it to be. Director Robert Lewis has seized upon it as though it were a nineteenth-century melodrama, stiffening it into artificiality at every crucial point. And a cast which on paper has considerable distinction performs in a strangely amateurish manner. Mildred Dunnock merely trots out again her well-established portrait of the tight-lipped neurotic mother, Nancy Wickwire plays the daughter-in-law as though rehearsing for *East Lynne*, and Ben Gazzara, already the most wooden performer on the stage today, surpasses himself as the amnesiac. The result is to make a small object almost invisible.

Newsweek, Sept. 28, 1964

Molière's *Tartuffe*

The Repertory Theater of Lincoln Center's production of *Tartuffe* is beyond question the best work yet to come from that beleaguered institution. Still, the production has serious flaws, and its positive elements are due precisely to the company's having called in outside help. But be grateful for small favors: this version of *Tartuffe* is a lively, energetic, and visually attractive offering, moderately well executed and all of a piece.

Tartuffe is one of Molière's central achievements, an indictment of hypocrisy and spiritual fakery so unsparing that it was banned for five years—1664–1669—as a menace to organized piety. We are of course under no such pressure; the figure of Tartuffe, the man whose theological cant masks an inordinate materialism, is thoroughly familiar to us, a proof of Molière's timeless insight. And so we can sit back and enjoy the spectacle of vice making an object lesson of itself and virtue painfully learning the ropes.

William Ball, the brilliant young director to whom the Repertory Theater has sent an SOS, has staged *Tartuffe* as broadly as is conceivable. As played by Michael O'Sullivan (another pro from outside), the title character, the impostor who exploits a pious but naïve rich man's earnest desire for salvation, is a grand comic figure. Antic, overblown, stylized, his legs splayed out, his jaws working with rococo malevolence, his lips narrow with puritanism or thick with sensuality, Tartuffe's transformations from savior to seducer are sudden and beautifully managed. And Ball has placed him in the center of a skillfully choreographed action, the supporting characters continually composing themselves into vivacious balletlike arrangements.

But Ball pays a penalty for his emphasis on physical animation. In making Tartuffe himself so bizarre and zany a figure he scants the rest of the play. Orgon, the rich man whom Tartuffe gulls, is a classic comic victim, innocent yet somehow getting his just deserts. But Larry Gates, under Ball's direction, plays him like the hero of a television domestic comedy—put-upon, dim-witted, and outside the main action. And in letting his cast indulge themselves in blatant horseplay—from frantic hand-wringing to belches and pratfalls—Ball has taken the easy road to popularity. Molière was marvelously able to fuse an exact sense of contemporary foible with an appreciation of eternal values (Richard Wilbur's verse translation beautifully captures this), but he had no desire to be the Olsen and Johnson of his time.

Newsweek, Jan. 25, 1965

Anouilh's *Colombe*

The great French director Jacques Copeau once defined directing as "the sum total of artistic and technical operations which enables the play . . . to pass from the abstract, latent state, that of the written script, to concrete and actual life on the stage." It goes without saying that Copeau's bare, functional definition applies only to *good* directing; bad directing is precisely that which fails to bring a script to life or substitutes a false life for the text's own. David Fulford's staging of Jean Anouilh's *Colombe,* for its part, is so inept and destructive as to constitute an act of embalming.

Colombe is middle Anouilh, both chronologically (it was written in 1950) and artistically. In this tale of a marriage broken by opposing conceptions of happiness, he was in a somewhat mellower mood than usual, his ironic view of existence softened by a line of graceful, gently farcical action. Yet the play is thoroughly characteristic in its use of the theater as an arena in which to study human behavior and its wry meditation on the nature of values.

The setting is a Paris theater around 1900. Julien, son of a famous and tyrannical actress à la Sarah Bernhardt, has married Colombe, a naïve, lovely girl. He leaves her in his mother's care while he goes off to do his military service. Three months later he returns to find that she has entered the very life he despises and wished to keep her from—that of the stage, with its cult of experience, sensation, pleasure, and personal assertion. For he is an idealist, with a strict sense of honor and duty, a man for whom pleasure lies in obedience to abstract values. Colliding with Colombe's desire for "life" and experience, these values can no longer sustain him or the marriage.

A play like this requires a supple and delicate directorial touch. But Fulford's hand turns out to be heavy, coarse, and brutal. His sins are multiple; but the central one is to turn Anouilh's vividly drawn theatrical milieu into a scene of grotesque camping instead of an area of ironic investigation. He has his actors play Anouilh's characters as gross buffoons, instead of stylized exaggerations of certain basic impulses. And he is wrong to emphasize Colombe's infidelity as sexual—actually, it is an infidelity to Julien's deadly abstractions. It must be said, too, that he is abetted in his crimes by a woefully incompetent cast and by an adaptation (by Denis Cannan) which doggedly spells out everything the playwright left implicit.

Newsweek, Mar. 15, 1965

Sartre's *The Condemned of Altona*

The resources of the Repertory Theater of Lincoln Center are still well below its aspirations, but its new production indicates that the gap is beginning to narrow. After *Danton's Death* and *The Country Wife*, two admirable choices from the classic repertoire, it now presents Jean-Paul Sartre's *The Condemned of Altona*, an important contemporary drama previously unperformed in the United States.

Sartre's play, one of his most complex if not his best, is marked by the extraordinary intelligence and eye for the crucial issues which are to be found in everything he writes. His theme cannot be stated succinctly; moving from morals to politics, from philosophical speculation to psychic inquiry, Sartre composes a new kind of tragedy, a black fable of human responsibility.

Altona is a suburb of Hamburg. There, in the great baronial mansion of the Gerlachs, a lordly shipbuilding family, the older son, Frantz, has immured himself in an upper room since his return from World War II thirteen years before. What begins as a domestic drama quickly expands to become a more resonant one, symbolic, philosophical, aimed at the age's deepest dilemmas.

Frantz has retreated, we learn, out of horror and guilt; he had been responsible for the torture and death of Russian partisans and in his room he carries out a Hamlet-like mad show, attempting to exorcise his demons by defending the age's and his own crimes to a tribunal of the future, whose inhabitants, he says, will be crabs. But as the play moves on it becomes evident others are "sequestered" too (the French title is *Les Séquestrés d'Altona*), that the father, dying of cancer, his daughter Leni, and younger son Werner are all isolated and sterile—the father through his arrogant use of power, Leni through her incestuous love for Frantz, and Werner through his fearful and unquestioning obedience to his father.

Sartre is not always able to bring these themes into coherent life; the play is choked and overloaded, its structure strained. But the quality of intelligence at work atones for a great deal. The production, under Herbert Blau's direction, does its best to keep that intelligence uppermost, but suffers from a mechanical quality, as though each scene and speech had been carefully blocked out and dutifully executed. And the cast is weak. Tom Rosqui portrays Frantz somewhat one-dimensionally, Priscilla Pointer's ability is radically overtaxed as Leni,

George Coulouris is heavily declamatory as the father. Only Carolyn Coates as the daughter-in-law has equipment equal to the task at hand.
Newsweek, Feb. 14, 1966

Molière's *The Misanthrope*

Americans never seem to get Molière right and probably never will, but the Circle in the Square's current production of *The Misanthrope* has enough going for it to make it very much worth seeing. If Stephen Porter's understanding of the play seems thin and his direction lacking in the animation so necessary to Molière, and if the majority of the cast can't manage the verbal rhythms and especially the rhymes, there's compensation in Richard Wilbur's splendid verse translation and, even more, in Brian Bedford's superbly supple and intelligent performance in the title role.

Before I talk about Wilbur's and Bedford's contributions, a word about the play and another about the production in general. *The Misanthrope* may be Molière's greatest work as well as a key to all his other plays, but it's also been perhaps his most misunderstood one. For several centuries, commentators as diverse as Rousseau and Goethe have offered their opinions of it and have been, for a range of reasons, largely wrong. Or rather, since there's not of course a precisely "right" *Misanthrope,* their exegeses have been inadequate, for the play is much more complex, denser, and "darker" than has usually been seen.

The grossest of mistakes is to view it as merely a comedy of manners; a more subtle and common error is to regard it as a study of misplaced idealism or of the inability to attain truth and "authenticity" in a world of formalized vanity. But Alceste, the misanthrope, is closer to Dostoyevsky's extreme world than to that of Restoration comedy or the universes of Shaw or Wilde. Instead of being a moral scourge or a prophetic if misguided seeker after honesty, he's a monster of egotism desperately seeking the love and admiration of those he professes to despise and yet unable to return that love or friendship. In Martin Buber's modern formulation, Alceste is the "I" incapable of recognizing the "thou."

Moreover, as Lionel Gossman says in the best single study of Molière I know (*Men and Masks*), he is a "comedian who acts as if he were not one, and who is completely trapped by his role." It's these aspects of the play that Porter mostly misses, although Bedford keeps working to reveal them. Porter, a rather square and somnolent director in the things I've seen him do, stages the play as though it *were* essentially a drawing-room comedy—Célimène's suitors, for example, are all much more foppish than they should be—although he does allow, or Bedford forces him to allow, some of the metaphysical pathology, the soulless monomania of the protagonist, to come through.

It isn't Porter's fault that most of his actors can't handle Molière's poetry. They don't mangle it, but they lose its intensity and movement, either by disguising it as prose or stressing it too much, coming down on the rhymes, for instance, as though to let *us* know that they know.

Still, Wilbur's lovely, witty rendering survives. Like his other Molière translations, this *Misanthrope* is a fusion of accuracy and justifiable liberties, the latter taken in the interest of lively contemporariness. Among the rhymes I jotted down (getting the rhymes right is one true test of a translator's success) were "Alceste" and "second-best" and "I'm not so interested as you suppose/in Célimène's discarded gigolos."

Which brings me to Brian Bedford. That he's English may or may not account for his skill in *speaking* verse and not either running away from or declaiming it, but it probably helps. As a reviewer has pointed out, his wig does make him look a little too much like Benjamin Franklin, but that's the only cavil I have. Bedford *knows* the play and the part; on the surface comically outraged, beneath that in black despair, his Alceste is extraordinarily complex but not fussily complicated. He squinches, stamps his foot, knots himself up, and then expands; he's sonorous, arch, and studiedly martyred by turns; offering us the literal verse, he extends himself to the deeper poetry, playing the truth of falseness. My encomiums runneth over.

Nation, Feb. 19, 1983

Part Two **Production Criticism:**

Shakespeare to Shaw

Zeffirelli's *Romeo and Juliet*

There was nothing in the Old Vic's *Macbeth* that could have prepared us for their *Romeo and Juliet* a week later. Quite the contrary: such was the ineptness of the first production that one would not have been surprised if the company had slipped quietly out of the country right afterward, its erstwhile reputation now shattered for good. But like a football team behind forty to nothing at the half, the troupe rallied and came back charging, the secret of the recovery clearly being a change of coaches.

The director of *Macbeth* was Michael Benthall, that of *Romeo and Juliet* Franco Zeffirelli. There is a great deal in a name here, since, as I have said, the only way to account for the transforming leap from one production to the other is by a switch in mentors, and in this case the fact that one man is Italian and the other English counts heavily. It may seem strange that it should count so much in the Italian's favor, for we know the kind of Vesuvian or *opéra-bouffe* Shakespeare Italy is likely to put on the stage. But this time the Italian hand was the right one; the play is one in which, as Henry James said, Shakespeare "Italianized his fancy," and if "Italian" means anything good to us it means lightness, wit, and life.

"English," on the other hand, means heaviness, fog, and, well, as far as the production of Shakespeare has recently gone, moribundity. Zeffirelli might, for that matter, have been from Dahomey: a fresh look from whatever source is what is wanted. His inventions are not infallibly useful nor is his wit always sure, but his sheer directorial vivacity, the quality of quick, almost headlong animation he makes *Romeo and Juliet* express, is in such great contrast to Benthall's opaque, creeping, clotted, textbookish *Macbeth* that we seemed to have come in a week from a cemetery to a festival.

Almost everything in this *Romeo and Juliet* moved under its own momentum; everything in *Macbeth* seemed to have been trundled out. The elements of Zeffirelli's staging at least tried to acknowledge what lay behind and what was to come, while in Benthall's the parts were hermetic, cut off from both history and future. The result was that *Romeo and Juliet,* the lesser tragedy, was much the greater experience.

From the opening curtain of *Macbeth,* when we are confronted with a backdrop that might have been blown up from an oleograph entitled "Stormy Skies," catastrophe is in the air. And it gets darker. The witches resemble backyard harridans and cavort like them, the Scottish warriors bumble around like members of an Elks lodge putting on *Macbeth.* As the play goes along, lump by lump, we do not even have the advantage of clear speech, which is of course what English productions are never supposed to fail us in. Most of the performers speak either too hurriedly or with a peculiar lack of resonance, some exceptions being Barbara Jefford, whose Lady Macbeth is quite a sound if not an exalted one, and Nicholas Meredith as Banquo. John Clements plays Macbeth with a tenacious hold upon the dozen square inches of imaginative (and physical) ground which measure his capacities or which have been allotted to him by Benthall—and I suspect the latter is the more important factor.

No, the whole production betrays that academic approach to Shakespeare which results in a display, a pageant, a set of readings shoved into motion, everything faithful to the text, but not to its spirit, lacking cohesion, continuity, and a submission of the parts to the whole. A series of tableaus, of stiff entrances and exits, of insular moments and arbitrary effects—and all because there has been no re-grasping of the drama as a single action, however complex (in the case of *Macbeth,* Francis Fergusson has described it, taking a line from the play, as "outrunning the pauser, reason"), and therefore requiring a single clear and unimpeded line of movement and expression if it is not to remain for us the thronging, fragmented, self-engorging spectacle that Shakespeare most often is in our theaters.

Zeffirelli's *Romeo* does exhibit such an unbroken line. He has made changes to that end: cutting down the speeches of Friar Laurence, omitting the scene with Peter and the musicians, having Mercutio die onstage; and he has filled the spaces in the text with lively if not always entirely appropriate action. But, most important, he has allowed the native speed of the play, its impetuosity and sense of onrushing fatality, to operate freely, and he has bound its elements together, so that at the end we know what this particular Shakespearian vision was: the fate of innocence and ideality at the hands of practicality and measurement, the former triumphing finally through having "held fast."

What keeps the production from being a superlative one, besides Zeffirelli's occasional lapses of taste (there is really no need to have quite so much horse-play in the interstices), is the quality of the performances, which while better by far than those of *Macbeth* are nevertheless not fully up to the job. The weakness is greatest on the lower levels: with Tybalt, Montague, and Capulet, the friar, and, especially, the nurse, whom Rosalind Atkinson plays in as burlesque a manner as she did a witch in *Macbeth*.

John Stride's Romeo and the Juliet of Joanna Dunham are better. They are both handsome and animated and at times their work together is tremendously appealing, their balcony scene (since everybody naturally asks) being distinguished by a freshness of movement, an unforced ardor, and the subtlest kind of alternation between playfulness and passion. Yet they tend, especially Dunham, to be less effective in their longer speeches and soliloquies, their bodies having reached a higher level of instrumentality than their voices, and this is one of the reasons why the production tends to lose some of its vigor and clarity toward the end, when the lovers are so often apart and lack each other's physical stimulation and reciprocating warmth.

The one performer who never once flags is Edward Atienza in the role of Mercutio. It is a commonplace that almost anybody can steal the show in that part, but Atienza is something special. He is pellucidly fine in his sardonic or bawdy duties, but he is most rare and beautiful in a place we do not ordinarily expect it, in his dying, where he manages with amazing sureness the transition from wit and sensuality and bucko spirits to accusing pain and horror. He is a model for one kind of Shakespearian actor, as Zeffirelli is for one kind of director.

Commonweal, Mar. 16, 1962

Gielgud's *Hamlet*

Over the centuries Shakespeare has withstood some relentless opponents—expropriators, bowdlerizers, death-dealing amateurs—but there were moments last week when it seemed as though the supreme dramatist was about to be given the *coup de grâce*. A dense cloud of irrelevance hung over the New York opening of Sir John Gielgud's production of *Hamlet:* ego, personality, and commerce appeared to have entirely obscured the possibilities of art. But when the curtain went up before an enameled first-night audience, the great majority of whom were dedicated enemies of the proposition that the play's the thing, ego and personality were left speechless in the face of an astonishing triumph of one of the arts of the stage.

It was anything but Gielgud's triumph or that of his "all-star" cast. For it belonged wholly and unassailably to Richard Burton, who turned out to be as masterful a Shakespearean actor as he had once been regarded in England. That Burton should have salvaged the production, after having been at the center of what was threatening to annihilate it, was the crowning irony in an epic of ironic developments. If *Hamlet* is destined during its sold-out run to place Burton before too many people who have come to see him for the wrong reasons, providence may see to it that a minority will attend for the right ones.

Whatever the audience, it is not likely ever to see a better Hamlet than Burton's, while it would have to look far to find a more inadequate and uninspired production of the play itself. These opposing forces convert the stage of the Lunt-Fontanne theater into a battleground on which a magnificently intelligent, resourceful, and unexpected interpretation of the Prince is perpetually denied an environment in which to flourish. In the end the struggle proves too much: the last third of Burton's performance diminishes in wit, force, and command. But you cannot maintain yourself in transcendence when everything around you is pulling heavily to earth.

The trouble with the production is not what had been anticipated: Gielgud's modern-dress version functions well as the container for the drama. He has staged it as though it were a final run-through, with the cast dressed in street clothes (Burton wears a black jersey and black trousers) and a minimum of props. While this does not fulfill his hope for a new freedom for the poetry, it at least doesn't perpetuate the banalities and distractions of such vulgarly "contemporary" Hamlets as Tyrone Guthrie's in Minneapolis last year.

What is wrong is precisely the direction. Gielgud seems to have exercised a minimum of control, having failed either to impart a shaping rhythm to the work or to release its elements into their intrinsic weight and edge. The suspicion is that, faced with a company largely lacking in the basic equipment for the job, Gielgud gave Burton his head and hoped for the best. In any case, with the exception of Gielgud's own recorded voice as the ghost, a splendid gravedigger by George Rose, and a narrow but honorable Gertrude by Eileen Herlie, the cast of this *Hamlet* is everywhere in flight from Shakespeare. Alfred Drake makes Claudius a flaccid schoolmaster; Hume Cronyn plays Polonius without crudity but also without strength or subtlety; Clement Fowler's and William Redfield's Rosencrantz and Guildenstern resemble nothing so much as clerks in a Madison Avenue clothing store; and Linda Marsh's Ophelia is distressingly below the level even of amateur theatrics.

Against this ensemble Burton offers an unprecedented Hamlet—a fusion of the grand manner of the role's great nineteenth-century interpreters with the most contemporary wit and indirection. Cutting through all the sanctified recent conceptions of the part, from the pallid intellectual to the neurotic son, he plays Hamlet to the full, as the complex, tortured but infinitely conscious, and, above all, animate figure of the text.

His timing is flawless, his range immense; he is fully up to the great diapasons of passion or despair. But what lifts his performance above that of any Hamlet in memory is his reinterpretation of the familiar. Time and again he takes a speech or an action we had thought fixed forever in an unshakable conception, and daringly hurls it into new life.

He is humorous when we expect solemnity and withdrawn when we anticipate aggression. When he tells Horatio that "there are more things in heaven and earth than are dreamed of in your philosophy," he smiles upon an inner perspective instead of pontificating. When he delivers his reply to Polonius's question about what he is reading, there is an incredibly exact and tension-filled space between each "Words" and an accompanying delicate step forward which thrusts the bare language into the heart of action. In the soliloquies his modulations among anger, despair, horror, and shrewd calculation are so sudden yet so precise and inevitable that the sense of discovery on the part of the onlooker is overwhelming. But the entire performance, until the singlehanded task becomes too heavy, is overwhelming, a revelation of what Shakespeare can be like, a monument to the actor's art, and a new base from which our imaginations can recover from their sleep.

Newsweek, Apr. 20, 1964

American Shakespeare Festival's
Richard III and *Much Ado*
About Nothing

Like Beethoven and Rembrandt, Shakespeare is an artist who spares people the necessity of caring about art. He vaguely satisfies the large conventional emotions, fills the gap between daily affairs and ultimate salvation, and is useful for beating down lesser but newer artists. The reason his plays are seldom done well in this country is that almost no one—audiences, actors, directors, or reviewers—ever thinks freshly about him, being content with what they have been told to think. But when they are done well, it is considered an outrage. Thus the Royal Shakespeare Company's revelatory *King Lear* is assailed for its "coldness" and the American Shakespeare Festival's *Richard III* for its excesses; what is wanted are good, solid, familiar textbook productions which arouse big, comfortable, familiar textbook sensations.

At his festival home in Stratford, Connecticut, Shakespeare has most often been presented this way, but the current *Richard* is another story. Greatly uneven, rash, clumsy, rough, a strenuous leap onto not always solid ground, it is still one of the few recent American Shakespeare productions which generates any excitement at all. There is an idea at work in it, a conception in action, and risks being taken; there is also love, and next to these things most Shakespeare we see appears especially mindless, slavish, and barren.

From the outset, when Douglas Watson drags himself on his side across the stage like a monstrous amphibian, it is clear that his Richard is going to be extreme, violent, and hugely enterprising. His voice is adequate, sometimes a major instrument, but it is his physical reality which dominates. He is a cripple unable to walk or stand without a harness from his waist to his built-up shoe. One hand is withered and deadly white, his hair is plastered down like a devil's forelock, his clothing is unrelievedly black. He capers, scrambles up walls, writhes in torment or hideous exultation; he bleats, whistles, and sucks his teeth. All this might have been gross or ludicrous, but it outfaces the dangers and emerges, all flaws forgiven, as a performance of force and daring.

The difficulty with *Richard III* is that this king who murders his way to the throne seems so absolutely and arbitrarily evil that the play threatens to slip into a nightmare of carnage. Yet Richard is "Hell's black intelligence," and

Watson's grotesque antics, within their sheath of sly wit and darkly lyrical declamation, are designed to show him this way: as evil intensely conscious of itself, engaged in its own free, strangely legitimate self-expression and self-dramatization. Watson does not always resist the temptation to strike for red-hot and gratuitous effects at the expense of a pattern and of the social as opposed to the metaphysical aspects of the play, and his supporting cast, with some exceptions, is not up to his standard. But plays live or fall on balance, through a central conquest, and this *Richard III,* for all its defects, lives with strength and harsh beauty.

Stratford's *Much Ado About Nothing* is less successful, though not a disaster. One of Shakespeare's most ingratiating comedies, it needs to be done with special lightness and grace, qualities the company may possess but has a hard time displaying. The tendency is to underscore everything—"this is *funny*, laugh!"—and to go off into private experiments. As Beatrice, Jacqueline Brookes conducts an especially odd experiment in monotony and glazed inattention, while Philip Bosco, who is an extremely talented performer, plays her partner Benedick with too heavy a hand. The rest is, once again, familiarity; the risks have all gone into *Richard.*

Newsweek, June 29, 1964

New York Shakespeare Festival's *Othello*

In a lecture on Shakespeare, Samuel Taylor Coleridge described Iago, who is as much the protagonist of *Othello* as the Moor, as being marked by "coolness, the coolness of a preconceiving experimenter." And in the play, Othello informs Iago that "My parts, my title, and my perfect soul shall manifest me rightly." Because Mitchell Ryan is incapable of playing Iago as Coleridge saw him, and James Earl Jones of playing Othello so as to manifest him rightly, the New York Shakespeare Festival's second offering is its second failure.

The production is crudely directed by Gladys Vaughan, who, like Festival directors before her, has staged a Shakespeare play without having investigated its special nature; she has simply set it moving lumberingly from scene to scene. Yet had Ryan and Jones held up, it might have pulled through. Ryan, however, lacks the detached and terrifyingly rational energy of Iago, proffering instead a grimacing, posturing characterization which can make him seem humorously wicked, or nasty, but never monstrous. And Jones, who has a rich voice and a fund of sincerity and physical élan, has too little technique for either Othello's original massive dignity, or collapse into jealousy, or final brokenhearted surrender to the blackness of a world where one cannot see or trust.

In an occasional movement—for example, Jones's slow, thunderous gathering of his broken powers to meet the revelation of Iago's evil—the production transcends its routine physical life and lack of intelligent shaping. And it has one more virtue: Julienne Marie, a musical-comedy ingénue making her Shakespearean debut, is a Desdemona of startling beauty and competence. She lacks full range and verges on the coy at times, but her clear speech, controlled intensity, and sense of the drama she is in make her unique among her cohorts. *Newsweek,* July 27, 1964

Lincoln Center's
The Changeling

Contrary to legend, drama critics do not enjoy being negative. If anything, their temptation is to indulge the theater's vices out of concern for its survival, and this temptation is reinforced by an American craving for positive belief and statement. Yet "positive thinking" can bring about the most negative condition: one in which standards are lost, the good is indistinguishable from the bad, and nobody knows what to think of anything. So it is with the current theater season. The fact is mournful and the impulse to evade it strong, but a dry rot is overtaking Broadway and its environs. Last week another arrival testified to the spreading malady.

The Changeling is the saddest event of a sad week. The Repertory Company of Lincoln Center was widely attacked last year both for its program and the quality of its performances, but we were told that better things were coming. The doubters might take perverse pleasure in their vindication, were it not for the fact that the second season's initial production is so deeply humiliating—to the company, its director, and—because it is a civic event—the public. When an audience literally cringes in embarrassment, when it can scarcely muster even the conventional rounds of applause, when it laughs at a play whose implacable terror is unmatched in all dramatic literature—then we are in the presence of a cultural disaster.

The blame falls inescapably on Elia Kazan. He has directed Thomas Middleton and William Rowley's great Jacobean drama of lust, intrigue, and murder without the slightest sign of understanding it, snatching instead at the chance for a few disconnected visual effects—madmen in an asylum—resembling those he has achieved in movies. The actors stumble about the stage like sailors on the deck of a torpedoed ship, farce alternates with melodrama and would-be satire in a muddled pattern.

Worst of all, Kazan has allowed actors pitifully unequipped for the job to display themselves, and given them no help at all. To hear Barbara Loden attempt the savage, passionate lines of Beatrice in an incredible little girl's voice, and to watch her almost shake with terror as the audience starts laughing, is one of the most painful moments in the recent history of the American theater.

Newsweek, Nov. 9, 1964

The Guthrie's *Richard III* and
The Way of the World

With a burst of civic pride and cultural enterprise, the city of Minneapolis two years ago launched the Minnesota Theatre Company, perhaps the boldest experiment in repertory undertaken anywhere in the United States in recent years. Cynics said that it could not last, not out there in the hinterland. But by last week the company was no longer an experiment; it had become as much of a fixture in the community as the first-place Minnesota Twins.

The season has grown from twenty to twenty-four and now to twenty-eight weeks; the chamber of commerce boasts about the company in its literature; every cabdriver knows his way to the handsome Tyrone Guthrie Theatre on Vineland Place; and Guthrie himself says of the group he helped to form and nurture: "Each year we become more of an institution."

Yet, when Guthrie leaves his post as artistic director at the end of the year, his successor and present deputy, Douglas Campbell, will face problems, all of them inherent in the operation of a large-scale repertory theater. Chief among them is the matter of training and keeping together a company, of creating a style, and, most subtly difficult of all, of determining how broadly popular to try to be, what concessions to make so that the seats stay filled. In the short history of the theater, the concessions have sometimes been rather heavy.

The current production of Shakespeare's *Richard III* is a case in point. Physically handsome, as all the group's productions have been, full of animation, loose and free, this *Richard* nevertheless is a failure precisely because it tries so hard to be a comfortable success. To play Richard as a basically comic figure, as Hume Cronyn does under Guthrie's direction, is of course one way of making the historical drama more contemporary. Yet the fact is that the play's cruelty, violence, and portrait of savage ambition are almost unrelieved, so that any humor distilled from it can only be of the blackest kind.

Cronyn's Richard is a television situation-comedy figure, an ingratiating villain at whom the audience is perpetually laughing because it knows that when he professes love or friendship or loyalty, he has that knife behind his back, the sly dog. And Cronyn milks these moments for all they're worth, smiling, rolling his eyes in mock innocence, imposing long pauses to make sure that the comic points have been made.

If another 1965 production, Congreve's *Way of the World,* doesn't come off, the fault is again one of direction. Restoration comedy needs a clearly articulated style, an especially confident approach; yet Campbell has staged the play as though his left hand distrusts his right. A superb performance by Zoe Caldwell as the languid beauty, Millamant, and highly competent ones by Jessica Tandy as the harebrained Lady Wishfort and Robert Pastene as the scheming Fainall are marooned in the center of a characterless production. Bits of *commedia dell'arte,* snatches of the grotesque, clownishness here, and posturing there, do not compose a style. And style is what the Guthrie Theatre is still mostly groping for. *Newsweek,* Aug. 2, 1965

Lincoln Center's *The Country Wife*

William Wycherley's *The Country Wife* is not an easy play to stage. Graceful but also savage, witty but also turbulent, it belies the popular notion that Restoration comedy is all elegant phrase-making and intricate amorous dalliance. Yet its savagery and turbulence lie well below the surface, and its language sometimes seems more suited to the library than the theater. To do it well requires more imagination and skill than the Repertory Theater of Lincoln Center now possesses.

Not that the production, the company's second of the season, is an embarrassment. There are no disastrous lapses of taste or conception, and while the acting is undistinguished there are no shameful performances such as marked the Repertory Theater's *Danton's Death.* What is chiefly wrong this time is not amateurishness but an absence of urgency, a failure to release the play's dark, cynical humor.

Wycherley, who was a familiar among the court wits of Charles II, was of an even more skeptical turn of mind than most of his fellow dramatists, and his play (first produced in 1675) deals as much with the dark side of social intercourse as with the merely foolish. Ostensibly built around the clash of innocence with worldliness, expressed through the encounter of a naïve country girl with a London rake, the play actually examines and indicts a whole range of social and moral practices, the hypocrisy of female "virtue," the deceptions people employ to hide their animal motives, the emphasis on appearances that mask corrupt activities. And he also subtly, and romantically, affirms the possibility of honesty and goodness, but only outside social institutions.

That the Repertory Theater's production, under Robert Symonds's direction, cannot do justice to this complicated work isn't surprising. But what is difficult to understand is why the play's humor should have so much trouble displaying itself. One or two scenes—an extended double entendre employing the word "china," the writing of a letter by the country wife to her would-be seducer—function spiritedly enough, but mostly everything is quiet, stately, decorous, and tame. Symonds himself gives a superior comic performance in a secondary role, Elizabeth Huddle is lively as the country girl, and twenty-four-year-old Stacy Keach is adequate as the rake, but the acting generally is not up to conveying the play's full values.

The best thing about the evening is the physical arrangements: a mock proscenium curtain that resembles a giant cardboard toy theater and a revolving, three-sided set that frames the action in the proper fusion of detail and artificiality. The Repertory Theater is at any rate beginning to learn how to use its unrivaled plant.

Newsweek, Dec. 20, 1965

Lincoln Center's *The Alchemist*

If the Repertory Theater of Lincoln Center is going to continue doing the classics, they'd better decide to trust them. One might think that Ben Jonson, for example, knew what he was doing in *The Alchemist:* writing a hard, intricate, icily lucid, and majestically amusing comedy about avarice in all its forms as well as a satiric sociological guide to the seamier and more exotic sides of Jacobean England. But Jules Irving, who has staged the theater's first production of the season, knows better: Jonson was really trying to write a madcap physical farce—a farce whose models would have been certain American film comedies of the 1920s and 1930s, had Jonson, back there in 1610, known they were coming.

Such mistrust is no doubt partly due to the company's demonstrated shortcomings. When you lack actors with the verbal strength and elegance and the suppleness of style to do a playwright like Jonson, you have them do what they can. And this means you have them do what anyone can—mug, screech, and take pratfalls, with these ear-splitting and eye-offending antics supported by periodic explosions from a Rube Goldberg-like machine representing the alchemist's preposterous confidence game.

In interpreting the play like this, Irving compounds his delinquency. Jonson's alchemist is far from an absurd figure: shrewd, calculating, coldly intelligent, this man who with two confederates sets out to exploit the gullibility of the world, this charlatan whose promises of alchemical means to fortune and pleasure trap a bagful of greedy innocents, is a disturbing comical creation. His very intelligence is the element which keeps the play from being a moral tract or a simplistic farce. For as the world goes, Jonson is saying, even a con man's intelligence and ingenuity are worthy of respect—the pained, grudging, amused respect paid to whoever can beat an acquisitive society at its own game.

The alchemist's name is Subtle, but Michael O'Sullivan turns him into a grotesque made out of Silly Putty. Shaping his features into a hundred unrelated grimaces, drawing vocally from such disparate models as W. C. Fields and Peter Lorre, he manages to put out the play's comic fire in his frantic efforts to fan it. And except for Michael Granger, Ray Fry, and most notably Philip Bosco in minor roles, the company follows his lead. Nancy Marchand and George Voskovec, for instance, are new additions to the company, along with O'Sullivan, and are performers of established skills. But caught in this atmosphere of wrongly inspired and sadly executed theater, they too surrender. Cut off from the principles and practices of the Jacobean stage, they turn to Abbott and Costello or Olsen and Johnson for inspiration, encouragement, and tips.

Newsweek, Oct. 24, 1966

APA's *The School for Scandal*

The APA (Association of Producing Artists) is a conspicuous example of making do. Such is the state of American repertory theater that the APA has been praised a long way beyond its merits. "Our best repertory company," is the most restrained thing most reviewers have been saying for years; well, America's best is about at the level of a middling English provincial company, and there is really no reason to rejoice.

The opening production of the APA's first full season on Broadway exhibits clearly its strengths and weaknesses. More a collection of competent-to-talented performers than a ground-breaking organization with a style of its own, the APA is at its worst in plays like Sheridan's eighteenth-century classic, *The School for Scandal,* which requires the kind of high style that eludes most American actors and some directorial imagination to rescue it from overfamiliarity.

The School for Scandal has been staged by Ellis Rabb (who is the company's artistic director as well as one of its leading performers) in an unexceptionable manner—a little mugging, just a whiff of archness and artificiality, the characters raised a careful notch or two to an agreeable level just below caricature—all standard textbook stuff.

Rabb lets his performers carry as best they can their particular shares of Sheridan's comedy about gossip and malice as ways of life. Some of them—Rosemary Harris as Lady Teazle, Keene Curtis as Sir Oliver Surface, Rabb as Joseph Surface—are deft and enterprising, but nearly everyone else seems to be working from memories of British productions, and this version suffers from a cautious, uncolored, pedantic approach.

Speaking of British productions of *The School for Scandal,* I actually saw one—not the memory of one—three or four years ago in New York. But skillful as the cast was, with all its gestures cutting the air finely, its speech meticulous and its costumes worn crisply and elegantly, and for all that the faultlessly eighteenth-century sets by Anthony Powell and the life exhibited on them were perfectly at home, I found the evening somewhat flat and pallid.

John Gielgud's direction struck me as lacking in inventiveness and vigor and his performance as Joseph Surface seemed deficient in the same qualities. Ralph Richardson, on the other hand, did a major job of interpretation as Sir Peter Teazle, although I'm not sure that his capering, antic, owlish deportment, and oddly spaced and husky speech, didn't clash with the more conventional declamation and high artifice of the others. I've yet to see a British or American production of this sentimental comedy of manners that will remain in my memory. *Newsweek*, Dec. 5, 1966

Breuer's *The Tempest*

> O brave new world
> That has such people in't.

I'd better say right off that I left at the end of the first act of the New York Shakespeare Festival's production of *The Tempest* in Central Park, which means I saw about 60 percent of the performance. In my defense, let me say that it was one of the worst evenings of the recent heat wave, and the Delacorte Theater, which lies in a sort of hollow among the hills, would have been better suited to *Don Juan in Hell*. But I'll quickly add that Lee Breuer's rendering of Shakespeare's wonderful last play was so outrageous (in the old-fashioned sense; no smart plea of having stuck it to the bourgeoisie is going to work here) that I'm sure I'd have taken off even if the park had become air-conditioned through a wave of Prospero's wand.

Assured later by colleagues whose sense of duty is finer than mine, or whose masochism is deeper, that Breuer's *Tempest* got no better after intermission, I feel justified in offering 60 percent of a review. Actually, what I want to do isn't so much to review this piece of folly as to put down a few thoughts about why it was perpetrated, why things of its kind are perpetrated so often these days, and what such directorial flights of fancy reveal about certain attitudes among us toward theater, the nature of art, and, since I might as well go the whole way, history itself.

Now even to question the practice of "modernizing" (hideous word) or "making relevant" (obscene phrase) classic dramas is to risk being accused by a type of avant-gardist of, at best, not being with it and, at worst, of being an enemy of the creative spirit in the theater. At the same time, who would want to be embraced by the Neanderthals whose presentation of Shakespeare rests on doing exhaustive research into Elizabethan England, studying the data we have on the Globe Theater, and, in general, acting like curators instead of interpreters? Well, to be any sort of useful critic means one has to resist bullying from whatever direction it comes.

But first some thoughts as I trudged toward Belvedere Lake. I'd heard some dismal reports from people who'd seen previews, the kind of thing I try to discount, but in this case I had my own grounds for apprehension. I'd seen enough productions of classics which were exemplary of avant-garde silliness (Richard Foreman's *Threepenny Opera* at Lincoln Center a few years ago, for instance) to expect only the worst from Breuer, a practitioner and theoretician whose work with the Mabou Mines had variously struck me as exciting, innovative, murderously boring, and profoundly obnoxious. Most to the point was Breuer's nearly deaf ear for language and his thoroughgoing anti-intellectualism rising from a populist, or pop, base. To turn Shakespeare over to him seemed to me to be asking for it.

A glance at the program was anything but reassuring. "Malaysian Dance Choreography" by Marion D'Cruz; "Gamelan Music Composed" by Barbara Benary; "Samba Music Composed" by Nana Vasconcelos. "The Samba Ensemble," whose names I won't list. Ariel played by eleven actors, whose names I also won't list. "Time: This Evening." "Place: An island in Central Park near Belvedere Lake." We were in for relevance without mercy.

The revels began. Raul Julia, whose Prospero, I have to say, was the best performance of the evening, probably because it was the least gimmicky, came on stage and started mixing some potion or other. A little boy ran out, and it took a while to discover that he wasn't part of the play but had escaped from his embarrassed mother in the audience. From the public address system came the strains of "Hi Ho, Hi Ho" and "Whistle While You Work." A toy helicopter figured in some action. The eleven Ariels swarmed on dressed as parachutists (later they would wear other raiment, including loincloths). A Japanese sumo wrestler appeared and stamped his feet before engaging Prospero (or was it somebody else?) in combat.

Then there sidled on a punk Caliban in shades, ragged jeans, and an open denim vest, and a Ferdinand in a white vinyl jumpsuit. They were followed by a Mafia group consisting of Alonso (the Godfather), Antonio, Sebastian, and Gonzalo, together with a couple of guards (the text says "guards" all right). They all wore various kinds of white suits and big-brimmed fedoras (later they would be stripped down to their underwear; it was really hot in the Delacorte, remember, and Shakespeare doesn't mention the weather) and the guards packed rods. Still later there was a scene with a Trinculo dressed like an 1890s madam and a Stephano whose attire I can't remember.

Caliban spoke in heavy punk-cockney accents, the Mafia guys in Mafia tones—though one of the guards was doing a streetsy Harlem number. Trinculo had modeled herself on Mae West, Stephano on W. C. Fields and Bert Lahr. And there were other pop takeoffs too numerous to mention.

If one had to set down not an *interpretation* of *The Tempest* but its thematic and imaginative constituents, which is all one can really do with any work of art, they would have to include: rightfulness and wrongfulness, usurpation and being usurped, avarice, ambition, the right uses of art and the wrong, restitution, relinquishment, the peace of age that has seen it all. Such is my sense of the play, for which I make no claim of originality, since I'm sure it's shared by many others. I haven't any doubt that Breuer shares it, too, for beneath the chic contemporaneity, the au courant put-ons and sendups, the dredging of pop culture, one could discern the rough outlines of traditional meanings, the consensus view of what is being *said* in the play.

Why, then, if the foregoing is true, does Breuer think it necessary to impose on these meanings and significances a mode of appearance, a fleshing out, one might call it, so radically and idiotically at odds with the original incarnation, Shakespeare's own choice of what would body forth his vision? The answer isn't hard to find. The assumption behind all "modernizations" in the theater is that the meanings and values of classic texts will be lost, have already been lost, through the alterations and destructions of time. And from this assumption another follows: that to "redeem" the classics, to enable them to live again, it's necessary to invent new appearances out of the iconography of present reality. Otherwise all is archaism, dim memory, sterile fidelity. "In its present form this play doesn't *speak* to us," is the motto.

Now faithfulness, literal faithfulness, can indeed be a vice, but what the modernizers don't seem to understand is that arid fidelity to Shakespeare is never really to the text but to an idea of the text and, worse, to an idea of what Shakespeare on stage must have been like. But we don't know much about that, and the area of liberty in directing Shakespeare now lies in just that lack of knowledge; you're free to invent what is plausible, what is dramatically sound *in itself,* as long, that is, as what you do doesn't undermine the text.

That Breuer's production undermines the text is evident at every point. What's even less forgivable is that it mocks the text, sending it up, establishing a jazzy superiority to it, as though Shakespeare, deprived of our electronic and other advantages, couldn't help having been a fuddy-duddy. This isn't simply a matter of the visual gimmickry and aural nonsense, the costumes out of *Rolling Stone* and Busby Berkely, the fashionable, irrelevant Eastern music alternating with the score of *Snow White*. Nor is it just a matter of characterizations. I'm not quarreling with Breuer because I think punk and Mafia are undignified or in poor taste but because they have no aesthetic weight. In Breuer's teeming brain there was doubtless the conviction that these figures were equivalents for Shakespeare's, when of course they're not, since to our imagination, which is all that counts in drama, they're merely faddish beings, creatures of the Zeitgeist.

But at the heart of what's wrong is precisely the infinitely vulgar, infinitely degrading warfare between the language of the play and the modes of expression on stage. To hear the great lines spoken in black or punk or hillbilly accents doesn't give an effect of universality but just the opposite; apart from losing the music entirely, losing the rhythms between speeches, such au courantism loses the significances too. It does this inevitably, simply through the enormous gap between what these varieties of contemporary speech ordinarily assume as their burden of utterance—what they're equipped to say—and what Shakespeare's speech was designed to do. The one thing we do know about his speech is that it wasn't "contemporary"; he didn't have a "good ear," he invented his language. (He invented his world, too. He didn't put in his program, "Time: Tonight; Place: a Theater in London.")

On numerous occasions the predilections of the kinds of speech being employed, or, less anthropomorphically, the limited imaginations of the pop stereotypes speaking Shakespeare's lines, result in truly hateful perversions of meaning. When, for instance, the punk Caliban bites off "the infections that the sun sucks up," he puts a heavy, sniggering emphasis on "sucks," an implication not lost on the audience, which wants relevance in everything, wants to "score," feel with it, feel superior; they are accomplices in the reduction of the imagination to what it can *prove* about reality instead of what it can reveal.

One can say that everything Breuer does is a type of pandering, a ministering to the audience's dislike of history and mistrust of the permanent. A stage director is in a position to treat works of dramatic art with such high-handedness and contempt; a museum director can't *repaint* Goya, an editor or publisher can't rewrite Stendhal. Since not even a director like Breuer can rewrite Shakespeare directly—by which I mean he can cut, perhaps, but he can't add lines or change existing ones—he rewrites around the text, in the presumed interest of saving it. But why do the play at all if you're afraid the language is dead (it isn't dead, of course; it never was "alive," it was never real speech but artifact)? Why *increase* the gap between language and bodies, if one exists? Why not leave it alone?

Maybe Shakespeare can't really be done on stage any more. More than a century ago Hazlitt argued that this was so. There *is* such a thing as dramatic literature. Plays can be read for pleasure; I get more from reading Shakespeare than I've gotten from all but a handful of productions. But those prove to me he can still be done. I think of Peter Brook's *Lear,* which was new and original, but untraditional in a way exactly opposite to Breuer's *Tempest.* What Brook did was to strip the play of all its conventional performance baggage, the panoply and pomp, offering a version so visually lean and austere that the language shone through as it hadn't in memory. He had made the play into something "rich and strange," but he didn't impose this. The richness and strangeness were there all the time; the characters didn't need modern counterparts to tell us who, in all their mystery and fecundity, they were.

Nation, Aug. 8–15, 1981

Roundabout Theater's *Misalliance*

Misalliance has never been one of my favorite Shaw plays. Even though it was written in 1909, long before Shaw's fecundity began to give out, it feels like a much later work and gives off a sense of having been composed of scraps and fragments and unfinished notions from his earlier dramas; Hypatia, for example, the rich man's daughter who wants to be independent, to be an "active verb," is Vivie Warren's pale descendant.

Misalliance is overwritten and overplotted, even for Shaw. More than any of his other major plays before the late 1920s, when we can begin to see his hand tremble, this comedy about the "rights" of children in relation to those of their parents relies on coincidence, arbitrary events, and a network of personal connections that seem to have been worked out with a slide rule. A bad or even an

ordinary production would succumb to the play's inherent difficulties: a confusion as to genre (settled in time in favor of farcical comedy), an overabundance
of thematic elements, and several Gobi-like stretches of Shavian rhetoric during which all our misconceptions about the drama-of-ideas are given a new
lease on life. Since Shaw's wit never completely deserts him, there is pleasure to
be gained, but the tenuous balance between epigrammatic sprightliness and
true feeling, such as is achieved in his best work, is never established here.

Since I hold this opinion, I wasn't in a hurry to see the current revival at the
Roundabout Theater. But then I began to hear some favorable reports about
the production. The adjective I kept hearing was "stylish," a word most often
used to describe a positive quality with no specificity to it. Stylish: having a
style. But what kind? In fact there is a positive quality to this *Misalliance:* the
performers seem to be enjoying themselves and nobody does anything flagrantly bad. But I didn't see any stylishness, or rather style, in the evening, principally because the performances were on so many different levels and failed to
cohere. There is a steep upward line from the shallow work of Nigel Reed and
Jeanne Ruskin as the young lovers to the splendid acting of Philip Bosco as the
underwear king with literary aspirations. Bosco, a solid Off-Broadway veteran,
is large, bearlike, supple, and vigorous. I kept my eye on him most of the time.
Nation, Nov. 28, 1981

Royal Shakespeare Company's
All's Well That Ends Well

All's Well That Ends Well has always been considered one of Shakespeare's poorer
plays, a "problem" comedy whose structural flaws and opacity of purpose have
led to its being infrequently performed or even read. The Royal Shakespeare
Company's current production, at the Martin Beck Theatre in New York City,

is the victim of this received wisdom, for, predictably, nearly all the reviews have praised the company's work while indicating less than enthusiasm for the play itself. The result is that a scheduled sixteen-week run has been curtailed for lack of business.

Now the point about received wisdom is that there's truth in it all right, but incomplete or unexamined truth. *All's Well* does have problematic aspects and loose ends; it also has wonderful thematic and linguistic elements that make it not just playable but a delight when played well, as it is in this production.

Moreover, the play's chronological position—the exact date is uncertain but is thought to be 1602 or 1603—places it very near *Hamlet* and *Measure for Measure,* the first of which it resembles in a number of verbal and attitudinal ways, while the second is its larger "sister." For this and other reasons, *All's Well* has a darker side than the category "comedy" usually suggests. Startlingly modern in its concerns, its themes are the conflict between age and youth and the discrepancy between appearance—one's "name," rank, and so on—and reality—one's virtue, what one is.

Ordinarily I'm put off, or worse, by updated Shakespeare, but this one works surprisingly well. Trevor Nunn has set the play in fin de siècle France and Italy (those are its original locales) and he and his designers have given it a most elegant mounting. The main set is a large, airy greenhouse; the costumes are crisp and even dazzling; the props—a wheelchair for the ailing king, an antique auto—don't feel anachronistic among the Shakespearean verse and ideas. And that verse is spoken by nearly every member of the cast with the special understanding American actors seldom possess.

Harriet Walter is a trifle uncertain as Helena, the young woman in quest of love and justice whom Coleridge called Shakespeare's "loveliest creation," and Philip Franks is somewhat too hectic as Bertram, the nobleman Helena wins after humbling his arrogance. But these are minor failures in a cast of exceptional skillfulness, among whom I might single out Margaret Tyzack as Bertram's mother, John Franklyn-Robbins as the king who befriends Helena, and Stephen Moore as Parolles, one of Shakespeare's great portraits of bluster and pretension, as his name indicates.

On a couple of occasions Nunn's penchant for special effects gets the better of him—for example, the smoke from a battle scene doesn't clear quickly enough and the next scene, which takes place at court, is played in a haze. But for the most part he and the RSC give us strong reasons to be grateful for this *All's Well*—and to mourn its shortened run in this country.

Nation, May 21, 1983

Part Two **Production Criticism:**

Beckett, Pinter, and English

Osborne's *Luther*

Nothing is more dangerous for a moderately gifted playwright, or a moderately gifted painter or novelist for that matter, than to wish to be more profound than he is capable of being, to put his accredited talent into a larger structure than it can fill or press his thought and imagination beyond what they can accurately fashion and steadily control. He has to extend himself, of course, or he won't know, but he also has to be prepared to discover what his limitations are. John Osborne has emphatically tested himself in *Luther,* and now he presumably knows, or at least some of us do. More of us would know if it had not been for the predictable response of the daily reviewers, who have found their annual *J. B.* early this season—a play of spiritual aspiration and pretension upon which they can bestow all their perpetually impatient adjectives like "inspiring," "ennobling," and "towering" and upon which no understanding whatever has to be expended, only rhetoric.

Not that *Luther* is nearly as bad as *J. B.* or Paddy Chayefsky's *Gideon,* to take another recent example of art by acclamation. It is better written than those dogged excursions into the impalpable, it has more passion and honesty behind it, and it exemplifies an unequal struggle with one's respectable material, not a pompous act of auto-elevation and adolescent aggression against the gods. If

Luther is a long way from being promethean, it is also very far from being foolish. But it is certainly not a distinguished or even a particularly good play, since it neither does what it sets out to do, nor accomplishes anything especially valuable by accident, nor maintains any sort of consistency at all, whether of style, tone, procedure, or vision.

Above all, it isn't a profound play; that is just what has to be seen about it. Its aspirations to be a large, sweeping, inclusive document about human nature and experience, to be exemplary and symbolic and implacable and hieratic, are continually undercutting its genuine, if modest and desultory, dramatic virtues. The failure is not so much one of language or gesture as of construction and thought: too many ideas float around without a destiny; too many impulses are given freedom and then curtailed; too much is left to history, to our instinctive appreciation of the a priori greatness of the subject; too little is dramatized in place of being merely paraded or announced.

That Osborne should have chosen Martin Luther as a subject is not so farfetched as it would at first appear. Luther, after all, is an existential hero, and Osborne an existentialist-minded playwright, who has declared his admiration for Jean-Paul Sartre and has built his own chief drama around the existentialist preoccupation with a search for identity and a repudiation of the given, unexamined, inherited situation which life all too easily, and society all too ferociously, keep us in so that we are prevented from becoming what we might truly be.

These were Luther's concerns, a good part of them unconscious surely. Whatever the theological implications of his rebellion, as a man and an historical nexus he represents a plunge back into existence, a recovery, or at least an attempt at recovery, of a personal sense and a private conscience. And he also embodies on a massive scale the principle of the necessity of forging values in action, however much uncertainty there will always be about the rightness of what one does. In one of the closing scenes of the play Staupitz, Luther's old superior, asks him if he was sure of the truth of what he had promulgated, and Luther's answer is no, he was not.

There is still more, by way of explaining why Osborne should have felt attracted to Luther. The latter was a man embattled with his father and with the established order, an *Umsterzmensch,* a man who wished violently to shake up the world without having a clear idea of what new form it is to take. *Look Back in Anger* is not, after all, so very differently oriented. But that play was limited precisely by its painful and detailed immediacy; Martin Luther as the protagonist of a drama affords distance, size, and perspective. A man whom Kierkegaard described as giving the impression that lightning was about to strike around him at any moment, but who was also, with his anguishes and infantilisms, his violence and brutal invective, his constipation and tortured entrails, the most earthy and earth-ridden of men, is a perfect hero for a play about the necessity and perils of action.

A perfect hero, that is to say, if you know how to metamorphose him out of history and into a figure for the stage. But that is just what Osborne doesn't know how to do, not nearly well enough at any rate. The most surprising thing about *Luther*, and what contributes so thoroughly to its weakness, is the extent to which Osborne has adhered to the historical facts. Almost all the salient and well-known physical events are here: the fit in the choir, the confrontation with the father after the near-disastrous first Mass, the nailing of the theses to the church door, the trial at Worms, everything but the lightning bolt which led to the decision to become a monk. But they have no new reality.

Besides this, every issue is touched on, but scarcely more than that. Osborne manages to get in something about the papacy, about Luther's psychological difficulties with his father, about indulgences, about the principle of faith justifying works, about the rising bourgeoisie, about the peasant rebellion which Luther helped crush, about his notions on celibacy and his strategies for facing the devil. Again whole sections of sermons are taken verbatim from the published works, and remarks that may be found in Luther's writings or in his *tischreden*, his table-talk, or that have been attributed to him, are scattered throughout the play as dialogue or reverie and unfortunately make Osborne's own language seem especially pale by comparison. And finally there is an excessive, pace-killing concern with verisimilitude, seemingly endless processions of monks chanting hymns, elaborate and digressive scenes of religious ceremony, as though Osborne, and director Tony Richardson, were trying to compensate for the amorphousness of the theme by borrowing ritual and grandeur from liturgical handbooks.

The effect of all this is, in the first place, to give the play the feeling of an historical pageant, accurate enough perhaps, inspiring if you are inspired by surface and leased bigness, but lacking in the kind of dramatic pressure which can only be applied by an imagination transforming its material. Almost nothing is transformed here; events, language, significance are simply appropriated, with the wistful hope that tragic beauty, relevance for our time, an existential call to arms, will somehow rise from the scene.

Nothing is thought through; Osborne's evident desire to be inclusive and epic and historically fair, to give the Church its due and Luther a corrective slap

or two, to recognize the importance of the changing social order and the problematic nature of Luther's psychic structure as it reflects our own, leads him to
touch on every side of every issue without creating a real dialectic (the meeting
between Luther and Cajetan, the papal emissary, is an instance of such a missed
opportunity, that between Martin and a knight who reproaches him for having
turned against the peasants is another). And his dream of making Luther complex and fateful, the way all our lives are or should be, to fuse history, personality, and spirit, is not accompanied by a capacity to do more than arrange them
as separate and unassimilated fragments within a drama which lacks coherence,
thrust, and definition.

A word about Albert Finney. He is as good as he has been said to be, possibly
not as subtle an actor as Paul Scofield or as vigorous a one as Laurence Olivier,
but for a man in his mid-twenties a remarkable performer who combines the
best qualities of each of the others. He does his best with the role and he is supported by an outstanding cast, among whom one should mention Peter Bull,
Frank Shelley, and John Moffat. But *Luther* cannot be lifted from its smallness
and sluggishness and essential mediocrity by even the most brilliant actor in the
world.

Commonweal, Oct. 18, 1963

Wesker's *Chips with Everything*

In the published version of Arnold Wesker's *Chips with Everything* there is this
dedication: "To John Dexter, who has helped me understand the theater of my
plays and directed them all when most others said they would fail."

Wesker does indeed owe an enormous debt of gratitude to Dexter, whose
staging of the play is an extraordinary example of one theater art coming to the
rescue of another. What has happened is that an extremely uneven, though always passionate and energetic drama has been given a compelling shape, a form

for its turbulence and a style for its wayward and somewhat inarticulate mas-
culinity. And it has been done not as compensation—to mask deficiencies or fill
in voids—but as fulfillment, the utmost in palpability and sensuous life being
extracted from a recalcitrant script. The "theater" of Wesker's play has been released from its sleep by a prince of inventiveness, wit, force, and unvarying taste.

The only other recent job of direction that compares with Dexter's is that of
Judith Malina on *The Brig,* and in fact the two plays have strong resemblances,
both being, at least on the surface, ferocious assaults upon military life and
both possessing central elements of movement and ritual action. But Wesker's
play is a great deal more complex than Kenneth Brown's, which in its thoroughly antiliterary mode of existence is a director's opportunity; to take nothing away from Malina, what Dexter had to do was fuse literature with gesture,
expression with expressiveness, to meet his text halfway instead of being able to
conjure up the drama from a set of notes.

The play is set in an RAF training camp, but though it spares nothing in its
contempt for military-mindedness, it is conceived more as an indictment of the
British class system than of the Air Force, which functions here as a microcosm
of the society beyond the gates. Wesker takes a group of nine young RAF conscripts, all but one of them from the lower classes, through their eight weeks of
basic training, and on its lower levels the play is a grimly funny, if familiar, revelation of the pains, terrors, and boredoms of military life. But Wesker is of
course after something much bigger. In time the conscripts' indoctrination becomes revealed as a particularly subtle and atrocious aspect of the system by
which the British ruling class maintains itself in power, through fear, the claims
and taboos of tradition, unnerving contempt, and liberality in nonessentials.

The ninth recruit is a wealthy aristocrat, in apparent rebellion from his class,
and the dramatic center of the play is his attempt, on the one hand, to ally himself with the proletarians, and his resistance, on the other, to the officers' calm
insistence that he has no choice but to accept his upper-class destiny and take
his place as one of themselves. In the end he is won over—not too convinc-
ingly, it must be said—through the exposure of his motive for aligning himself
with the troops: on his own social level he faces extreme competition, but
among the men he can be a leader and even a messiah.

Wesker, whose first three plays were a trilogy about Jewish working-class life
in London, has improved considerably over those sometimes vivid but more often doctrinaire and tendentious works. But he is still seldom convincing when
he is being polemical and an angry young socialist. "How I hate civilians," he
has his Colonel Blimpish commanding officer say. "They don't know; what do

they know? How to make money, how to chase girls and kill old women. No order, no purpose . . . I'd sacrifice a million of them for the grace of a Javelin fighter." It is hard not to believe that this is taken from a pronunciamento, just as it is hard to accept the absolute rigidity of the British class lines as Wesker draws them.

But he is almost entirely convincing when he is being personal and is imaginatively searching for a new basis of social relations or lamenting not so much the forms of society as its qualities that conspire to hold men apart, its soullessness and vacant functionalism. Then his language serves admirably, either as shrewd comment or robust declamation or anguished and lyrical indictment and dream. He can become stiff and rhetorical but he is continually being saved by his more honest passions and perceptions and of course by his director's mastery of how to give those their proper life.

The abortive friendship between the aristocratic recruit and a sensitive working-class boy, a relationship which explores one of Wesker's central and most fecund themes, unfolds in scenes that are as well written as almost any in recent British drama. Here Wesker is concerned with the distance between the intellectual and the laborer, or, more symbolically, between mind and body or values and feeling. And the whole painful split and sense of betrayal are brilliantly kept from dwindling off into hopefulness or prescription. "You're a hypocrite—a hypocrite you are," the boy tells his well-born fellow-soldier. "You take people to the edge . . . and then you run away . . . you lousy word-user you . . . you clever, useless leftover . . . you call us mate, but you're a sacred old schoolboy . . . a bleedin' slummer."

For this scene, as for the less verbal ones, Dexter has created a pattern of direction that could not have been improved upon. It keeps language in balance with movement, imposes a line of controlled and rhythmic physicality, maintains a beautifully accurate pace, and offers a sensuous texture which is a long way from the gimmickry and visual extravagance of so many Broadway plays these days—of Tony Richardson's *Luther*, for example, where a false and irrelevant surface makes a weak play even more unpleasant.

Dexter's cast, it scarcely seems necessary to say in this era of English performing supremacy on our stages, is a splendid instrument of his will, with only one or two minor and temporary defections. Together, the director and his company have brought off a minor miracle; they have carried a playwright into his kingdom, a small realm which is still vulnerable and uncertain of itself, but full now of the capacity to live and extend its conquests.

Commonweal, Oct. 25, 1963

Pinter's *The Room* and *A Slight Ache*

Harold Pinter is a talented playwright who has yet to demonstrate his capacity for going the imaginative distance. His only full-length play, *The Caretaker,* conjures up an impressive atmosphere of psychological threat and metaphysical portent, but dissipates its own mystery halfway through. His short plays, on the other hand, retain their mystery to the end, but fail to move past atmosphere into a solid universe of dramatic event. In *The Room* and *A Slight Ache,* Pinter's strengths and deficiencies are equally on display, and they add up to an evening unquestionably worth attending, if not exactly worth shouting about.

The Room is Pinter's first play, written in 1957 when he was twenty-seven and full of a beginning playwright's unrealized impulses. One suspects his chief impulse was to carry the antinaturalism of Beckett and Ionesco to the point of satire. It doesn't come off: excessively irrational and arbitrarily motivated as the action is, it remains straightforwardly mystifying instead of mockingly so.

In a seedy London room live a hulking, cretinous truck driver and his drab, garrulous wife. He eats his breakfast and leaves without a word, after which the wife receives a succession of visitors who fill the room with undefined menace. The janitor stops by and the two have an eerie, demented conversation. A young couple ask about the room, which they have been told is for rent. Finally a blind Negro comes with a message for the woman to "come home"; when the husband returns he kicks the Negro to death as the woman clutches her eyes and moans, "I can't see!"

Frances Sternhagen as the wife, Clarence Felder as the husband, and Ralph Drischell as the janitor give this slim exercise a taut, skillful reading. Yet for all its effects of ambiguous danger and despite its final blatant symbolism of corruption through violence, the play is chiefly notable for Pinter's ability to turn domestic speech into a species of alarming discourse. When the janitor tells the woman the Negro wishes to see her, she replies, "But I don't know anybody . . . we've just moved into the district." "But he doesn't come from this district," the man says. "Perhaps you knew him in another district." Her answer is "Do you think I go around knowing men in one district after another?" The effect is to charge the quotidian word "district" with obscure but disturbing metaphysical and psychic meanings.

A Slight Ache is a more substantial work. Another couple, this time upper-middle class, find a filthy old matchseller standing motionless for days outside their country house. The husband, a pedantic, passionless man, feels threatened by the presence, but the wife is oddly interested. They invite him in. Standing bent over like a crumbling ruin, silent throughout, he becomes the agent of their passage into the visible manifestations of their inner realities. The husband collapses into the deathlike being of the matchseller, while the wife lavishes on the foul old man the love that has been suppressed in her. Sternhagen, Drischell, and Henderson Forsythe as the husband do a splendid job, and carry the experience safely past, although just past, the borders of discovery and significance.

Newsweek, Dec. 21, 1964

Wesker's *The Kitchen*

Life is no bowl of cherries in Arnold Wesker's *The Kitchen*—it's ten thousand bowls of everything from sour soup to stale cream puffs. In Wesker's 1961 play, given its first American production last week, the English playwright has used the vast, gleaming, steaming kitchen of a large restaurant as a microcosm for the anthill society of modern life with its oppressive routine of mindless and demeaning work.

Wesker is the most ideological of the breakthrough generation of playwrights who, led by John Osborne, trampled angrily through the drawing rooms of stultified English drama in the mid-1950s. He is a socialist artist in the tradition of William Morris and John Ruskin, who believes that art is an active weapon in the struggle to enrich the lives of the millions on the treadmills of mass society. Like Joan Littlewood with her *Fun Palace,* he is working toward his ideal of Centre 42, a project designed to bring culture to all of the people, and not just to what Wesker calls the "incestuous elite."

As a playwright Wesker's closest American counterpart is Arthur Miller, but he has several advantages over Miller. One is his youth, and the directness and freshness that go with it. Another is the fact that the vestigial but very real class tensions in Britain allow Wesker to write in a straight tradition of "proletarian" naturalism, without recourse to symbolic subterfuges. It is the tradition which in Russia has been perverted to "socialist realism," but which in Wesker still has an almost astounding sincerity and vigor.

Watching Wesker's relentlessly "real" people brings home the realization of how idealistic is this desire to transfer reality to the stage, sharpening its texture and its tongue so that it will speak and move its audience to change their hearts and lives. But in this early play Wesker is far from succeeding. His platoon of chefs, cooks, slaveys, butchers, busboys, and waitresses has been recruited too patly from the melting pot of class, nation, race, and character. There is the Italian boss, at once stingy and paternal, who can't understand why his troops should be dissatisfied; the Greek porter whose pride is in "making" things, like radios; the unnamed chef who reads his newspaper and lets things simmer; the French Negro cook with a racial chip on his cleaver; the smilingly cynical German cook who finally goes berserk with routine and frustration; the good-guy pastry cook who is crammed full of good-guy despair because people don't communicate.

Wesker sees sharply, knows a lot, and is true-hearted; he shows the lethal hysteria that can foam up through the surface of ordinary lives. But his play doesn't go deep enough or far enough; it misses the true shock that the energy of real insight always ignites, and its explosions become mere cherry bombs of sentimentality.

The Kitchen is the first directorial effort of Jack Gelber, who became a part of American and international stage history with his 1959 play, *The Connection*. He skillfully steers his twenty-nine actors through Ed Wittstein's inferno of urns and ovens as they chop, boil, bake, sauté, serve, squabble, and swab their way (with imaginary food) through the sizzling, sweating, screeching crescendos of lunch and dinner. He gets especially good performances from Rip Torn as the breaking-point German, Conrad Bain as a misanthropic meat-cutter, and Muni Seroff as the blue-suited boss of the stained and spattered crew. But Gelber shouldn't have tried to force-feed the play into an American setting. It is too obviously the product of a European milieu and sensibility, and references to "Rego Park" sound pretty silly mixed with English slang and the fancy-footed horseplay of soccer fans.

Newsweek, June 27, 1966

Pinter's *The Homecoming*

Everything Harold Pinter writes bears his special mark. Even his weaknesses are simply the price he pays for originality and power. Along with John Arden he is the most significant playwright now writing in English, a dramatist who has created an unmistakable world and whose energies go to the heart of present-day experience. His new play, *The Homecoming*, marks a new phase for Pinter, one of seemingly greater objectivity and "realism" and less mysteriousness-in-a-vacuum; without being entirely satisfying, it confirms his reputation and in fact puts it on a new plane.

Seldom has a playwright been better served by a director than Pinter is by Peter Hall, or by a more brilliant acting ensemble than that of the six performers from the Royal Shakespeare Company who make *The Homecoming* a theatrical occasion not to be missed. On a superb set by John Bury—a great, gray, barely furnished living room in a decaying London house, with a long shadowy staircase rising in the rear—Pinter's brutal, dreamlike action unfolds with such precision, so unerring a grasp of style and movement, as to constitute a lesson in the dramatic arts and a reminder of how exciting theater can still be.

The house is occupied by four men. Max (Paul Rogers) is seventy, a lusty, foul-mouthed bully. His son Lenny (Ian Holm) is in his early thirties—sharp, ironic, ruler of a stable of prostitutes. A younger son, Joey (Terence Rigby), is a large, oafish, would-be boxer. Max's brother Sam (John Normington) is sixty-ish, a pale, drab man proud of his ability as a chauffeur. Into this all-male ménage comes Teddy (Michael Craig), the eldest son, a philosophy professor in the United States, on his first visit home since his departure six years before.

With him is his wife, Ruth (Vivien Merchant), whom the others have never seen. Cool, enigmatic, rather elegant but also quietly sensual, she immediately becomes the focal point of the play. The atmosphere has been charged with hatred; for half the first act we seem to have had a portrait, in the manner of Tennessee Williams or Edward Albee, of domestic horror. But the play now shifts. We are no longer witnessing a psychological or sociological investigation but a ritual, a strange encounter of elemental passions and dreams within a closed universe of the mind.

In a quintessentially Pinteresque scene built upon an ashtray and a glass of water, around whose trivial shapes the densest implications accumulate, Ruth and Lenny establish themselves as participants in a moral combat, mythically sexual, uncompromising, touching the deepest places of the self. "I'll take it" (the glass), Lenny says in an unaccountable act of menace, to which Ruth replies, "If you take the glass . . . I'll take you." And from then on the play is about who takes whom, that is to say whose capacity for reality asserts itself most decisively and whose fantasies—in which the truest attitudes toward existence are embodied—win out.

Their ritual carries Pinter's people to a world beyond morality. At the climax Teddy is calm and unruffled when his father and brothers propose to his wife that she remain with them to fill the hole in their womanless lives, the only requirement being that she work as a call girl to help the household budget.

Teddy does not react "humanly" to this monstrous proposal because it is not monstrous in the terms and conditions of the play. For there is no logic to what has happened, no continuity with the accepted behavior of people. Like those in *The Brothers Karamazov,* a book that seems to have greatly influenced Pinter, the characters of *The Homecoming* are incarnations of human faculties, dividing among themselves the great possibilities of attitude and approach to existence.

When Ruth accepts the proposal, she has made a move toward the greater actuality of the family. For her husband Teddy is an abstract man, an overhygienic consciousness, while she is nearly elemental physicality. Earlier he has told her that he wants to go back to America where it's "cleaner." And Lenny has chided Teddy on his life there, on "the old campus," a world of Bermuda shorts, ice water, coeds, and "all the social whirl." "We live a closer life here," Lenny adds in an understated and ironic summing up of what their fierce, carnivorous but unmasked and unevasive community represents.

When the play ends, Ruth has made it clear that, far from being the exploited one, she is the one in command. To Joey she will be a mother figure, to Lenny a whore, to Max a special kind of wife. For she has agreed to satisfy their fantasies, which have at least the virtue of expressing the deepest archetypes of human experience, while her husband stands for the evasion and fear of physical actuality.

What keeps the play from being a masterpiece, a full jump into a new dimension, is Pinter's failure fully to integrate these last developments. They seem tacked on, rushed into action, reserves called up for fear the main force hasn't done its work. Further, there is a hesitation in Pinter's construction, a wavering between fully fleshed characterizations and bare, symbolic ones, a slight failure to mesh his levels of portrayal. But these are small deficiencies in what is

otherwise an extraordinarily impressive play, one whose equal we are not likely to see at all soon.
Newsweek, Jan. 16, 1967

Beckett's *Rockaby*

Samuel Beckett's writing long ago reached a point where one could scarcely expect it to get any sparer, more concentrated, or, for that matter, shorter. Not for more than fifteen years has he produced a work remotely fitting our definition, of "full-length," and this is true of his fiction as well as his theater pieces. Since the early 1960s, the former has consisted of exercises of no more than five pages (some are as short as a single page), while the theatrical writing, as well as that for radio and television, has been made up of tiny, precisely choreographed and physically stripped playlets, or "dramaticules," as he calls some of them.

But in Beckett's case, length isn't the consideration it usually is in the literary and theatrical worlds, or should I say the publishing and producing universes, where writers of short stories are pressed to do novels and writers of short plays are informed that there's no market for their work, since nobody is going to pay for even a "delightful" or "important" twenty minutes or so at the theater. Beckett is a master of literature and drama, perhaps *the* master since Joyce and Brecht, and he can get away with anything. While nearly everybody else moves toward size—the "big" novel, the "major" play—he seems to proceed steadily in the opposite direction, toward quiddities and beyond, toward the vanishing point.

Of course, he stops just short of that, so close, though, that you can hear the silence on the other side. *Rockaby* is about the same length as his other recent works for the theater or television or radio, the pieces collected in *Ends and Odds,* for instance. It's about fifteen minutes long in performance, the reason, I imagine, why it isn't getting a regular commercial production, but instead is being sponsored by various universities. It had its premiere at the State University of New York at Buffalo on April 8, marking Beckett's seventy-fifth birthday (a celebration was held). It then played for three performances (I saw the middle one) at La MaMa under the sponsorship of New York University's Center for French Civilization and Culture, afterward moving to the State University at Purchase, New York. I don't have a clear idea of what will be happening with it next, but it isn't likely that anyone reading this will be able to see it for some time to come.

And that's a pity. For *Rockaby* is a marvelously beautiful piece of work, for all that it barely exists, which may be just the point. Against all the noise that assails us, the words that continuously wash over us, in life and in art, here is something minuscule, austere, essentially unseductive and remote. It is so disinterested that it makes you feel—if it's possible to say this about a work presumably intended to affect audiences—first, just sufficiently fed and, then, not like a target but an eavesdropper, a privileged one.

Like so much of Beckett's work for a long time now, *Rockaby* "concerns" death or, rather, dying. I put "concerns" in quotation marks because the word isn't at all accurate to describe what the play is doing, but no other word from *Roget's* would be of any more use. This little play, reminiscent in certain ways of *Krapp's Last Tape* and *Not I,* isn't *about* death or dying so much as it's a distillation of, an almost pure utterance from, a condition of contemplation of finiteness, finality. One more variation on Beckett's overriding theme, or obsession, it forges a voice to speak into the silence, that voice which is all we have to hold off, for as long as we can, oblivion and the end of it all.

On a rocking chair a woman sits, an old woman dressed in an old-fashioned long black dress with shiny black spangles and a high collar, a little black toque on her head. She starts to rock while a voice on tape (clearly her own) speaks, or rather softly intones a recapitulation and threnody. "Close of a long day," it begins, and proceeds to review a life and prepare for its end. In the kind of symphonic movement familiar to us from Beckett's earlier work, most notably *Not I* and *Happy Days,* certain phrases occur, are dropped and are picked up again: "going to and fro"; "time she stopped"; "all eyes, all sides, high and low"; "another like herself . . . a little like."

The voice speaks of her having been seated by the window, "her window . . . facing other windows . . . other only windows . . . all blinds down . . . hers alone up." It is as though she is the only one still alive, or perhaps the only one still willing to look out at the world in search of another. The voice talks of her mother, who it seems died in the same chair after having "gone off her head . . .

but harmless." Two or three times the voice stops, and the woman in the chair croaks "more" and the tape resumes. Finally the life and the play run down, the head begins slowly to droop, the chin falls on the chest, the eyes close, and the spotlight goes out.

Rockaby is directed by Alan Schneider and performed by Billie Whitelaw, a British actress undeservedly little known in this country. She has had a great deal of experience in Beckett plays and seems to me a perfect interpreter of his subtle, uncompromising intentions. To fill out the evening, Whitelaw reads a story by Beckett called "Enough," a lamentation by a very old man. Though not one of Beckett's finest works, it is more than adequate for this purpose. The reading takes about twenty minutes; the whole program, with intermission, lasts about an hour. Was what we had seen and heard drama? As I walked out, under a spell, it didn't occur to me to ask.

Nation, May 9, 1981

Churchill's *Cloud Nine*

Cloud Nine is the first work of Caryl Churchill I've seen or read. I'm pretty sure it's the first of her plays to be produced here, but that ought to change. She is not quite as accomplished perhaps, or as firmly in control of her material, as some others among the new echelon of British dramatists—Howard Brenton or Stephen Poliakoff, say—but may just turn out to be the most gifted of all. *Cloud Nine* has its dull spots and periodic lapses from coherence, but also an admirable wit and energy and a depth of human acceptance that put it very much above any other new drama I've seen in months.

From what I know about her, as well as from some internal evidence in this play, Churchill is a feminist of a rather determined sort. But even though the work is informed by certain feminist attitudes, as well as by a strong sympathy for lesbianism, there is nothing ideological or sexually didactic about it at all.

Nor is there anything pugnacious or defensive. If the play makes a plea, it's of the implicit kind that emerges from any work of imagination that perceives human behavior accurately and generously. And it's our sexual turmoil—the history of attitudes toward sex and the changing, beleaguered patterns of our experience of it—that constitutes Churchill's vision.

The play is in two distinct acts, the first set in Africa in 1880, the second in London in 1980, although, as the program says, "for the characters it is only twenty-five years later." The point is that three central characters have leaped over a century of social and moral change while having physically "lived" only a quarter of that time. In the African section, a British colonial family, as pukka as can be—they begin by singing "Then gather round for England, come rally to the flag"—are put through a series of farcical and parodic events, chiefly consisting of various homosexual and heterosexual entanglements and, to coin a necessary word, cross-entanglements. All unfold within clouds of Victorian guilt and hypocrisy, even though, as I said, it's done farcically, and with a rhetoric of hard-breathing Victorian euphemism.

In London, a century later, the characters carried over from the first act, along with some new ones, are in a drastically changed sexual and psychic climate. Couplings are of course far easier to effect, euphemisms are no longer necessary. Homosexuality, both male and, especially, female, is prominent and requires no apology or furtiveness. What has happened is that at the deepest level, roles are no longer so rigidly defined, either socially or in matters of sex. And so the characters circle and clasp one another, exchanging hungers and anxieties, coming to "know" themselves better. Not that they're happier or psychically richer than their predecessors—Churchill is too responsible a thinker for that—but they're less constrained and so, perhaps, less false.

Still, modern sexual fashion has its own kind of falseness, so that if the first act is full of inflated, evasive talk the second has some wonderfully chic chatter. "All I want to do is give you orgasms," a man tells his wife, and another character says to a lover, "you don't seem to realize how insulting it is to me that you can't get yourself together." But the second act moves steadily beyond such parody to culminate in some very moving recognitions of the way desire is besieged by doubt, pleasure by guilt. There's an especially fine monologue in which a woman describes her movement from shame about masturbation to acceptance of its satisfactions and, as in her case, its occasional necessity. At the end the speaker embraces a figure from the first act, a representation of her own early repressions. The action is conciliatory, accepting, the culmination of what Churchill's wide, unjudgmental imagination has been arranging all along.

A cast of seven acts this intelligent play with vigor and enthusiasm, playing several roles in most cases and getting past an infrequent obscure or uncertain spot in the text without faltering. I particularly liked E. Katherine Kerr and Veronica Castang, and the only performance I didn't like was that of Don Amendolia as a little girl. But that was really a matter of casting rather than performance. In several other cases men play women's roles and vice versa, which fits in well with the play's ruling notions, but the sight of a large, hairy-legged man in a short skirt and with his thumb in his mouth half the time quickly became irritating and then obnoxious. Apart from that I had nothing but admiration for the way Tommy Tune directed and the way the evening went. *Nation,* June 27, 1981

Fugard's *"Master Harold"*

. . . and the Boys

Among the white writers who have dealt nobly and tirelessly with apartheid in South Africa, Athol Fugard has a secure place. The protagonists of his plays (uneven in quality as these may be) are blacks or persons of mixed race portrayed with great sympathy; or they are whites who are connected to them by affection and good will and disconnected by psychic and social pressures. Such is the relationship within Fugard's latest play—a quiet, simple tale, finely wrought, and one that represents a considerable step up from the vague dramaturgy and rather preachy moral tone of his previous play, *A Lesson from Aloes.*

"Master Harold". . . and the Boys takes place in 1950 in a somewhat shabby tea room in Port Elizabeth, the setting for several Fugard plays. The date marks the time when racial matters in South Africa were beginning to settle into the extreme conditions that prevail today. It was also the time when Fugard, nearly twenty, was presumably becoming fully conscious of the situation.

Willie and Sam, two black employees who are waiting for the tea room to open on a "wet and windy afternoon" before their day's work begins, are joined by Hally, the seventeen-year-old son of the woman who owns the place, and the three proceed to enact a moral and political drama of subtle, painful intensity. The black men are forty or so, and it immediately becomes evident that they enjoy a close, easy relationship with the boy, who, we learn, spent a great deal of his troubled childhood in their company. They joke, banter, reminisce, work on a school assignment of Hally's; the atmosphere is warm and intimate.

"I almost wish we were still in that little room [where he would visit the men]," Hally says. "Life felt the right size in there . . . wasn't so hard to work up a bit of courage. It's got so bloody complicated since then." The "complications" soon start to show themselves, beginning when Hally learns from a phone call that his father is coming home from the hospital. The father is a cripple and an alcoholic, and the son can't bear the thought of his return. Stricken by anger and shame, he turns on Sam, the more articulate and complex of the two black men, engaging in what clinically could be called "displacement."

While never less than literate and well crafted, the play up to this point is slow in developing real dramatic energy, but now it finds its vigor. The long scene in which Hally repudiates his friendship with Sam becomes a confrontation of cultures, moral systems, and levels of humanity. In this scene Fugard accomplishes what all playwrights wish to do: he makes his characters representative and universal; they are made to yield general truths out of their specific circumstances. The thing is beautifully done: the rhythm of the encounter rises in its painfulness and tension, subsides, rises again and reaches an almost unbearable moment in which far more is at stake than the connections between two particular human beings.

In his shame and gathering psychic blindness, the boy lashes out. When Sam urges him to remember the respect he owes his father, Hally warns, "be careful . . . you're treading on dangerous ground . . . mother's always warning me about allowing you to become too familiar. You're only a servant in here." *In here.* The place is a moral one, the location of prejudices, ancient fears. When Hally tells Sam to "start calling me Master Harold," and Sam replies, "if you make me say it once, I'll never call you anything else again," we witness the death of personal love and also of social hope. And when, after Hally goes still further in his need to humiliate the black man, and Sam says, "You've hurt yourself, Master Harold . . . you've just hurt yourself bad," we become aware of the extent of the moral injury.

"Master Harold" . . . *and the Boys* had a limited run in its recent world premiere at the Yale Repertory Theatre, but it is certain to come to New York City. One hopes that in its reincarnation it will have the same actors who played Willie and Sam at Yale. Zakes Mokae as Sam and Danny Glover as Willie are extraordinarily good: they press for nothing, underscore no emotions, but simply ride easily along the swell of the textual wave or, in keeping with one of the plot elements, move like supremely gifted ballroom dancers. Zeljko Ivanek as Hally and Fugard in his capacity as director are distinctly inferior to them; Ivanek is much too brittle, too given to abrupt, jagged moments, and Fugard exhibits an often shaky directorial hand. Nothing fatal here, but there's room for improvement.

Nation, May 1, 1982

Pinter's *The Hothouse*

In 1958, after *The Room* and *The Dumbwaiter* had been produced and after *The Birthday Party,* his first full-length play, had been pretty well savaged by the London critics, Harold Pinter wrote a second long work and then shoved it into a drawer. Some years later, Pinter explained his suppression of this play by calling its characters "cardboard," among other negative judgments. Within the last year, though, he seems to have had a change of heart. The world premiere of *The Hothouse* took place in March in Providence, Rhode Island, where it was produced by the Trinity Square Repertory Company. This production, directed by Adrian Hall, the group's artistic director, has now come to New York City.

Anything by Pinter asks for attention, and I for one am happy to give it. I watched and listened, I took notes, and by the end it seemed to me that Pinter was right the first time; the play, while not exactly an embarrassment, is deficient in almost every dramaturgical and intellectual respect. Its central metaphor is strained and unconvincing, its procedures are chaotic and opaque, and its language—Pinter's great virtue, after all—is five or six cuts below his general level. I've asked myself what I would have thought had I not known who had written this piece, and had to admit that I probably would have left after the first act.

That would have been a mistake, but only a slight one. After the intermission, *The Hothouse* picks up briefly, before finally letting down with a rather resounding thump. The vigor that's generated for a while at the beginning of Act II arises almost entirely from a single character, and when he is left with nothing to do, the play surrenders to its inherent debilities.

The setting of *The Hothouse*, referred to merely as "The Institution," is clearly a psychiatric hospital. We are shown the director's office, a sitting room, chain-metal doors, and some stairways; the patients, who never actually appear on stage, are up above. These patients are known by numbers instead of names, and indeed the whole atmosphere is intended, one assumes, to convey the distant, terrifyingly impersonal power of the State (a shadowy "Ministry" figures in somewhere) over its people's lives. Sure enough, several generous or fawning, but in any case superficially educated, reviewers were pleased to describe the proceedings as "Kafkaesque," which I can assure you they're not.

Kafka would never have given his characters names like Lush, Lobb, Tubb, and Cutts (there are also Roote, Lamb, and Gibbs), a nomenclature derived from an idea—influential in the late 1950s and doubtless owing much to Beckett's Nagg, Nell, and Krapp—of what "absurd" and unrepresentational characters should be called. And Kafka would never have been so obvious in his schema of events; *The Hothouse* is full of activities that spell out with painful heaviness Pinter's imaginative intention, from scenes of electric shock therapy, arbitrarily imposed, to a culminating "massacre" (played out offstage) in which the patients wipe out the staff almost to a man.

This early play does have some traces of Pinter's stylistic hallmarks: his famous repetitions, for example, and his wonderfully shrewd eye for banality. But these things are buried in a text that feels as if it's been composed of scraps of intuition and perception, theories or rumors of psychic and political oppression, instead of a real vision of them. In none of Pinter's other plays, including the three that preceded this one, is there such lack of clarity (by which I mean imaginative control and not narrative openness) or such straining after effects.

The Hothouse has been described by several reviewers as "fiercely funny," but it isn't. It does have one quite funny stretch, some ten or fifteen minutes at the beginning of Act II, but this segment's humor may have as much to do with a single performance as with the script. George Martin plays Roote, the director of the Institution (an archetypal Colonel Blimp), with great vigor and panache. Violent, coy, fawning, and imperious by turns, Martin is the model of bureaucratic madness. "I've given up visiting the patients," he says. "It's not worth it, it's a waste of time." When he opens a bottle of Scotch he immediately throws the top into the wastebasket; when he addresses the staff on Christmas night it's a masterpiece of fumbling pomposity. But Roote drifts out of the play after a while, and nothing comes along to fill the hole.

Nation, May 29, 1982

Hare's *Plenty*

No matter how far Britain sinks as a power or how enervated its social existence becomes, British playwrights continue to surprise us; the theater in England keeps being renewed. There's been an interplay between drama and political conditions there for the last twenty-five years, ever since John Osborne's Jimmy Porter complained that there were "no good, brave causes left." *Look Back in Anger* released a tremendous burst of theatrical energy which, after a lull, has resurged in a new generation of dramatists who are even more directly political than were their predecessors—Osborne, Arnold Wesker, John Arden, among others. A subject, a basis for fierce complaint, a ground for imagination, an instigation to creative assertion, politics, or sociopolitics have vigorously informed a whole new group of playwrights more gifted than the corresponding generation in the United States.

David Hare is among the most talented of these younger writers—who include Howard Brenton, Stephen Poliakoff, Heathcote Williams, and Barry Keefe—and *Plenty* is the sixth of the seven full-length plays he's written. It's also probably the best, although it suffers from a central structural defect (to which I'll return). The play was first produced at London's National Theatre in

1978, and its leading performer, Kate Nelligan, was chosen as that year's best actress by the British critics. Nelligan, who is Canadian, is making her first American appearance in *Plenty* and should be a prime candidate this year for our highest awards.

The play moves back and forth in time and place during the years 1943–62, shifting between London and other English cities and wartime France. Nelligan plays Susan Traherne, who at seventeen was parachuted into France to work with the Resistance. The experience had been terrifying but also exhilarating—life was at its most intense and everything counted. "I met people for an hour or two," she remembers, "and I saw the best of them." When she returns home after the war, everything is flat and drab. The English are "loveless," she says, and remarks that "the people who stayed behind" now "seem childish and a little silly." Above all, England is without energy or vision; though promised "Peace and Plenty," the British have been reduced to scraping by.

"I want to move on," Susan says after her return. "I want to change everything and I don't know how." What she does do is become an advertising copywriter, a job in which success is "a matter of pitching my intelligence low enough"; she tries to have a baby with a man she's chosen for the task, and later marries a diplomat she doesn't love. From then on, she responds to life with bitterness and random violence. A last attempt to recover the lucidity and sense of purpose she'd once had is an abject failure. A one-time fellow Resistance worker has looked her up after twenty years, and they spend a night in a seedy seaside hotel. It doesn't work. The man, now a business executive, says, "I hate this life we lead," and she can only agree. The play ends with a flashback to 1944 in newly liberated France. "We have grown up," the young, ardent Susan says. "We will improve our world."

Plenty is continuously absorbing, never banal or obvious, and there are many moments of keen perception and fine emotional complexity. Yet there's something wrong at the center. Hare never does decide what is the cause of Susan's malaise. On one hand there are England, society, the meanness and absence of ideals; on the other is the protagonist's psychological pathology. "I have a weakness," she says at one point. "I like to lose control." And in one crucial scene her long-suffering husband tells her, "You are selfish; you are determined to destroy other forms of happiness."

We agree with him, and our sympathy for Susan is tempered by that awareness. Yet the character is one of the great roles in recent English-speaking drama, and, especially as it's performed by Nelligan, it triumphs over the play's confusions. The production also triumphs over some occasionally inept staging (by Hare as his own director): annoyingly long blackouts during which scenery is trundled on; a much slower pace at times than there ought to be. But Nelligan is transcendent. With her clear profile and look of aristocratic intelligence, her husky supple voice, her absolutely firm stage presence, she makes *Plenty* the most memorable occasion of the season so far.

Nation, Nov. 27, 1982

Churchill's *Top Girls*

The season has been such a Sahara that I'd particularly looked forward to Caryl Churchill's new play *Top Girls,* since her *Cloud Nine* was one of last year's most impressive works. Flawed, uncertain of its structure, it nevertheless stood out against the general unimaginativeness and relentless domesticity of so much recent drama. In light of that, my disappointment in the new play is more than ordinarily acute.

Churchill, who has been on the edge of the new movement in British playwriting, is not an important figure but someone to take account of. She's a feminist, a political skeptic on the left, a student of literature and history whose writing is distinguished by the fertility of its ideas and their relative freedom from ideological rigidity. But as the price of her intellectual fecundity, her plays tend to be dramaturgically wayward, confused, incoherent.

Cloud Nine was able to overcome its structural and thematic debilities through its vigor and some witty writing, but *Top Girls* is unsalvageable. After a long opening scene in a vein of complete fantasy, the play abruptly switches tone and manner, moving at first into stylized naturalism and then, in a long concluding scene, into naturalism of a thoroughly straightforward kind. Before the evening's over, a half-dozen motifs or subjects have been thrown out for our consideration, but not one provides a central organizing principle, and none are adequately embodied in the dramatic action.

The first scene brings six women together for lunch in a London restaurant rather unsubtly called La Prima Donna. One of these is Marlene, the organizer of the affair and the only "real"—that is, contemporary—character in this scene who will appear throughout the play. The others are drawn from literature (Chaucer's Patient Griselda; Nijo, a royal concubine from medieval Japan who wrote an autobiography), art (Brueghel's Dull Gret, who in armor leads a charge through hell), religious myth (the apocryphal ninth-century Pope Joan), and history (the Victorian traveler Isabella Bird).

The five proceed to tell their "stories," with Marlene as a sort of talk-show host. At first they trample on each other's lines, but then settle into some sort of conversation. It's not clear what it all adds up to, but I take Churchill's meaning to be that they've "come a long way" into consciousness, as one character puts it, that their real or invented lives are exemplary of women's responses to their situations, which range here from Griselda's and Nijo's meekness in the face of exploitation to Gret's and Pope Joan's toughness and bellicosity.

It's opaque and far-fetched in conception, but there is some funny writing (Joan briskly orders "canneloni and salad"; Nijo says, "I'm not a cheerful person; I just laugh a lot") and at least one moment of substantial feeling. This occurs when Joan is describing having been stoned to death for having borne a child. But there's much too little of that. From the beginning I was on the playwright's side, rooting for the thing to come alive, seizing the occasional moments of enjoyment—until my patience wore out and I longed for the curtain.

The scenes that follow take place either at the offices of the "Top Girls" Employment Agency in London or at Marlene's sister Joyce's house in Suffolk. Marlene has just been named director of the agency; she is a "top girl," a winner in a man's world, and her implicit model is Margaret Thatcher. The danger of worldly success, Churchill seems to be saying, is that it hardens you, men and women alike. In the long final scene, Marlene bitterly quarrels with her sister, who has remained at home, an "underachiever," but who has the last accusatory word on Marlene's ungenerous, "I'm all right. Jack/Jane" attitude.

There are a few flashes of wit and intelligence in this scene, as there are in the first, but where the restaurant sequence is obscure, the segment at Joyce's house is all too transparent. Churchill here lets her critical social eye glaze over with resentment and her political acumen degenerate into easy indictments. And what a jumble we're left with! It's rare to find a play that works so actively against its own potential virtues.

Nation, Feb. 12, 1983

Beckett's *Ohio Impromptu,*
Catastrophe, and *What Where*

Samuel Beckett's plays have grown increasingly short, to the point where "playlets"—or "dramaticule," as he's called at least one—is a more appropriate term for them. Beckett is the great master of less is more, of the fertile silence and the echoing nuance; no other living dramatist is so free of cant, sentimentality, and verbal fuss.

If he now sometimes gives the impression of parodying himself or, less harshly, of working and reworking familiar materials, it doesn't much diminish my pleasure in his work. The three playlets that make up the current Beckett bill at the Harold Clurman Theater offer us nothing really new—except perhaps a somewhat more explicit note of political concern than before—but they're nevertheless a delight to see and hear.

Ohio Impromptu, which was written for and first performed at Beckett's seventy-fifth birthday celebration at Ohio State University a couple of years ago, is a two-character piece in which a reader, R (beautifully played by David Warrilow), reads to a listener, L (Rand Mitchell), a tale of love fading and finally dead. The first line is "Little left to tell"; the last is "Nothing left to tell." Between those so characteristic utterances lie the story and something more: the fact and nature of storytelling itself, of literature, something composed, sent out, received.

Visually, *Ohio Impromptu* is striking, if a little portentous, as are all three plays, which Alan Schneider has directed with strict fidelity to stage directions but a trifle too much atmosphere. The two men sit at right angles to each other at the end of a long table, in the center of which is a black, wide-brimmed hat. Both have long white hair and are dressed in long black coats; they shield their eyes from the light and remain almost immobile throughout, except for an occasional rap on the table by L, which serves to start the reading again after a pause. The men are mirror images of each other, the point being that so are writing and reading: the tale told, the tale heard.

Catastrophe is dedicated to Vaclav Havel, the dissident Czech playwright, and is perhaps Beckett's most overtly political work. A "protagonist," clearly a figure for the writer or artist, is fixed under a spotlight as a black-robed living statue, which a "director," an impresario-like personage in fur hat and fur-collared coat, and his "assistant" arrange, tinker with, fuss over ("Whiten his hands," the director orders) in an almost pure allegory of exploitation. At the end an oration is heard from an invisible audience as the piteous creature sags from his frame. The piece reminded me of Kafka's story "The Hunger Artist" (the chief difference being that in the earlier tale of the artist as performer and scapegoat, the action is voluntary, whereas here it's the result of extreme coercion), and of the Pozzo and Lucky speeches in *Waiting for Godot:* the mind at the end of a rope, intellect enslaved.

If any of these plays is self-parodic it's *What Where.* The characters are named Bam, Bim, Bem, and Bom, and there are lines like "We are the last five" (there's Bam's "voice" too) and "I am alone. Time passes. That is all." The shadowy characters move in dim light enacting a tale of some mysterious assignment to get "him" to say "it" after having been given "the works." "What must he confess?" is asked several times but never answered.

A clue is that the main figure, a prosecutor or inquisitor, keeps editing his words. He says something, expresses displeasure at it, starts again, calls it "good" and goes on. Another allegory of writing and reading, with "the works" referring to an oeuvre and also to the old gangster term for murder, the point being that writing and literature can be used to deceive and oppress. I won't push it. The play's last lines are "That is all. Make sense who may." Even in this slight, rather forced exercise, Beckett is too dense and both grimly and playfully enigmatic to be forced into single meanings.

Nation, Aug. 6–13, 1983

Part Three **Book Reviews**

George Steiner's *The Death*
of Tragedy

Near the end of this long essay on the decline of tragic drama George Steiner expresses a credo that might more serviceably have appeared at the beginning. "I believe that literary criticism has about it neither rigour nor proof," he writes. "Where it is honest, it is passionate, private experience seeking to per-suade." You can't ask for anything fairer than that, but it might, as I say, have better been told to us earlier, criticism of this kind not being to everyone's taste.

It is, with slight reservations, very much to my own taste, I had better say be-fore I go further; without at all gainsaying the achievements of the textualists, I believe we need more of this kind of "old criticism," as Steiner has elsewhere de-scribed it, provided it's understood that something quite different from Van Wyck Brooks or J. Donald Adams is meant by the term. Steiner is no literary sociologist or patriot, nor is he a Houseman poised at his mirror ready to slice his throat at the memory of some devastating line. You will find here almost as close a reading of texts as is being performed at Chicago or Gambier, Ohio.

You will also find as brilliant, thorough, and concerned a contemplation of the nature of dramatic art as has appeared in many years. Steiner doesn't have a profoundly original thesis, which along with the self-imposed limitation on his subject—there is scarcely any discussion of comedy—keeps me from placing his book in the company of such ur-works of recent drama criticism as Eric Bentley's *The Playwright as Thinker,* Francis Fergusson's *The Idea of a Theater,* and H. D. F. Kitto's *Form and Meaning in Drama,* but *The Death of Tragedy* seems to me to rank not far below.

Steiner starts from the obvious fact that there has been no high tragic art since Corneille and Racine and the Elizabethans, and from the only slightly less evident truth that the history of the drama since then has been largely a simultaneous flight from the tragic and an unending attempt to resurrect it. There have been magnificent approaches—he cites Milton's *Samson Agonistes* and the plays of Schiller—immensely fertile suggestions—some of Byron's works for a "mental theater," the plays of Kleist and Büchner—radical efforts to revitalize the genre by using the resources of other arts—Wagner's massive experiment. And there is the almost miraculous achievement of Ibsen, "the most important playwright after Shakespeare and Racine."

But there has been no breakthrough; the possibilities Ibsen opened up for a new kind of tragic drama have not been seized upon, and tragedy, in any of the imprecise but commonly understood meanings we give to the word, has not been found possible.

Steiner, it should be said, doesn't presume to offer an airtight definition of tragedy. He describes it as having to do with the "fact of catastrophe," and as a "deliberate advance to the edge of life, where the mind must look upon blackness at the risk of vertigo"; he argues that it does not "speak of secular dilemmas which may be resolved by rational innovations, but of the unalterable bias toward inhumanity and destruction in the drift of the world," and notes that it is "the form of art which requires the intolerable burden of God's presence." All of which helps us to know and to accept his premises.

His chief premise is that what gave the death-blow to tragic drama was the great change in Western habits of mind that occurred in the seventeenth century, the change from symbolic, allegorical, mythological modes of perception and cognition to rational and scientific ones. "After Shakespeare the master spirits of western consciousness are no longer the blind seers, the poets, or Orpheus performing his art in the face of Hell. They are Descartes, Newton and Voltaire." And needing as does no other form of art the presence in human affairs of the supernatural, the sacramental, the ideas of divine retribution and pre-ordainment, as well as an overriding sense of the irrational, tragic drama succumbed before the gradual emptying of these notions and their receding hold on men.

As I have said, this isn't strikingly original. But what gives Steiner's book its great value is the almost unbelievable erudition he brings to his account of the process (multilingual, he provides excellent translations of his quotations from French and German), the subtlety and acuteness of his analysis of particular plays and the enveloping atmosphere of rich seriousness which his critical approach distills.

I haven't space to do more than mention some of the questions he treats: the nature of neo-classic tragedy; the unavailing attempt of the romantics to restore the tragic ideal; the deadening effect of Shakespeare's example on the English dramatists who came after him; the anti-tragic nature of Christianity; the rise of the novel as the literary form most able to express the new age of reason and secular values; the existence of poetry as the traditional vehicle for tragedy, and the growth of the possibility of its replacement by prose.

This last theme brings Steiner to a consideration of recent efforts to recapture the spirit of classical tragedy, either through verse dramas or the recasting of Greek myths or the two together. Yeats has some splendid moments, he says; Eliot catches a shadow of the real thing; but they don't bring it off; and when we drop below their level we are faced with embarrassment. "The verse tragedies of modern European and American poets are exercises in archaeology and attempts to blow fire into cold ash."

The weakest sections of the book are those on contemporary drama. Not that there's anything wrong with Steiner's basic judgment on poets in the theater (although he does fail, inexplicably, to mention Lorca). The trouble is with his leitmotif, which begins to operate in these last pages as a dogma and a principle of exclusion. "The classic leads to a dead past," he says. "The metaphysics of Christianity and Marxism are anti-tragic. That, in essence, is the dilemma of modern tragedy."

But what is left is just what Steiner fails to take up sufficiently or else downgrades: the possibilities articulated by Chekhov; the theaters of Strindberg and Pirandello; those of Camus and Sartre; the revolutionary new stage of Beckett, Ionescu, Adamov, and Genet. Brecht alone seriously interests Steiner among recent writers who have made any kind of advance. I can't quarrel with admiration of Brecht, but I think there are other promising directions opening, including the possibility of a radical revaluation of our entire concept of tragedy, such as is being worked out in the novels and critical writings of Alain Robbe-Grillet.

This partial myopia stems, I think, from an understandable desire to protect a thesis, and also from a subtle mistrust of consciousness in the drama on Steiner's part. It is the sort of thing that leads him to make the remark that over the characters in Schiller's *Don Carlos* "there hangs too vivid a cast of thought. Schiller would be among the first of those whom Eric Bentley referred to as the 'playwright as thinker.'" This is a tiresome mistake; Bentley meant nothing like that. What he did mean is that the playwright thinks, that thought is as necessary to him as imagination and that from Ibsen on dramatists have tried to re-create a theater of depth and significance by thinking even more acutely and strategically than before.

But I don't want to leave on that note. There is no critic without a blind spot. And the virtues of Steiner's book are such that the blindness is more than compensated for by a dozen sources of light.

Commonweal, May 12, 1961

Lionel Abel's *Metatheatre*

"I have tried in this book," Lionel Abel writes, "to do two things: one, to explain why tragedy is so difficult, if not altogether impossible for the modern dramatist, and two, to suggest the nature of a comparably philosophic form of drama." One is impressed even before the attempt gets under way. To write on drama in America is to review, which means that in all but the exceptional case you have to have a reviewer's mind and soul and therefore an almost total incomprehension of such questions as Abel poses. Or else it is to produce texts and histories and academic articles, which means that you are much more likely to find yourself talking about masks, or Shakespeare's comic characters, or social ambiguity in Arthur Miller. As for the few open, unclassifiable, and engaged critics we have, the continuing and consuming job is to preserve the very notion of drama as an art, against the thinness of the native evidence and the hostility to thought which our theater, even more than our other cultural institutions, exhibits like a badge of identity.

Elsewhere—in France, for example—such inquiries as Abel's are much more common; even the stints of daily reviewing are sometimes made the minor occasions for them. Where you don't have to spend your time and vigor establishing that drama is an art, you can talk about what kind of art it is and about its dilemmas; and where the distinction between art and commerce is clearer, there is a great deal less confusion about the area and function of criticism. The critic discusses art, and some other kind of authority discusses business. Here, though, we are painfully held down to the elementary considerations: what to do about Broadway, popularity versus the imagination, can thought be dramatic, how to write or not write a play.

The result is that writing on the drama which changes our ideas, sharpens our responses, or expands our consciousness is extraordinarily rare in this country, much rarer than such criticism is in poetry or fiction. Isolated and intermittent books that combine scholarship, force, a sense of the past, and contemporary insight, such as Eric Bentley's *The Playwright as Thinker* or Francis Fergusson's *The Idea of a Theater,* instruct us and keep the possibilities open, but at the same time they remind us that we have almost no place to put them.

This loneliness of vision and idea affects the works themselves, and accounts, at least in part, for certain qualities and attitudes of Abel's book: its aggressiveness, which is that of the prophet without honor in his own country; its self-assurance—amounting at times to cocksureness—which is that of the mind protecting itself against homelessness and cultural insecurity; and its dogmatism, which is often the ricochet from an opposing dogmatism, that of inherited beliefs and organized refusal to encounter change and to mobilize the mind to encompass it.

"I do not ask to be listened to, even if wrong," Abel tells us at the outset, "on the ground that my way of being wrong is interesting or idiosyncratic. I claim to be right." Among the areas where the claim is staked out is the problem of *Hamlet,* settled in this book "once and for all"; the exact approach to Beckett and to Brecht ("No, I do not think this is the point of *Galileo* at all, even if Brecht thought it was"); the precise and unvarying constituents of tragedy; and the nature of the entire complex change that has come over Western drama since Racine—elucidated in a formula. Abel's intransigent and grandiose independence also carries over into his style. At times his prose is marvelously supple and accurate. Owing nothing to academic totems, New York cult, or the circus of the ego, his best critical writing is informed by an urgent sense of the primacy of tight logical structures for containing aesthetic phenomena, and animated by a rare concreteness of response. But at least as frequently his writing is bewilderingly elliptical and compressed, tangential and foreshortened, full of premises without conclusions and conclusions without origins, and marked by assertions of meaning whose cogency is undermined by Abel's refusal to set down an approach to meaning, to trace the passage between ideas.

> Why are time and its effects so important to Beckett? Because, I suspect, of his nostalgia for eternity. Should we not be, at the very least, the playthings of eternity and not merely the playthings of time? Such is the question Beckett poses in his plays, thus suggesting that the actual characters are themselves the scenes of an invisible action: the action of time, which might be eternal itself, or the surrogate, although we cannot be sure of this, for eternity?

Metatheatre, then, is a battle between author and reader, and Abel's stature requires that his reader be as militant, or at least as strategy-minded, as he is. There is, one doesn't hesitate to say to Abel, no absolute truth in matters of criticism, the encounter is everything, and a mind that is interestingly wrong is surely to be preferred to one that is dully right. In the face of Abel's central claim to be right and his unwillingness to be thought of as interesting, I think him mostly wrong, but more valuable than if he were frugally right.

Abel's argument that tragedy disappeared from the theater after Racine is something that only those who think *Death of a Salesman* a tragedy would want to dispute. No plays of the past three hundred years have qualified as true tragedies by the standards that have been maintained and that derive from Greek, Elizabethan, and French classical examples. Still, Abel's approach is much more radical than other recent ones, for he restricts the definition of tragedy so that it leaves room for far fewer plays than even the most exacting criticism has allowed in up to now. In this new and narrow dispensation, Shakespeare is permitted to have written only one tragedy—*Macbeth*—Racine one or two, Corneille, Marlowe, and the other Elizabethans none at all.

There is nothing unconsidered (although there is something inevitably peevish) about Abel's exclusion of so many plays which have always been taken for tragedies—of *King Lear,* for example, about which Frank Kermode has recently said that "for everybody, [it] is the greatest and most inclusive of tragedies." Nothing can be a tragedy for Abel unless it meets his strict conditions. "Sophocles, in *King Oedipus at Colonus,*" he writes, "set forth the two essential movements of tragedy: in the first play about Oedipus, the protagonist is destroyed; in the second play, having lived through tragic destruction, he becomes divine, a daemon."

The definition is of course consistent with the events of *King Oedipus* and with those of several other plays Abel discusses, and in his hands it becomes an effective instrument of analysis and revelation as long as he is attending to just those works. But when he carries it over to other plays a resistance immediately springs up which his arguments are never able to overcome. It becomes clear that he has committed in a new form the classic error of making one kind of tragedy the norm or pattern for all others, of imposing a unity within which the objects he is handling will not rest obediently.

His insistence that tragedy can only unfold as the destruction of a protagonist who is then raised to power through suffering simply ignores all those plays in which such a process cannot be traced—the *Hippolytus, Hecuba,* and the *Bacchae* are examples. And his assertion that it cannot be written without the possession of a set of "implacable values" similarly brushes aside those plays in which implacable values do not lie behind the events, but rather developing values, as in the *Oresteia,* or turbulent or disintegrating ones, as in much of Euripides or Shakespeare.

Beyond this, one wishes to say that it is not values which distinguish tragedy from other forms of drama so much as actions, or rather action itself, which is precisely what is implacable—fateful, complete, irreversible, and felt to be at the center of existence. And it is the impossibility of our feeling action to have this character, of possessing the sense of existence as at the same time necessary and disastrous, that has made tragedy itself impossible, since the breakup of those coherent worlds where it was the most implacable vision of implacability and the gravest form to contain fatality.

But though Abel's formal description of tragedy is too limited, too formalistic and idiosyncratic, the fact that he has produced one, that he has made it so uncompromising and backed it with such vehemence, is a valuable accession to us. And this is because there is no area of drama criticism which is more ambiguous than the consideration of tragedy, even in regard to the generally accepted plays, none that allows more sentimentality, slackness of vision, and imprecision of ideas to flourish. Abel is one of the rare critics who see tragedy as stringent, rooted in history, and entirely anti-romantic; it is the romanticism of so much of our thinking about the form, our wish to see it as something ennobling and therefore a justification for all our lesser activities, instead of as a stern mode of awareness, that has plagued us for so long and permitted the canonization of inadequate creations.

There is more than the meaning of tragedy at stake. There is also the fact that drama criticism has lagged behind drama, that we have not yet elaborated an understanding of the ways in which the theater, at least the theater that has maintained itself as an art, has filled the metaphysical and aesthetic gap left by the disappearance of tragedy. And this is the area of Abel's second thesis, which rises directly out of the first. In his essay on *Hamlet,* a piece whose suggestiveness and originality are just able to redeem it from a debonair dismissal of *all* previous interpretations and a consistent misreading of whatever holds out against the theory, Abel sets about building his bridge between the end of one kind of form and sensibility and the beginning of another.

If the bridge is too narrow and if Abel commits the same reductive and highhanded acts on the near side as on the far, it is nevertheless one of the few serious attempts we have had to uncover the nature of the change. Abel sees Hamlet as the first self-conscious character in drama. And though this emphasis results in a failure to see the play whole, it also enables him to throw light on its central problem. If Hamlet is self-conscious, Abel says, it is because Shakespeare was self-conscious; he wished to write a tragedy in an age when tragedy was becoming impossible, and his protagonist, uncomfortable in this kind of play, was forced to "write" his own, to dramatize himself. The result was a "metaplay," the first in drama.

I think that Shakespeare did write a tragedy, one within which the new fact of self-consciousness had to be incorporated, but in any case, Abel's ideas about the character of Hamlet and the existence of a new element in drama become the basis of his theory of metatheatre. The new drama is characterized, Abel says, by two principles: one, that the world is a stage, and two, that life is a dream. That is to say, the philosophic drama that evolved after tragedy is the product of the modern self-conscious playwright's inability to accept the world as real. Metatheatre, unlike tragedy, dramatizes not the world but the consciousness, of which the world is felt to be a projection. It is the form most suited to an age from which implacable values have vanished, experience has become cut off from cosmologies, and the self has been left at the center of its own dream.

"I have asked myself," Abel writes, "can I be the first one to think of designating a form which has been in existence for so long a time . . . ?" Yes, he is the first, to designate it at any rate, but what he has named does not rest quietly under its new title. The fact is that, like Abel's notions of tragedy, the idea of metatheatre is extremely useful when it is employed to examine those plays it happens to fit, and is either irrelevant or obfuscatory everywhere else.

It is especially helpful when applied to Pirandello and Genet, two dramatists whose theater is "about" theater as much as it is about life, and who have used theatrical illusion to examine the nature of illusion itself and locate it in relation to events. It is worse than useless in regard to playwrights like Shaw and Ibsen, both of whom Abel has in fact to derogate because their plays will not lend themselves to his theories. (How reductive Abel can be is demonstrated by his remarks on *Ghosts,* whose "real subject" is not the "rigidity of Norwegian middle-class society," but rather the fatal rigidity of ideals in a world of fact.) And though his concept of metatheatre enables him to cut through a great deal of cant about Brecht and Beckett, it also threatens to turn his discussions of them into cranky bits of special pleading.

His reading of Brecht rests on the notion that Brecht was not interested in moral truth but in proclaiming and defending basic physical existence, the human body "in its assertiveness, natural ecstasy and desire to endure." This is an original idea and a valuable approach to Brecht, but it is not the only one and Abel's insistence that it is makes his reading more difficult to accept than it need have been. When he turns to Beckett his absolutism is still more damaging. Urging his interpretation, to the exclusion of any other, that *Endgame* and *Waiting for Godot* are "directly and undeviatingly about Joyce and Beckett's relation to him," Abel comes close to being merely perverse.

But then Abel is forever running this risk. That he always eventually escapes it is testimony to the boldness and intensity of his ideas, whatever their waywardness, and still more to his powerful responsiveness to drama before the logical and categorical processes get into motion. Even in his most outlandish essays, those on *King Lear* or Beckett, for instance, this openness to aesthetic experience keeps the losses from being complete. And in those pieces where the theorizing is suspended—his review of *J. B.* and Djuna Barnes's *The Antiphon,* where he brilliantly demolishes the pretensions of modern verse drama, or of *The Connection,* in which he exactly delineates the strange new antipleasure and destruction of the gods that Gelber's play announces—there is no critic of drama who can surpass him.

The point, I think, is that where you feel compelled to be on top of all aesthetic reality, to urge your views instead of your taste, and to be right because so much is flagrantly and complacently wrong, you are going to suffer from the deprivation of room, patience, humility, and tentativeness that criticism requires. The problem of tragedy is not to be settled in a formula, nor is the nature of the metaphysical change that has come over recent drama to be accounted for by simply taking the prefix off "metaphysical" and attaching it to the arena of the change. "The greatest failure of insight," La Rochefoucauld wrote, "is not falling short of the goal, but passing it." In his brilliant, bellicose, capricious, and unrelenting attempt to make a place for his insight in American thinking about the drama, Abel has certainly gone far past the goal. It remains

to say, of course, that we are better off than if he had not addressed himself to any goal at all, or to a trivial one. But the damage is there.
Commentary, Oct. 1963

Eugène Ionesco's *Notes and Counter Notes*

After Eugène Ionesco's first play, *The Bald Soprano,* opened in Paris in 1950 it ran for weeks before audiences that sometimes numbered fewer than ten. What these adventurous spectators saw was a revolutionary drama which had abandoned the chief conventions of naturalistic theater—recognizable characters, coherent plot—and used language to mock language and logic to make logic seem insane. Like all upsetters of tradition, Ionesco has since been dismissed, derided, or treated as an errant child. But while his works may never fill scalpers' pockets, they are performed throughout the world, and his reputation is secure. With Samuel Beckett and Jean Genet, he is a playwright who has changed the contemporary stage.

Perhaps the most subtle way his detractors have found of deflecting Ionesco's thrust against the ramparts of conventional theater is to have pinned a label on them. He is now as identified with the "theater of the absurd" as Ibsen was with the "theater of ideas." The result, as with Ibsen, is that he is widely seen as an exemplifier instead of a creator, a theatrical real-estate agent instead of a colonizer of new lands. But while Beckett and Genet, almost equally victims of labeling and categorization, have remained silent about their work, Ionesco has spoken and written extensively and with lucidity in defense of his, especially of its right to be considered on its own terms.

These declarations—essays, notebook entries, texts of speeches and interviews—collected in France in 1962, have now been translated by Donald Watson and published in the United States as *Notes and Counter Notes.* They compose, perhaps, the most eloquent statement of a playwright's aims and attitudes we have had in years. Throughout, one theme is dominant: "I do not teach," Ionesco writes, "I am a witness; I do not explain, I try to explain myself." In his wild, remorseless dramas, people are killed with the *word* "knife," a corpse continues to grow, men turn into rhinoceroses, and objects proliferate dementedly. He has embodied a personal vision far transcending psychology or sociology or politics: a vision of man made giddy and terrified by the precariousness and vulnerability of existence.

"I feel that life is nightmarish, painful and unbearable," he writes. "Look around you: wars, catastrophes and disasters, hatred and persecution, confusion, death lying in wait for all of us . . . we struggle . . . in a world that appears to be in the grip of some terrible fever . . . Have we not the impression that the real is unreal . . . that this world is not our true world?"

This sense of unreality, of action having no coherent basis and language serving to disguise meaning as much as express it, informs his plays and marks their break with a theater of narrative progression and verbal directness. This theater depends on an acceptance of order and consistency in our lives. But for Ionesco it is precisely such unexamined acceptance that freezes us and limits our freedom. "We need to be virtually bludgeoned into detachment from our daily lives, our habits and mental laziness, which conceal from us the strangeness of the world . . .. art means the revelation of certain things that reason, everyday habits of thought conceal. Art pierces everyday reality. It springs from a different state of mind." It is above all the comic state of mind that Ionesco believes makes the "unendurable" able to be borne—"Laughter comes as reprieve: we laugh so as not to cry."

Much of the book is taken up with Ionesco's replies to critics, among them Kenneth Tynan, who accuse him of a lack of social commitment, but who seem to him to be themselves "in search of messiahs." Even more detailed are his explications of the role of the avant-garde. Far from being arbitrarily new and different, he writes, the avant-garde is always concerned with a return to an earlier tradition, a rediscovery of primal forms and powers which have gone dead through clichéd language and gestures. "The theater is the prisoner . . . of conventions, taboos, hardened mental habits . . . To renew one's idiom or one's language is to renew one's conception or vision of the world."

In his new apartment on Boulevard Montparnasse, filled with 2,500 books and several dozen rhinoceros figurines, Ionesco spoke last week with *Newsweek*'s Yorick Blumenfeld. "My book," he said, "is mostly a response to those critics who could not, or did not want to understand my plays because they up-set their preconceived notions of the theater. There must be freedom of art."

The fifty-one-year-old playwright was forceful in his admiration of Beckett, whose work "is increasing in richness and diversity," and skeptical of the term "theater of the absurd." At present, he said, he is working on two plays, one of which he would not describe—"I am only in the period of research . . . like an explorer in a deep jungle looking for clues"—the other a drama about the Lon-don plague.

At the end of the interview Ionesco remarked that he was "becoming a mon-ument" and displayed a copy of *Rhinoceros* used by American high-school stu-dents learning French. Then he asked: "What is the use of becoming a monu-ment? Look, the first question at the end of the first lesson is 'What is a grocery store?' " And he burst into wholehearted laughter.

Newsweek, May 11, 1964

Eric Bentley's *The Life of the Drama*
and Robert Brustein's
The Theatre of Revolt

The health of an art is never in exact relationship to that of its criticism. Where art is moribund or immature, criticism may draw temporary replenishment from raids on the past, or define itself against a day of renewal. But in general it is naïve to expect criticism to flourish where its subject has a perennially thin life, and the history of drama criticism in America bears this out.

In an atmosphere where static and mindless theatricality squeezes out the imagination—where, in fact, the nearer plays approach the urgency and deci-siveness of art the more menacing they appear to audiences and popular review-ers alike—the critic of insight and efficacy is an intermittent presence at best.

Never more than one or two salient weekly commentators writing at the same time, a handful of widely spaced books of value—Stark Young's *The Theatre*, Eric Bentley's *The Playwright as Thinker*, Francis Fergusson's *The Idea of a Theater*—such has been the substance of drama criticism in this country.

What feeds the little we do have is the European drama: text, occasion, theme, possibility, the theater of Europe are what the few intelligent American critics mostly write about, reserving a small stock of seriousness for Eugene O'Neill, Tennessee Williams, and whoever, like Edward Albee, comes along with an achievement beyond the pack's. It is what, for their different purposes, Eric Bentley and Robert Brustein write about in these new books, the publication of which in the same week is a notable event, since two such original, complex, important works on the drama are ordinarily separated by half a generation in our culture.

The two authors have a great deal in common. Both have figured centrally in that splendid, lonely chapter of American intellectual history, the *New Republic*'s tradition of unimpeachable drama criticism, which was carried on for so long by Stark Young. Bentley served the magazine from 1952 to 1956, and Brustein has been there since 1959. Both, in addition, are professors of dramatic literature at Columbia, where among other duties they alternate in giving that school's big survey course in drama since Ibsen. Yet, to our great advantage, their books—however much they share fundamental aesthetic assumptions and a community of taste—are thoroughly divergent in subject, style, procedure, and tone.

The Theatre of Revolt is Brustein's first book. A series of essays on eight major modern playwrights, it is organized, as its title implies, around the theme of rebellion, which he sees as the impulse and ambiance that radically distinguishes the recent stage from what he calls the "theatre of communion."

"By theatre of communion," he writes, "I mean the theatre of the past, dominated by Sophocles, Shakespeare and Racine, where traditional myths were enacted before an audience of believers against the background of a shifting but still coherent universe. By theatre of revolt, I mean the theatre of the great insurgent modern dramatists, where myths of rebellion are enacted before a dwindling number of spectators in a flux of vacancy, bafflement and accident."

His eight subjects—Ibsen, Strindberg, Chekhov, Shaw, Pirandello, Brecht, O'Neill, and Genet—do indeed yield themselves, in one or another degree, to an elucidating notion of this kind. They were all dissidents, profoundly at odds,

as makers of plays, with the theaters of their time and, as artistic conscious-
nesses, with the basic values of their societies. Moreover, although Brustein
tends, wrongly I think, to see this as a corrupt or decadent form of the Romantic thrust that he regards them all as exemplifying, the greatest among them
were seized with a rebelliousness against the conditions of existence itself. One
may quarrel also with his inclusion of O'Neill, who, as he admits, was a failure
as a rebel and only came into true art when he lowered his sights and shaped a
domestic drama of acceptance, and with his exclusion of Eugene Ionesco and,
especially, Samuel Beckett. But these are minor strictures on a book of exceptional strength and usefulness.

Brustein's particular exegeses are, almost without exception, brilliantly ordered and persuasive. He is especially fine on Ibsen, whose "drama is the biography of his rebellious spirit," Chekhov ("while the surface of his plays seems
drenched with tedium vitae and spiritual vapors, the depths are charged with
energy and dissent"), Brecht ("his failure to be a Utopian ideologist is his triumph as a dramatic poet"), Shaw ("if he is fading from us today, then this is because he stubbornly refused to examine, more than fitfully, those illusions he
held in common with all men"), and Pirandello.

But what is undoubtedly the crucial accomplishment of the book, and its
chief significance, is that for the first time on a thoroughgoing scale contemporary drama has been brought into the larger intellectual and aesthetic history of
our time. "It is atop the broken hierarchies, discredited values, and collapsed
institutions of traditional culture that the modern dramatist meditates his revolt," Brustein writes. What has long since been a commonplace about poetry,
fiction, music, and the graphic arts, has now, with his book, come to declare itself about the age's serious drama as well.

The Life of the Drama, Eric Bentley's first book since 1947, apart from collections of reviews and fugitive essays, is a very different sort of undertaking. The
quintessence of his long theoretical and practical experience of the theater, it
can be read as an extension of the work done by Young in *The Theatre,* and by
Bentley himself in *The Playwright as Thinker.* Informal in tone, drawing heavily on analogical and illustrative material from the life outside theater, upsetting
conventional ideas at every turn, it is a remarkable exploration of the roots and
bases of dramatic art, the most far-reaching and revelatory we have had.

Bentley describes what he has done as a "study of the life of the drama in
which, without denying the meaning great drama ultimately has, I start out
from the drama's 'low life,' its points of contact with our mundane existence,
where this is furthest from ideology and ideals." In this respect his book is

sharply divergent from Brustein's, whose investigation is precisely into the "highest" meanings of plays. But the two books are complementary, not antagonistic; between them, drama criticism exercises its widest and most supple powers.

Bentley's examination enters into every aspect of dramatic creation, from plot and character to the role of thought, the nature of the actor's contribution, and the forms of dramatic composition, which he divides, traditionally enough, into melodrama, farce, comedy, tragedy, and that contemporary mode we call tragicomedy. But there is nothing traditional about his findings; nowhere does he rely on assumptions he has not tested: everywhere his book reveals that freedom from academic constriction on the one hand and populist rhetoric on the other, which is so much rarer in our drama criticism than in the study of any of the other arts.

Intricately fashioned, proceeding from the broadest ground to the most transcendent conclusions, *The Life of the Drama* scarcely lends itself to summary. But its central thesis is that "the flowers of dramatic art have their roots in crude action," and everything follows from that. This belief of Bentley's underlies the hundreds of liberating and luminous *aperçus* and formulations with which the book is filled:

> "The playwright's first intention . . . is to create existences."
>
> "The actor's fundamental contribution is not mimicry but vitality."
>
> "Two rules for budding playwrights: if you wish to attract the audience's attention, be violent; if you wish to hold it, be violent again."
>
> "The dramas that attain the highest intensity of feeling will be found, one and all, to be, like *Phaedra,* elaborate structures, into the making of which went a remarkable mind."
>
> "Melodrama is the Naturalism of the dream life."
>
> "Higher forms transcend lower forms, they do not repudiate them."

The final pages, on the nature of modern tragicomedy, constitute the best refutation of the argument for "positive statement" in drama that I have seen. "In our time," Bentley writes, "if the man of letters [read: man of mind and conscience] hears himself uttering the big affirmations, he has to ask himself if in seeking his salvation he has not got himself well and truly damned. Now when the affirmations are suspect, negotiations may be more honorable. In these circumstances, the negative attains the force of the positive."

Bound to the physical and the contingent in a way that the other arts are not, lagging behind the philosophic and aesthetic changes that each age undergoes, barely catching up in the next, its theoreticians having to expend inordinate energy simply keeping its credentials as an art in view—the drama has for more than a hundred years been a supplicant at the door of the House of Ideas. At no time has it been given a more sympathetic hearing and, as a consequence, a more impassioned advocacy, than it is getting right now. With Brustein's and Bentley's books, thinking about the drama has finally entered into its maturity in this country.

New York Herald Tribune Book Week, Oct. 4, 1964

Herbert Blau's
The Impossible Theater

It will be a miracle if Herbert Blau's book doesn't put off both classes of readers who could best profit by it. In some ways the most important, certainly the most passionate statement of what it means to try to fuse art and theater in America, *The Impossible Theater* has two central handicaps: it is devastatingly honest, which will estrange most professional theater people, and it is clumsily written, which may disconcert those intellectuals whose search for style extends everywhere.

Well, those are the risks Blau takes. He is anything but a cautious man; if he were cautious, he would not be the co-director of what is undoubtedly the best, most adventurous, permanent theater group in the United States, the San Francisco Actor's Workshop. Among other things, this book is a history of the Workshop, but that means it is also the history—rash, candid, vigorous, and disarmingly vulnerable—of a mind at work in an area where mind has always been anathema.

"Our theater remains a stronghold of non-ideas," Blau writes, as one leading premise of his book, and you cannot have the slightest quarrel with him. He writes also: "The failure and fatuousness of the American theater . . . the pieties substituting for vision on and around Broadway . . . [acting] in which most of those who are working are ashamed of what they do." The indictment builds and you go on agreeing, until finally, in a magnificent break with the pieties themselves, Blau says what lovers of the drama and observers of the commercial theater have long wanted to say, a great, purgative outburst of indignation and contempt: "There are times when, confronted with the despicable behavior of people in the American theater, I feel like the lunatic Lear on the heath, wanting to 'kill, kill, kill, kill, kill, kill!' "

This is extremely shocking, of course, but how salutary! For it is precisely the American theater's continual refusal to tolerate any shocks to its self-esteem, coupled with our genteel newspaper criticism which will not or cannot see how the theater drags miserably behind the other arts in America, that, as George Jean Nathan remarked, has been a major cause of its perpetual adolescence.

It was out of disgust with the commercial theater's corrupt standards and mindless procedures that in 1951 Blau, along with Jules Irving, founded the Actor's Workshop. Their rough inspiration, sociologically if not aesthetically, was the Group Theater of the 1930s. "Our first mission," Blau writes, "was to establish the ground upon which we could believe in our own talents, encourage rapport, and subsequently act together to recover the passion lost [after] the demise of the Group."

From its first production, Philip Barry's *Hotel Universe*, to its recent offering of Brecht's *Caucasian Chalk Circle*, the Workshop has come a long way, artistically and physically. It survived, as Blau candidly says, "in spite of the general neglect and even civic suspicion" it encountered in San Francisco. And its survival constitutes an epic of passionate yet crafty dedication to the possible, a tightrope set between the poles of an unready but educable audience and a risk-taking, uncertain, and ceaselessly self-discovering company.

What was achieved, or is in the process of being achieved, is a "permanent theater of identifiable character," which is what the rest of our regional theaters, in which out of despair over Broadway we place so much hope, have so far failed to attain. The directors of these theaters may learn from Blau how to survive, but only through attention to his spirit, not through fidelity to his practice. For *The Impossible Theater* makes it very clear that survival is a matter of the most agonizing rapprochement between one's artistic desires and the realities of one's physical situation. That is why the theater is so nearly "impossible";

its dependence upon audiences, its thousand practical impediments, its impure structure in combat with the pure impulse of the artist, all conspire to make it a battleground where victory is at best always fugitive.

Blau devotes much of the book to his own role as director of specific plays. "The director," he writes, "if he is fulfilling his function, is a Socratic gadfly, questioning the text, the actor and the stage itself, referring them all back, and himself, to the concrete evidence of the world." In his analyses of plays as diverse as *Lear* and *Endgame* he is continually making that reference back to the world, especially to the particular world of crisis and cold war with which the Workshop's life is coeval. His belief is that the theater is the "public art of crisis," and this determines—overdetermines, one is sometimes driven to feel—a great many of his interpretations and exegeses.

To use "the theater as an image of the Cold War and the Cold War as an image of the theater" affords a powerful hold on some contemporary psychic and social realities, but it also leads Blau into a narrowness which sometimes ends by politicizing the plays, converting works as perennial and unlocal as *Mother Courage* and *Waiting for Godot* into mere instruments of defense against present social disorder and malaise. Thus, after a brilliant analysis of Beckett's play, Blau feels compelled abruptly to tamp it down into a narrow political space, leaving the reader with a sense of injury and loss.

There is a loss, too, in Blau's style and literary manner. It is a loss, in the first place, of clarity, due primarily to an inability to refrain from introducing *everything* he knows or feels or has read about a subject. He quotes twice where once would do, and once where his own words would be better. He uses four adjectives where two already constitute a supererogation. And he is frequently carried away by his feelings into apocalyptic clichés: "Existence is a mortal wound. Man is his own disease."

And yet, difficult, awkward, overwritten as it often is, *The Impossible Theater* makes nearly all books on the state of drama in America seem pallid and evasive by comparison. In its unclassifiable way it marks the start of honesty and seriousness in our thinking about the theater that we have and that we might, with courage, ardor, unselfishness, and stamina such as Blau's, some day come to possess.

New York Times Book Review, Dec. 13, 1964

Jerzy Grotowski's
Towards a Poor Theatre

Nobody knows better than Jerzy Grotowski how, in the theater even more than in the other arts, the likeliest fate of original ideas is a swift congealing into formula, and how what one proposes as spirit is almost unfailingly seized on for conversion into property. Stanislavsky, Grotowski recently remarked, "was killed by his disciples, and I think I am going the same route." Disciples are of course idolaters; much more interested in usefulness than in truth, they kill by *handling,* by the manipulation of intellectual acts and the wielding of consciousness as though it were materiel. Stanislavsky was brought down by the construction of a "method" out of his liberating ideas, Antonin Artaud by a hypostatized and self-conscious "theater of cruelty," and Grotowski, the third great original theater mind of the century, will be laid low by having his "poor theater" turned into a blueprint.

The present volume, which had been available in English only in a paperback edition published in Denmark in 1968, contains nearly everything a would-be disciple might want. Translated by various hands, the book is composed of Grotowski's most important theoretical pronouncements—speeches, essays, interviews—together with descriptions by him and others of his Polish Laboratory Theater's training procedures and exegeses of its main productions by Ludwik Flaszen, the group's literary adviser. It also contains a number of photographs of these productions and of the actors' preparations for them.

Read in the right spirit, which is to say without avarice or the itch to exploit, *Towards a Poor Theatre* is a book of unequaled significance not only for the theater but for something a great deal more central: the state of our thinking about the nature of aesthetic creation and about the place of imagination in an increasingly utilitarian world. For, in investigating and elaborating a new and immensely rigorous enterprise for the stage, Grotowski has at the same time enunciated a new general aesthetic, or rather has resurrected and deepened a notion of artistic action which our age had almost buried. In a period when "life" is the seductive dimension and imagination is recommended mainly as utility, his ideas about the absolute independence of art and its existence as counterstatement have the exact revelatory force and self-confidence of a blow against fashion and so of a potential deliverance from temptation.

This temptation and the possibilities of release from its corruptions are what Grotowski is all about. Everything in his activity and thought—the evangelical calls to order and implacable repudiations of established practice, the extraordinarily exacting training methods, the inflexible "élitism" of his group's career in public—rises out of his disengagement, from the pressure toward *culture,* the process by which art is turned into domestic object and commodity. More decisively still, it rises from his rejection of the notion that art ought to be converted life, a matter of enhancement, reflection, or interpretation of experience, instead of an increment and an opposition to what we ordinarily undergo. In his "poor theater" what has been sought is action and gesture "between dream and reality," original statement, the creation of theatrical truth through the release of "pure" impulses attained by an escape from the "exact imitations of human reactions and calculated reconstructions."

The "poverty" of this theater lies in its elimination of everything the stage doesn't need, all the accoutrements and paraphernalia—costumes, make-up, lighting, sound effects, sets, a strictly defined playing area—that enable it to avoid its unique and "irreplaceable" reality: the "actor-spectator relationship of perceptual direct . . . communion." To prepare to mount this requires an attitude and morale so radically different from the prevailing theater's as to constitute the state of mind of an almost wholly new kind of artist.

"We are not after the recipes," Grotowski writes, "the stereotypes which are the prerogative of professionals. We do not attempt to answer questions such as: 'How does one show irritation? How should one walk? How should Shakespeare be played?' . . . Instead, one must ask the actor: 'What are the obstacles blocking you on your way towards the total act which must engage all your psycho-physical resources, from the most instinctive to the most rational?' I want to take away, steal from the actor all that disturbs him. That which is creative will remain with him. It is a liberation. If nothing remains, it means he is not creative."

The basis of Grotowski's aesthetic ideas, as this book makes abundantly clear, is his conviction that life exhibits itself in its "natural" condition as a set of clichés and stereotypes, which means that the preliminary task of the actor—and, by extension, of any artist—is to resist the temptation to be "lifelike." Beyond this he has to come upon new forms, precisely those that life has been unable to propose on its own, and this is possible only through a series of sacrificial acts. By means of these movements of repudiation of stereotypes, this patient passive waiting for the discovery of what lies behind "the mask of common vision," the actor transforms himself from a "courtesan," one who woos the public through polished techniques for the display of "beauty and gymnastics," into someone "holy."

Words like "holiness," "profanation," "monastic," and "sacred" are prominent in Grotowski's vocabulary, along with another apparently antithetical kind of diction: "autonomic," "ideoplastic," "tropistic." It is in just this confrontation of the dissimilar and even violently opposed orders of value and experience that these words suggest, in their juxtaposition and interpenetration, that Grotowski's theater takes on its nature and shape. He is distinguished by his ethic of creative purity and sacrifice, but this ethic is given weight and exemplary being by the most rigorously scientific "research" into the body's possibilities and the most accurate articulations of what is discovered.

Grotowski has described the artist's effort as one composed of "sincerity and precision." The former is a moral and spiritual category, the latter a technical and instrumental one. It is the absence of one or the other quality that characterizes so many artistic enterprises today. In the theater sincerity alone is likely to result in lax humanitarianism such as the Living Theatre's; precision by itself leads to Mike Nichols. Grotowski's "secret" is that he has been both sincere and precise; he has fought to obtain the painful and not yet known truth beneath appearances and to develop clear signs for their manifestation. There is nothing programmatic in this effort, nothing that can be put directly to account. If anything, it provides a most radical and inspiring education in *what not to do;* but that of course is something disciples have the greatest difficulty in understanding.

New York Times Book Review, Feb. 8, 1970

Martin Esslin's *The Peopled Wound*:
The Work of Harold Pinter

Martin Esslin is a critic whose usefulness lies less in original thinking or insightfulness than in lucid exposition, the kind of critic who possesses thoroughness in place of brilliance, breadth instead of depth. His book *The Theater of the Absurd* (which gave that unfortunate term its currency) may have made every interesting play of the century seem to have been written by the same person, as a fellow critic observed, but it had value as a source of information and as raw material for the gaining of perspectives on a phenomenon more complex than Esslin knew. The same thing was true of his long study of Brecht, a work mostly firm and reliable as long as it dealt with the facts of the plays and the life, but often soggy and unconvincing whenever it turned to exegesis and interpretation.

Esslin's new book, one of the first full-length studies of Harold Pinter, begins on an apologetic note. "Is there any justification," he writes, "for a book on an author who . . . [is] not yet forty years old?" Whereupon he proceeds to offer us a book which, if justification can be won by completeness, indefatigability of research, and attention to detail, will clear him before any imaginable board of inquiry.

The book's embarrassingly literary title is itself an indication of how far he has ranged. It comes from a line in an essay by Pinter on Shakespeare, written at around the age of twenty, when Pinter was a beginning actor and sometime poet. Esslin tells us a great deal more than most of us had known about Pinter's origins in the Jewish East End of London and about his subsequent life and career, most of the account being in the form of a chronology that has its solemn-silly moments: "1957. Pinter leaves Hackney Down Grammar School . . . 1958, February, Pinter takes a flat in Chiswick, London." But the book hasn't set out to be a biographical study and Esslin soon gets down to his main business, an extraordinarily exhaustive, painstaking going-through of all the plays, with excursions into the early poetry, the later film scripts, and an unfinished novel, *The Dwarfs*.

His method is the extremely conventional one of providing detailed summaries of the events of each play and then moving on to elucidate and make interpretations. One thing this does is make it easier for the reader to determine where he ought to follow attentively and with trust and where skepticism ought to take over. If you aren't familiar with a particular play of Pinter's, Esslin is a reliable guide to what happens in it. (He is especially valuable for his summaries of discarded or unfinished plays and those written for television but altered for the stage.) But once past that, we enter the realm of Esslin's ideas about Pinter, and what is needed is a critique of *them,* or rather of what Esslin does with them.

These are the main ones: Pinter's basis is in a deceptive realism, one that presses toward nonrealistic ends; he has a special kind of ambiguity and illogic coherent with those of experience itself; he uses language as "poetry" rather than as a mere dispenser of cognitive or physical information; he makes crucial use of pauses, repetitions and silence in order to get at the meanings behind speech; he creates "metaphors" of the human condition and "archetypes of cosmic significance" instead of anecdotes or circumscribed, easily assimilated tales.

Now there is nothing very original in all this and nothing seriously to dispute. At his best, working among these notions, Esslin is able to offer some helpful illustrations of how Pinter's dialogue achieves its effects and some minor illumination of the way he departs from traditional dramaturgy. But Esslin has larger ambitions, without the critical equipment or the imaginative power to realize them, so that his book, for all the general adequacy and rightness of its governing ideas, distills in the end a peculiar sense of stagnation, a miring in the approaches laid down by terminology, and has the earnest, unlimber, uninventive tone of a doctoral thesis.

After his clean, accurate descriptions of the plays' events, Esslin most often winds up in vague, rhetorical conclusions such as these:

> "Pinter's plays present us with a situation, or pattern of interlocking situations, designed to coalesce into a lyrical structure of moods and emotional insights."
>
> ". . . the over-all effect is one of mystery, of uncertainty, of poetic ambiguity."
>
> "A play like *The Birthday Party* can be understood only as a complex poetic image. Such an image exists, simultaneously, on a number of levels. A complex pattern of association and allusion is assembled to express a complex emotional state."

Besides the fact that *The Birthday Party* is no such achieved poetic image (one of Esslin's worst failings is his inability or refusal to see the real defects of Pinter's early plays and consequently to see how greatly he has developed), such sentences as these, with their atmosphere of the seminar room, offer no true way into the work nor, what is most important, any heightened awareness of its presence, its specificity and singular existence.

Esslin's excessive concern for establishing what serious drama criticism has known for a long time—that plays should not be mere stories but structures of experience and that verisimilitude is a guarantee of nothing—makes one wonder if his book isn't, consciously or not, addressed to those cultured bourgeois audiences for whom Pinter is a perplexity but who would love to get him right. For such readers the continual presence of words like "metaphor," "archetype," and "ambiguity" is a coercion toward acceptance, an instrumentality of adult education, whereas anyone more sophisticated will understand that such terminology tells us very little of what Pinter is really doing or how he is different from all the other writers whose work is metaphorical, ambiguous, and archetypal too.

On occasion Esslin seems able to see this himself, with the result that he offers interpretations, which is to say he stuffs the categories he has erected with possible meanings and theoretical significances. At these times he plunges right past his own early statement that "Pinter very rightly refrains from commenting on the 'meaning' of his plays." The interpretations he arrives at are in nearly every case either clearly wrong, or right but reductive: *The Homecoming,* for example, is surely "about" something more or other than an Oedipal situation, *The Caretaker* is more (or less) than a metaphor for the relations of fathers and sons.

These fixed readings are less prominent in the book than Esslin's tendency to encircle the plays with terminology and his narrow experience of them as sensuous, independent, unprogrammatic works. This limitation is what lies behind Esslin's pervasive judgment that Pinter's art is finally about "alienation," the difficulty of "verification of identity," "noncommunication," and the like. Judgments of this kind, which rise from theories of literature instead of full encounters with it, are never able to account for the fact that, as in Pinter's case, the works themselves are not alienated, succeed in establishing certain kinds of identity, and are capable—which is precisely the miracle—of communication. *New York Times Book Review,* Sept. 13, 1970

Bertolt Brecht: Collected Plays,
Edited by Ralph Manheim
and John Willett

By now Bertolt Brecht has been fully accepted into cultural history, where his presence continues to give difficulty to pedagogues and others with a stake in clear, orderly classifications. No important contemporary playwright has inspired such vehement polemic; none is more resistant to schemes of interpretation. His extraliterary life, notable for a highly idiosyncratic Marxism and a capacity to improvise commitments, has been thrown back at his art or used to help justify it. The alternative portraits are of Brecht as wily, self-serving, a hoodwinker, or as infinitely resourceful, a master strategist of survival. The one thing clear is that his influence on the theater, which derives as much from his theoretical writings as from his plays, has been rivaled in our time only by those of Stanislavsky and Artaud.

Brecht has suffered from the same kinds of misreadings and distortions as they, the same reduction to the programmatic. As Stanislavsky was narrowed to a formulary "method," and Artaud to an exploitable motif of "cruelty," so Brecht has been closely framed by his ideas of "epic" theater and of "the alienation effect" as a principle of acting. He sometimes seemed to help the process along, but he was to learn from his own practice as a playwright and director that these notions worked as anything but blueprints. Perspectives on stage art, constituents of a dramatist's morale, like his more diffuse idea of a theater to oppose the "culinary"—his term for popular commercial drama—they operated as possibilities for a resurrection. Like Stanislavsky's and Artaud's, as well as Jerzy Grotowski's at this moment, Brecht's theoretical writings ought to be read as prophecies and calls to order more than as the platform of a technocrat.

At the same time his plays ought to be read and seen as both more and less than the exemplifications of his ideas. At different periods they moved with different rhythms and toward diverse imaginative objectives, but throughout his work we can discern the radical tension, which never left him, between opposing conceptions of drama's uses. The received wisdom about Brecht is either that he triumphed over his didactic and ideological impulses through a powerful *prédilection d'artiste*, or else that tendentiousness was the very thing that brought him down. The truth is that he brought about a revivification of drama through a new fusion of feeling and idea—and of the private and the public—and that this accomplishment emerged from the contradictions of his being and would not have been possible without them.

In any case, Brecht is there, large, complicated, and very far from having been exhausted. And since a good or even an endurable production of any of his plays is extremely rare in America, we can be grateful for the prospect of having his complete works placed before us in a uniform series of new translations into English. The enterprise is what is usually described in literary circles as an "event," and in this instance the term is not so hyperbolic. The collected works of significant writers like Brecht are much more likely to be published in Europe or England (where this project originates) than in America, where such completeness, conceived of as a duty to culture and a tribute to a man, is hardly fashionable.

The plan is for nine volumes of plays, one of poetry, and one or two of prose (presumably the writings on theater and *The Threepenny Novel*), the second volume to be released a year from now, with the others coming along at half-yearly intervals. If the format of this first volume is followed, each will contain texts that are as "definitive" as the editors can obtain (Brecht was notable for never regarding any of his plays as finished and for continually reworking them) with variant readings, notes, Brecht's own pronouncements on the plays, and editorial comments.

Volume One is made up of all the plays of Brecht's first or "Bavarian" period: the six years from 1918, when at the age of twenty he completed his first play, *Baal*, to 1924, when he left Munich for Berlin, a talked-about young playwright in search of wider conquests. The other plays include *Drums in the Night*, the work which gained him his first recognition, *In the Jungle of Cities*, and the very free adaptation of Marlowe's *Edward II* which he wrote with Lion Feuchtwanger. The book also contains five one-act plays, none (as far as I know) hitherto translated and none of more than historical interest.

Both *Drums in the Night* and *Edward II* stand apart from almost all Brecht's other work in being what might be called intrinsically antipolitical, pure visions of oppression by the movements of power, the former grimly comic in tone, the latter the closest thing to a tragedy Brecht ever wrote. *Drums* deals obliquely with the Spartakus rebellion of 1919, and its irreverent attitude toward that event was to trouble Brecht later, as some of his remarks reprinted here make clear. *Edward II* turns Marlowe's tale of a king ruined by his "friendship" for a young man toward a much more explicit homosexual theme and toward a far blacker species of consciousness. Both plays are worth knowing, but the two in this volume that are indispensable are *Baal* and *In the Jungle of Cities*. In the face of prevailing opinion, a case can be made that these plays are among Brecht's greatest and may even outlive the so-called "big," late works like *Mother Courage, Galileo,* and *The Caucasian Chalk Circle.* Certainly they are Brecht's most mysterious dramas, most wayward and "unconscious," as well as most purely poetic. *Baal,* one of the more remarkable first plays in stage history, owes a great deal to the most astounding first play of all, Georg Büchner's *Danton's Death.* And just as our fetish for growth and progress, even in artistic matters, has kept us from seeing that Büchner's genius, though he died at twenty-three, was complete and not merely precocious, so Brecht's *Baal* is ordinarily thought of as the greatly interesting but immature work of someone destined for larger achievements.

It may be. Yet *Baal* contains nearly all the elements of Brecht's future work, without that slight sense of the schematic and didactic we can detect in the last plays, in this early dream of a figure both blessed and cursed, a hugely sensual "animal" who lives outside society and morality and dies of life itself—the "disease"—and in *In the Jungle of Cities,* a drama about an unfathomable, nightmarish "fight between two men in the gigantic city of Chicago," Brecht drew on resources of violent lyricism and imaginative daring he was never again to command so fully. Immeasurably the most difficult of his works, they continue to be the least susceptible to the orderly processes of criticism, the least likely to be turned from art into the illustrations of ideas.

They are also, naturally, the most difficult to translate. Brecht's complex verbal sources, from urban slang to street ballads to formal literature, have made all his works hard nuts for translators. In keeping with the spirit of the "event," I would like to be able to announce that these new versions are greatly superior to anything we now possess, that for the first time we have Brecht satisfyingly in English, etc. But that isn't the case. On the evidence of this first volume, the Pantheon series is going to provide a supplement and an alternative to the less formal and less complete one published by Grove under Eric Bentley's editorship, but it isn't going to replace it.

A bit cleaner, more colloquial (all translators should ponder the benefits of contractions), having the advantage of some recent findings by Brecht scholars, the new versions are welcome, but not as any kind of revelation. What I mean, to confine myself to *Baal,* is that William E. Smith's and Ralph Manheim's "sexual intercourse is dirty" is preferable to Bentley's and Martin Esslin's "the union of bodies is a filthy thing" and "you're too full of schnapps or too full of religion" to "you have either too much brandy or too much religion in you"—but the distance isn't anything to marvel at. The Bentley-Esslin version has in fact an occasional edge over the new one: "love is better than mere pleasure" makes more sense, for example, than "better to love than to enjoy."

But, barring the flagrantly inept or inaccurate, translations should be allowed to exist as possible readings, not scientifically determinable ones. The new series is valuable not for the reconsiderations it brings about or for any wholly new perspective, but because it takes Brecht as seriously as he ought to be. To leave nothing out, to offer the plays in the company of the changes Brecht made and his own thoughts about the works, is to give us what we need to begin to do him justice.

New York Times Book Review, Jan. 24, 1971

The Letters of Sean O'Casey,
Edited by David Krause

He described himself in the titles of several of his books as a "green crow" and a "flying wasp," but the image of Sean O'Casey that's fixed in my mind is of a more ungainly sort of winged creature: a crane or stork, a great flapping, squawking, long-necked, near-sighted bird with Adam's apple bobbing in rage or indignation. O'Casey pretended to—and sometimes possessed—the homely uncorrupted sagacity of the crow of our animal tales, and regarded himself as called on to administer stinging wasp-like rebukes to social and artistic complacency. Yet as this ponderous volume of his correspondence demonstrates, he was often simple-minded rather than innocently wise, and querulous, even mean-spirited, instead of intellectually valorous.

There's nothing to be surprised at in this: we expect a man's letters—*a for-*

tiori a writer's—to reveal his dissonances and contradictions. Still, in the matter of O'Casey something of more than psychic or moral interest is at stake when we find him displayed to us in this informal way. Anomalies and contradictions abound in his writing and in the zone of estimation that surrounds it. What is his place, this troublesome, erratic, autodidactic Irishman? Was he really one of the great modern playwrights, as so many textbooks and so much popular consideration would have it? I remember the litany from my student days: Ibsen, Strindberg, Chekhov, Shaw, O'Casey, O'Neill—the recent masters.

His towering importance is naturally assumed by the editor of these letters. David Krause is the author of a serviceable if indulgent literary biography, *Sean O'Casey: The Man and His Work,* which has just been reissued by Macmillan in an expanded edition, and he has worked with astonishing diligence to track down nearly every scrap of correspondence O'Casey ever wrote. This volume, 1910–1941, is to be followed by two more going up to O'Casey's death in 1964, the whole enterprise being likely to come to more than 2,500 pages. "A heroic figure," "the radical conscience of the modern theater," "a generation ahead of his time," Krause says of his subject, and one would like it all to be true, if only to justify such stupendous labor.

But it's not true. O'Casey can't bear the weight of such an apotheosis, which threatens by reaction to diminish his limited achievement. There are too many bad and even deeply embarrassing plays in his oeuvre (*Within the Gates, The Star Turns Red, The Bishop's Bonfire,* et al.) and too many aesthetic sins of naïveté, rhetorical excess, sentimentality, and tendentiousness in all but his very best work: *Juno and the Paycock, The Plough and the Stars,* the late and only half-successful *Cock-a-Doodle Dandy.* I suspect that O'Casey's inflated reputation in the textbooks and in certain theatrical circles is largely a set of extra-artistic circumstances: the sterility of the English-speaking theater in the twenties when he came to prominence with his "Dublin" plays at the Abbey Theater; his ferocious battle with censorship; his own "dramatic" story—slum childhood, self-education, lifelong nearblindness, self-exile.

If the letters have value, then, it's not in the mode of revelation about what-lies-behind-greatness, etc., but (it doesn't seem to me insulting to say) in a more prosaic vein, that of insight into a flawed career. The peculiar violence of O'Casey's circumstances, his beleaguered physical and economic condition, his struggle with Irish prudery and provincialism, make him something other than a fully representative literary figure, but he is representative in having been frequently unconscious of the true nature of his work, in having felt simultaneously misunderstood and touched with glory, and in having doggedly insisted on his inspiration even when it was leading to imaginative disaster.

"Writing letters is a talent the gods have denied me. I must have been a secretary in a previous existence," he writes in 1925 to Gabriel Fallon, an actor-friend to whom many of the most personal letters are directed. Yet he obviously relished it, and though there is indeed something secretarial in the dutifulness with which he sets down the details of his own career, there is also an attractive energy in the way he goes about it. He lets nothing get past: he pounces, groans, fulminates, lyricizes, protests. And always in the substance of what he writes, or in its subtext, is the assertion (or question) of who he is, what he has done.

The letters are to friends and acquaintances, of course, but there are also a great many to newspapers and magazines, constituting the text of O'Casey's lifelong public debate. They begin when he is thirty and for some years, until he turns seriously to writing plays, mostly concern his political ideas and activity. (Most of the early ones are signed S. O'Cathasaigh: christened John Casey, he Gaelicized himself in his mid-twenties, adopting his final name when *The Shadow of a Gunman* was accepted by the Abbey in 1923.) As he begins to think of himself as a writer the letters touch more and more on literary matters and from then on move easily among politics of an increasingly radical kind. He writes finally about the theater and, to intimates, about the details of his besieged existence.

Impetuous to defend himself, he rushes headlong at every criticism. His letters to journals where he has been attacked are full of impassioned (though not usually very seductive) claims for the value of his plays or ideas, together with frequently vituperative assaults on his detractors' intelligence and, in some instances, sanity. Of an opponent in a controversy over *The Plough and the Stars* he writes: "Mrs. Skeffington is certainly not dumb but she appears to be both blind and deaf." To the poet Æ, in the latter's capacity as editor of the *Irish Statesman,* he says: "Calm yourself, calm yourself, and try to force a definite thought or two out of the congested mass of nonsense in your nut."

He himself is "altogether too vehement to be a good critic," as he tells a friend. But the awareness doesn't prevent him from being a sedulous and savage one. Except for Shaw, who befriended him, and Joyce, he detests his Irish contemporaries. Of Sean O'Faolain and Frank O'Connor he writes that "they go along in literature like two little neatly dressed colleens, arm in arm, out for a walk." And from London, where he settled in 1926, he anathematizes the entire English cultural establishment in a letter to Fallon of 1929: "What these Literary and Art controlling posers want is to be chained together and made to look at Punch and Judy shows, visit Circuses, stare at Revues, and do years of hard labor dancing Jazz. Then there might possibly be a glimpse of God for them."

There was a basis to his complaint. British culture between the wars was in fact desiccated and nowhere more so than in the theater. Yet in its cocksure invocation of popular forms with their presumed vitality and childlike directness the passage is revealing of one strand of O'Casey's opaque self-estimation as an artist. He considered himself a "natural" singer, a voice from the streets, making a virtue of his lack of formal background, and seeing himself as the victim of a conspiracy of highbrows. "I can honestly say that I don't care a tinker's damn about art," he writes in 1938 to George Jean Nathan, who had become his advocate in America and later a close friend, "simply because I know nothing about it. But I love the way I imagine the Greeks wrote [and] the way I know the Elizabethans wrote."

Admirable sentiments. The trouble was that O'Casey's ambitions after his "naturalistic" period demanded something tougher than such splendid innocence. He wanted to experiment, to mix structures and styles, to be more "poetic." Yet his sensibility and theory of drama, grounded in what he acknowledges in a letter to be a strange equality of admiration for Shakespeare and Dion Boucicault, were scarcely up to the job. With *The Silver Tassie* in 1928 he fell into some of the most flagrant delinquences—bathos, ideological cant, pseudo-poetic rhetoric—of the then dying Expressionist movement, and most of his plays from then on exhibit the same malfeasances.

The controversy over the Abbey's rejection of *The Silver Tassie* is fascinating and instructive. (O'Casey had the entire correspondence published in the *Observer*, and Krause reprints it here.) Speaking for the Abbey's directors, W. B. Yeats told O'Casey that the play suffered from both inadequate technical prowess and imaginative unconvincingness, to which O'Casey, furious, replied that "you seem . . . to be getting beautifully worse. . . . There are shallows in you of which no one ever dreamed." On O'Casey's behalf Krause asserts that "it is still an open question whether Yeats was right or wrong about this challenging work." But the question isn't open: Yeats was right, and though, as Krause says, O'Casey was treated shabbily, there was no failure to discern his genius.

Convinced, though, that the play had been rejected because of its disturbing originality, O'Casey seized on and built up a role as prophet unhonored. He was given ample material: the bannings of his plays in Ireland and Boston, the abuse of outraged jingoists and bluenoses. But political irreverence, anticlericalism, and sexual honesty aren't enough to constitute literary genius. Good as his best work is, emotionally accurate as it occasionally can be, O'Casey's theater mostly lacks that mysterious agency by which experience is shaped by form into new consciousness. His six-volume part-fictional autobiography, to which these letters serve as an addendum and a check, is perhaps the most durable of his contributions.

When Ibsen heard in Rome of the critical outcry back home against *Peer Gynt* he wrote superbly to a friend that "the definition of poetry will have to be changed to conform to my play." Ibsen's critics were artistically obtuse; O'Casey's were simply morally dense. He was not ahead of his time: to see this one has only to compare his "experiments" with those of Brecht and Pirandello, who wrote during much of the same period.

In any case, this book shows him reacting with extraordinary persistence and violence to the low-level critique which, sadly, was almost all he was offered. I don't want to give the impression that there is nothing else in these letters: O'Casey could be a warm, shrewd, witty, and generous correspondent, all of which qualities are in full evidence. But he misunderstood the nature of his imaginative powers, and that is the important cultural fact. In one of the last of these letters he writes to his American agent: "I've never written anything that didn't cause a dispute, a row, a difference of something." He was right, but the disputes were mostly ephemeral, the differences pitifully small.

New York Times Book Review, Mar. 16, 1975

Henrik Ibsen: The Complete Major Prose Plays, Translated and Introduced by Rolf Fjelde

A few years after Henrik Ibsen's death in 1906, Rainer Maria Rilke saw his first production of a play by the great dramatist (*The Wild Duck,* as it happened) and wrote from Munich to a friend that he had come upon "a new poet, one to whom we will go by path after path, now that we know there is one." As an artist, Rilke went on to say, Ibsen was "a man misunderstood in the midst of fame, an entirely different person from what one hears."

What one heard then, and what continues to be heard as we celebrate this year the 150th anniversary of Ibsen's birth, is talk of a hard, wintry imagination, a craftsmanship exercised with narrow, even mechanical precision, a consciousness centering itself on public "problems." To identify Ibsen as a poet in the wider sense of the word, as Rilke was one of the first to have done—even Bernard Shaw, Ibsen's fervent admirer and evangelist in England, saw him chiefly as a social critic—is to free him from the false aspect of his eminence, from his being largely thought of as an uncoverer of communal secrets, an exacerbated prophet, a high-minded prosecuting attorney.

He was in fact all those things to a degree, but he was none of them at the heart of his genius; they are not the basis of his permanence, not what moved Pirandello to say that "after Shakespeare, without hesitation, I put Ibsen first." He was "objective" in certain respects, extraordinarily accurate about physical details, the shrewdest observer of behavior, but the objectivity and canny eye were tactical, were in the service of a passionate engagement with the truths of his own divided being: he once described his work as dealing with the conflict between "desire and duty." He was the perfect exemplar of Yeats's dictum that art is the result of a quarrel with oneself and not with others. "I have never wrote," Ibsen once said, "because I had, as they say, 'found a good subject.' Everything that I have written has the closest possible connection with what I have lived through inwardly. . . . In every new poem or play I have aimed at my own spiritual emancipation and purification."

He knew the truth of Rilke's judgment, that he was a poet mistaken for a moral mathematician, and would have set the record straight had he been able. In 1898, when he was seventy and at the height of his celebrity, he told the guests at a testimonial dinner given him by the Norwegian Society for Women's Rights, to whose members he was of course a hero for *A Doll House* if for nothing else: "I have been more of a poet and less of a social philosopher than people have generally been inclined to believe. I thank you for your toast, but I must decline the honor of consciously having worked for women's rights. I am not even quite sure what women's rights really are. To me it has been a question of human rights."

This disclaimer has not yet entered into public or even most academic awareness, any more than has his true imaginative size. The recent revival of interest in him is surely due almost wholly to the purported feminism of *A Doll*

House and, to an only slightly lesser extent, of *Ghosts, Hedda Gabler,* and *The Lady from the Sea,* as well as to the questions of political and commercial morality raised by *Pillars of Society* and *An Enemy of the People.* He is still, in other words, a social philosopher to us, a writer tied to issues.

The overriding value of this new set of translations by Rolfe Fjelde, apart from the general excellence of the English versions themselves, lies in its having brought together, in chronological order, all the plays on which Ibsen's false reputation has been founded. The chronology is important, much more so than in the case of any playwright of comparable stature—Chekhov, say, or Brecht. Toward the end of his career Ibsen asserted that "only by grasping and comprehending my entire production as a continuous and coherent whole will the reader [as was true of most important dramatists of his time, Ibsen's plays were much more widely read than seen on the stage] be able to receive the precise impression I sought to convey in the individual parts of it." In his introduction Fjelde writes that "it is in obedience to this injunction to see at least the major prose plays as a subtly and significantly interconnected dramatic cycle that this present collection has been designed."

Fjelde neutrally describes as "prose" plays what have been more familiarly, and misleadingly, known as Ibsen's "social" ones, the sequence of twelve dramas beginning with *Pillars of Society* in 1877 and ending with *When We Dead Awaken* in 1899. His early stage works had been chiefly in verse and were mainly historical dramas based on the Norse sagas or on Norwegian legends. In the 1860s, while in self-imposed exile in Italy, after he had fled his countrymen's provincialism, their "cold, uncomprehending eyes," he had written the great verse epics, *Brand* and *Peer Gynt,* from whose themes—the too stringent soul and the too expansive one—he would never cease to draw.

"Brand" had won him his first real recognition in Scandinavia, but at least as much for its political implications, its call for a spirit of Norse independence and personal sacrifice, as for its artistic grandeur. *Peer Gynt,* while greeted rapturously by a minority, had been attacked ferociously for its "slander" of the Norwegian character and, even more vehemently, for its "ugliness," its dazzlingly new disjunctive style which, as so often happens in artistic history, was thought to be no style at all.

In a superb riposte to his critics, Ibsen wrote at the time that "if my play is not poetry, then it will be; the definition of poetry will have to be changed in Norway to conform to my play." But the reception of *Peer Gynt* (in published form; neither it nor *Brand* was to be produced for many years) was greatly disturbing to him. He had always had a high estimate of his potential role as a shaper of consciousness—he would offer his own struggles as exemplary—and this seemed threatened now. He turned therefore to a mode through which his work could become more available, at least on its surface. Later he would write that "I came to regard verse as wrong . . . verse has been most injurious to dramatic art . . . the aims of the dramatist of the future are almost certain to be incompatible with it."

Whether or not this was a rationalization at the time, he was to be proven right—and to be the chief instrument of the proof—and the result of his turning to prose was to lay the foundation for what we think of as modern drama. But the shift was strategic, not a question of a profound change of sensibility; the poetry became hidden, retreating under the surfaces of domestic event, and composed of a mesh of implications, hints, cross-references, silences, and guarded metaphors. Toward the end, in the last few plays, the poetry moved to the front again, not formally, but as newly recovered lyricism and directly elegiac statement.

The quarrel wasn't between poetry and prose, conceived as antithetical modes of imagination, but tactically, between verse and naturalististic speech. Ibsen once described the poet as the person who "sees," and pointed out that the word "theater," in its Greek derivation, means a "place for seeing." Like the Greeks, he thought the theater ought to be a place where one saw past the details of action into the structures of existence. In this regard, Henry James, a very early admirer, said that "like all first-rate minds" Ibsen's subject was "primarily an idea" and that in his case the idea was of "the individual caught in the fact."

This is the governing idea behind the specific notions of plays such as *A Doll House, Ghosts,* or *Hedda Gabler.* On the surface they deal with social or psychological themes: male chauvinism, the devastations of rigid moral systems, neurosis in an aristocratic woman, and so on. But at a deeper level they move past the status of case histories to enter a realm of universal dramatic truth. Their "stories" are of human beings trapped within sets of conditions from which they can extricate themselves only by discovering their own reality. Nora's accession of knowledge is that she does not know who she is, Mrs. Alving's that she has participated in an elaborate lie, Hedda's that her romantic hunger has left her unable to live. And these are poetic circumstances, not sociological ones.

It is a pity that Fjelde says nothing about this development in his brief general introduction and even briefer, indeed perfunctory, prefaces to the individual plays. He is a rather indifferent critic, it has to be said; like Rilke he esteems

Ibsen's covert beauty, but he does very little with it. There is a lack of discrimination in his estimate of the various plays, a failure, for example, to see that *An Enemy of the People* (one of Ibsen's' most popular works, to be sure) is beyond question the weakest play of the cycle, the one most afflicted with a didactic virus, the "easiest" and most transparent. And he has a tendency to see all the plays from a narrowly psychological perspective on the one hand and an inflated cosmic one on the other, with a vocabulary suited to both stances: "hyperaesthesia of the total self," "world-process," "frontiers of the mind," and so on.

More important, although he rightly sees the prose plays as thematically connected, he fails to do more than touch in the most fleeting way on the vital dialectic, the oppositions and reversals from one play to another, that gives the series its truest unity. *Ghosts,* which Ibsen said "had to come" after *A Doll House,* is a vision of psychic imprisonment after its predecessor's movement of liberation. The critique in *The Wild Duck* is of that species of self-righteousness and moral interference which is a main aspect of *An Enemy of the People. The Lady from the Sea* offers a perspective on the possibilities for sustained, responsible existence that will be denied the protagonist of the play that comes after it, *Hedda Gabler.* And *John Gabriel Borkman* is an alternative or opposing vision to that of *The Master Builder,* a lament over ill-fated, lordly ambition coming after a play that celebrates a movement to the transcendent limits of a destiny. Of all this, there is scarcely a word in Fjelde's comments.

Still, the translations are the thing here, and if Fjelde is not the most astute of critics, he is certainly a translator to whom we ought to be grateful, for he has given us as fine a set of renderings of these plays as we are likely to get for a long time. His is the fifth major body of translations of Ibsen into English (there have also been a number of scattered translations by various hands). The first, William Archer's stiff, earnest Victorian ones, reigned in the English-speaking world for many years before they were replaced, or at least augmented before World War II, by Eva LeGallienne's, which though rather flowery had the virtue for us of being more or less American in idiom. During the last twenty years we have had the nearly complete works by James Walter MacFarlane and all the prose plays by Michael Meyer; both these translators are English, and there is little to choose between their careful, intelligent renderings.

The increment in the Fjelde translations isn't a spectacular one, because there is no question of his having vastly improved on previous crude efforts or of discovering uncorrupted texts or the like. The body of Ibsen's work is quite firmly fixed, its sense has been conveyed to us before, and so has much of its subtle verbal splendor. Fjelde does make a small, important correction, translating Ibsen's best known title as *A Doll House* (not *A Doll's House*); for the original Norwegian, *Et Dukkehjem,* conveys the play's sense of a place where all the inhabitants, not just the protagonist, live like children, the point Ibsen made in his remarks to the Norwegian feminists.

The gains are small but cumulative and are in the direction of a more thoroughgoing Americanization of the texts than LeGallienne was able to accomplish, and of a greater "actability," as the theatrical term has it. To begin with, Fjelde has turned almost every "it is" and "will not" into a contraction, a step on the path toward more plausible speech, but one that even the best British translators have taken only sporadically. He has, naturally, eliminated nearly every Anglicism from the texts, expressions such as "my dear chap," "fancy that," and "let them have a good lie in," and substituted in these and other less egregious cases an American vocabulary with a proper colloquial, though not at all fashionably up-to-the-minute tone.

A passage from the first act of *The Master Builder,* in three translations, will serve to demonstrate the improvements. First Archer:

SOLNESS. Is it long since you found out that I was married?

HILDA. I have known it all along. Why do you ask me that?

SOLNESS. Oh, well, it just occurred to me. What have you come for?

HILDA. I want my kingdom. The time is up.

SOLNESS. What a girl you are!

HILDA. Out with my kingdom Mr. Solness! The kingdom on the table!

Next Meyer:

SOLNESS. Have you known for long that I'm married?

HILDA. I've known all along. Why do you ask that?

SOLNESS. No, no, I just wondered. Why have you come?

HILDA. Because I want my kingdom. The time's up now.

SOLNESS. That's a good one!

HILDA. Stump up my kingdom, master builder! On the table!

And Fjelde:

SOLNESS. How long have you known I was married?

HILDA. Right from the start. Why do you ask about *that?*

SOLNESS. Oh nothing—just wondered. Why have you come?

HILDA. I want my kingdom. Time's up!

SOLNESS. You're the limit!

HILDA. Give us the kingdom, come on! One kingdom, on the line!

The changes are small and often subtle, especially between Meyer and Fjelde, but multiplied many times they add up to clearer surfaces for all the plays and a livelier, more speakable dialogue. One more example: in Fjelde's translation Hilda tells Solness that she can't buy any clothes because she's "completely broke." Archer has it "I have run through all my money," LeGallienne "I'm all out of money," and Meyer "I've spent all my money." Any actor will confirm the superiority, as theatrical speech with no injury to meaning, of Fjelde's version.

There are losses here and there, as one might expect. Tesman's whispered line in *Hedda Gabler*, after the news of Løvborg's death, is given by Fjelde as "Oh, Hedda, we'll never come clear of all this," while Meyer has it more exactly, if a bit more verbosely, "Oh Hedda, we shall never be able to escape from this." In the same play one misses, too, Meyer's delicious nickname for Tesman's aunt, "Juju," which Fjelde has as the more prosaic "Julie." And "pals," Meyer's word for Thea's and Lovborg's characterization of their relationship, is more evocative than Fjelde's "companions."

But these are infrequent lapses. There is a steady beauty in Fjelde's work, a quiet fidelity, and, on the occasions when they are called for, qualities of intense lyricism and accurate invention. Rebecca West speaks in *Rosmersholm* of an inner peace she had known, "a tranquility—like an island of sleeping birds, up north, under the midnight sun." Hilde tells of once having seen Solness "high up in the spinning sky." Borkman describes his ambition as having made him feel like "a voyager in the air." There are no such things as definitive translations; language changes, perceptions controlled by language do. But it's hard to imagine better ones for now than these.

New York Times Book Review, Apr. 16, 1978

Margaret Brenman-Gibson's
Clifford Odets: American Playwright, The Years from 1906 to 1940

I've always been puzzled by Clifford Odets's last name. It seemed characterless, lacking a national origin, though it did of course lend itself to that wonderful pun: "Odets, where is thy sting?" Now in Margaret Brenman-Gibson's preternaturally lengthy biography of the playwright, I learn that the name was devised by Odets's father, Louis, who, wishing to disguise his Jewishness, or at least his Russian-Jewishness, excised the first three and last two letters of his real name, Gorodetsky. This is useful to know.

There are other useful facts to be gleaned from this book, but I'm not sure they're worth the exhausting effort getting at them entails. Mrs. (or Dr.) Brenman-Gibson (she's a practicing psychoanalyst who is married to the playwright William Gibson) is no minimalist. Her book runs to nearly eight hundred closely printed pages and covers Odets's life only until 1940 when he was thirty-four; his last twenty-four years will be the subject of a second volume. If this is anywhere near the length of the present book, Brenman-Gibson will have produced what must be the longest literary biography we possess, with the exceptions of Leon Edel's *Henry James* and Joseph Blotner's *Faulkner.*

Edel's work, if somewhat overpraised, is clean and shapely, while Blotner's is swollen with irrelevant detail. But at least he had the justification of his subject's importance, while Brenman-Gibson doesn't. Try as she will, she can't give Odets the stature she needs for him. He remains interesting because of the hurly-burly of his life and his representative status as a figure of the cultural 1930s, but his plays are fast sinking from sight, if indeed they haven't already disappeared. Brenman-Gibson herself says of Odets that he was "plagued by the terror that he was a mediocre talent, too eager to please," and if "mediocre" is a bit harsh, at least in the context of his times, the fear was essentially warranted.

To read Odets now—his plays are almost never revived—is to see a dramatic substance and style disintegrating before your eyes. Time has worked its erosions. The plays are severely dated, from their political optimism to their superannuated slang. One cringes at a passage like Leo Gordon's peroration in *Paradise Lost:* "I tell you the whole world is for men to possess. Heartbreak and terror are not the heritage of mankind! The world is beautiful . . . men will sing at their work, men will love." And one is scarcely less discomfited by all the "gees," "goshes," "swells," "feeling blues," and so on that are scattered throughout the texts. It's clear now that Odets triumphed in an especially naïve period, both politically and in regard to the level of American theater art. He seemed new, to have the common touch, but time has exposed him as a melodramatist.

One senses that Brenman-Gibson suspects this but has suppressed the notion. After all, such stupendous labor is an investment that demands protection. (At one point she describes herself as a "clinician-biographer who is cheering for" her subject's "growth as an artist.") Brenman-Gibson knew Odets and has been given access to the astonishingly voluminous materials he left—letters, diaries, notebooks, drafts of plays, scraps of writing of all sorts—and to the recollections of many people who knew him well. These include Harold Clurman, the Group Theater director who for years was Odets's closest intellectual collaborator; Elia Kazan; Stella and Luther Adler; and Luise Rainer, whose disastrous marriage to Odets makes up one of the book's more absorbing episodes.

So much research has been necessary because Brenman-Gibson writes "psychobiography," an approach that seems to aspire to the total re-creation of a life. She is a disciple of Erik Erikson, who has called her book "a breakthrough in life history writing." Perhaps it is, but it's certainly no breakthrough in drama criticism or general cultural investigation, for that matter. Seizing the issue, Brenman-Gibson begins by quoting Freud's well-known remark that "psychoanalysis must throw down its arms" before the mysteries of art, and then proceeds to try to prove him wrong. Instead she confirms him. This happens because she lacks what nearly every psychoanalytic writer on art has lacked—an aesthetic sense—and so commits the common intellectual sin of such enterprises: to mistake motives for artistic actualities.

In her discussions of Odets's plays she practices a type of thematic inquiry in which the importance of a work's motifs is the essential thing and where abstract categories of moral or social value override questions of imaginative complexity or original vision. She doesn't examine or elucidate so much as label. She writes of *Awake and Sing!* that it's a "rich allegory which celebrates the grand passions of life, of death, and of resurrection" and calls it a "bubbling play, sizzling with interior plot and conflict." She speaks of the "rich, compassionate emotional flow in *Golden Boy,* with its layers of meaning, its cornucopia of American image, of symbol, of character." This isn't criticism but press-agentry, and of a rather illiterate kind at that.

Brenman-Gibson's few efforts at criticism are no better. Odets, she tells us, for example, "projected . . . complex identity-elements into the conflicting characters, the external resolutions in the play representing his internal integrations." If it were only that simple. But playwriting, or any literary act, isn't a means of therapy, or is only incidentally that. Dramatic characters are just as likely to "represent" a writer's disintegrations, and in any case such methods as Brenman-Gibson's tell us nothing about the quality of the work. Above all they offer nothing about why Odets's plays, so striking to his contemporaries, should feel entirely melodramatic and dated now.

Failure as a critic doesn't mean that Brenman-Gibson has failed in every other area. And, in fact, some of the purely biographical sections of the book are competent enough, even if they're much too long. (Do we really need endless letters from Clurman to Odets reprinted in their entirety? Do we need to know what Odets bought at the grocer's one afternoon?) Still, if you can get through this clot of detail, Odets's life does have interest, primarily because of its exemplary, or cautionary, nature. He was a prime instance of success coming too soon and praise too abundantly; like Arthur Miller after him, he was a victim of the hyperbole that afflicts so much of American life.

Brenman-Gibson traces Odets's earliest years in Philadelphia and New York as the oldest child of a passive, melancholy mother and a blustering, boorish father (who once called Odets the "dummest [*sic*] chunk of humanity" he'd ever known); his early years as an actor; and in his mid-twenties, his joining the Group Theater, for which he was inspired to begin writing plays and which was to be his spiritual and organizational home for some years. This volume ends with Odets already a successful but unhappy screenwriter. Throughout these years Odets is shown furiously struggling in "a war . . . between the aristocrat and peasant" in him, between his masculine and feminine sides, and between his Jewish and American identities.

Speculative as all this is, Brenman-Gibson's "life-history" might have succeeded as straightforward, if uninspired, biography had she not had a grander ambition, nothing less than to connect her subject's experience and fate to "the larger sweep of developing history." The results are ludicrous. "The worldwide scramble for a division of the . . . spoils spawned a successful revolution in Russia in 1917," Brenman-Gibson writes, "and the governments of other nations were in terror of similar movements." And again, in "the tense summer of 1938 . . . President Roosevelt was urging all Americans to pray for peace, and there was still no script of the new 'dentist play' from Clifford."

But what's even more ludicrous is the way Brenman-Gibson lectures on history apart from Odets. We're told that Adolf Hitler was originally named Schicklgruber, and that Charles Lindbergh (a daring young pilot who . . . etc.) was nicknamed Lucky Lindy. We are told about Sacco and Vanzetti as though we never heard of them; Shakespeare is presented as *William* S. in case we didn't know. There's a naïveté here, an innocence that's almost winning. But it doesn't do much for poor Clifford Odets, the best playwright of his time *faute de mieux,* whom we leave in the grip of guilt and avarice in Hollywood, waiting, as I suppose we must, for Volume Two.

Saturday Review, Nov. 1981

Arthur Miller's *Timebends: A Life*

Arthur Miller—Honest Art, the Abe Lincoln of our theater, the craggy, earnest, clumsy, roughhewn spokesman for the common man, the playwright of "American liberal folklore," as Eric Bentley called him—has after his huge early triumphs (*one* huge triumph, in reality) lived through many vicissitudes, public and private, gone on doggedly writing plays (most of which have had dispiriting commercial and critical fates, in this country at least) and has managed to outlast his detractors (of which, to a degree, I've been one). Now he has written his autobiography, which might have carried the subtitle "The Making of an Icon," were not Miller too aw-shucks modest for that. It has been greeted by some ecstatic notices: "stirring," "rich," "humane," "a classic," "autobiography as art," "among the great books of our time."

Well, of all those adjectives and apostrophes the only one that seems to me warranted is "humane," although you could say that the book *is* "rich" in anecdote and gossip. Yet despite the hyperbole, *Timebends* has its virtues. Just as in the life, there's a rugged stamina in the story of the life, a determination to see it all through and get it all down. And though the characteristic weaknesses of Miller's writing for the stage are here in abundance—awkwardness, sentimentality, false lyricism, psuedo-philosophizing—his characteristic virtue is also present, the quality I think best accounts for his indestructibility in the face of nearly thirty years of mostly failed dramas: his decency, his "humanity."

Honest Art. A good man, a kind one. Not an original mind or a powerful one but, yes, a man of the people, if by that we mean the writer as homely representative, rather than guru, sage, or shaper of what we used to call "beauty." Such a writer articulates, stammeringly most of the time (but that's just the charm—he's *like us*), our fears and aspirations, confusions and doubts. In this respect Miller resembles those American writers like Dreiser and O'Neill whose very struggle with language in the task of enunciating or imagining experience is one basis of their appeal.

Miller has never been subtle, elegant, revelatory. I remember participating in a panel on *Death of a Salesman* at Brandeis University in the 1960s. The event got off to a disconcerting, hilarious start when a real salesman, invited to give his professional opinion of Willy Loman, indignantly protested that, first, he wasn't a "salesman" but a "sales representative" and, second, that he never went out on the road but did all his work on the phone. Then came a discussion of whether or not *Salesman* was a true tragedy. After some learned, lofty palaver by myself, Robert Brustein, and a Brandeis drama professor, a middle-aged woman rose in the audience and said, "Tragedy, shmagedy, all I know is that I never cried so hard in my life."

Never cried so hard. Not for that woman or Miller the notion of "thoughts that lie too deep for tears." The basis of *Salesman*'s permanence, as has often been pointed out, is its exposure of the dark side of the American dream, something that elicited not pity and terror in the classic formula but pity alone. And this strong emotion, not to be analyzed or gainsaid and not to be extricated from its confusion with self-pity, the liberal's occupational disease, is what holds the play in existence and enables it to lend a sort of justification to those other, far lesser works *All My Sons, A View from the Bridge, The Crucible,* and *After the Fall*—works that keep on being revived despite their manifest inadequacies or embarrassments.

In *Timebends* Miller unwittingly throws light on the phenomenon of his own reputation, which is, after all, a central question: Why, with so many post-*Salesman* detractors among the "higher" critical establishment, should he be so big? Speaking of O'Neill and Odets, he says of the misunderstandings and false claims to which their work has given rise, "As always we were trapped into estimating writers by what they apparently stood for rather than by what they were actually doing, by the critical propaganda surrounding them rather than by their literary deeds."

I think Miller has been the subject of such propaganda by his admirers, the "popular" critical establishment. There's no venal or cynical motive behind it, but it's propaganda all right, stemming from our perennial need to have *important* writers, including (or especially) dramatists, with the result that in Miller's case one fairly solid work has been extended to look like a whole career.

Miller begins *Timebends* with descriptions of his rather privileged early life in New York (he was born in 1915)—"and so the years . . . were marked off by rhythmical repetitions—the funerals, weddings, and bar mitzvahs, the cycle of games"—and attempts to account for his literary ambitions, a main element being his oedipal relations with his uneducated father: "To become a reader meant to surpass him, and to claim the status of writer was a bloody triumph."

He moves on to describe his coming of age during the Depression, the birth of his antifascism and largely romantic socialism, college, the first plays, the first marriage, the arrival at great fame with *Salesman*. After that the story becomes how he deals with that fame—how he deals, too, with the string of failed or disappointingly received plays, with his marriage to and break-up with Marilyn Monroe, with his confrontation with the House Un-American Affairs Committee; there are notes on his third marriage, to Inge Morath, his experiences as president of PEN, the international writers' organization, and, with much reduced detail, his life for the past twenty or so years.

Throughout are interspersed reflections on life, the world, America. Most are banal, obvious, or lachrymose: "America's unacknowledged religion was self-destruction"; "Where was the heart of evil if not in us?" "Deep down in His heart God is a comedian who loves to make us laugh."

Following no strict chronology, doubling back on itself (hence, I imagine, the ugly, coined title-word) so as to bring the inner life abreast of the public one, the book is by turns dull, informative, windy, honest, affecting (the Marilyn section, in part), pretentious, funny, and, always, "sincere." Throughout, some passages of straightforward description aside, one must contend with the pitfalls of Miller's style.

Time and again language fails him, metaphors go awry, clots form in the prose. He speaks of an uncle "who seemed to search for me in his eyes and made me feel extant," says of Orson Welles on the radio that "he seemed to climb into [the microphone], his word-carving voice winding into one's brain," avers that in 1947 "the yang and yin of existence had gone slack," and asks "how many times before memory catches up with the latest swelling of the ideal and squashes it with cynicism before it can mature?" Then there's his pretentious, pseudo-philosophical mode: "The ultimate human mystery may not be anything more than the claims on us of clan and race, which may yet turn out to have the power, because they defy the rational mind, to kill the world;" "Socialism was reason, and now it was in fascism that the rank pool of instinct collected, with Hitler and Mussolini and later . . . Franco reaching down to the dark atavisms within man to rule by unreason and war"; "Was coherence the triumph, the system's manifestation and therefore God's okay, while our flux of choices merely soothes the entrepreneurial loneliness of the untribed, self-warring soul?"

These examples of bad writing (chosen almost at random) aren't quoted to dismiss Miller but to get his verbal ineptness on record so I can argue, first, that his admirers are either blind to it or wonderfully forgiving; and, more important, that in this misty world of good intentions and comforting *sincerity*, it doesn't matter. In *Timebends* good writing isn't at issue, just as whether or not *Salesman* is a tragedy isn't pertinent to what people *feel*. For those to whom language doesn't matter but only intention, to see Miller inexpressively seeking expression is, as I said about his whole career, if anything a source of sympathy.

Nowhere is this more true than in his pages about Marilyn Monroe. He writes of "some sublime, trackless spirit in this incomprehensible young woman." "The sight of her," he reports, "was something like pain, and I knew that I must flee or walk into a doom beyond all knowing." Later we learn that "she had no common sense . . . but something holier . . . a vision of which she . . . was only fitfully aware: humans were all need, all wound." This is soggy stuff, but it more than satisfies the craving for *big* emotions: heartfelt, glamorous, portentous messages from *one who knew her,* one who *cared,* and who, having had the luck and the burden to have had such a *rich* existence, still has the common touch and can articulate it all for us. Miller's thoughts about Marilyn and about everything else become, vicariously, our own.

Timebends will be of particular interest to people of the theater because of what it reveals of Miller's self-estimation as a dramatist and his thoughts about the state of recent dramatic art. I've spoken of his modesty, and I hold to that: Miller is anything but a monster of ego. Yet how can he help being carried away by his idolization after *Salesman*? He reports that Lee J. Cobb told him, "This play is a watershed . . . The American theatre will never be the same." Maxwell

Anderson's wife, Mab, declared, "It's the best play ever written," to which Miller adds, "it would be said often in the next months and would begin to change my life." More to our point, he recalls that when he was starting to write the play, "I had an indescribable feeling of a new form; it would be both infinitely compressed and expansive and leisurely." Such exaggeration and inaccuracy are forgivable in the case of *Salesman,* but with the other plays his comments seem to me to bear almost no relation to the works.

Of *The Crucible* he writes, "what I sought was a metaphor, an image that would spring out of the heart, all-inclusive, full of light, a sonorous instrument whose reverberations would penetrate to the center of the miasma." Discussing *A View from the Bridge,* he speaks of "the stress between the play's formal, cool classicism and the turmoil of incestuous desire and betrayal within it." Of *After the Fall* he argues, "The play was about how we—nations and individuals—destroy ourselves by denying that this is precisely what we are doing." At the end of *The American Clock,* he suggests, "we should feel, along with the textures of a massive social and human tragedy, a renewed awareness of the American's improvisational strength . . . the feel and energy of a democracy."

What such rhetoric reveals, besides Miller's inability to distinguish actuality from intention, is just the kind of pretentiousness, the grasping for profundity, for "large" themes and bold passions, which marked O'Neill's work for most of his career. And just as O'Neill misunderstood Strindberg, his chief modern influence, so Miller misreads Ibsen, his own main early source. Writing about his "adaptation" of *An Enemy of the People,* Miller calls it a "message-work" and says that his extensive alterations of the text were designed to find "its application to our moment in America—the need, if not the holy right, to resist the pressure to conform." This of course entirely misses the ironic aspect of Ibsen's play, it's perception that the nonconformist is more than likely to mask a ferocious egotism behind his service to "truth."

Though his fame hasn't dimmed, Miller has for years felt left out of the course drama was taking, left "behind," we might say. But Miller sees it differently: It's drama that's gone wrong, while in his lonely way, he tells us, he has kept the faith. When he wrote *Salesman,* "It was a time when the heroic had all but disappeared from the theatre along with any interest in the tragic tradition itself." Later, as drama shifted more radically from naturalism and pseudo-poetry, his disaffection grew: "In art, style was the thing, not content," he writes, regretting "the fascination not with what was being said but how."

His complaint deepens as "style" seems more and more to take over from "content, that false division which conventional minds always throw in the face of the new. Against neurosis, decadence, and despair he holds up "the broad marble brow of the Greek vision." "The time would come," he writes, "when story-telling would seem old-fashioned; the Bomb had blown away credibility in all such continuities. The world would end with neither bang nor whimper but two people on a slag heap each trying unsuccessfully to make out what the other was implying."

The caricature here of Beckett's plays, the sententious business about the Bomb, the implicit appeal to those eternal verities our age is supposed to have subverted—all this tells us more about Miller than about his ostensible subject. He *has* been left behind, by the keenest movements of dramatic imagination. There's been no conspiracy against him on the part of "academic" or "intellectual" critics, as he several times says or insinuates in the book; with a few noble exceptions his work has largely dismissed itself.

In *Timebends* he writes about what being a dramatist meant to him: "Playwriting was an act of self-discovery . . . it was a . . . license to say the unspeakable." And that's just the trouble; in most of what Miller has written he hasn't uttered the unspeakable, but the eminently sayable, the obvious, the expected, or else "adventurous" notes falsely struck. His eminence would seem to prove that enough people have been content with that.

American Theatre, Feb. 1988

Part Four **Profiles and Legacies**

Bertolt Brecht Once Again

More than twenty years after his death, Bertolt Brecht remains a peculiar case, an unsettled question. He was an *exception,* a man nothing like our conventional notions of the artist-hero, and therefore an impediment to any clear, orderly intellectual history of his times. No important writer of the twentieth century was more "public" than Brecht, more intricately and aggressively involved in the gritty details of social and political actuality; none was more pragmatic in his conception of the artist's role. "I am a teacher of behavior," he once said, and meant by that a practical guide, not a seer or master. Practicality seemed to be everything to him: would a play do what he wanted of it, would an action in the realm of art have the right effect in the realm of politics?

This level-headedness and concern for efficiency, these artisan's virtues, seem to stand against the splendor and irreducible mystery of his best works. The beautiful waywardness of *Baal,* his first play, written in 1918 at the age of twenty, and *In the Jungle of Cities* (1921), the resonant moral wakefulness of *Mother Courage* (1939) and *The Good Person of Setzuan* (1940), the great ballads—half lowdown street-singing and half formal eloquence—these are the strange accomplishments of someone who said that he "should have liked to be a cabinetmaker." This split, if it really is one, is the basis of the continuing debate about

Brecht, a hectic discussion of the relationship of his political commitments to his aesthetic vision, of his theories to his practice, and, most subtly, of his moral nature to the stringent critique he made of everyone else's.

What isn't in question is that Brecht was one of the central influences on the postwar theater, a theoretician and practitioner whose importance can be measured as much by the opposition he has aroused as by the inspiration that has flowed from him and animated many stages. Nearly everything "objective," which is to say unromantic and unsentimental, in the contemporary theater stems in part from him; aside from Beckett there is no recent playwright more "modern," less accommodating of the deadening past. Or so those of us believe who admire him without serious reservations.

Yet to a fellow playwright such as Ionesco, Brecht was an enemy of the imagination precisely because of his claims to objectivity and his apparent rationality. To a critic such as Herbert Lüthy, he was never "able to indicate by even the simplest poetic image or symbol what the world for which he was agitating should really look like." And Hannah Arendt, while justly praising him as the greatest German poet of the age, thought his reputation as a playwright inflated, and wished to write off all his dramatic works because of those last seven or eight years before his death in 1956, when he was a quasi-official cultural figure in East Germany.

Like so many others, Arendt completely misunderstood Brecht's Marxism, calling it "ludicrous" and "doctrinaire," when the evidence is that, with the possible and only partial exception of the so-called "didactic" plays of the late 1920s and early 1930s, it was almost entirely undoctrinaire, a supple principle of inquiry and an anchor in the factual world, not a storehouse of dogma. In another area, against the widely held view of Brecht as a canny cultural operator, a ruthless exponent of his own interests, Arendt described him as a man "scarcely interested in himself," so identified was he with epochal issues and ideas.

It was Brecht's fate to be perpetually mistrusted and attacked by opposing sides. To Georg Lukács, the Marxist ideologue, he was a dangerous exemplar of artistic indulgence, a formalist and carrier of the virus of "modernism"; to Thomas Mann, the classic artist-seer, he was an uncouth activist. Brecht could handle Lukács and other detractors on the official left by tirelessly exposing their pettiness and retrograde thinking. (After his visit to Russia in 1935 he wrote about Soviet literary critics and historians that "they are frighteningly unproductive, venomous, personal, authoritarian and servile at the same time.") But Mann's lofty stance infuriated him. In an exchange of letters he once wrote: "It is in our natures that you should fight in a gentlemanly and I in an ungentlemanly way. You, for instance, are not intent on my destruction. I am on yours, though."

Bellicosity of this order is likely to be interpreted according to one's larger opinion of a man, and so it was with Brecht. To admirers it was a mark of his seriousness, to detractors an indication of his colossal egotism. But Brecht's self-regard was hardly a simple matter. Feeling himself besieged and oppressed, at first by a conventional society and a regressive cultural establishment, later by an exile that cut him off from his roots, and always by misunderstanding, he asserted himself, struck at others, was wily, made unreasonable demands, played both sides at times, veered and tacked and managed his way through. His personality had the tasks of both protecting his genius and making it felt. He survived, a truth about him that a great many idealists and political moralists have never stopped resenting.

And he continues to cause resentment by resisting classification. At twenty, he wrote to Caspar Neher that "I am a materialist and a bad hat and a proletarian and a conservative anarchist," and a few years later he told another friend that "I must have elbow room, be able to spit when I want, sleep alone, and be unscrupulous." He was referring to his relations with women, but this was true in other parts of his life as well. The portrait that emerges is that of a man in constant need of female devotion, who on the one hand treated women with deference and even tenderness and on the other would draw up "contracts" with his mistresses, "detailed agreements intended to govern the relationship . . . and preclude from the start false claims and expectations."

The much-disputed final years in East Germany had a contractual aspect to them, too. The Communist regime gave him his own theater and company, the first one he had ever had, and for the most part left him free. In turn, Brecht gave the regime intellectual validity. He had a "skeptical commitment" to it, often criticizing its actions and never wholly acquiescing. "Doubt moves mountains," he once remarked. "Of all things certain doubt is the surest." The elegant reversal was characteristic of his methods, just as the most stringent unsentimentality was of his being. Shortly before his death he wrote a poem to serve as his epitaph. It begins this way: "Here, in this piece of zinc, lies a dead man, or his legs and head, or still less of him, or nothing at all, because he was an agitator." Having spent his life battling illusions, it was not likely he would have any in his own case.

New York Times, Dec. 17, 1978

Appraising Stanislavsky's
Legacy Today

In one of those apparent cultural coincidences that are actually the result of broad intellectual currents that cross national boundaries at certain moments, the year 1898 saw both the founding of the Moscow Art Theater by Konstantin Stanislavsky and Vladimir Nemirovich-Danchenko, and Freud's starting to write *The Interpretation of Dreams,* the book that formed the foundation of all his future work.

In the *Tulane Drama Review* some years ago, John J. Sullivan, a psychologist with an interest in the theater, argued that the starting of the MAT and Freud's book were responses and contributions to certain radically changed conditions of the European mind: a new consciousness of the self, especially of its interiority, and a new awareness of the relations between body and mind. On the basis of these intuitions, Freud embarked on a "scientific" revision of nearly all human self-knowledge; Stanislavsky's goals were more modest and circumscribed, but the results of his investigations in his chosen domain nevertheless proved to be far-reaching.

A few months ago, Lee Strasberg (1901–1982) died after a long reign as head of the Actors' Studio and an even longer one as Stanislavsky's chief interpreter (or, as some think, misinterpreter) in this country. With his death, an era has come to an end; so, this would seem to be a good time to ask some questions concerning the place of Stanislavsky in American theatrical practice, most centrally in the training of actors.

How pervasive is his influence? What is the present status of his ideas and their probable future? Is Stanislavsky-oriented training suited to types of theater wholly outside the naturalistic canon, theater such as he never could have imagined? Is there, in fact, after all these years of controversy and interpretation, anything we can safely call a Stanislavsky system and in what does it consist?

Some of these questions were posed—and some answers suggested—at a recent convention in New York of the American Theater Association, an organization whose membership is drawn from many sectors of the noncommercial theater, but principally from academic areas. Among the several hundred panel discussions at this annual week-long meeting, some of the most heavily attended were directly devoted to Stanislavsky. Since the training of American actors has increasingly shifted from private studios, the bailiwicks of gurus and disciples, to an academic or, in some cases, an academic-conservatory milieu, the opinions expressed at the convention can be taken as reflective of the current thinking about acting in this country. Many of the famous old studios go on—Stella Adler, Herbert Berghof, the Neighborhood Playhouse, the Actors' Studio—but more and more of our most successful young actors are emerging from places like Juilliard, the Yale School of Drama, Carnegie-Mellon, the University of Wisconsin-Milwaukee, and the California Institute of the Arts.

Given the history of Stanislavsky's influence here—a history of misinterpretations, distortions and, above all, fierce internecine warfare among the various self-appointed evangels of his purported "system"—the degree of unanimity revealed at the convention signaled a new stage in American perceptions about his significance. As among various Freudians and neo-Freudians, there was a fundamental consensus on one basic point: By now, Stanislavsky seems to be accepted as the point of departure for all contemporary thinking about acting, the central figure whose fundamental premises are accepted, whatever the disagreements about details of his philosophy.

At a panel discussion called "Acting: Alternatives to Stanislavsky," for example, Bob Hobbs, a professor of acting at the University of Washington, set the tone with his opening remarks. "There are no alternatives to Stanislavsky," he flatly asserted, "Stanislavsky has said it all." He was joined in this opinion by another panelist, Leslie Reidel, an acting teacher from the University of Wisconsin-Milwaukee, who called Stanislavsky a "given." Ted Hoffmann, the theater critic and scholar who teaches at New York University, went so far as to remark that "we almost never even mention the name Stanislavsky in our courses. It's understood that he lies behind everything."

Such agreement, however, has only been attained after considerable qualification and revision of the early, often overheated enthusiasms. The history of Stanislavsky in America begins in 1923, when the MAT made its first visit to the United States. The tour was a revelation. At the time, the practitioners of American theater were mired in a tradition of routine artifice, without thoughtfulness, risk-taking or innovation. What they saw in the MAT productions were a new, "truer" way of acting, a consciousness—detailed, exacting, inspiriting—of the theater *as an art,* and what would be most significant for the future of the American theater, the promise of a system or method for implementing these ideals.

The tour was the beginning of Stanislavsky's hold on American theater—

and also of misreadings and partial readings of what he meant. To many self-appointed acolytes and evangels of the master's wisdom, Stanislavsky was either a mystic in possession of runic secrets or a great psychologist—a view in the name of which many perversions of his teachings were committed. Perhaps one of the most important accomplishments of the ATA convention was a kind of demystification of the man himself. Stanislavsky, for his own part, was nothing if not sober and realistic in his approach to acting, and though he dove into the psyche for his methods, he knew and was troubled by the primitive nature of the psychology at his disposal.

Yet, the essence of his achievement is undoubtedly that he laid the basis for a psychological understanding of acting and fused it with a deep sense of drama as aesthetic truth. "The fundamental aim of our art," Stanislavsky wrote in *An Actor Prepares*, "is the creation of [the] inner life of the human spirit and its expression in an artistic form." To retrieve the truth that had been lost in the theater, Stanislavsky proposed something one would have thought remarkably obvious: that actors ought to understand how men and women actually behave physically and psychologically. Nothing more than that, but also nothing less. Stanislavsky's strongest legacy, said Libby Appel, the dean of theater at the California Institute of the Arts, the one that functions most concretely in acting programs today, is his concept of "action and objective." Like T. S. Eliot's well-known doctrine of the "objective correlative" in poetry, Stanislavsky's idea was that an actor should move from a subjective feeling to its manifestations by physical means.

But ironically, it was precisely this emphasis on inner truth that became a major source of the misunderstandings of Stanislavsky in this country. The psychological emphasis, apart from the fact that it satisfied a perennial American appetite for self-knowledge, especially if it could be attained through a "method," was a doctrine well suited to the psychological plays that filled our theaters in the 1940s and 1950s.

In fact, Stanislavsky stressed that the need for personal truth in acting had to be balanced by attention to texts, to imaginative realities outside the actor's immediate experience, to entering "the world of the play" as a whole. One of the salutary results of the recent shift from studios to academic milieus has been the restoration of the balance to include texts of plays, their overall structure and ideas as well as the actor's individual motivation, in the consideration of the theatrical work. In many theater programs today, acting students are given courses in textual analysis, often by critics and scholars—something almost unheard of under the reign of the "master-teachers" in their studios. To know the play one performs in, to see it as a whole and not just from the perspective of one's part in it, is something all responsible teachers of acting nowadays demand from their students. This change of emphasis has probably also been prompted by—and is more appropriate to—the "theater of ideas" that became predominant in the past several decades. The plays of Beckett or Pinter, for example, demand a more intellectual, a more analytical approach than did the dramas of relationships of the earlier period.

Another aspect of Stanislavsky's "method" that had been disregarded by his early American exponents was his insistence that the art of acting couldn't be served without the keenest development of the actor's physical resources. During the great days of the Actors' Studio, for example, along with its genuine accomplishments, there was a scandalous neglect of training in voice and movement. These days, such training is required and expected almost everywhere—and again, is particularly necessary for the physical, almost ritualistic forms of performance (the Living Theater or the Open Theatre are early examples) that flourish in some branches of experimental theater.

Indeed, it may be the nature of Stanislavsky's greatness—as well as his flexibility—that his thinking took into account, at greater *or* lesser depths, nearly every aspect of what goes into the making of an actor. He himself was the first to point out that his thoughts and observations did not constitute a "system"; but none of the philosophies of acting that have arisen either in opposition or in seeming indifference to his approach have so far been able to displace it. It was thought at one time, for example, that Bertolt Brecht's theories of acting, in their stress on detached "objectivity," were inimical to Stanislavsky's. Yet, Brecht saw no opposition between the two approaches and several times praised Stanislavsky in the highest terms.

Similarly, when Jerzy Grotowski's radical ideas about theater, especially about the actor's "holy" vocation, with its demand for extraordinary physical and psychic labor, swept avant-garde theatrical circles here, they momentarily threatened to dislodge Stanislavsky. Yet, Grotowski made a point of calling Stanislavsky his "master" and ascribing his own seemingly revolutionary thinking to Stanislavsky's basic principles.

Perhaps the one area where substantial doubts remain about the efficacy of Stanislavsky's methods is in the training of actors for what we may call the "new theater," from the works of Richard Foreman and Robert Wilson, to the Mabou Mines. Although, of course, Stanislavsky had nothing to say about such art, there is nothing intrinsic in his thinking that can't accommodate the most extreme changes. And at the moment, in terms of preparation for the more experimental forms of theater, there seem to be no rival methods of training. Earl Gister, associate dean of the Yale School of Drama and head of the acting program there, says that "in the first place, *all* actors today use a methodology that is based on Stanislavsky," nor is there, in his opinion, "any way to train people specifically for such work." The avant-garde may of course use nonactors, which is to say people who haven't been trained at all, "but all the bases for so-called 'new theater' work," Mr. Gister claims, "are in Stanislavsky."

Paradoxically enough, then, now that the hold on Stanislavsky by his self-appointed legatees has been relinquished, or broken, and the confusions about what he *really* meant have largely dissolved, the teaching of acting in America under his aegis seems to have entered a richer period. This isn't to say that he spoke the last word, that new discoveries of a psychological or physiological kind won't alter or modify some of his specific doctrines or recommendations.

No longer a fetish, he may obtain his greatest value as a guiding spirit. D. H. Lawrence once wrote that artists learn from their predecessors not so much exact, fixed techniques as a "morale" of art-making. In his probity and devotedness, his reasonableness and fire, Stanislavsky surely continues for us that task of instruction.

New York Times, Sept. 5, 1982

Jest, Satire, Irony, and Deeper Meaning: Thirty Years of Off-Broadway

My main title is that of an 1822 play by Christian Dietrich Grabbe, who may have been, spiritually, the first Off-Broadway, or better still Off-Off-Broadway dramatist. An exercise in spleen, provocation, and arrogant despair, *Jest,* etc., was the work of a young and nearly unknown writer seeking his place in the sun. In the course of this crowded, wayward piece, Grabbe mocks conventional theater practices and audiences, as well as reigning playwrights like Schiller and

Kotzebue, has the decency to tick off his own pretensions, and excoriates the prim and obtuse theater critics of his day. Looking for a rubric or two under which to organize this impossible assignment, I thought at once of Grabbe and added a few more qualities and actions to fill out the picture.

My task (or so I've been told) is to introduce a commemoration and celebration of the thirty years during which the *Village Voice,* through its coverage and its Obies, has been amorously, at times haggardly, involved with Off- and Off-Off-Broadway, the first of which begat the second and may be said to have been effectively, if not literally, born only a short time before the awards that are annually and ceremoniously, and, sometimes, in lean seasons, grudgingly bestowed upon both parent and child.

(A *New Yorker* cartoon—from the late 1950s, early 1960s? It's a Helen Hokinson and in it two of her suburban matrons have approached a traffic cop in Times Square. The caption reads: "Officer, can you direct us to Off-Broadway?")

The Shortest Possible History, or Pre-History, of Off-Broadway.

About 1906, groups begin to form to do social-minded plays such as Broadway would have no truck with (the Progressive Stage Society) or to serve immigrant audiences (the Neighborhood Playhouse). With varying artistic and ideological agendas there follow at intervals over the next forty years the Washington Square Players, the Provincetown Playhouse (much early O'Neill), the Negro Players (self-explanatory), Eva LeGallienne's Civic Repertory Theater, the Jewish Workers' Theater (almost self-explanatory), the East and West Players, the Ukrainian Dramatic Circle, and Orson Welles's Mercury Theater, to list only some of the best known or most piquantly named.

Nobody has thought to call this activity "Off-Broadway," though the "Little Theater Movement" catches its nature. None of these theaters survives the war. When that's over, things pick up again, on a widely scattered front and a mostly amateurish basis, such as had been largely true before. Nearly all these theaters and productions away from Broadway minister to narrow constituencies or are exercises in pathetic self-expression, like vanity publishing. Nevertheless, enough is going on for Actors' Equity to lay down rules in 1950 for 199- and 299-seat theaters outside the midtown area.

Someone coins the term "Off-Broadway." Its history as a matter of morale if not of fact is often said to have begun in 1952, when the newly founded Circle-in-the-Square successfully produces Tennessee Williams' *Summer and Smoke.* But its truest history, the one that's supposed to justify this supplement, begins in 1955 when someone on the *Voice* awakes from a grandiose dream and proclaims, "Obies!"

Until just before this time, like most of my "sensitive" contemporaries, I had little regard for drama as it had been made known to us in America, and even less for theater, which at the time was synonymous in our minds with Broadway's banal "magic." Then several things happened. I saw *Waiting for Godot,* which had inexplicably strayed onto the Great White Way (it didn't last long; the absurdity of its being there soon made itself known and Beckett would not again be displaced uptown); read Eric Bentley's *The Playwright as Thinker,* with its revelatory news that there were modern European dramatists who were artists on the same level as Kafka or Proust or Yeats; and came upon the Living Theatre, then working in cramped quarters up near Columbia.

And then there was the *Voice.* After recovering from the near-wreck of my hope that this new journal would be both passionate *and* intelligent about the incipient phenomenon of a new or newer theater, the occasion of my crisis of faith being Norman Mailer's populist putdown of *Godot,* surely one of the more flagrant misjudgments in our cultural history, I found myself looking to the *Voice* as Off-Broadway's cicerone, recording secretary, prosecuting and defense attorneys, and judge. But this took time; I didn't think there was enough *there* yet.

The chronology of the mind is never as determinable as that of palpable events. I've been speaking of Off-Broadway's prehistory and emergence into something ascertainable and susceptible of description, but when did it begin its existence as an idea, a state of mind and rallying cry, when did it start to offer the full sense of an alternative? Having assumed in this essay the role of a representative or deputy for general consciousness, I'll go on in that capacity now.

My own sense of Off-Broadway as a possible site for a new and wider potency for the theater, a place (to which no traffic cop could ever point the way) where there could be fidelity to visions, room for risk, for more than ad hoc skill, for invention and fertile chance, is inseparable in my memory from those events I described before that led me to begin taking theater seriously. But I do remember some central occurrences. One was the production I saw in 1955 of Pirandello's *Tonight We Improvise,* which the Living Theatre did at its uptown loft, another was Turgenev's *A Month in the Country,* which Michael Redgrave directed at the Phoenix Theater in 1956.

But the turning point, the birth of love and gratitude, came for me on a fall night in 1959. Once more it was the Living Theatre, this time at its new place on 14th Street. The play was Jack Gelber's *The Connection.* Did it win any Obies? I haven't the facts at hand. But I date the existence of a changed American theater from that night (a year before Edward Albee's *The Zoo Story* had nearly persuaded me that the miracle had occurred). And that *The Connection* was dismissed or reviled by every "uptown" reviewer, which is to say all those for whom Broadway and the Theater were all but identical, added to the sense of an alternative.

What was I looking for in those years? I'll put it as compendiously as I can: style, antipsychology, antidomesticity, a noncommercial spirit, Europe.

The noncommercialism was mostly a delusion from the start. What was really present for a while were simply *lower prices* than Broadway's, until the gap began to narrow so that another impetus came for the débouché into Off-Off. Still, throughout the scene there were always groups or isolated souls for whom poverty seemed, sometimes romantically and sometimes not, to be a desideratum, even a sine qua non, for the work they felt called upon to do.

But maybe "noncommercial" is the wrong term. It wasn't that I expected people to work for nothing, in a sort of glorious asceticism, but that on Broadway *everything* pointed to money, was subsumed under it; skill was money, fame was money, *ideas* were money. Here and there away from Broadway you could find relatively nobler motives, pockets of sacrifice and idealism. For the rest it was a matter of penury and obscurity waiting for the redemptive moment: someone with power and wherewithal will *see us.*

Our dislike of psychology and the quotidian in drama was bound up with our quest for style—the visible details of an aesthetic, I'd call that—and with what Europe had come to represent: emboldened imagination, the extension of dramatic possibility, language as problematic and unpredictable (and so a deliverance from comforting or comfortably disturbing dramatic tales), the questioning of drama itself in order to free it from its dead past.

The only American playwright I really admired at this time was Williams, for his dangerous lyricism and movement toward emotional extremity. Everything else was sentimental or pretentious or inept as writing (I saw O'Neill in all these ways); everything was what I already knew and couldn't use.

Then after *The Connection,* or, in the interests of impeccable history, *The Zoo Story* (Albee's best play), Off- and Off-Off-Broadway gave us a great number of plays we didn't have to feel embarrassed or disgruntled by, and some in which we could take much pleasure. As opposed to our theater, American drama has never caught up with European (I dislike the metaphor of pursuit, competition, but let it stand). Apart from Williams, Sam Shepard is our only recent dramatist I'd think of putting in the same rough zone as Beckett, Genet, Ionesco, Pinter, Arden, Handke, Bernhard, and Kroetz.

But who under the admittedly ferocious sun of theatrical judgment would turn up his or her nose at Maria Irene Fornes, the early Ronald Tavel, Rosalyn Drexler, Jean-Claude van Itallie of *America Hurrah* and *The Serpent,* Robert Lowell's *Benito Cereno,* David Mamet, Kenneth Koch's *George Washington Crossing the Delaware,* the early Rochelle Owens, Robert Montgomery's *Subject to Fits,* Ronald Ribman's *The Journey of the Fifth Horse* (And, alas, who remembers—O Tempora, O Mores!—such bright names of the early years as Loree Yerby, Robert Hivnor, Jack Richardson, Doric Wilson, Soren Agenoux, and H. M. Koutoukas?)

With scarcely any exceptions, then, the best American playwrights and plays of the last generation and longer have come to our attention away from what I'm becoming increasingly unhappy at having to call Broadway: the word's too easy, too ideologically stacked; it makes for imprecision and loss of nuance. Well, away from Midtown (as a value judgment, not a location), from the Theater of the Majority, from Walter Kerr, *Variety,* Show Biz, visiting buyers, and refulgent names which stand in the place of talent.

And the Europeans? After *Godot,* Broadway (there's no way around it) saw fit—I recognize the anthropomorphism—to receive *Rhinoceros,* Ionesco's most "accessible" play to that point and, wouldn't you know it, the one with which his decline begins, and since then a scattering of Swiss, Balts, Croats, South Africans, Germans, and Harold Pinter, along with a couple of more youthful and less gifted Britishers, have been given widely spaced cracks at the Big Time and our consciousness.

But, going back, Büchner, Ibsen, Strindberg, Chekhov, Pirandello, Brecht (yes, yes, *Mother Courage* and *Arturo Ui* were briefly on Broadway; disastrous productions), Wedekind, Lorca, Ghelderode, etc., and, going forward, Beckett, Genet, Arden, Bond, the Austrians and Germans I named earlier to my contemporary pantheon, Pinter's *shorter* plays, Ionesco's more difficult ones, Botho Strauss, et al., et al.—where would we have found them? Not that they were often done well, but as someone once said about something, it's a wonder they were done at all.

What's been true of drama has been even more true—less debatable—of changes in theatrical practice and philosophy, altered notions of acting and performance, new thinking about what the stage might be for. All of this has taken place away from ... Is it possible to think of Foreman and Wilson and the Mabou Mines, the Bread and Puppet Theater, the Wooster Group, and Charles Ludlam as having originated or been sustained in any other milieu than the one where in fact they rose and, more or less, flourished? Can we think of Performance Art (whatever else we think of it) as a mode and product of the Theater of the Majority? Were buyers and theater parties interested in Artaud, Grotowski, Meyerhold, the Open Theater's "transformations," Tadeusz Kantor?

Lest anyone think I have nothing but praise for O-B and O-O-B, I offer some strictures and indictments. There was a near infinitude of boring occasions over these thirty years, theatrical epiphanies of appalling dullness, and there was widespread lack of skill, sometimes compensated for by ardor and ideality but more often not. And also: self-indulgence; juvenile acting-out; theory run amok; false gurus, fake avant-gardism, dreary imitations of Beckett, Ionesco, Pinter; a dispiriting hunt for modern "myths"; an equally dispiriting idea that you could devise "rituals" as though they were party games; an obnoxious belief that if you shouted "Love!" and "Freedom!" loudly enough you would bring them about; and other instances of nonsense, witlessness, and *dreck.*

Artaud was radically misunderstood and misapplied. I remember participating in a panel discussion on him in 1962, when his vogue was just beginning, and Mary Caroline Richards, the translator of *The Theater and Its Double,* warning the packed audience (which would have none of it) that Artaud ought to be taken with twenty-five grains of salt. And I remember Grotowski commenting on Richard Schechner's *Dionysus in '69* that "touching isn't communion."

I remember, too, Joseph Papp's pretensions and erratic taste, but also his fierce entrepreneurial skills, and the *Voice's* capriciousness and occasional bad writing, but also its enthusiasm and championing of so much that would otherwise have expired. I remember my perpetual ambivalence toward the whole scene, that infuriating, indispensable venue for theater.

I was inserted directly into the symbiosis between Off-Broadway and the *Voice* soon after I started writing drama criticism in 1961. I was an Obie judge in 1962–63 and 1963–64 (and again in 1981–82; is there any such span wider than mine? "Can there be misery [he yawns] loftier than mine?"—Hamm, *End-game*). In those days there were only three of us—my colleagues were Gordon Rogoff and Michael Smith—and this was of course a measure of the relatively modest number of productions we felt a desire or an obligation to see. As late as 1966 Smith could write that "half a dozen plays or more . . . are produced every month on Off-Off-Broadway's . . . principal stages"; the term O-O-B had been coined a few years earlier by, I believe, Jerry Tallmer.

Smith could not have foreseen what would come about: a demented proliferation of plays, pieces, shows, readings staged and unstaged, *Versuche—*

Brecht's word: "stabs," theatrical sorties—along with the pressing into service for their exhibition of every imaginable, and unimaginable, space, many of them in hitherto unthinkable corners of Manhattan.

Later I worked with the Open Theater, a central presence during those heroic years of the 1960s, and later still playwrights I had taught at Yale, or who at any rate had passed unscathed through my hands there—Robert Auletta, Albert Innaurato, Chris Durang, Wendy Wasserstein, Ted Talley, William Hauptman, Harry Kondoleon—came into visibility Off- and Off-Off-, and former students of mine—Michael Feingold, Eileen Blumenthal, Alisa Solomon—became critics for the *Voice*. I have memories and a stake in it all.

I'm bringing this piece to an end. As I said, it's been an impossible assignment. I've left out too much, my opinions are subject to execration, my interpretations, to head-shaking. But it's too late now. I sort through the past, sifting my recollections, and among the crowd these begin to separate themselves out:

Judson Church in the early 1960s; Al Carmines and Larry Kornfeld; the lovely Gertrude Stein plays, *What Happened* and *In Circles;* Rosalyn Drexler's *Home Movies,* the first musical of the absurd; Ronald Tavel's *Gorilla Queen;* Irene Fornes's *Promenade.*

Grotowski speaking at BAM in 1967 and Erika Munk and I marveling at the threat his ideas posed to the assembled and frantic New York directors and acting teachers; *The Constant Prince* and *Akropolis* at a church on Fourth Street, my eyes opening to what theater can really be.

William Ball's *Six Characters* at the shabby Martinique, a model of how to do Pirandello.

The symposium at the Quaker Meeting House in Gramercy Square at the end of the 1960s, when the Living Theatre, back from self-exile and gone apocalyptic, evangelical, and false, causes a near riot by assaulting and reviling an audience most of whose members are only searching for a place to deposit their good will.

Judith Malina's wondrous direction of a mediocre text by Kenneth H. Brown, *The Brig,* an example of how the physical stage, which Brecht said usually "theaters everything down," can sometimes theater them up.

Che, the play closed by the police in the early 1970s; after witnessing it, I could tell my children that I'd been present at the first simulated defecation and actual urination on any American stage.

The lobby of a small theater in the East Seventies where at intermission of Tennessee Williams's *In the Bar of a Tokyo Hotel* Harold Clurman and I look embarrassedly at each other, mourning the death of a career.

Beckett's *Rockaby* at La MaMa, with Billie Whitelaw, fifteen or twenty minutes of such quintessential drama as to raise the notion of less being more to the status of a categorical imperative.

Kantor's *Wielopole, Wielopole,* also at La MaMa: dusty yellows and grays, giant puppets, outcry and obsession, the hieratic and the lowly: memory.

A *Metamorphosis in Miniature* at the tiny Cubiculo, "freely adapted" from Kafka's story and exemplary of how to make a dramatic equivalent, not a theatrical version, of a piece of great fiction. We gave it an Obie in 1982.

The *Voice* was present at these occasions and all the others. Sometimes wise, sometimes foolish, it was there. It's earned this celebration.

Village Voice, May 21, 1985

Jean Genet, 1910–1986

Jean Genet died the other day at the round age of seventy-five. I have to reach for him in memory, recover the sense of him that had been so strong when his works were coming out; his last play, *The Screens,* appeared in 1960, and his fiction was all done by then too. For those to whom it's only cultural rumor, I need to say that he was as central a figure in the theater, and in consciousness generally, as anyone during the 1950s and 1960s. As late as 1970, when he appeared on the Yale campus during the Black Panthers trial in New Haven, we nudged each other excitedly when we saw him and expected apocalyptic wisdom, though none came.

An astonishingly short man (five foot two: the same height as his mentor and exegete, Sartre), stocky, with a bashed-in nose like an ex-boxer's, he was there to lend his prestige to the Panthers, who wisely didn't look this gift horse in the mouth. For he had once written, "I do not love the oppressed. I love those whom I love, who are always handsome and sometimes oppressed but who stand up and rebel."

He made himself felt as part of a climate in which notions of ritual, violence, and cruelty—in the meaning of Artaud, with whom he had some affinity—were animating the practices of fiction and theater. A transvaluator of values to an extreme beyond Nietzsche, a bearer of news from the dark side, he had written to all good citizens like us that "each object in our world has a meaning for me different from the one it has for you. I refer everything to my system, in which things have an infernal significance."

His system, he told us, perhaps at Sartre's prompting, began with his desolate childhood: "Abandoned by my family [mother a prostitute, father unknown], it seemed natural to me to aggravate this by love of boys, and this love by theft, and theft by crime . . . thus I refused decisively a world which had refused me."

There are those who saw this as an elaborate rationalization, and Genet's whole work as a manipulation, of fashionable negation and despair. It wasn't true, even though he indeed saw keenly into our, and his own, bad faith and not so secret guilts. "We shed our sicknesses in our books," D. H. Lawrence once wrote, which is what Genet did. In *The Miracle of the Rose,* he wrote that his aim in the book was "to relate the experience of freeing myself from a state of painful torpor, from a low shameful life taken up with prostitution and begging . . . under the sway of the glamour, . . . of the criminal world. I freed myself by and for a prouder attitude."

It's impossible to separate the homoerotic basis of his writing—and the position of homosexuality in the world that condemned him—from his aesthetic procedures. For drama in particular he helped set free the nature of theater itself: the use of "mirrors," substitutions—of roles for roles, images for people, appearance for things. He was the poet-exposer of the nature of power, real and imaginary, in modern theatricalized society. His plays were frightening, dizzying perspectives where nothing was trustworthy and where hatred was more than a literary emotion.

Yet this exponent of the perverse, who said that he admired the pimp for being "the man who has not been taken in by love," had his prouder, nobler attitude as well. Nothing from the realm of "humane" art, the universe of virtuous discourse, surpasses in beauty and humble generosity these words of Jean Genet's: "Talent is courtesy with respect to matter. It consists in giving song to what was dumb." "My victory is verbal," he once wrote, and left us its memorials.

The Village Voice, Apr. 29, 1986

Eric Bentley . . . and Me

A man is walking alongside me whom I recognize from a few photos I'd seen on dust jackets or in the papers. He's taller than I'd imagined, a lot taller than was Brecht, after whom he's vaguely (and, it occurs to me, as a sweet sort of tribute) modeled his appearance, to the extent, anyway, of wearing his hair in bangs. It's a beautiful late summer afternoon and Commercial Street, the main drag of Provincetown, is crowded with strollers, some of them going back and forth, as in a Mexican *paseo.* A celebrity alert is in effect, and to me he's one of the biggest celebrities of all.

As he pulls ahead of me I tell the people I'm with who he is and that I've decided to introduce myself to him. So I do. I rush forward, step in his path and say, "Mr. Bentley, it's a pleasure to see you here." Then I tell him my name and add, "I've admired your work for a long time."

Not that long, if the truth were known. This was the summer of 1962. I had been writing about the theater only since the fall of the previous year, having been asked (on the strength of my style, one review of some new translations of Ibsen, and, I suppose, a faith in my capacity to learn) to be the drama critic of *Commonweal.*

I was an unlikely choice. I hadn't formally studied drama or theatre; my only practical "experience" lay in having acted in some nondescript plays in school and summer camp. Until a few years before I hadn't even any particular interest in the stage. In this respect I resembled the great majority of my intellectual contemporaries, for whom drama, as we'd encountered it in this country, was an art distinctly inferior to fiction or poetry. We might, of course, make an exception for a Shakespeare or a Chekhov, but we saw their work more as literature than as theatre (the way it's still seen by English or comp. lit. departments). Besides, they survived from a past that had somehow been able to spawn a true dramatic art; that no longer existed, we thought in our airy sophistication, seeing so-called modern drama as pretty much a wasteland.

So what I wrote about and thought about, too, when I started to do those things professionally, were poems, stories and novels, as well as general cultural ideas. It may be too much to say that Eric Bentley's books, especially *The Playwright as Thinker,* singlehandedly made me open my eyes to the aesthetic and intellectual possibilities of the stage (seeing *Waiting for Godot* in 1954 also played a big part in my awakening), but his writing was surely among the chief propulsions I had at the time.

He was what we didn't then call a "role model," and whether or not my becoming a drama critic was an accession to the culture, I haven't any doubt that Bentley had the same kind of revelatory effect—an effect like a clearing of vision, light entering where murk had been—on many others that he had on me: students of the arts, ordinary literate persons, and even, presumably, in time, hardened theater professionals.

Is it surprising that the latter group put up the strongest resistance to letting themselves be enlightened? I didn't read *The Playwright as Thinker* when it was first published in 1946, for that was during the extreme phase of my unconcern for theater, but some years after I did read it and was so greatly inspired that I did a little research into the book's contemporary reception.

It was scarcely a publishing "event," though it got a few respectful, and one or two laudatory, notices. The responses it mostly aroused within the theater universe and its satellite universe of journalistic theater coverage ranged from the scornful, shocked, and appalled to, at best—maybe at worst—the condescending. If I remember rightly, the reaction in the academy wasn't much warmer.

I'm taking some liberties with the actual language of what we might call the establishment rejoinder to *The Playwright as Thinker*, but the burden of it was this: How can this man's approach be right? How can playwrights be thinkers, when everyone knows that they're *feelers*? They deal in emotions, not ideas—don't they? Well, don't they?

No they don't, not the way you mean. More than any other critic, Bentley gave to the theory and observation and potential practice of theater in the United States—he certainly gave it to me—a means of overthrowing so wrongheaded and baneful a distinction. Francis Fergusson added to the work of demolition and reconstruction, but Fergusson was much narrower.

Mind and body, thought and feeling, ideas and emotions—such crude and injurious antitheses have a long history of causing intellectual blight in America, nowhere more flagrantly and debilitatingly than in the theater. In his quirky way, Edgar Allan Poe was the first to hint at the malady; Henry James (whose drama criticism is still too little known) refined the diagnosis and prescribed for its cure; and Bentley carried the understanding into our own time and expanded it.

The points he was making in *Playwright* and that he elaborated on in the writing that was to follow are, in essence, that drama is, or has been, an art as dense or supple or reverberant or mysterious or vigorous or disturbing as any other; that like other artists, dramatists *think* in the ways proper to their art; that thinking in art is the process by which raw, unmediated emotion—with its treacheries and deceitfulness, its inducing of blindness—is made present to the mind, placed, explored, and brought into relation with both experience and imagination. Brought, in other words, into *consciousness.*

When Pirandello said that what was "new" about his plays was that in them he had "convert[ed] intellect into passion" (he might equally well have said that he had bound them together, made each an aspect of the other), he may have been overstating his originality. He had had great predecessors, but the remark, and the action it described, were accurate and startling enough in the conditions of the theatre in his day.

Intellect and passion had always been complementary, reciprocal; but the received wisdom of the theater, even in its admiration for the "classics," persisted in seeing them as contrarieties. This is what lay behind Walter Kerr's infamous dismissal of *Godot* as a "philosophy lesson," not a play; and it's what lay behind the established opinion, widely disseminated in my youth (and still hanging on here and there), that, for example, Ibsen was all intellect or "ideas" and no passion, Strindberg all brute feeling and no mind, and Chekhov, well, the comfortable, silly notion had it, he was neither passion nor thought but some drowsy, moody, "bittersweet," wispy thing in between.

Pirandello, Ibsen, Strindberg, Chekhov, Brecht, to a lesser extent Shaw—these were the playwrights of the modern era whom Bentley's book rescued for me from obscurity, misreading, obloquy, or, maybe deadliest of all, the academic. In its pages, too, I came for the first time upon their great neglected nineteenth-century ancestors (all Germans as it happened): Kleist, Grabbe, Büchner supremely; and dramatists I'd only known as novelists or poets: Zola, Yeats, Lorca. For that matter the book introduced me to theoreticians and practitioners I hadn't known or had barely heard of: Appia, Gordon Craig, Antoine, and so on; and critics: Stark Young, Shaw, and Beerbohm in that aspect of their careers. I was educated by this book.

In time I was able to see that *The Playwright as Thinker* had faults: a somewhat jerry-built structure, occasional opacity, some loose ends, mistakes of judgment or interpretation here and there, a few errors of fact. But when my first infatuation had cooled down and I was able to see these things, I put them all down, and continue to ascribe them now, to the circumstances under which Bentley wrote. He was an explorer, a pioneer, and such people by definition don't have accurate maps and precise instruments but must work their way through the terrain partly by touch, a feel for what is there, an openness to what may surprisingly be uncovered, a sense of the relation of things happened upon to the previously known. Errors, distortions, omissions, even blunders are inevitable.

Even so, the book holds up remarkably well, and though *The Life of the Drama* may be a better book—certainly it's better organized and more assured—it can't displace *Playwright* from the center of my affections. Something else occurs to me, which is that the book seems to have served (as Bentley said *Brand* and *Peer Gynt* did for Ibsen) as the "quarry" from which he drew the materials for most of what he would later write.

Over the years I've read just about everything Bentley has published, having had to catch up with the books that appeared during my time of indifference to the theater. I haven't always been persuaded (the book on Shaw didn't convince me that its subject had done quite what Bentley said he did), and I've sometimes found myself dissenting from some theoretical propositions—about the nature of melodrama, for instance. But I've been wonderfully instructed, made wiser about drama and the stage.

I think of that series of chronicles he published in the 1950s—*In Search of Theatre, The Dramatic Event, What Is Theater?*—his weekly criticism between covers, along with some occasional pieces. Has there ever been journalistic reviewing in America so supple, witty, deep, and unaccommodating? His was the chief voice of reason in—or about, or against—the American theater during those years; he was its tireless, learned policeman, as Shaw described one of the critic's tasks.

I start to reach for the books, which I always keep on a shelf near my desk, but then I realize that I don't need to refresh my memory, for it can readily offer me any number of exemplary pieces. I think first of "Trying to Like O'Neill," still the shrewdest estimate I know of our (alas!) best playwright. Then they start crowding up: "Doing Shakespeare Wrong"; "The China in the Bull Shop" (a witty tribute to Stark Young, a predecessor at the *New Republic*); "Craftsmanship in *Uncle Vanya*"; "The Stagecraft of Brecht"; "Tennessee Williams and New York Kazan" (a finely balanced assessment of the playwright and an equally astute evaluation of the director's virtues and delinquencies); "The Broadway Intelligentsia" (mostly the people who think playwrights are feelers); "Is Drama an Extinct Species?" with its prescient remarks on film as an aesthetic threat to the stage.

When it came time for me to write my own book, *The Making of Modern Drama,* I was dismayed to find myself with the impulse to quote Bentley on every other page. So I did a volte face; falling deeply into the Anxiety of Influence, I kept shutting him out of my mind. Although Eric wasn't old enough to be my biological father, spiritually, intellectually he was my progenitor, and if I couldn't kill him, even metaphorically, I could at least keep thrusting him away. Still, hard as I tried to do this, I remember my editor commenting mildly on the frequency with which comments of Bentley's did turn up in my text, and my replying that there simply were cases where I wasn't able to say better, or with any degree of originality, what he'd already said.

Eventually the times outdistance us all, so it isn't surprising that in recent years Bentley has dropped away from what we call "developments" in the theater, or they've skipped beyond him. Then, too, much of his energy has gone into his own plays and performing: the critic stepping down into the arena after watching it for so long with an eye that nothing escaped. Politics have occupied him more directly than before, political reality, whose presence in drama had been one of the uncomfortable truths he had unearthed and laid before a theatrical world which would much rather not have seen it.

Though my political values aren't that far from his, I don't share all his particular positions and I sometimes find myself irritated by his diatribes. But he's earned them, and it's alright. Everything's alright. He's seventy now and I want to tell him, and as many readers as I can garner, how much he's meant to me. With all the awards our self-congratulatory theater is forever bestowing on itself, there ought to be one for him. But, then, he'd probably turn it down; in his high-pitched, hesitant voice he's say something elegantly wry, maybe paraphrase Brecht to the effect that any institution that needs heroes is in bad shape. Well, we were in bad shape and we needed him.

American Theatre, Oct. 1986

"A Man Misunderstood
in the Midst of Fame":
Henrik Ibsen

My title comes, of course, from a letter Rilke wrote to a friend in 1910 or 1911 I think it was, after he had seen his first Ibsen play, *The Wild Duck,* as it happens. Rilke went on to say that Ibsen was "an entirely different person from what one hears," and by person he surely meant, as he did by the misunderstood "man" in that letter, artist, writer. In the same letter Rilke called Ibsen "a new poet, one to whom we will go by path after path, now that we know one." This, of course, reminds us of Ibsen's own well-known remark to the Norwegian Society for Women's Rights on the occasion of their dinner for him celebrating his 70th birthday in 1898, that "I have been more the poet and less the social philosopher than people have generally been inclined to believe."

He could see this misunderstanding and deal with it, as he had dealt with others. But did he foresee what would happen after his death? In the popular mind as, more complexly and formally, in the academic and critical minds as well, his plays would be honored, rejoiced in, discredited and misconstrued in perhaps equal measure, and raked over. You remember how, when *Peer Gynt* was first published in Norway, long before it was performed, it was misread and resented as an indictment of the Norwegian character, just as *Brand* had been in part misread in Scandinavia as a document of nationalistic or regionalistic fervor? Well, *Peer* could have been seen as an indictment of Norwegian character, but only in the sense that Norwegians presumably shared in human nature. Was it really an indictment at all? Or was it a half-joyous, half-lamenting piece of imagination whose instigation lay within its creator, not in society?

"To write is to sit in judgment on oneself," Ibsen wrote, the most famous of all his *obiter dicta.* So, who was Peer, and who Brand, if not their author? Who, for that matter, were Nora *and* Torvald, Hedda *and* Tesman, Rita *and* Allmers? One of the ways we distort drama (as we do fiction) is to see the works as the stories of their protagonists, great suns around whom circle the lesser stars and moons: when the truth is that the imagination in its triumphs fills its skies with equilibrium and reciprocity.

"My task is in the description of humanity," Ibsen also said with characteristic immodesty—if we want to call it that. And even though, when on an ordinary psychic or emotional level—a secular one, we might say—outside aesthetic and dramaturgical considerations, he could be bitter toward his countrymen for real or imagined slights, could be quarrelsome and even petty, in his art there are no fulminations, no grudges. The energy and shaping vision were directed against the intractable (or seemingly so), the hugely problematic in human experience and behavior, against self-deception and mendacity as perennial realities. Yes, and also against idealism in its threat to unaccountable and vivid life, its menace to particularity, and against utilitarianism, the other side of that.

If we chart the wilderness of misconception that has surrounded Ibsen's work in our century, we find it readily dividing into two main tracks: the interpretation of him precisely as a social philosopher and not a poet and, not so well-known, a form of obtuseness, the inability to see the *miracles* of just those works, the last ones, in which poetry—informal poetry we might call it to distinguish it from the formal verse of *Brand* and *Peer Gynt*—emerged with astonishing directness as Ibsen's dramas more and more shed the disguises of the earlier "social" plays, the tactical verisimilitude, the strategic intricacies of plotting.

In her early misguided stint as a drama critic, Mary McCarthy gave exemplary expression to the belief that the last plays represented a radical falling-off, a waning of Ibsen's powers, and while these days this view is much less often enunciated with quite such cocksureness and much less likely to go unchallenged where it is advanced, it's an opinion that's still around. "*The Master Builder, Little Eyolf, John Gabriel Borkman,* and *When We Dead Awaken* are windy, inflated, vague, shapeless, and unconvincing. They are . . ." (a shudder or sneer accompanies the designation) ". . . *symbolic.*"

I once called McCarthy's critique "The Quintessence of Mis-Ibsenism." And I think MisIbsenism, in various gross and subtle forms, is still being promulgated. Bernard Shaw himself, despite his heroic efforts on behalf of his predecessor, was (*pace* Eric Bentley) in certain respects a MisIbsenist and may be held responsible for some of the continuing emphasis on what I would call Ibsen's conscious and partial intentions: Ibsen as social commentator or analyst, cosmic moralist or cultural scold, even prophetic voice in the world-historical arena—strands of such roles and functions *can* indeed be discovered in the plays; but to see them as dominant, to construe them as what the plays are chiefly doing, is to attenuate, diminish, and finally eliminate the fertile *mystery* of Ibsen's art.

Now, it isn't fashionable to speak of mystery in connection with Ibsen. The most that's usually done is to talk about problems, ambiguities, or swatches of opacity, notably in plays like *Rosmersholm* or *Little Eyolf,* say; but really in all of them, including, I suppose, *Catiline* and the Viking plays. And these problems and areas of indeterminacy are assiduously being "worked on" in an effort to clear them up. I don't quarrel with this. Up to a point, I greatly respect such scholarly and critical endeavor: but only up to a point. What *lies beyond* the grasp of academic and critical inquiry is what I am most interested in and what I want most to stress. It's scarcely a certified way of doing intellectual business in regard to dramatic history—or any other history for that matter—to argue for *less* understanding rather than for more, but that is what I want to do.

First of all, let me make my terms and propositions clear—surely the accredited way of proceeding in these matters—after which I hope you will see that I am not a know-nothing and that at least I love Ibsen. Not wisely, it may be, but well. By "mystery" I don't mean anything occult or cultic, anything deliciously vague, and I certainly don't mean anything wholly unknowable. When I argue against trying to understand too much, I'm not hoping for irrationality or mindlessness. I am not transcribing S. J. Perelman's remark that "I don't know anything about medicine but I know what I like." Far from it: if I felt this way I would not have written criticism myself. I don't remember who it was who said—ah, yes, I *do* remember—Denis Donoghue in a recent book said it— "Mystery in the arts, artistic mystery, is what remains after Reason has done all its necessary and possible work." And this is a view to which I have always subscribed. And I would add to this definition—or illumination—the idea that the residue left after the intellect has done its job is the space that's been cleared for imaginative and moral possibility, *and* (we must always remember with special alertness in the case of Ibsen) that the *aesthetic* realm deals far more with possibility than it does with actuality. In a sense, it does not deal with actuality at all. This space is precisely what distinguishes art from other human activities, the closest parallel—and I don't want to scant the differences—being religion. No, I'm not against interpretation, but *over*interpretation.

I want to preserve and celebrate what remains and can't be codified into either useful intellectual knowledge or consoling wisdom. After interpretation, *beyond* interpretation. I may seem to have strayed from my ostensible topic, "Ibsen and the Modern Drama," but I don't think I have. I call it up again, now, in a context of perception and response which I think may be more useful—or at any rate less tedious—than the detailed recitation of the already known, such as hewing to an explicit subject would have been bound to incite. I take it for granted that all of you are familiar with the main elements of Ibsen's plays and what we so loosely call "modern drama"—which is just why I don't want to do more than sketch that place here. Ibsen is "the father of modern drama" as Büchner may be said to be its grandfather. His influence has been pervasive. That a writer as different from him as Pirandello could say that Ibsen was "unquestionably the greatest dramatist since Shakespeare" testifies to his stature, but more usefully to the way keen, original minds could open themselves up to Ibsen's own originality. This is better than giving him classic status, for that runs the risk of domesticating and denaturing him, turning his work from art into culture.

Specifically: more than anyone else, Ibsen took the theater he inherited from melodrama to drama, from spectacle to aesthetic vision, "well-madeness turned to moral uses" as Eric Bentley so astutely pointed out. (As he pointed out so many things so astutely.) Plot turned to revelation, character turned to fate. Perhaps, above all, Ibsen, more than any other playwright of the nineteenth century, gave seriousness—not grimness—I, too, see the comic side—seriousness to drama as an art; moved it forward a plane beyond its ordinary, vulgar uses and placed it on a level with the other arts—a level it had not occupied for several hundred years. We can speak of Ibsen having returned the theater to its soul the way all innovation does in all the arts. It's been said that he brought about a rebirth of tragedy; but he also brought about a rebirth of drama that *matters.*

Certainly drama of social and moral awareness has roots that go back much farther than Ibsen's work; but his are the roots that most directly nourish us. Yet I've noticed that I don't say "moral" or "social" investigation or inquiry or explicit call to order. If anything distinguishes Ibsen from his imitators or epigones, it is that his work is full of consciousness, bitterly won consciousness, rather than being full of "subject," "theme." "I never wrote a play because I had, as they say, a good subject," Ibsen once wrote. Whereas with the lesser writers in his tradition, subject is most of it, if not all.

I just spoke of Ibsen's tradition. But what is that? Is it fair to speak of a double tradition? The obvious one of the so-called "social" dramas and the more hidden or subtler one of the last, more immediately personal and poetic plays? And what about the "tradition" of *Brand* and *Peer Gynt*? In either case—or all of them—to return to my theme, *mystery* obtains. It was Eric Bentley, once again, who said that Ibsen looks easy, but is difficult. We can pursue this and find that what is easy in him are just those elements that are amenable to research and interpretation. I don't mean to suggest that such things aren't hard work. My point is that they eventually make works yield to scrutiny, make them lend themselves to formulation. And what is hard is what resists being thoroughly known, mystery, in short. In this regard I think of the remarkable insight Henry James had into Ibsen—remarkable, because James was as far as he could be, temperamentally, socially, and artistically, from Ibsen. James spoke of Ibsen's "independence, his intensity, his vividness, the hard compulsions of his strangely inscrutable art."

It is the conjunction of those two words, "strangely" and "inscrutable" that is so arresting. Why, to begin with, should Ibsen be inscrutable? Well, that is just what is strange. The plays—and remember that James was writing about the early and middle prose or social plays—were more, and other, than they seemed. They *seemed* to be "social" or "ethical" or "psychological" studies: to constitute a typology of human behavior within more or less familiar boundaries. But, as James saw and expressed in another memorable phrase, they were really about what he called "the individual caught in the fact." How marvelous that is! And how mysterious!

I think of all the instances—No! I have to choose. Nora—and Thorvald, too; Gregers Werle. Even Stockmann. Mrs. Alving, Osvald, and Manders; Rebecca and Rosmer; Ellida, the lady from the sea, which I think may be the most mysterious of all of Ibsen's plays—along with Little Eyolf. Solness and Hilde, Borkman and the sisters; Rubek and Irene—right to the end. Individual and fact; spirit and materiality: the trap of existence. The only playwright of the century who saw as deeply into this mystery as Ibsen, was Chekhov. Shakespeare and the Greeks grappled with it too, of course: Beckett wrestles with it now. But, for several hundred years, the *mystery* of existence was largely shunned and modern drama, at its best, has restored it, has—the word is so small for what it denotes—restored it to its *kingdom.*

Now I was struck last night (as I am always struck at symposia of this kind) by the multiplicity of questions beginning "Why?" *Why* does Allmers repudiate his book? *Why* does Rita want to keep him only for herself? *Why* does Solness climb the tower? *Why* does Hedda kill herself? Motives: the hunt is always for motives. This is, of course, a result of the naturalistic mode of shaping things and looking at them; but it is also a stock-in-trade of critical inquiry. As blatant as the older psychological mode or, as we find, as the newer philosophical or "archaeological" one. Now, the crucial fact is that, as Brian Johnston has said, characters in drama are not motivated the way people in life are—though there can't be an absolute opposition between these things. "Psychological plausibility is what's required—and *all* that's required," Chekhov said. The truth is, that to track down motives, whether they're psychological or structural—*pro-*

cedural we might call it—is to risk being reductive, risk dismissing the aesthetic in favor of the "real."

The question isn't one of motive, psychology, but of living action: ontology, being. And the quarry isn't explanation but *presence*. To be in the presence of the work, that is what reading or spectatorship or listening, is. To help toward the "presence" of the work—that is criticism.

I've only time for one example of what I'd call reduction by motivational explanation—or, rather, one example of how such explanation can injure the integrity of the work, or reduce its presence. Hedda's suicide. How many explanations of that have we had. In an ultimate sense, I don't "know" why Hedda kills herself. I can't explain it to the satisfaction of psychiatrists, sociologists, or wholly rationalist critics. All I can do—all I *must* do, is think about it, absorb it, and, insofar as I am a critic, write about it. Forgive me if I quote what I *have* written in this regard. "Hedda's suicide is neither an exemplary nor a cautionary act as it seemed to Shaw, nor the outcome of clinical pathology, but a despairing, strangely courageous movement of the self to cut through an *impasse*—to have faith where one could not have a life." This does not explain anything but perhaps it may help to frame an attitude in which the action may thus be received. I think that, as I've said, art is about possible realms. The best metaphor for art I know is Ibsen's: "a castle in the air, but one built on strong foundations." The castle is the imagination, the foundation the life the imagination exalts, transforms, interrogates, condemns, and adds to.

I'd like to end by quoting three greatly dissimilar figures. Italo Svevo wrote in *The Confessions of Zeno* that "health can't know itself even if it looks in the mirror. It's only we invalids who can." Modern drama, of which Ibsen is a progenitor, like modern fiction and poetry, may be said to have been, and to be, largely about ill-health, in Svevo's sense. In order to choose a metaphor from Ibsen to elucidate Svevo's meaning I would pick this: "to be inhabited by ghosts." In this perspective, the unhealthy are those for whom inauthenticity, in such large part created by ghosts, is a continuing presence and threat. For the healthy there are no ghosts; there are no gods or demons either. I would like to keep Ibsen an invalid, infected with the ghosts he fought against. I don't want to make him healthy. Jerzy Grotowski once said that in life, the first task is to be armed; in art, it is to be disarmed.

Too much explanation, too narrow an explanation: in Ibsen's case, too zealous a desire to reduce the mysteries and make him as knowable as life outside his art, will be to re-arm him, make him safe. And one more: Kierkegaard tells the story of a man who passes a shop window in which is displayed a handsome, sturdy chest of drawers, together with a sign that says, "For Sale." He's instantly enamored of it, goes in, asks the shopkeeper its price—and is told that it isn't on the market: the only thing that is for sale is the sign that says "For Sale." My fear is this: I see a field on which all of Ibsen's plays are being readied for presentation. In the foreground someone holds a sign that reads "Ibsen Studies." The sign begins to grow until it blocks out the activity in the background—the plays, the life, the art.

Theater Three, Fall 1986

The Second Coming of
Tennessee Williams
(1911–1983)

The story is told that when André Gide was asked who was France's greatest writer, he replied, "Victor Hugo . . . hélas." In the same way, the answer to a question about America's best playwright might be, "Eugene O'Neill (or, to some minds, Tennessee Williams) . . . alas." Though both responses express sorrow, the cases are different. Gide's point was that Hugo, a forceful but not especially profound or original writer, was so wrapped in the apparel of literary fame that he dwarfed all other reputations, whereas the point about O'Neill and Williams is that our history of writing for the stage, writing seriously, is so thin and insubstantial compared to Europe's as to make them our masters by default.

The two suffer from the invidious effects of such comparison, particularly among those we might call the theater intelligentsia. In both cases, their gifts existed in the midst of grave deficiencies, embarrassments of an intellectual and esthetic order. In the oeuvre of both, very few plays measure up to—indeed, most fall drastically short of—the standards established by the dramas of Ibsen, Strindberg, Chekhov, Shaw, Pirandello, Brecht, and Beckett. Still, I myself firmly believe that Williams was our best playwright, *at his best.* The qualification is necessary because at his worst he sank below even O'Neill at *his* worst.

Yet why play the rating game? In the matter of Williams, about whom we've all been reminded by the presence on Broadway of *Cat on a Hot Tin Roof* with Kathleen Turner (and earlier this season by Peter Hall's production of *Orpheus Descending* with Vanessa Redgrave), he should not be allowed to drift off, a fringe figure, a dubious case, to some third or fourth tier of theatrical renown. For it's not too much to say that Williams brought American drama to maturity in a way that not even O'Neill had done. Williams once said he wanted to air out all those "closets, attics, and basements of human behavior," which is just what he succeeded in doing. He brought a darker, more violent side to our stage imaginings, brought the unconscious into prominence; after him there was no clear artistically obnoxious line between normal and abnormal, no excuse for evasion. One specific triumph was that he changed the way women are portrayed on our stage, offering us articulate and powerfully erotic beings where the ordinary range had been between charmers and bitches.

If through some writings of mine I've played a small part recently in what has clearly become a case of Williams *revidivus,* or Williams as Phoenix (the title of a review of mine in the early sixties; a year or two later, as unstable as he was, I wrote another entitled "Mistuh Williams, He Dead"), if, as I say, I've had anything to do with his newest flowering, I'm gratified, but I still get a little weary of arguing with people about his place in our admittedly sparsely populated theatrical pantheon. Why is it, I wonder, that so many otherwise sensitive people are unable to appreciate Williams; why do their ears turn to tin in the presence of the more than occasional beauties of his writing? And why can't they forgive, if that is the problem, his melodramatic excesses and sentimental flaccidities when they so readily forgive O'Neill or Arthur Miller theirs? Could it be that something we thought long vanished retains its potency, a bias connected with his mostly disguised yet never wholly hidden homosexuality, to use a word from the period in which he established himself?

Is he being arraigned for having been gay, or, more likely, for not having stepped fully—and prematurely—out of the closet? The politics of sex have been known to create strange aesthetic opinions. Whatever the truth in this region, there's another, most likely even more pertinent bias: against his Southernness, what seems to many the overripeness of his temperament and vision, their deadly honeysuckle fragrances. The denigrations go on, not confined to the sorely vulnerable works of his last twenty or so years, but extending back to touch on the putatively golden age. In the same way that it's hopeless to try to convince someone that a particular joke is funny, it's ludicrous to try to *prove* Williams's virtues as a playwright; tin ears are tin ears, and blindness won't be cured by arguments. But my impulse is to keep chipping away at the wall of negativity that still partly surrounds him, or at least to discover its basic materials.

Apart from the morally offended—a second generation of prudes—Williams's detractors show several faces. There are those who detest mystery, who want all things explicable and explicated, within works and as we contemplate them: works without shadows or incompletions, everything coming from the most lucid places of the imagination. But Williams, though a lot less muddled than is often thought, was less lucid than he was fevered; like O'Neill, he isn't to be strictly judged by the clarity of his thought or the depth of his philosophy. He was a lyrical voice; he sang, sometimes hitting atrociously false notes, but at least as often striking an exact, astonishing rightness of utterance.

The mysteriousness of Williams's best work lies first in its having tapped unconscious—chiefly erotic—sources (he was the first American playwright to do this with verve and consistency) and then in what we might call its "residues," what remains after everything that can be has been accounted for through sociological or psychological inquiry. *The Glass Menagerie* has one of these fertile residues, *A Streetcar Named Desire* has, and so in varying measure have plays like *Suddenly Last Summer*, *The Eccentricities of a Nightingale*, *Cat on a Hot Tin Roof*, *Orpheus Descending*, and *The Rose Tattoo*.

The main question about Williams's rhetoric—his strong point, as structure wasn't quite—is this: how do the lyrical passages (in the dialogue, not the stage directions, which, poor things, suffer most from his uncritically romantic side) relate to the more functional ones, or, to put it another way, how does his poetry—after we've distinguished that from his poeticizing, his self-confessed chief debility—maintain its elevation in the midst of the prosaic? The poetry is sometimes besieged, for Williams's narratives, the "stories" that can be extrapolated from the texts, are occasionally at war with his language, events not always cohering with verbal textures; *Sweet Bird of Youth* is an especially egregious example of this. And a second group of detractors likes to pounce on such deficiencies.

Sometimes, for example, the sociology in Williams becomes too heavy, too much like a polemic. This is the case in *Sweet Bird of Youth,* where along with some of his sloppiest construction—three acts in no sort of organic relation to each other—the brutal politician has an air of caricature. Yet *Sweet Bird of Youth* has much for us to honor. Alexandra Del Lago, the aging actress trying to outrun oblivion, is a splendid creation—"When monster meets monster, one monster has to give way, *and it will never be me*"—and Chance, though more pathetic than tragic in his doomed virility, still commands attention. We stay with him right through those famous last words to the audience: "I don't ask for your pity, but just for your understanding—not even that—no, just for your recognition of me in you, and the enemy, time, in us all." A tightrope walk between bathos and authentic emotion, those words, but as so often in Williams they manage to stay aloft.

I asked a question about what I called Williams's "rhetoric," but I haven't the space here even to try to answer it. I only want to point out that in Williams, lyricism is sustained, anchored we might say, by accuracy of perception and a keen ear for the rhythms of ordinary speech. It doesn't come from aspiration, the *wish* to be eloquent, the thing that disfigures a dramatist like Maxwell Anderson, or O'Neill when he's laboring, but as a natural mode of imagination. This particular imagination's findings, the dark or "perverse" subjects of the drama, put off the puritans, as from an opposite stance they do the rationalists.

Is there any doubt now that Williams's chief subject is love, love sought for, love denied, traduced, beleaguered; love at the mercy of greed, the heart under assault by rapacity? And love as sex, sex as love: at his best—redeeming phrase!—Williams brought the American theater to maturity, and not least by giving a dignity to sex such as, sentimental people that we are, had previously been afforded to love alone. I think this is why it doesn't matter what Williams's own sexual nature was, or the true "preferences" of his characters; that Proust was gay doesn't in any way invalidate the majesty of his musings on what he presented as heterosexual love.

In *Sweet Bird of Youth*, Chance Wayne says that "the great difference between people in this world is not between the rich and the poor or the good and the evil . . . [but] between the ones that had or have pleasure in love and those that hadn't." This is a ruling motif in Williams and never better dramatized than in *Orpheus Descending*. But the noteworthy thing about love's pleasure in Williams is that the erotic, while remaining an arena and an atmosphere, moves in his imagination past the purely physical to become the representation and agency of affirmation, generosity, and a noble resistance to time's ravages.

To be thwarted in the quest for love is the main source of suffering for Williams's characters—Amanda Wingfield, Blanche DuBois, Maggie of *Cat on a Hot Tin Roof*, Lady of *Orpheus Descending*, Alma of *Summer and Smoke* (how Williams, like Chekhov, extended himself into the feminine!)—but what lift his plays above a notion so subject to banality are the thick textures of his social portraiture, especially that of his Southern experience: the redneck, the know-nothing, the stricken Southern belle, the big daddy, the blanched and the florid, and, like Carol Cutrer and Val in *Orpheus Descending*, the "fugitive kind" who struggle against appropriation.

Williams transcended the local in his art, which is why his Southernness, whatever we may think of it, is the occasion of his writing, not its theme or definition. He once wrote that "I have always been . . . interested in creating a character that contains something crippled . . . nearly all of us have some kind of defect," and he went on to say that he felt closest to those of his creatures who were "desperate to reach out to another person." Nothing easy for the mind here, nothing resembling our familiar psychobabble about the need to "work on" our personalities or establish "mature relationships." As Shaw said about Ibsen, Williams gave us "ourselves in our own situations," the first of our playwrights to do this and still the most eloquent. He deserves our gratitude and continuing attentiveness to the life for the theater he fashioned out of his own beleaguered one.

If you don't know what the American theater was like when Williams first came into it, you can't know what he meant to so many of us. From the beginning he was an original, not simply a more "talented" writer than his contemporaries but a different breed, an artist where the others were craftsmen. We used to joke about his name, wondering why he didn't call himself "Alabama" or "Mississippi," but we understood the exotic edge he sought to gain through that place name. He didn't need it; he was exotic from the start. In the dismally cautious, safely "liberal" atmosphere of American drama, the Southern wildness, the sexual perversities and ferocities, the dangerous quality of what he dreamed gave his plays heat—their mingling of corruption and emotional accuracy—touched us far more deeply than did any "reasonable" American drama.

It's hard to keep in mind that Williams was once our most scandalous dramatist, "the one," as he wryly said of himself, "who writes all those dirty plays." I suppose there are still a few moralists around who make faces at the mention of his name, but otherwise his "disturbing" subjects have long since been assimilated into theatrical and public consciousness—though the cannibalism of *Suddenly Last Summer*, spoken of in the play and absurdly made partly visible in the film version, has hardly become a common theme.

But the rest of it, the hunger for erotic contact (but seldom simply for the erotic), the secrets of lust, the range of sexual phenomena from adultery to

sadomasochism, the castrations and abortions, above all the homosexual dispositions and implications, sometimes disguised as heterosexual arrangements
(well, Proust did that magnificently, too)—all this no longer has any power to
shock. That is why it's so important to remember, or understand for the first
time, the bloodless atmosphere of the American theater at the time—the late
1940s, the early fifties—Williams made his dangerous, irreverent appearance.

Drama has been called the "impure" art and if Williams's is notably impure,
the best of it retains, or more accurately seems to have regained, a legitimate
place in our affections and esteem, whatever the skepticism of the absolutists.
After a long period of decline, the result primarily of the series of inferior and
sometimes catastrophically bad plays he kept desperately turning out for the
last few decades of his life, his reputation, insecure as it continues to be, appears
to be on the rise. Still, I remember the night over twenty-five years ago when,
walking out of a Broadway theater, I smiled ruefully at a remark by one of my
colleagues: "The gravy train doesn't stop here anymore." We'd been to the second night of *The Milk Train Doesn't Stop Here Anymore,* and it was clear to us
that Williams was in flight from his own powers, that he was in fact beginning
to parody them.

From then on the decline was rapid. I remember another night at the end of
the 1960s when another colleague, Harold Clurman, and I looked at each other
sadly and without speaking during the intermission of a greatly embarrassing
play by Williams called *In the Bar of a Tokyo Hotel.* He continued to write; the
work continued to be embarrassing. After a while you had to make an effort to
summon up memories of the excitement you once felt at the prospect of a new
Williams play. I make the effort now.

Over the last six or seven years since his death in 1983, three or four dozen
productions of his plays have been produced by theaters around the country; a
new biography by Virginia Carr, the biographer of Carson McCullers, will be
published by Scribner's in the next couple of years; and an exhaustive two-vol-
ume literary biography by Lyle Leverich is in the works. There have been several
large-scale television presentations (the most recent an unfortunate *Sweet Bird
of Youth* last fall with Elizabeth Taylor), and Williams has returned to Broadway in considerable triumph, or at least with much fanfare, with *Cat on a Hot
Tin Roof,* a production that, though overlong and unevenly acted, allows the
text to survive its playing.

The way that a text can be said to "hold up" is that it resists being confined to
its period, something Williams's less harsh detractors like to do with nearly all
his plays; the harshest deny him any virtues at all except perhaps for a wan ex-

oticism. What may date in Williams are details, local references, the catch phrases and iconography of an era, but not, in his best or better work, his deep motifs, his obsessions, the singularities of his vision, his having written for actors roles with real weight and intensity. Even less likely to date are the pleasures his dramatic language can now and then give—unsurpassed by any American dramatist.

The consensus is nearly absolute as to what his best works are: *The Glass Menagerie* and *A Streetcar Named Desire.* After that, opinion tends to splinter. In my own case I see a little below those two plays another quite admirable pair: *Suddenly Last Summer* and *The Eccentricities of a Nightingale,* Williams's rewriting of and improvement on *Summer and Smoke.* And below them, managing to hang on to some minor territory of theatrical permanence, or semipermanence, are *Orpheus Descending, The Rose Tattoo,* and *Cat on a Hot Tin Roof,* with *Sweet Bird of Youth* and *The Night of the Iguana* asking us to look as kindly as we can on their severe frailties, with *Camino Real* remaining visible as a noble if almost totally failed experiment.

Not surprisingly, the best of Williams's plays are the best constructed—their dramatic progression marked by economy, coherence, and the absence of wayward issues competing ruinously for the playwright's attention. They are also the ones most free from intellectual fog, into which Williams, like O'Neill, was so prone to disappear. They're freeest, too, from false lyricism, a vocabulary of pseudo-poetic longing as well as pained amorousness, and from flaccid melancholy, or a sorrowfulness so free-floating it can attach itself to nothing instructive. (Williams, who had rather more self-awareness than he's usually credited with, once told an interviewer that his chief debility "has been a tendency to what people call . . . to poeticize, you know.") The last hapless plays, with their angels, ghosts, apparitions, and avatars of Williams himself as suffering poet and doomed lover, are full of these qualities of maimed dramatic speech, though they can crop up in his work at any time.

But when he's using his ear well (the "ear" in a good playwright, or novelist for that matter, is never for the details of speech but, again, for its rhythms) and his emotions are under artistic control, the language in his plays is as inventive and evocative as any we've had. Blanche DuBois's painful yet self-serving memories, Tom's speech in *The Glass Menagerie* about going to the movies, or Val's in *Orpheus Descending* about the bird that sleeps on the wing: all three are characterized by a splendid fusion of imaginative verve and exact diction. These examples, however, are dramatic high points, arias that anyone familiar with Williams's work will know. It's in the humbler speeches, dialogue that neither soars nor celebrates, that Williams's forever beleaguered mastery of language can best be heard. Out of a wealth of possibilities two little speeches from *The Eccentricities of a Nightingale* make the point.

One is by Alma after her father has told her of her mother's "cold spite" and said that such women shouldn't get married. Alma: "I know, but they do, they do. They are the *ones* that marry! The ones that could bring to marriage the sort of almost—*transcendental tenderness* that it calls for—what do they do? Teach school! Teach singing! Make a life out of little accomplishments." The other is by the father to Alma: "Little things like that, an accumulation of them, Alma, little habits, little mannerisms, little—peculiarities of behavior—they are what get people known, eventually, as—*eccentrics*. And eccentric people are not happy, they are not happy people, Alma."

The rhythms, the strategic repetitions, the exactly chosen emphases and beautifully functioning hesitations—all this quietly demonstrates Williams at his craftsmanlike best. But often in the last plays, he fell into dialogue of an almost hysterical incoherence, as in this outburst from *The Red Devil Battery Sign,* perhaps his worst play: "Yes! Human! To enter my life something human is special, this day, this night, this place, suddenly—you—human! Here! What?" The speech is by a character called the Woman Downtown, whose abstract name suggests the Expressionistic influences (more broadly, the dated avant-gardism) to which Williams came to succumb in his fever to get past the naturalistic limitations—as he, reluctantly, and others, cruelly, saw them—of the plays of his heyday. A late two-character short play, *I Can't Imagine Tomorrow,* has, for example, a woman named One and a man called Two, indicative of the "experimental" tics that more and more came to afflict his writing.

The itch to do something technically "new" was likely the result of the scorn in which his later realistic plays were increasingly held by sophisticated critics. During the 1950s, when Williams was flourishing, the European avant-garde—Beckett, Genet, Ionesco, Pinter—was seizing the imaginations of Americans concerned with the laggard condition of our dramatic art. And even those writers' (distant) American cousins, Edward Albee in his earliest work and Jack Gelber in *The Connection,* had begun to shift attention from Williams's "old-fashioned" dramas. But this old-fashionedness, the quality of bold, sequential narrative and mimetic fidelity, is just what makes for Williams at his best.

If Williams maintains his place in our theater it's because his frequently elegant imagination is its own justification. To see *Cat on a Hot Tin Roof* now is to become aware again of how that imagination worked. Proof that in Williams the erotic is seldom present for its own sake is abundant in *Cat.* Brick's anguish over his possible homosexuality, his and Maggie's marital Armageddon, are subsumed under a much larger and more complex rubric: that of "mendacity," lying about oneself and to the self. Thus in Williams, sexual passions always conceal and at the same time give body to themes of besieged spirit, loss, anguish, and the demands of moral integrity. The erotic is the scene of defeat and despair but also at times of affirmation and generosity. The "heroes" in his plays are those who, however faulty or maimed in other realms, remain fully human in this one; his "villains" are the envious, the vindictive, the converters of love into use.

For all his flamboyance and cunning egotism, Williams was wild with self-doubt (as well as with hypochondria, his mad self-dramatization before the idea of death as though he thought himself the *only* person slated to die). That might have been justified in the later years and in fact helps account for his desperate return to the theater year after year with inferior plays. But it certainly wasn't justified when, at the height of his powers, he sabotaged himself over and over in attempts to please friends and placate detractors. He substantially rewrote *The Night of the Iguana,* for example, after it had opened in Chicago and been berated by Claudia Cassiday, gossip columnist and drama critic (!) for a Chicago paper.

Perhaps best of all, Williams rewrote *Orpheus Descending,* over many years, from *Battle of Angels,* his fifth full-length play but the first to be produced professionally, in 1940 in Boston, where it was a thorough failure. When it was reincarnated as *Orpheus* in 1957, Williams wrote: "Why have I stuck so stubbornly to this play? Well, nothing is more precious . . . than the emotional record of [one's] youth," and he added that "I have finally managed to say in it what I wanted to say." A comparison of the two texts is, like Chekhov's turning *The Wood Demon* into *Uncle Vanya,* a lesson in a dramatist's growth.

Williams kept the skeleton of the earlier play and some minor dialogue, throwing out a silly flashback and an absurd plot fulcrum, deepening his characterizations, eliminating romantic soft spots, and adding several powerful images, the Choctaw Cry of the Conjure Man and the story of the bird that lives its "whole life on the wing" and sleeps "on the air." One mark of Williams's genius was his ability to integrate controlling metaphors into his dramatic tales—the broken unicorn in *The Glass Menagerie,* the word *mendacity* in *Cat on a Hot Tin Roof*—instead of offering them, as so many lesser writers do, as symbolic plums stuck into real cakes. Only a few of his imaginative flaccidities remain, mostly confined, again, to his stage directions: "The confectionery blooms into a nostalgic radiance, as dim and soft as memory itself."

Possibly most important, he changed the nature and history of his female protagonist, while making his male one, Val Xavier, much more complex. In turning Myra of *Battle of Angels* into Lady, an Italian, he was following his own *Rose Tattoo,* whose Serafina distills a Mediterranean earthiness, and in establishing a strong moral and social ground for Lady's hatred of her redneck husband, he beautifully fuses his themes of erotic love under siege by envy and of the spirit assailed by small-mindedness and cruelty.

Probably worst of all, Williams allowed Elia Kazan, who had directed his early successes, to persuade him seriously to injure *Cat on a Hot Tin Roof.* Kazan convinced the dramatist that he couldn't let the character of Big Daddy drop out of the play early in the second act, since the part was being played by a star, Burl Ives, and the audience would resent his absence. Williams meekly wrote Big Daddy back into the script, then some years later again published both versions, soliciting the reader's opinion. The consensus: Kazan might have been commercially astute but Williams had been artistically correct.

There are more such stories I could tell, most of them common, if not public, knowledge. For all his éclat, Williams was perpetually embattled with the theater; he was better than it deserved or knew what to do with. It's a commonplace to say that the theater exists on a boom-or-bust mentality, but it's nonetheless true, and Williams was one of its exemplary victims. The theater praises its practitioners too soon, too much, and too indiscriminately, and infects everyone with the mad itch for smash hits. For a dramatist to sustain an artistic career, as distinguished from a merely commercial one, therefore isn't easy.

Well, Williams, who believed *everything* that was said about him, is dead now, and matters begin to sort themselves out. At some point in the 1970s, the years of Williams's decline and despair, several students of mine called on him in Key West. It was a pilgrimage. They revered his earlier work and had the crazy idea they could persuade him that he didn't have to prove himself anymore, that the love they and others felt for him wasn't going to leak away. You really don't have to write anything else, they told Williams; you've already given us more than anybody. He was grateful, pleased, disturbed, and defensive. He fed them and sent them on their way. Yes, their mission was naïve, even foolish, but they were right; he did do enough. It's what *I* would have wanted to tell Tennessee Williams, and what I want to tell him now: You gave us more than any other American playwright.

New York Times, Apr. 29, 1990

Joseph Chaikin: Seeking the
Words to Recapture
a Past and Shape a Future

The American theater has never produced a complex theoretician or visionary mind on the order of Stanislavsky, Artaud, Brecht, or Grotowski, nor until the late sixties or early seventies any stage company with a distinctive, internally evolved style and artistic philosophy. Joseph Chaikin may not be of the stature of the prophetic Europeans I have mentioned, but his ideas and example have done as much to bring maturity to the stage here during a ten-year period as those of anyone else I know, just as his group, the Open Theatre, has come closer than any of our other companies to the spirit of the great, principled, risk-taking European ensembles.

The Open Theatre was established in New York in 1963 by a number of young actors, writers, and directors of whom Chaikin quickly became the charismatic figure (a description he would no doubt disavow). He was twenty-eight, an actor disenchanted with the institutionalized stage, who had studied unprofitably with numerous teachers and had finally benefited from a three-year association with the Living Theatre of Judith Malina and Julian Beck. What he learned there, however, was nothing technical; then as always, the Becks were only remotely interested in questions of actor-training. They helped him instead to a way of regarding theater as force and revelation, as antidote to bourgeois existence; and it was these notions, together with a quest for style, that moved the new company once it stepped into its life.

It was resolutely, sometimes apocalyptically, opposed to the commercial stage. "My intention," Chaikin wrote in *The Presence of the Actor*, "is to make images into theater events, beginning simply with those that have meaning for myself and my collaborators; and at the same time renouncing the theater of critics, box office, real estate, and the conditioned public." For the most part the group was able to hold itself outside commerce and so fill an exemplary role for many young theater persons, although it was thrown into something of a spiritual crisis by the unexpected popular success of works like *America Hurrah* and, to a lesser degree, *The Serpent.* In 1970, the accumulating strains to which such enterprises are always subject caused the Open Theatre to divide, a smaller group under Chaikin retaining the name (until 1973), with the others reconstituting themselves as the Medicine Show.

Chaikin himself is a thoroughly political man, an undoctrinaire radical, and the Open Theatre was always political, without, however, being tendentious or aggressively ideological. Still, they paid what might seem to be a price. The tension that arises from the necessity to find, elaborate, and defend a style at the same time as you try to bear witness to sociopolitical values gave the company a certain inconclusiveness, an unevenness, and at times a naïve look that are all in sharp contrast to the smoothness and self-assurance of the commercial theater when it is working at its mechanical best.

But that is one point and justification of groups like Chaikin's. Only those for whom art isn't exploration and struggle but simply a feat of skill that is brought off or not, can give their ultimate esteem to high sheen and the absence of doubt. For Chaikin the theater is endlessly in process, its goals forever shifting, its accomplishments never more than tentative, its means perpetually having to be interrogated. In *The Presence of the Actor,* he wrote, "we ask questions . . . and in response we experience a dynamic silence. In effect we are joined to each other . . . by what we don't understand." Against romantic belief, an artist is one who, like Joseph Chaikin, tries to make visible that mutuality of incomprehension.

I was introduced to Joseph Chaikin's Open Theatre early in its existence by Gordon Rogoff, who told me about a new group whose work he suspected would interest me. It did indeed, and before long I found myself thoroughly involved in the enterprise. After a time Rogoff and I became full-fledged members of the company, being listed on the program as "advisors." This meant that we functioned roughly as what we would now call "dramaturgs," though the word and the activity were scarcely known in those days, in the United States at least.

If I'd had to define my work and responsibilities on a job résumé, it would have gone something like this: advised on plays the group might do or had decided to do; served as critical eye on the "experiments" being conducted in acting and, especially, in ensemble playing; gave informal talks on many aspects of dramatic and theatrical history, aesthetics, the philosophy of performance, and so on; contributed to the formulation and articulation of the Theatre's credo—what it eschewed (psychology, naturalism, the quotidian, the "culinary" in Brecht's usage) and what it aspired to ("myth," revelations of the unconscious, the submission of personality to art, spontaneity, visionary force).

I learned as I "taught." I learned even more when I directed plays by Megan Terry and Maria Irene Fornes for the Theatre. What was so exciting about those days in the loft on Spring Street was that nearly everybody in the group was without prejudice in regard to ideas about theatre and drama, unless you can call our rejection of conventional theater a "bias." We were really rather like Grotowski's Laboratory Theatre (about which at the time none of us knew more than rumors) in that we kept testing things, seeing what worked and what didn't, making "stabs" (Brecht's *Versuche*) into the possible nature of drama and performance.

For me, who had been almost wholly abstract and theoretic in my approaches to the newness I wanted in theater, working with the Open Theatre was a ground, an anchor in the physical; I felt myself implicated in living substances instead of notions. Or rather I became committed to trying out notions, moving constantly between theory and practice. We all did that, and I think it was what distinguished us from other groups, at that time and since, who simply wanted to do "good" plays or who had a special, usually ideological, concern. At the time, in those early years, we thought of ourselves in fact as a leading edge of theatrical revolution in New York, not smug or arrogant about it but carried by the élan that came from being new, adventurous, and unfettered by congealed tradition.

As to the effect we had on others, our place in theatrical history, to be formal about it, I think it falls into two categories. On what might be called the technical or procedural level the Open Theatre did of course influence subsequent theater in a number of ways: by its work on "transformations"; its ensemble ideal; the idea of creative reciprocity between playwrights and actors. Perhaps more significant, although scarcely amenable to research, the Open Theatre was a source of morale for many. I remember how often people would say to me, after seeing one of the productions we began to do in late 1964 or after watching work in the loft, how excited they were by the things themselves, what they'd witnessed, but still more by the spirit behind it all, the enthusiasm, the zeal. And they were energized, too, by something else: a new or renewed sense of possibility.

Twenty-five years or so later, I sit at the back of a large, low-ceilinged room on the eighteenth floor of a building squeezed in among the porno shops and fast-food places of West Forty-Second Street in Manhattan. The studio belongs to the Women's Project, the producers of *Night Sky,* a new play by Susan Yankowitz opening Wednesday at the Judith Anderson Theatre down the street. Today is the first read-through. Around a nondescript table are six actors, the playwright, the stage manager, Ruth Kreshka, and the director, Joseph Chaikin. I've known Yankowitz and Joe Chaikin for many years, though friendship hasn't brought me here so much as the fact that they figure in a remarkable set of circumstances.

Besides directing the play, Chaikin is its thinly disguised subject: an astronomer who is seriously injured in a car accident. When he started work on *Night Sky,* he was finishing a stint at the American Place Theatre, performing in a program of two one-character plays whose subject, even less hidden, he also is. One of them, *The War in Heaven,* he had collaborated on with Sam Shepard; the other, *Struck Dumb,* he had worked on with Jean-Claude van Itallie. Still another play, *The Traveler,* by van Itallie, deals with Chaikin's condition.

His condition: on May 8, 1984, during his third open-heart operation, he suffered a massive stroke. When he surfaced, it was with a new existence: that of a victim of aphasia, which literally means "without speech," deprived of words and their relationships, to one degree or another unable to read, write, speak, or understand what's said. Accompanying the vocal disaster was a mild paralysis of his right side.

Calamitous for anyone, it was especially so for an actor, which Chaikin had been since his teens, and scarcely less grievous for the director and teacher he'd also been. "Theater is my life, my family," he has said, and for twenty-five years he'd been at the center of new theatrical visions and methods. These ranged from the antirealistic innovations of the Open Theatre and its later incarnation, the Winter Project, to his iconoclastic performances as Hamm in Beckett's *Endgame,* Galy Gay in *A Man's a Man* by Brecht, and the title role of Büchner's *Woyzeck,* among others. From his teaching, a runic observation such as "there are zones of ourselves which have never lived yet" contributed to the making of a cult figure, a guru.

Now, though, during the read-through of *Night Sky,* he is somewhat uncomfortable. When the actors finish, he sits rather tensely for a moment and then, as though leapfrogging or side-stepping the inhibitory power of his affliction, starts talking, telling an anecdote about a professor who became a "surgeon brain." Aphasics often reverse phrases, abandon sentences halfway, speak mostly without articles, prepositions, or connectives, mix up syntax. "I couldn't walking," he tells the group, then quickly changes it to "walk." But most of what he says (he talks mainly today about aphasia) is, with a little effort on everyone's part, intelligible if foreshortened.

Throughout the reading he has been playing with an unruly pile of papers and now he hands out copies of what he calls a "brain map" someone made for him. It's a circle with some ganglia-like lines and words identifying areas of brain function: "moods," "emotion," "speech." Then he passes around a large calendar with mysteriously lovely astronomical photos. "I'm obsessed with this," he says . . . wrongly, and touchingly, stressing the first syllable.

Yankowitz says that Chaikin, with whom she'd worked at the Open Theatre, had asked her to write a play about aphasia, and it was his idea that the protagonist be an astronomer, a woman felled in mid-career. Anna, who struggles, after the car accident, to speak, cries: "I am aphasia! Aphasia! No retard! No mental! Bud cot in brain! Million aphasia United Stars. One million!" In a speech at the City University of New York accepting the Edwin Booth Award in 1987, a talk he had painstakingly written out and that began: "Thank you. I cannot speak well, but thank you, from my heart," Chaikin had revealed what might be the link he sees between his disorder and the heavens. "So much feeling between words," he said, "it's endless . . . enough for endless planets and stars."

Now, at fifty-six, he, too, like the astronomer Anna, has had to work his way back from scratch. At his apartment in Greenwich Village recently we spoke ("The word still scares me," he said). For a time, his only word was "yes," which he sometimes meant, though it often came out when he meant "no." "Talking is always a sacrifice," he confided, yet he did it energetically enough, his speech an amalgam of the clipped and staccato with the hesitant and repetitious. A short man with "the body of a Russian peasant," as a friend described him, he has amazingly lucid blue eyes, which lighted up when he darted from the room to fetch the white plastic leg-brace he had worn for a while; fitting it on, he limped a few steps.

Then he talked about meeting the playwright Robert Bolt, the victim of a similarly disastrous stroke, whose only word at first was an obscenity. Bolt, he went on, had said about his aphasia that "it's awful and it's lovely," which Chaikin, assenting, recast as "it's heaven and it's hell." Inferno lay in being exiled from the world, paradise in coming back to it, truncated, partly estranged, yet with certain sharpened awarenesses (he speaks of a heightened sense of color, for example) and with new devotedness.

Chaikin began regiments of rehabilitation with speech and physical therapists. Gradually he recovered full mobility. Then words returned, singly and in clumps; expression—wounded, incomplete, badgered, as in significant ways it still is—built itself up again. But within a few months, he said, he knew that as an artist he needed some more radical program than the usual one for aphasics. So when Sam Shepard, visiting him in the hospital, suggested they resume work on a collaborative piece they'd dropped, this time incorporating the trauma, he jumped at it.

In 1978 he had worked with Shepard on two pieces, *Tongues* and *Savage/ Love,* but then they had been on the same bodily plane. Without articulating it at the time, Chaikin wanted to use this new work, which became *The War in Heaven,* for therapy but also for something more subtle. It would be the first step in employing his lost, ravaged art in the process of healing; he wanted to attack the devastation with the instruments of which it had all but stripped him.

From then on he slowly assembled a new career, neither a replica nor a shadow of his former one. With Nancy Gabor, who directed the American Place student program, he began to give acting and directing workshops, at Case Western Reserve University, the Theatre School of Milan, Daytop (a New York drug rehabilitation center where he worked with families "acting out" their chaos), and at his apartment. He directed *Waiting for Godot,* and with Gabor *The Bald Soprano* and an evening of monologues from Adrienne Kennedy's plays. But the only real acting he did was *The War in Heaven* and *Struck Dumb* in Los Angeles last year. "At first, he was nervous," Gabor says about the workshops and the directing. "But I pushed him."

As I wait for him to perform this double bill at the American Place Theatre recently, I remember his saying that acting is now more difficult for him than teaching or directing, less "useful." ("This will be my swan song," he had told me.) The audience this evening is made up in good part of friends and associates, and I suspect they share my emotions. An aphasic actor? I know that speech for him tonight will be spared the beleaguerments of ordinary conversation, since he has fixed texts he will read, yet I'm apprehensive all the same.

As the performance makes its way, his speech is strong, almost wholly intelligible, with some nice characteristics remembered from before: a slight evocative breathlessness now and then, imaginative pauses. But he ends many lines on a peculiar interrogatory note, hurries some syllables together, says *ob*-sessed again, and is a bit off in the rhythms. What's more, the two pieces' abstractness and somewhat strained lyricism make for a certain monotony. Still, knowing what has happened to him, knowing him, sustains one's attention; if the drama is less in the works than in the occasion, there isn't much to regret in that.

In contrast to the impressionistic pieces in which he's been acting, *Night Sky,* the play he's directing, is essentially naturalistic. Because Chaikin can't fully grasp abstractions now, Yankowitz thinks he prefers to direct more "objective," more physically and emotionally localized material. Watching him at another rehearsal of the play, one senses, too, that because he doesn't have many full sentences now he seizes on discrete words or phrases, investing them with implicit thoughtfulness, concentrating his directorial advice in them.

He tells an actor who plays an astronomy professor to show more enthusiasm for his work: "infection ('infectious,' we all understand) . . . teaching . . . stars!" To an actress he says about an action: "not problem . . . tender," drawing the last word softly along. And he tells someone else: "it's simple . . . but not simple." The actress Joan Macintosh, who has worked with him before and who plays the aphasic astronomer in *Night Sky,* speaks of his "incredible patience and good humor" and the way he allows her freedom to explore the role. "When he gives us notes," she says, "it's almost always a distillation of complex thought." I, too, see this. After an actor has inadequately said "I love you," Chaikin takes "love," hefts it, breathes on it, endows it with its proper gravity.

On the wall of his apartment is a watercolor of the actress Eleanora Duse. "She's model for me . . . and two others," he says. I ask him who and, surprisingly, he replies, "Olivier, Brando." I suggest that Duse represents morale, devotion to the actor's art, Olivier technique, and Brando energy and physical presence. I'm relieved when he nods vigorously. Then he suddenly says: "Words are important . . . 'love' . . . 'truth' . . . shouldn't be mixed up with 'eating candy,' commercials."

In the summer of 1988, the year before he died, Samuel Beckett, whom Chaikin deeply admired and with whom he had established a friendship, suffered a moderate stroke. While recovering, Beckett wrote a poem called "Comment Dire" in French, which he later translated into English as "What Is the Word" and dedicated to Chaikin. At the end of the American Place twin bill Chaikin read this poem. Its last lines are:

> Folly for to need to seem to glimpse
> afaint afar away over there what
> What—
> What is the word—
> What is the word.

New York Times, May 19, 1991

Index